AMERICAN NEGRO FOLKTALES

Collected with Introduction and Notes by

Richard M. Dorson

ISBN: 978-1-63923-734-0

Printed: March 2023

Published and Distributed By:
Lushena Books
607 Country Club Drive, Unit E
Bensenville, IL 60106
www.lushenabks.com

ISBN: 978-1-63923-734-0

To the memory of James Douglas Suggs and to other friends who speak in these pages

Preface to New Edition

The present volume is drawn from my two previous books of Negro oral narratives, *Negro Folktales in Michigan* (Cambridge: Harvard University Press, 1956), of which almost all the tales are reprinted, and *Negro Tales from Pine Bluff, Arkansas and Calvin, Michigan* (Bloomington: Indiana University Press, 1958), from which about half of the contents are reproduced. I have also reprinted the following tales from articles I published in folklore journals: "Grandmother Whipped" and "Dead Man Sits Up" from "Negro Tales of Mary Richardson," *Southern Folklore Quarterly*, VI (1956), 5-26; "Who Ate Up the Food" and "The Elephant, the Lion, and the Monkey" from "Negro Tales [of John Blackamore]," *Western Folklore*, XIII (1954), 77-97; "The Baptist, Methodist, and Presbyterian Preachers" from "Negro Tales from Bolivar County, Mississippi," *Southern Folklore Quarterly*, XIX (1955), 104-116; and the A, E, O, and P texts from "King Beast of the Forest Meets Man," *Southern Folklore Quarterly*, XVIII (1954), 118-128. In addition I am printing four previously unpublished tales, "The Fight" from Joe D. Heardley, "On the Cooling Board" from Walter Winfrey, and "The Mermaid" from Sarah Jackson and Mrs. E. L. Smith.

In this new edition I have taken the opportunity to do some rearranging of the chapter groupings and to update the notes. For one instance, I have dropped the chapter "Fairy Tales" in *Negro Folktales in Michigan* as too loosely integrated, and introduced a new chapter on "Fool Tales." In the notes I have added references to the works of Abrahams, Brewer, and Crowley, which have appeared in the meantime; to Baughman's published index, previously referred to in its dissertation form; and to the revised editions of Stith Thompson's motif index and the Aarne-Thompson type index. Also I have written a new general introduction.

TABLE OF CONTENTS

Part One
THE SETTING

I ORIGINS OF AMERICAN NEGRO TALES

One of the memorable bequests by the Negro to American civilization is his rich and diverse store of folktales. This body of oral narratives took form on Southern plantations during the dark days of slavery and has expanded and traveled north on the lips of colored people in the last hundred years. By contrast, the white population has inherited no firm tradition of ethnic folktales. Ever since the Grimm brothers in 1812 first revealed the abundance of European peasant stories, the folklorists of every country in Europe have enjoyed a succession of field days. But no Grimms have made their appearance, or can appear, in Uncle Sam's America.

The reasons why are fairly clear. Americans are not ethnically homogeneous, and their history is far too short for the new homogenized American that Crèvecoeur spoke about to have become a reality. Various colonizing and immigrant groups—Pennsylvania Germans, Louisiana French, Spanish-Mexicans in the southwest, Italians and Poles in northern cities—have preserved their own transplanted narratives in their own tongue. But the colonizing Englishmen of the seventeenth century had largely lost the folk art of storytelling. They retained vivid legends of witches, ghosts, and the Devil, but they had ceased to relate magical fictions of stripling heroes and enchanted castles. In the American colonies and the new republican states, a mobile class of independent farmers replaced the communal peasants of Europe, and European storylore has always flourished among the peasantry. Then, too, in the modern world new forces were at work to inhibit the older forms of oral narration: the forces of popular education, industrial and urban growth, and mass communications. Storytelling did not and never will die, but the nightlong novelettes replete with marvelous adventures have yielded to snappy jokes, witty anecdotes, and conversational city legends.

Only the Negro, as a distinct element of the English-speaking population, maintained a full-blown storytelling tradition. A separate Negro subculture formed within the shell of American life, missing the bounties of general education and material progress, remaining a largely oral, self-contained society with its own unwritten history and literature. In 1880 a portion of this oral literature for the first time became visible to the mass of Americans with the publication by Joel Chandler Harris of *Uncle Remus: His Songs and His Sayings*. Harris was a journalist in central Georgia who worked on the first plantation newspaper, *The Countryman*, and then spent a quarter of a century on the staff of the *Atlanta Constitution*. In its pages he launched the character of Uncle Remus, the favored elderly slave of the old plantation who fascinated the little white boy of the house with his Brer Rabbit stories. Harris was not the first to report on the wealth of Negro oral expression; for instance, William Owens discussed "Folk-Lore of the Southern Negroes" in *Lippincott's Magazine* in 1877, calling attention to the special popularity of the "Story of Buh Rabbit and the Tar Baby." Owens declared that the fables of talking animals, which formed the bulk of Negro folklore, were "as purely African as are their faces or their own plaintive melodies."[1] Harris repeated this assertion, when he suddenly found himself a literary celebrity and a presumed authority on folklore. To his admirers and inquirers he protested that he was both an accidental author and an incidental folklorist. Yet he could be dogmatic on the sources of slave tales. "One thing is certain—the Negroes did not get them from the whites: probably they are of remote African origin."[2]

Subsequent collectors and scholars reaffirmed this belief in the African basis of American Negro tales and spirituals. The term "Afro-American folklore" passed into standard use in the late nineteenth century. No one thought to question so obvious a matter, since the Brer Rabbit stories differed markedly from any yarns known to the whites, since the slaves had come from West Africa, and since the published collections of African folktales contained a high quota of animal characters. When American anthropologists such as Melville J. Herskovits and his students turned their attention to Africa, they reinforced the thesis of African origins with the best scholarly credentials. In his much praised work, *The Myth of the Negro Past* (1941), Herskovits chastised the white supremacists who denied all cultural inheritance to the Southern slaves and placed them on the level of childlike savages. Rather, he contended, and cited evidence from his own field researches in Dahomey, the slaves had been torn from proud and ancient kingdoms with highly developed institutions and arts.

Meanwhile, intermittent collecting broadened and deepened the known repertoire of Negro folktales in the United States. Harris himself had not sought to reproduce literally the narratives he heard in middle Georgia. The plot outlines sufficed for his literary purposes. While the excessive dialect he placed in the mouth of Uncle Remus and Daddy Jake seemed a sign of realistic portrayal, the writers of local color fiction in the nineteenth century regularly employed phonetic dialect as a literary device to emphasize the quaintness of regional characters. Still, the Uncle Remus books did tap oral folklore and inspire methodical field collections. Two volumes of unadorned tales soon appeared—*Negro Myths from the Georgia Coast*, by Charles C. Jones, in 1888; *Afro-American Folk Lore, Told Round Cabin Fires on the Sea Islands of South Carolina*, by Mrs. A. M. H. Christensen, in 1892—both stressing animal stories. The emphasis on the south Atlantic coast and islands was continued by Elsie Clews Parsons, the active feminist and anthropologist who published numerous shorter and longer collections of tales from 1917 to 1943. Her most substantial works presented repertoires from the South Carolina sea islands, the Bahamas, and the Antilles. Parsons first brought to light previously unreported kinds of tales popular among Negroes, particularly jests and numskull stories. Two Negro collectors, Zora Neale Hurston and J. Mason Brewer, further extended the spectrum of Negro oral narratives by calling attention to the dramatic cycle of episodes pitting Old Marster, the planter, against John, his favorite slave, and to other genres such as supernatural accounts of "hants" and jocular anecdotes about preachers. Zora Hurston, a gifted novelist who died penniless in a Jacksonville hotel room, gathered tales in middle Georgia; Brewer, a university teacher with a master's degree in folklore from Indiana University, harvested stories from North and South Carolina and the Brazos bottoms of east Texas.

By 1952, when I began my own collecting, a sizable store of American Negro folktales had reached the printed page. Yet the extant collections fell short of the needs of the folklorist. Both Hurston and Brewer gave some literary gloss to tales, and neither provided the comparative notes that identify traditional narratives. The scholarly Parsons did annotate her texts, but she did not utilize the great *Motif-Index of Folk Literature* of Stith Thompson (1932-36), published late in her career, although she did make use of its companion tool, *The Types of the Folk-Tale* (1928). Since her time both of these ingenious indexes, which make possible the tracing of folktales to their family tree, have been considerably expanded by Stith Thompson. Parsons fully accepted the Africanist theory and arranged her tables of contents to place first the tales of clearly African provenance, but since she concentrated her activities on the island network of the Caribbean and the Atlantic seaboard, her collections only partially represent the mainland. None of these collectors identified their narrators properly, if at all, and they tell us nothing about individual styles and repertoires.

In 1952 and 1953 I recorded over a thousand oral narratives from Negroes born in the South. To travel into every state of the South and to establish contacts there would require a prolonged investigation, but in fact I performed my main fieldwork in Michigan, Negro communities had formed there from Southerners migrating north, and the storytellers I met came from Mississippi, Alabama, Louisiana, Georgia, Tennessee, North Carolina, Missouri, Arkansas, West Virginia, and Texas, and they had traveled and lived in many other states from New York to California. The most fertile raconteur, James Douglas Suggs, had resided in thirty-nine states. On one occasion I ventured south to collect in Pine Bluff, Arkansas, and Mound Bayou, Mississippi, and discovered that various of the Arkansas narrators were born in Mississippi, North Carolina, South Carolina, Kentucky, and Tennessee. These thousand stories, then, well represent the full storehouse of American Negro folktales. From this batch of tape-recorded and dictated narratives I have selected typical specimens, grouped them according to their central themes and characters, supplied data on all the narrators and described the most talented and prolific in some detail, and furnished comparative notes indicating the traditional nature of the tales. From this information one can render new judgments on the sources and content of Negro stories.

The first declaration to make is that this body of tales does not come from Africa. It does not indeed come from any one place but from a number of dispersal points, as the comparative notes make clear. Many of the fictions, notably the animal tales, are of demonstrably European origin. Others have entered the Negro repertoire from England, from the West Indies, from American white tradition, and from the social conditions and historical experiences of colored people in the South. Only a few plots and incidents can be distinguished as West African. Each tale has to be studied separately to discern its history. The "Old Marster" cycle appears to be a solid block of narratives, but upon examination they are seen to flow together from a number of separate channels. On one occasion I played a tape recording of Suggs to Melville Herskovits, who exclaimed, "Those are some remarkable African tales!" Shortly after, I played the same tape to Stith Thompson, who exclaimed, "Those are some remarkable European tales!" These comments reflect the strong biases of the two masters, whom I equally admired. But the question of origins is susceptible of proof, and the proof of European origins lies in my notes.

Comparing the motifs known in West African folktales with those in my own collection, I have found a correspondence of only about ten percent.[3] Of the twenty-two African motifs found in the over two hundred motifs in my tales, only one is not known in Europe. This is K1162 (an index to these motifs appear on p. 380), "Dupe tricked into reporting speaking skull, is executed for lying," which does provide an African core to one popular American Negro tradition. But this case is exceptional. Not a single example is listed for J17, "Animal learns through experience to fear men," and yet this was the story I encountered most often on my field trips, far more frequently than Tar Baby. The Type Index reports instances of this tale (Type 157, "Learning to Fear Men") throughout Europe. Another fiction, "The Mermaid," that I collected in eight well-structured variants has not previously been reported in Europe or Africa or anywhere else. However, the conception of a mermaid with magic powers is European. Again, the witch of Negro Americans clearly follows the English rather than the African idea of a witch. Such a typical West African motif as G271.1, "Juju man cures bewitched boy, takes witch out of his heart and puts it in rock," never occurs in the United States. On the other hand, some of the court records of the Salem witchcraft trials of 1692 closely match my 1952 tape recording in Calvin, Michigan, of conversation about witches who ride human beings.

A second observation concerns the geographical area of American Negro folklore, which overlaps with, but yet remains distinct from, other New World Negro folklore. Joel Chandler Harris recognized from the first that dissimilar stories were told in central Georgia and coastal Georgia, and he sought to enlist collectors on the coast. One of his fictional storytellers, Daddy Jake, had come directly from Africa, and recited in a different idiom from Uncle Remus. In the present century Lorenzo Turner has shown the number of African words retained in Gullah, the name for the dialect spoken by ex-slaves and their offspring living along the Georgia and South Carolina coast.[4] In her Caribbean island-hopping trips, Elsie Clews Parsons collected some unmistakably African tales dealing with an unresolved dilemma, but this tale type is unknown on the mainland. Another noted folklorist, Martha Warren Beckwith, assembled a whole volume of Anansi the Spider stories in Jamaica, but Anansi fails to set foot in the United States, bowing out to Brer Rabbit. The conclusion emerges that the New World Negro repertoire falls into two groups of stories, one pointing toward Africa and one pointing toward Europe and Anglo-America. The Atlantic and Caribbean islands and northeastern South America comprise the first block and the plantation states of the Old South the second block. But both story stocks draw from multiple sources.

Two recent publications of Negro tales, one from the Bahamas and one from North Carolina, can confirm this point. In his admirable study and collection, *I Could Talk Old-Story Good: Creativity in Bahamian Folklore* (1966), Daniel J. Crowley supports the Africanist view of Elsie Clews Parsons advanced in her own Bahamian collection of 1918. With many more comparative materials at his disposal, Crowley places the old-stories from the Bahamas in the West Indies family of tales, sharing the stock characters and magical beings, the opening and closing formulas, the pattern of inserted songs and nonsense verses, and the episodic plots. The usual cast of characters includes B'Rabby, the tricky rabbit or man; B'Booky, the foil to B'Rabby, who takes different forms; B'Anansi, originally a spider among Twi-speaking Africans but now a mischievous boy or monkey; Mr. Jack, a youthful hero; and Mr. King, a bumbling dolt. Of this pantheon, only B'Rabby has his counterpart in mainland Negro folktales. The popular narrative of B'Rabby stealing the butter from his fellow workers by pretending to play godfather, or the account of B'Booky duping B'Rabby into playing his riding horse so that B'Booky can impress the girl they are both courting, are exceptional instances of stories shared by the Bahamian and mainland Negroes. By contrast, J. Mason Brewer's *Worser Days and Better Times, Folklore of the North Carolina Negro* (1965), fits at once into the now familiar traditions of the Southern Negro. Here are short, rapidfire anecdotal fictions about Old Marster, talking parrots, discomfited preachers, and slyly innocent colored folk. Some of these tall tales, jokes, and ghost stories circulate equally in white and Negro circles.

A third general observation applies to the changing character of the Negro folktale repertoire within the United States. The note of social protest has come to sound more overtly, both in historical accounts of the white man's injustice and in wryly humorous jests of race relations. As colored people move north, the forms and style of their oral expression alter to catch the rhythms of the urban ghettos. In his collection of Negro narrative folklore from south Philadelphia titled *Deep Down in the Jungle* (1964), Roger D. Abrahams has placed on record the powerfully obscene staccato jokes and long rhymed toasts heard in poolrooms, dives, and slum apartments. Brer Rabbit has become a fast-talking, sporty hipster in the reshaped Negro lore of Harlem, Watts, south Chicago, and other metropolitan ghettos.

The Negro folktales presented here are of course much more than a body of entertaining stories. They open the door into a submerged culture finally moving into its rightful place in American life. From this subculture have arisen personalities who are household names today: sports champions, entertainers, politicians, intellectuals. One or two generations back their families lived in the South of conjure doctors and chanting preachers reflected in these tales. The young Negro professor chatting gaily and cleverly with his white colleagues seems a product of the same academic environment as theirs, and a master of the same jargon, but in a moment, if you know his world, he will switch—not without some surprise at your knowing—to the other world of his birth and childhood and tell of his illiterate grandmother in Alabama who has seen the spirits and knows all about signs and omens. The contrast between the two worlds may appear to oppose affluence and poverty, education and ignorance, fortune and misfortune. But from another perspective one may perceive deep resources of mind and imagination and tongue in the traditions of colored folk unknown in the pallid lives of college-bred white people. The folktales of Negro Americans are one expression of those resources.

[1] Quoted in Stella Brewer Brookes, *Joel Chandler Harris—Folklorist* (Athens, Ga., 1950), p. 155.

[2] Julia Collier Harris, *The Life and Letters of Joel Chandler Harris* (Boston and New York, 1918), p. 162, quoted in Brookes, p. 23.

[3] This comparison is made on the basis of Kenneth W. Clarke's "A Motif Index of the Folktales of Culture Area V, West Africa" (unpublished doctoral dissertation, Indiana University, 1957).

[4] Lorenzo Dow Turner, *Africanisms in the Gullah Dialect* (Chicago, 1949).

II THE COMMUNITIES AND THE STORYTELLERS

1. MICHIGAN

Calvin

On a raw Friday afternoon in early March 1952, I drove down a blacktop and gravel road into Calvin Township, a farming settlement in southwestern Michigan. The countryside looked bleak and hostile and the frozen brown fields wore a sullen face. Outwardly the rectangular farms, red barns, and clumps of cattle suggested a typical community of husbandmen. But in one startling respect Calvin differed from her neighbors; most of her thousand souls were Negroes. They owned and tilled the loamy soil of Calvin, or commuted to surrounding cities for daily jobs, or rested here in retirement. Negroes held all the township offices, and Calvin boasted the only township supervisor of color in the state of Michigan. Before the Civil War, freedmen had drifted into Calvin, invited by Quakers or settled by white fathers, and slaves had fled there on the underground railroad. Booker T. Washington visited Calvin at the turn of the century, and praised this example of agricultural progress independently achieved by his people. During the depression years a new tide of immigrants had streamed into Calvin— Southern-born fugitives from Chicago's South Side anxious to live and buy land in a Negro village. The established families, whose children had inversely sought their futures in the big cities, frowned on these darker, poorer, less educated newcomers, and tension had developed as Michigan landowners faced Mississippi laborers.

Calvin attracted me as a testing ground in my quest for Negro folktales up North. In spite of all the substantial collections from Southern states, no one had ever sought folk tradition from the five million Negroes who now lived in a new black belt from New York to Chicago. Had the rich repertory of Southern tales taken root in chilly climes? Did storytelling still flourish as a vital part of Negro culture? How did the folklore of colored families born and bred in the North compare with that of the transplanted Southern migrants? These questions led me to Calvin, and subsequently to other Negro areas in Michigan.

On first appearance Calvin looked unpromising indeed for collecting purposes. No cluster of shops or main street offered an opportunity for casual meetings and inquiries, only a bleak crossroads where a gloomy store faced a boarded-up town hall. An invisible people lived behind the empty fields and scraggly woods, protected even against automobile intrusion by deep thick mud that turned the back roads into morasses. Two points of contact with the community lay available to me: the tavern, a quarter of a mile from the four corners, which I hung around diligently; and the churches, which I attended prayerfully. Learning about the strong new Adventist group in the township, I found my way on Saturday to their trim white meetinghouse, and on Sunday drove through mud to the century-old Chain Lake Baptist Church. Right after the Adventist service a stiff, pear-cheeked lady rushed up to me, thrust some religious literature into my hands, and began speaking volubly. She was Carrie Taylor Eaton, daughter of a slave, the first Negro girl to graduate from the Indiana high schools and enter Indiana University, known as a local poetess, fluent, sharp, shrill, race-bitter. We met again later, when she introduced me to a few storytellers. At the Baptist service, sparsely attended that chilly day, the minister called on me to speak from the congregation, and I stated briefly my interest in the local history and background of this unique community. Once more someone sought me out, a deacon named Fred Steele, who had assisted on the centennial booklet of the church a few years before, and would like to help me gather the local history. For several days we snaked back and forth through the farms and homes of Calvin, talking with elderly survivors of the oldest families, while I probed vainly for traces of folktale.

These were a strange people, the descendants of Calvin's Negro pioneers —caught between cultures, thin of body, yellow in color, reedy of voice, sapped of energy. Some could easily pass for white, and several showed discomfiture at my questions about their past. The township supervisor, a pudgy little man who worked in the county rest home, supposedly a jocular fellow, shifted uneasily during our brief interview, said his folks came from Ohio, and dismissed me with "We're a forward-looking, progressive people here; we don't look back." Others, less conscious of their position, spoke candidly and even brutally about their own and their neighbors' genealogies, tearing apart the polite veil of Ohio origins to reveal direct connections with slavery. One of the pioneers had fled to Calvin as a fugitive slave, shooting his master, crossing the Ohio River at night, and receiving the applause of farmers on the other side for his act of murder. Another family was descended from a Confederate general who had bought his mulatto son a farm in Calvin. One old settler, after getting his free papers, bought the slave girl he loved and came North with her; ever after, during a domestic spat, he silenced her with "Shut up, Lizzie, remember I bought you."

Beyond these family traditions, however, no visible links with Southern Negro culture remained. My only glimpse of storytelling behavior developed on a visit Steele and I paid to Oscar Saunders, the last representative of Calvin's first Negro family, whose fortunes had ebbed away. Fred Steele greatly relished these conversations, for though Northern-born he ranked beneath the first families, being a later, darker arrival, and savored each gossipy revelation of their slavery origins. In Saunders he found a kindred spirit, also resentful of the aristocracy, and the two fell to chatting and joking in high spirits; when somehow the conversation turned to ghost stories, the two matched eerie experiences in a breathless flow, slapping their thighs and rocking with laughter at the unnatural scares that had sent them flying from deserted houses and overgrown pathways. Here seemed some fragmentary survival of the olden lore; did it point to larger, richer pockets?

My fifth night at Calvin I sat alone in Ab and Edith's tavern puzzling over my strenuous unrewarding days in the field. As far as the Northern residents were concerned, my quest appeared thoroughly futile; the best informed old settler had simply pulled down the county history and begun reading passages about Calvin's beginnings. One genuine animal folktale had crept into my notebooks, from St. Elmo Bland, a massive ex-furniture mover stricken with Parkinson's disease, who stared fixedly before him and spoke with childlike slowness about his youth in Mississippi. Carrie Eaton and her sister Lulu Powell had recited snatches of folklore stories; they were Missouri-born, but raised in Indiana. My few leads all pointed to Southerners, although as yet I had made no effort to reach these newer migrants.

At this juncture Edith brought me a fish sandwich and coffee and began conversing amiably. In spare moments I dropped regularly into the tavern, for a beer, or a lunch, or the weekend dances that brought colored people from as far as Chicago and northern Indiana, just to let myself be seen, and also to strike up acquaintances with the regular bar loungers. Tonight this policy bore fruit, for Edith began talking in rapid-fire confidence. Large, sallow, harried, and maternal, Edith knew intimately the town of her birth, whose iniquities flowed past and through her doors, and she prattled on about mixed matings, crimes of passion, and other scandalous bits, until abruptly pausing, she confessed, "We didn't know what to make of you when you first came here; there had been two federal detectives around not long ago, to break up a marijuana ring, and some thought you were from the FBI. But I told them, No, you must be a writer feller like you said, because you had those two patches on your sleeves, where you'd worn out the elbows from writing on a desk." And Edith pointed to the reinforced leather patches on my jacket, sewed on, luckily, just the month before. Becoming now quite friendly, Edith asked how my work was progressing, and could she help. I admitted to disappointment and wondered if she could suggest some likely Southerner for me to see.

"You might call on Suggs down at the four corners past the Community Church," she mused. "He's from Mississippi, and he's a good talker. His wife don't hardly know she's alive; they've got ten kids, and can use any help you give them; I took some clothes to them once when they were living in a chicken shed. Be sure to say Edith sent you."

Thanking Edith, I drove right down to Suggs's house, faced with cheap brick siding, and found him smiling expectantly at the stranger. "I hear you know lots of stories," I said at once. "I know a million of them," he responded with a wide grin and, standing on the grimy floor with his numerous barefoot daughters peering out from the bedroom, we swapped yams for two hours straight. Suggs proved the best storyteller I ever met. For whole days, from morning till midnight, he dictated tales to me, or recited them into the tape recorder, faultlessly and with great gusto. "I hear a story once and I never forget it," he boasted innocently. Alert-eyed and smooth-skinned in spite of his sixty-five years, with a husky melodious voice, Suggs resembled a champagne bottle about to fizz, his expansive buoyancy barely corked by the restraints of society. Relax them a trifle, and Suggs erupted into fable, anecdote, jest, and minstrelsy; eventually he volunteered nearly two hundred narratives and twenty-five songs.

The evening after I met Suggs proved lucky too, when, at the end of a wearying fruitless day, Fred Steele took me to the E. L. Smiths. They had come out of the South, and Steele kept referring dubiously to the lady as "awfully fogy." On our entrance a voluminous woman with lustrous features and a courtly little man all seamed and wrinkled, rose from their dinner and enveloped us with hospitality. They pressed us to dine with them, narrated tales, and talked continuously; Mrs. Smith overpowered the men with her vocal energy and, for nearly an hour, standing all the while, she delivered a monologue on how the spirit of a brown man had brought her from Chicago to this farm in Calvin with its magically healing spring. The Smiths exuded supernatural lore and belief about witchcraft and hoodooism and God's vengeance; they fitted each other like two pieces of stovepipe, one taking up where the other left off, and kept the collector dizzy and furiously scribbling. With such lively informants the recording machine clearly could help, and one memorable evening it snatched from the air an animated conversation strewn with witch and hant tales.

Just as I was setting up the machine, a stranger entered, a slight, fragile old lady, trailed by two little grandsons. This boded ill for my recording session, but no interruption could have been better timed. The newcomer perfectly complemented the Smiths, for Mary Richardson, raised in Tennessee and Mississippi, shared their culture and could exchange occult mysteries with them long into the night. This wisp of a woman, her nose squashed in by hoodoo evil (as she would later reveal), and her bones always sore with "arthuritis," possessed indomitable spirit and salt, and fairly crackled with spry sayings and arresting accounts.

In Suggs, the Smiths, and Mrs. Richardson, I struck gold. These four Southerners overflowed with traditional lore, and their words were enriched by earth-drawn phrases and melodious tones. They sang, rhymed, intoned, mimicked, reproduced the sounds of witches, birds, trains, animal calls, and human cries. All believed in hoodoo, spirits, and the literal word of the Bible, whose store of marvels they continually cited to underpin their own wondrous tales. Other Southerners in Calvin shared these traits to some degree, and the answer to my initial query soon became evident, and would be supported by fieldwork in other communities. A wide gulf separated the Southern-born migrants from the Northern stock; often miserably poor in the world's goods, these plantation folk were richly endowed in cultural tradition; their vibrancy and animation contrasted curiously with the general listlessness and business obsession of the old Northerners. "How come these folks up here got so little *spirit?*" Mrs. Richardson once queried.

Suggs I saw most of, and he became adept at dictating narratives to me or reciting them for the tape recorder.

Unquenchable, fraternal, Suggs still wore the badge of the minstrel entertainer, breaking into story, jest, song, and even dance when the spotlight swung his way, vastly enjoying applause. But in another mood he turned crackerbox philosopher, and moralized on human behavior in simple Biblical terms. Stopping at the tavern with him one evening after a recording session, I saw Suggs in his element—greeting a dozen people with voluble enthusiasm, kidding, swapping jokes, giving and getting the laugh—and one readily understood how and why he accumulated stories. The candor of his conversational sallies left me agape. He remarked to a dumpy, whitish woman how fat she had gotten, then asked how her husband Frank was making out since his last attack, when it sure looked like he was going to die. Seeing Frank, a tall unshaven man with an old felt hat sitting at the bar, Suggs yelled out, "Looked like you were going to leave us last winter, didn't it, Frank?" and Frank weakly smiled assent. But Suggs's genuine good humor disarmed everyone, and left a wake of smiles in the crowd.

The role of collaborator with the college professor delighted him, and he once confided that several persons in Calvin had complained to Edith for sending me to Suggs instead of to them. After I mailed him a photograph of the two of us standing before his shack, he carried it about constantly and displayed it to all comers in the tavern. Finally he made a touching gesture. Calling for the first time with my wife, I beheld him emerge resplendent in a pressed navy-blue pinstripe suit, white shirt, and tan hat with uncrushed brim, walking on eggs in his self-consciousness, but mighty pleased too. "There's no cause for me to dress up on the job or at the tavern," he explained, "and of course I'm not cou'ting no more. But I can look good when I go out visiting with respectable folks."

Mary Richardson proved to be my second best narrator, next to Suggs, giving me fifty-four stories, of which I printed twenty-three in *Negro Folktales in Michigan*. In addition, she knew sayings, signs, and beliefs in dense profusion.

Mary was born in North Carolina between Wilson and Selma, on an eighty acre farm owned by her father, who was part Creek. "I'd have to go back to the Bible to get the date," she says, but believes that she turned seventy-one on March 18, 1953. However her family moved to Clarksdale,

Cohoma County, in northern Mississippi in March, 1881, when she was seven, which would make her seventy-nine in 1953. "My father read in the paper where Mississippi land was so rich you didn't have to manure it; so he sold out and emigrated."

Mary only went to school for a day here and there. "I don't know as I got one year of school if all the days was put together. I went one day in North Carolina, and I stood up and cried all day; it was a mean teacher, and I was afraid of him. He crocked me up and down the head with a lead pencil. It was the longest day God ever made, that first day I went to school. I was hungry, tired, sick, and had a headache where he struck me up and down the forehead with that lead pencil and hollered 'E\ When it come to 'rithmetic and subtracting I'd get lost, like the dog on the rabbit's tracks. But for a piece or a speech I'd be right up there with the good scholars."

Mississippi proved disappointing to Mary. "I didn't like the situation in the South. A person should be judged on what they is, not make angels out of white and devils out of black. I got tired picking such big crops for so little, on halves." So she began moving north, along the route of many other Deep South Negroes, farming in Arkansas and Missouri with her first husband. She married Mose Hale in 1922—"no license"—and moved to Chicago with him and their four children in 1930. "We got divorced about a year after. I got tired him drinking, th'owing away the money. I decided I could live better in a breshpile than with him hunting me." In Chicago she earned her living sewing and doing housework, and married Eddie Richardson from Mobile, Alabama, in 1943. The next year they bought a little farm in Calvin, where Mary could live "near the earth, like the rabbit. I'd rather stay here and fry frogs." One son, Nathan Hale, lives on the hill close by her and works at Studebaker in South Bend, two others are in Chicago, and a fourth is a preacher in Decatur, Illinois. She cannot join them as she loses her old age pension if she leaves Michigan. Eddie was severely? crippled in one arm and one leg, and Mary did all the chores, planting and pulling the com, feeding the hog and chickens and dogs and cats, when I met them. Still she kept her tiny home spick and span. On my last visit to Calvin, in September 1955, we found her living alone. Eddie had been taken to a hospital in Chicago with a serious kidney ailment, and she despaired of seeing him again. She had given up her livestock but still tended her cornfield. At dusk she "barred up" the house, and kept it dark to appear deserted, sleeping with a gun under the bed. "I'll stay here as long as

I can burn bread," she told us. "Then I'll go up to the red house on the hill [the old folks' home] and get acquainted with those folks."

A marvelous narrator of realistic occurrences, Mary excels at the supernatural belief tale rather than the humorous fiction. She thoroughly credits witchcraft and hoodooism, and will tell for true, as specific localized events, folktales that other informants relate for amusement. Her repertoire thus contrasts with that of John Blackamore (published in *Western Folklore*, XIII, 1954, pp. 77-97, 160-169, 256-259), whose twenty-eight texts, which run to the animal and Old Marster tale and the racial jest, correspond with hers in only two instances. Mary Richardson specializes in the strange and macabre experience, and sometimes the listener cannot be sure whether she relates fact or fiction.

Benton Harbor

"Before my peach tree started bearing, I drove up north to get some fruit at a new settlement called Town Line Road. It lays on the Benton Harbor town line. They had colored folks from every state in the South coming in there."

This chance remark by Mr. Smith led me to Benton Harbor, a rapidly growing industrial and fruit shipping center of some twenty thousand people, an hour's drive northwest of Calvin toward Lake Michigan. Swarms of Southerners, both colored and white, had moved to Benton Harbor in the last few years, to work in the foundries and on the surrounding orchards and farms. Summer pickers drove up from the deep South for the annual cherry and apple and peach harvests, and Arkansawyers placarded at home by promises of a better life came up for good. After a storm had desolated southern Arkansas, the mayor of Benton Harbor dispatched trucks to the stricken area laden with food and supplies and bearing posters, "Benton Harbor is a good place to live and work." The great ambition of an Arkansas Negro was to own a car with a Michigan license. Overnight Negro colonies had sprung up around town—the tough section known as "the Flats" south of Eighth Street, the genteel neighborhood west of Paw Paw Avenue, the army barracks used for newcomer housing along Fair Avenue called "the Project," and the rude collection of shacks on the southern outskirts of the city named New Bethel or Town Line Road. One old-timer could recall the day he first came to Benton Harbor and found only a handful of Negro families for company, while now half the town was colored.

Driving to Benton Harbor for the first time, I asked a gas station attendant for the colored section, and he pointed across the highway to the barracks. The sight of so many apartment units clustered side by side cheered me, after the arduous trekking through the muddy back-roads of Calvin, and I visualized easy access to a continuous string of informants. The case proved otherwise. This barracks community, transplanted and rootless, uneasily adjusting to Northern city life, lacked social warmth and *esprit de corps;* people did not know their nextdoor neighbors, and no gathering places existed to promote acquaintance; the dingy barracks huddled and compressed body and spirit. I found storytellers, but with more effort and pains than one would have thought.

My chief luck in Benton Harbor came through the unexpected twist of circumstance so characteristic of field work. A series of feeble leads had brought me to the living room of Idell Moore, a tall, lithe young mother of six children, including one moaning baby who had just fallen off the bed. While a Western movie blared on the TV screen, she narrated a fine version of The Devil's Daughter. But Idell had her hands full, and suggested I see her bachelor brother, Joe Booth, who had heard the same stories from their father in Arkansas. Joe, who lived in a grubby gray house close by the Project, proved most friendly, taller and slimmer even than his sister, thin of face, cavernous of grin, perpetually on the verge of explosive laughter, and apparently the perfect storyteller. Oh yes, he assured me, he had always been the life of the party, telling one joke and toastie after another all night long. Fine, would he tell me some? Joe tried, but couldn't think of a one. I prompted him with some sample tales, which he appreciated hugely, but they failed to trigger him off.

We lapsed into an embarrassed silence; Joe cudgeled his brains helplessly, and gave up. He had been taking a correspondence course in air conditioning, and thermal units had driven all the stories out of his head. Suddenly he called to somebody in an inner room, "Hey, John, come out here and tell this fellow a story." A heavy-set, dark, and impassive young man appeared, in the act of tying a tie over a fresh shirt, and began to dictate a folktale to me in a deadpan voice. He told two in fact, dressing all the while preparatory to going out, and I scribbled them in my notebook until he went out the door. That was my introduction to John Blackamore, a master at long circumstantial narratives delivered with unerring detail, but in so flat a monotone I never bothered to record him.

On subsequent visits Blackamore dictated tales seven and eight hours at a stretch, effortlessly and inexhaustibly. On closer acquaintance he appeared less stolid and imperturbable, and revealed a jocular and mirthful vein. John worked hard, at his regular foundry job, hauling loads in his truck, and renting rooms in his house and garage. A sporty new Chevrolet convertible testified to his rising status. Arkansas-born and Missouri-bred, John had come north in 1946 with his father, and speedily adjusted to the Northern tempo. "I haven't told any tales since I left Missouri," he said; "no time for it up here."

Friendly Joe Booth steered me to another star storyteller, calling him on the phone and insisting that by all means I visit Tommy Carter. He proved a personality sure enough, youthful, dapper, narrow-faced, suave in manner and soft in speech, self-assured and easy. Tommy had been around; he had left his home in Mississippi and found a waiter's job in Florida; traveled throughout the Deep South as a confidence man selling mojos (lucky hands) at five dollars apiece until the law caught up with him; broadcast for a radio station in Georgia; played in a jazz band, and had finally come to roost up North. Each time I came to Benton Harbor, Tommy had a different job: welder, garbage man, bellhop in the hotel where I stayed. He talked smoothly, and related slavery-time folktales with a pretty touch.

Not till a second trip to Benton Harbor did I reach my original target, the settlement on Town Line Road, a dismal collection of shanties and shacks lying on an unmarked dirt road. "It's too rough out there for me," one of my friends in the barracks remarked. Walking around the deeply rutted roads, and viewing the nondescript dwellings, I sensed a general debility and sloth, rather than any roughness; three old men I spoke to, hanging about the mailboxes, seemed near witless. Town Line Road had grown up haphazardly, from Arkansas and Missouri migrants, and lacked any community spirit, or even a legal name. All my inquiries and attempts to make contacts proved fruitless, until chance uncovered one remarkable family of informants. Someone gave me the name of Brown Lee, whom I found in a squalid cupboard of a shack, possessing only a verminous bed and a stumpy chair. Brown Lee and a friend sitting in the doorway jumped up hospitably, proffered me the chair, and fell to gossiping and storytelling most amiably. Impressively wrinkled, hawknosed, bulb-eyed, Brown Lee in his slouch hat and rags made an arresting figure; he ranted like an oldtime preacher, discoursing on the iniquities of mankind, the white man's cruelty to the black, and his own hard lot. Brown Lee appeared a much abused man, but a different opinion shortly reached my ears.

Wandering through the dilapidated settlement, I approached the very last structure at the edge of the fields, in whose doorway stood a somber woman of wide girth. Having no entree, I simply called out to ask if she knew stories. Surprisingly, after my rebuffs and blank looks that day, she said yes matter-of-factly, asked me in, and launched directly into an attractive variant of How the Buzzard Got his Bald Head. Sarah Hall spoke in a soft, mellifluous voice, oddly incongruous with her bulky shape and sullen look. She soon broke off from story-telling, and commenced a savage onslaught against her ex-husband, who turned out to be none other than Brown Lee. He had abducted two of their children, sent the boy to reform school and put the girl in a detention home. Brown Lee called Sarah a whore, and stopped the church at Benton Harbor from helping her. Yet she had bought him a house (the shack I had just visited), for a hundred dollars. Now that Sarah Hall had a good home of her own, and another man, he had hoodooed her father and uncle to death, and sworn to get her next.

At this point in her diatribe her youngest daughter walked in, Effie Dean, a bright, solemn, well-scrubbed child of ten, and at Sarah Hall's behest began reciting folktales with grace and poise. Effie's chubby twelve-year-old sister Barbara, and Odessa too, a racy-looking filly I met once later, on her release from the detention home, told stories, and this family group (all Arkansas-born) would yield prize texts. Proper storytelling flourished in this household, and Sarah Hall sharply corrected the girls if they omitted the signature endings which, in the old days, concluded all fireside tales.

Covert

At Benton Harbor I heard about Covert, some twenty miles north in the next county, which had in recent years gone Negro. From the state highway that split the village nothing unusual could be seen, just the customary gas stations, cafes, garage, post office, and tavern to service the surrounding farmers. But most of the people on the sidewalk or hanging around the tavern were colored. Overnight, Negroes had bought up properties in Covert as they came on the market, and won the town. "See that old feller shuffling across the street," a lounger on the tavern steps confided to me. "When the white folks put up the big two-story building down yonder for sale, he bought it, paid eight thousand dollars cash money. No one knew he had a button; he just did odd jobs, janitor work, raking leaves. That's how it is; the colored come in and the white go out. Why, some of them look as if they came straight over from Afriky." And my friend, who said he was part Indian, sniffed contemptuously. Later I was told, however, that he was first cousin to a very dark man sitting nearby.

In little Covert with its shifting population the color line had fast receded. Late in the evening I found myself writing the tales of Ray Brooks, a husky, benign colored man, in the grimy apartment he shared with a white woman and her two children. Earlier, gray-haired Edward Mills pointed out to me, from the porch of his little home facing the highway, a figure striding along the road with a sack of groceries. "That white woman came to Benton Harbor from Arkansas with her husband and four children. She was working in a plant, when she saw a colored feller whose looks she liked. She asked to be introduced, and took up with him, and left her white husband and kids and married him. A good-looking woman too—and she's from the South."

Covert yielded its share of storytellers, all Southern migrants, and on my second visit produced a star. Joe Dee Heardley, Louisiana-born, of an Irish father and a "Jewmaica" Negro mother, had just come to town from Grand Rapids, to open a barber shop. Short, light, curly, and unquenchably merry, Joe spouted forth quips, gags, and repartee in a furious stream, all the while posing, gesturing and gyrating, without apparently ever missing a clip of the shears. The barber shop was his stage, and the waiting customers his captive audience. Only the slightest suggestion was needed to direct Joe's patter toward tall tales, jokes, and riddles.

Idlewild

A flourishing summer resort visited by celebrities like Joe Louis and Lena Home, Idlewild sports a glossy reputation unique among Negro communities in Michigan. I chose to drive up one day late in September, when the resorters had vanished, in order to see what year-round permanence existed here. Empty hulls of gaily painted hotels and lake floats and roadside taverns reflected the summer's fun, and at first sight this appeared a ghost resort. Beneath the tinsel, however, a large Negro population had come to roost, fanning south from Idlewild the four miles to Baldwin^ county seat of Lake County, and thence another eight miles farther down to the all-Negro settlement of Woodland Park, established from the overflow of a second, less publicized summer colony. Real estate promotion had first enticed Negro Chicagoans to the cutover lands bordering on Idlewild and Spring Lakes; now pensioners had moved out to retire, or summer fruit pickers lingered on in the winter, fishing and hunting, and commuting to jobs in distant cities. Already the Baldwin high school was 50 per cent Negro.

One short visit disclosed Southern storytellers among the caretakers and all-year-rounders who wandered along the deserted lanes of Idlewild. Lee Curtis, a solitary widower with steel-gray hair and powdery cheeks, had come here from Chicago ten years before, wishing to retire to a country spot; he knew tales from his youth in Tennessee and Kentucky. "I've told lots of stories to my boys. My wife left me six to rear up after she died, and evenings they'd say, Daddy tell us some stories. And I'd tell one rigmarole after another—telling jims, they call it. My boys caught it from me, and I ain't got a boy that can't tell jims and stories."

Curiously, Curtis used the name Efan for the roguish slave conventionally called John, a use duplicated only by Suggs among all my informants.

A grocery store nestled among the shuttered hotels showed signs of life, and walking in, I saw a fleshy old gentleman with thick glasses and frizzy hair sitting idly by the counter. He proved to be Charles Brown, born in Zachary, Louisiana, in 1888, and he agreeably told me three tales right off the bat. One of these, the Fight between the Two Strong Slaves, proved a special prize, for it reflected slavery attitudes on the old plantation in revealing and ingenious fashion.

Inkster

A friend in Detroit, hearing of my interest in Negro communities, mentioned nearby Inkster. A visit disclosed a substantial development, grown up since the 1920's, when a few colored folk spilled out from Detroit in search of a home and a lot. With the great Negro migration to Detroit's defense plants in the Second World War, and the impossible housing conditions in the city, many Southerners sought shelter at Inkster, and the government constructed barracks for the overflow. Now over sixteen thousand souls reside in Inkster, the early comers in their own homes and cottages on the east end, the late arrivals packed into drab "project" units on the west. Main highways bound Inkster on all sides, and a cement road cleaves her in the middle, forming a minor Main Street, with barber shops, grocery stores, a pawn shop, and a pool room. On the western boundary, Middle Belt Road, stands the Club Vogue, a lush night spot filled on weekends with well-dressed colored patrons come to dance, drink, listen to a highly souped-up band, and watch mobile performers. A new million-dollar school had just opened, to serve the bursting area. Inkster wears a casual and self-assured air, in contrast to the rawness of Baldwin and Benton Harbor.

Lacey Manier gave me the inside history of Inkster, in which he has played a leading part. Although I dropped in unknown and unexpected on a Saturday night, directed by a grocer, Mr. Manier received me cordially and talked until midnight about his beloved Inkster. Tall, athletic, long-faced, volatile, he bounded around the room pouring forth local history (buttressed with scrapbooks), original verses, anecdotes, and toasties. When reciting one of his own rhymes, which had won him considerable local reputation as a toastmaster, he cocked his head, raised his voice, and broke into a mincing verbal jogtrot.

Well Inkster is a busy little town out Michigan Avenoo,
Where the people live happy and are very seldom blue.
They raise their chickens and they plant their corn
(The kind you eat with your meat
And the kind that's been distilled),
Until every lot is filled.
But they go to church on Sunday
And practically every night,
And both old and young they have their fun
And seldom have a fight.
They have their clubs and their fraternity organization,
With one thought in mind, to get ahead,
Seem to be their determination.
They prune the flowers and cut the grass
To attract the visitors when they pass.
And they never worried about the Blue Eagle,
Not even from the start,
Because I know that the records show
That Inkster has always played its part.
Now some folks brag about the city,

But I'll accept Inkster for mine,
And shall expect to find better times in Inkster.
These honest sentiments expressed Mr. Manier's pride in the progress of his town. He had sold the property bought by the first colored family in Inkster, in 1923, and had moved out himself the next year. Manier had come north from Nashville in 1916 to work for Oakland (now Pontiac), and promote fights on the side; "Jack Johnson was my trainer." Soon he turned to promoting Inkster, organized its first political club, and secured the deeds and abstracts for its first two churches (now there are thirty-six). Inkster was incorporated in 1927, but falls into Nankin and Dearborn Townships, so that it musters about 45 per cent of the voting strength in the townships. Through the efforts of the Inkster Community League, two of the four Councilmen, four of five school commissioners, half of the police and fire departments, and 85 per cent of the teachers, are colored. "A quarter of a million Negroes in Detroit never elected a Councilman." So sophisticated politically had Inkster become that in 1951 a new young Negro group broke off from the Community League, put up a rival candidate for the Council, and split the Negro vote so successfully that neither was elected.

A number of Southern storytellers cropped up in Inkster, but as usual one overshadowed all the rest. "There's an old crippled feller around the comer can spin lies all day long, and keep you laughing fit to bust," a casual acquaintance said, and so led me to Walter Winfrey. His robust frame hobbled by arthritis and his heavy face clamped in pain, Winfrey sat rigidly in his wheel chair and matched jokes and stories with all comers. Strangely, he showed little outward pleasure in yarning, but pumped out anecdotes almost mechanically, in a fertile flow. Born in Camden, Arkansas, in 1891, he had worked in sawmills, played professional baseball, served in the army, and come to Detroit in 1922, for the good pay he could make handling two-hundred-pound boxes in the transmission line at Ford. Arthritis ended his working days in 1946, but savings, pension, and insurance eased his old age, and he made some extra cash selling cases of beer stored in his refrigerator to white and colored customers. With time on his hands, his narrative talent paid dividends in delighted auditors. "All my life I had fun telling lies," he explained, to account for his repertoire, "in the sawmill, traveling with the ball club, in the army, at the factory; even in the hospital we'd go around from one room to another swapping lies." And every visit I paid him he punched out ten to fifteen stories, matching me tale for tale, while his wife and grandson and roomers and friends gaped at this fizzing fountain of comical lore.

Mecosta

Russell Kirk, my colleague and close friend, author of an epochal book on *The Conservative Mind*, told me about the little-known Negro settlement around Mecosta. Some of Russell's fine fictional pieces painted the hard, bleak life of sandhill farmers in this stump-fence country where his grandmother and great-aunts lived. Yankee homesteaders had passed Mecosta by, leaving its sandy soil for Ojibwa Indians, immigrant Poles, and free Negroes to parcel out after the Civil War. I drove up with Russell one cold weekend in February to learn what I could about these pioneer Negro families.

The tiny village of Mecosta lies in west-central Michigan, in the heart of the cutover stump country. Negro landowners are scattered through Mecosta and her neighbor townships, Remus and Millbrook and Blanshard, and so, unlike their counterparts in Calvin, lie submerged beneath the dominant whites. My task in reaching these outlying families was happily simplified through Russell's connections. His uncle, the township supervisor of Mecosta, took me directly to Herschel Cross, an historically-minded member of a pioneer Negro clan. Silvery-haired and handsome, Herschel talked fluently on crops and farm problems. In the course of our visit he happened to mention a sister, who had a Ph.D. from Radcliffe, had published three solid books on international law, won a Fulbright Fellowship to India, lectured at the Sorbonne, and served on a UNESCO committee. Yet she had been born and raised among these desolate sand barrens.

Herschel Cross proved most helpful, guiding me to his older kinfolk and other octogenarians in the area, setting them at ease, and then sitting back to savor the gossipy folk history which they poured forth. When seventy-seven-year-old George Norman, swarthy and mustachioed, sat on a hay bundle in the middle of a field his uncle had homesteaded, and told us his great-grandfather had wedded a white woman in Virginia with hair as red as fire, Herschel slapped his thigh and whistled in amazement, "So that's where all those redheaded Normans come from!" A bizarre genealogy unfolded from one after another old settler, as we poked into their past; the light skinned spoke of German and Scottish and Polish ancestors, the dark of slave and Indian forebears. European and African, free and bond, white and black, had mingled dramatically in these families, and often husband and wife or mother and son looked complete aliens to each other. Slowly the hidden history came to light.

Two lines of ox-team Negro homesteaders converged on Mecosta in the 1870's. One came from Ohio, where freedmen congregated after leaving the lower South, the other from southern Ontario, the destination of fugitive slaves who would return to the United States after the thirteenth amendment. But uniquely among Michigan's Negro communities, Mecosta had lain undiscovered by colored people outside, and no Southerners had streamed in from Chicago and Detroit to replenish the original Negro stock. Rather, the young generation abandoned their farm homes for city careers, to return annually for the great family gatherings, or the traditional Old Settlers Reunion. Over a hundred Normans gathered for their 1953 celebration, and a fortnight later some five hundred Mecosta pioneers and their descendants met as usual in the county park that a runway slave named Isaac Berry had first homesteaded. On a wooden platform, framed by tall hardwoods and bordered by School Section Lake, sat a score of Negro pioneers, none less than seventy-five, to whom the assemblage paid honor. Following the custom, the old settler who had returned from the farthest point received a prize, and this year it fell to a traveler from Oregon.

With respect to my original inquiry, the migration of Southern Negro folk tradition to the North, Mecosta offered an excellent proving ground. Not a single Southern-born colored person lived in Mecosta. Did the old storylore survive at all?

It surely had not passed into the European strain, who now belonged to and married "visible" Negroes, because somewhere a drop of Negro blood had entered their veins. They stared blankly at mention of Old Marster or hoodooing or Mr. Buzzard.

By contrast, Uncle Amos Cross responded immediately. The patriarch of a fruitful tribe, born at Remus in 1870, the year after his folks moved north from Ohio, Uncle Amos spoke proudly of his slave father, who grew up in Loudoun County, Virginia, and planted a noble family in this Michigan stump country. Taking down a sixty-one-year-old photograph, Uncle Amos showed me a picture of himself as a young man, surrounded by his parents and seventeen brothers and sisters. Of them all, only he still lived. Straight and tall, hollow-cheeked and deep-voiced with age, Uncle Amos rumbled genially about runaway slaves and the white women who had followed them north, and he lightened the talk with a few oldtime folk jokes.

A spry old lady, herself the daughter of a fugitive slave, proved to be even older and more vocal than Uncle Amos. At eighty-nine, Katy Pointer wore no glasses and performed a full day's housework; deceptively she resembled the European descendants, with her light color (received from her mother) and small features, but her father, Isaac Berry, had run away in 1859 from his master in Missouri in a harrowing escape she related to me with strong emotion and minute detail. Obviously she treasured the words of her father—one of Mecosta's best known pioneers—and had absorbed from him the realistic, humorous and supernatural traditions of slavery life. While maintaining a superior attitude toward Southern Negro superstitions, Katy had nevertheless memorized all the buried treasure and hoodoo tales confided to her by a friend from Georgia.

And still another child of a slave linked the old South with this high North country. Reputed to be Remus' most successful Negro farmer, Will Todd looked like anything but a man of business: short and stumpy, with a mouth full of broken teeth, reddish cheeks, a small mustache, and a rhythmic twangy voice. He too had heard his dad tell of slave degradations; once his father had to lick off with his tongue manure splashed on a white horse. He must have heard other matters also. Standing under a grove at the Old Settlers picnic, he twanged animatedly about his own powers as a bloodstopper, and described occult healers in the vicinity who had mysteriously cured him and his kinfolk of painful ailments. Clearly Will, though Michigan born, had breathed in much of the plantation culture.

Mecosta ended my quest, and confirmed my earlier findings. Southern Negro lore had moved north indeed, but only with migrants cradled and nurtured in the yeasty Southern traditions, or with the few still-living children of slaves. Northern-born Negroes, growing up among cities and factories, supercilious toward their Southern brothers, had severed and discarded their folk heritage, and the new migrants grow farther from it as they take on Northern attitudes. But while Negro emigration keeps flowing northwards, the warm springs of leisurely Southern storytelling will continue to bathe the wintry latitudes.

2. ARKANSAS

Pine Bluff

Although folklorists in the United States enjoy no such facilities as speed up collecting, say in Ireland, they can create favorable field situations. Sympathetic institutions, agencies, and key individuals may open up routes to the prized informants one usually seeks by haphazard meanderings. Such was my experience on a field trip in southern Arkansas, when in eight days (June 23-30, 1953) I netted one hundred and sixty Negro folktales, in an area new to me and where I lacked any acquaintances.

A speaking engagement at the Arkansas Folklore Society had taken me down to the University of Arkansas, deep in the Ozark hills. Before returning north I wished to supplement my Michigan Negro lore with some Southern Negro comparisons. But the enthusiastic group I met at Fayetteville, and their leading collectors, Vance Randolph and Otto Ernest Raybum, specialized in folklore of the rolling Ozark country, where few Negroes lived. A Negro graduate student I fell in with at the student union suggested my seeing the president of the Arkansas Agricultural, Mechanical and Normal College, Lawrence A. Davis, who was taking a summer course at the University. President Davis spoke with me most cordially, saying he had himself written a master's thesis on Negro folk sermons, and came to hear my talk on "A Fresh Look at Negro Storytelling." The young and energetic president proved a benefactor indeed; he invited me to headquarter at his all-Negro college in Pine Bluff, explained its situation in the heart of the cotton-growing flatlands, where colored folk lived densely, and telephoned ahead to make arrangements for me. Accordingly I drove two hundred and fifty miles southeast, and took up residence in the new modern student union building, where I lived among Negroes, being the only white person on campus.

Except for the hundred-degree heat, this base of operations served my purpose admirably. President Davis had requested his director of public relations, the painter John Howard, to assist me; Mr. Howard, urbane and impressive, introduced me to other faculty members, who pooled their wits in my behalf. The A. M. and N. College was established in 1875 as a Negro agricultural college, but since the presidency of Lawrence Davis it has expanded, physically moving to its present attractive semi-circular campus, and intellectually moving toward a broader humanities curriculum. As is usually the case with a faculty group, close bonds with the "folk" did not exist, but the college community provided me with some initial contacts in town, chiefly professional men, and still more important, approved my credentials and made possible my smooth entry into a tension-ridden society. (An anthropologist friend of mine teaching in the South once complained that he and his students were unable to pursue field work among Negroes because of white suspicion and pressure.) Furthermore, by being around and visible for a period of time, I constantly reminded my hosts of my quest, who came up with suggestions which had not occurred to them on our first meeting.

A friend and former teacher of Mr. Howard's living close by the college turned out to be a star narrator. Reverend Silas Altheimer, a wrinkled, sharp-featured, soft-spoken, lightskinned old man, still remembered clearly the slavery-time tales he had heard from his mother. His father had come from Germany to farm in Arkansas, and developed the plantation which grew into the village of Altheimer, twelve miles outside Pine Bluff. There he met the ex-slave woman who bore him a family. "They didn't stop their old habits after slavery time, you know," the elderly man said in his gentle way. Despite his long educational background, Reverend Altheimer had absorbed completely the traditions of Southern Negro culture, and related comic fictions, grim accounts of slavery life, and supernatural legends. Surprisingly he believed in hants and hoodoos, and argued spiritedly with his son about a ghost-ridden orchard behind the ancestral home; the boy contended the strange screams and shakings were psychic phenomena, while his father stoutly maintained they were hants. At the end of each visit Altheimer said he knew no more stories, but after we talked a little on my return he remarked, "That brings one to mind," and was off again.

Between interviews and scoutings I cooled off at the Lion's Inn, a cafe on the edge of campus where most of the college community drifted in at one time or another to snack, drink iced tea or Cokes, and listen to a thunderous jukebox. The owners, Mr. and Mrs. A. A. Mazique, soon understood my mission, and introduced me to likely prospects. Shrill and voluble Mrs. Mazique loudly trumpeted my demands for old tales, and Mr. Mazique, a large, curly-haired Louisianan with French blood, told me a couple himself, and suggested a splendid storyteller, E. M. Moore, who lived right by the college in a small cottage. All the faculty knew Moore, an engineer with a fluent tongue, and seemed puzzled at their oversight in not giving me his name. Moore had owned one of the most beautiful homes in town, but sold it to finance a new type of excavator he had invented. His Indian blood showed clearly in oval features and short black hair, and he spoke in the tones of an elocution teacher. Why Moore had not immediately occurred to the faculty circle soon became apparent, for his stream of anecdotes sidestepped the conventional plots about Brother Rabbit and Old Marster, to center on the racial situation, in realistic and wryly humorous fashion. Actually Moore was relating a seldom collected narrative form, the Negro tale of social protest.

Sitting around one evening in the Lion's Inn when my leads had run out, I met A. J. King, Jr., a youthful graduate of the college, wiry and energetic, who interested himself in my project at once. He had noticed and remembered the announcement of my lecture at the University in the Little Rock paper, because it dealt with a Negro subject. He said that he was a West Indies Negro, and so smarter than the Southern-born Negro, and he talked in lively fashion, keeping the group around him convulsed with laughter. That night he drove me out to Barnes Settlement, where he taught school, and introduced me to an eighty-nine-year-old grandmother, Maria Summers, as a likely prospect. But young King himself gave me more tales than the matriarch.

One day Mr. Howard assigned the college photographer, Geleva Grice, a tall, bushy-haired young man, as my guide to inspect the outlying villages. He took me to nearby Altheimer (named for the Reverend Silas's father), to see the Negro farmers and their families come to town on Saturday afternoon, a cherished custom of the Southern Negro reflected in folktales. A wide, dusty highway separated the depot from a string of low, flat-roofed stores joined to an arcade screening the pavement from the burning sun. A dense crowd shuffled slowly up and down under the arcade. Among the stream of brightly clothed Negroes stood out an island or two of sunburned white farmers and a gang of Mexicans, imported under contract to help with the rice and cotton planting. Grice knew no one in the throng, so we went up cold to two colored men talking quietly by themselves and asked if they knew stories. Naturally they looked at us with surprise, but one of the pair (a master mason just returned from a score of years in Chicago), directed us to Ben Jones in Gethsemane, who could keep us listening from morning to night. This seemed like a dodge to get rid of us, but the man insisted, and gave us directions, and off we went, nine miles of mostly gravel road through flatlands all planted to cotton, until we reached the gas station that passed for Gethsemane, and found Ben Jones at home on his farm (he didn't own an automobile), a fairskinned, jaunty Irishman to all appearances, with a twinkling tongue sure enough, popping out jokes and tales in a steady flow, many of them "rough."

One morning a professor of foreign languages I had met casually asked how things were going, and would I like to talk to his class. I wanted this particular opportunity, and Professor Oliver Jackson kindly introduced me to his freshman composition class of some twenty students, half of whom were older women, presumably in-service schoolteachers, and urged them to assist me in gathering Negro tales. I told some samples, and after the class six students came up to contribute stories of their own.

Right from the first Mr. Howard and other faculty members suggested I visit the colored Old Folks Home. Previous collecting experience had taught me that this idea, seemingly so plausible, contains little merit. Your informant must first of all possess a keen and active mind and tongue, and institutionalized old people are often senile and witless. But since Mr. Howard had made the appointment for me, I drove out east of town through an increasingly ramshackle colored neighborhood, until I reached the home, a clean, fresh-painted little building set back from the road. Reverend Mrs. Toler greeted me, the founder of the home and minister of its adjoining chapel, an active, durably built lady with a remarkable career of teaching, preaching, and social work in the Deep South. She writes in her magazine, "I started on my mission one cold day in March, 1942. I was told of one Mrs. Ollie Hill who lived alone. She was like Job, full of sores, bedridden; a very unpleasant odor met me at the door. I was glad to bring her with me, bathe, feed and care for her."[5] So started the project that Mrs. Toler had now built up into a well equipped nursing home able to care for one hundred persons. Her inmates covered most species of human pathos, the paralyzed, the blind, the feeble-minded, a man who could only crawl, another who couldn't sit, the forgotten, the forlorn, the destitute. Mrs. Toler had culled the few not bedridden for the storytelling party, and these gathered in the chapel expectantly. In the ensuing exchange, as I anticipated, I did most of the talking and they gave little response, a handful of short texts, each followed by an outbreak of childish laughter. But the day was surprisingly saved by Mrs. Toler herself, who tried to stimulate the group with some excellent tales from her own background in the Mississippi hills, including my only version of the well-known West Indian type, In the Cow's Belly. This experience strengthened my conviction that the best informants possess superior mental gifts.

For all the assistance the college circle gave me, my richest strike in Pine Bluff came from a chance contact before I even reached the campus. The Courtneys, a father and son and their wives, belonged socially and economically to the small wage-earner class, below even the tenant farmer, who chopped and picked cotton by the day, and did what odd jobs one could in a city. Tobe Courtney had just gotten to his feet after eleven months on his back from a stroke, and sat all day on his little porch in a rocking chair; his wife Sally worked in the fields; their son John, who lived next door, although a big, sturdy-looking fellow, held an incurable cancer in his stomach, according to a doctor's letter he showed me, and could do only light jobs like paper-hanging or a little barbering on the side; his wife Julia was nursing a fourth baby and confined to the house all day. Each of the four told me stories, making up a large and absorbing family collection, and yet at first meeting the auspices appeared wholly unfavorable.

Arriving late my first evening in town, I checked in at a motel, and wandered around the nearby streets after supper. I had chosen a Negro section to stop in, and through the evening haze could discern figures seated or standing on the porches that fronted each squat dwelling. My first attempt to start a conversation failed, but my second scored a ten strike. I asked the white-haired, roundfaced old man rocking in a porch chair if he knew any tales. "No," he answered, "I stopped telling them since I became a Christian convert in 1915." In a few minutes however I had invited myself onto the porch, and chatted amiably with Tobe Courtney the rest of the evening. Tobe spoke with laborious slowness, but he had a good deal stored in his head that gradually transferred to my notebooks during the week. Tobe could do nothing except sit on his porch and greet passersby, clasping and unclasping his hands spasmodically, and his wife or son had to dress and undress him, so feeble were his arms.

Tobe soon forgot his earlier objection to storytelling, and brought me deep within his own folklore-laden surroundings. Sitting with him one afternoon on the porch, I saw a briskly walking stranger stop short, inquire as to Tobe's health, and then suggest he treat his twitching hands by splitting a frog down the middle and tying one half to each wrist; as the frog died, the misery would leave. After the man had gone, I asked Tobe why he didn't try the remedy; because his wife and son were both terrified of frogs, he said, and he couldn't tie them on himself, with his stroke. Another time, talking of witches and spirits, he mentioned a case of witchcraft that had befallen his wife, and summoned forth the timid woman, worn out from the cotton fields, who described the episode in full detail without a moment's hesitation. At one point big, ambling John Courtney, Tobe's son who lived next door, and spoke as softly as his father, drifted over, and related to his dad a vision of buried treasure that was obsessing him. John could not place the spot, but Tobe recognized it instantly. A chance reference Tobe made to a Baptist revival being held a couple of blocks away resulted in my accompanying him that night. The only white person present, I marveled at the fervent spontaneous singing of the congregation, the hortatory talents of the ministers, the tears of the mourners, and the shouts of the happy. Whoever has attended a Southern Negro revival will understand the wealth of Biblical allusion in the daily speech and the Scriptural folktales of Negroes, and the chanted interpolations these so frequently contain.

After hearing John's hidden-treasure dream, I turned his way and found that he quite exceeded his father as a narrator. In spite of his labored, rambling way of talking, John knew his texts thoroughly and in extensive detail, and his deadpan delivery sent his audience into spasms of laughter. One night I recorded half an hour of John's narration, and surprisingly his wife Julia also contributed a couple of tales into the microphone, although John had stated that she knew no stories, being a good Christian woman. Julia at first seemed on the severe side, a sturdily built, efficient, positive woman, quick of gesture and speech, the complete opposite of John. Her two stories, crisp and idiomatic, stuck in my mind, and now I found myself dropping back to see Julia. She talked six times faster than the average person, so she said, and while nursing her baby burst into a streak of storytelling that had me writing till my fingers cramped. My last evening in Pine Bluff I stopped in to record Julia, and the excitement that recording always generates stimulated John to produce fresh tales, and even old Tobe thought up another, and I recorded and wrote until after midnight. As I shook hands to say goodbye, Tobe said, "I was proud to have you visit me," with a moving sincerity that quite embarrassed me; all four Courtneys came to the gate and waved as I drove away.

Another relationship I formed off the street deteriorated instead of improving. Wandering around the heavily Negro section of town by the railroad depot, I spotted two lean men of middle age on a bench in front of a rooming hotel, and attempted to strike up a conversation. I had however failed to notice their white canes, and one had to explain to me they were blind. He could tell by my voice that I was Northern, and white. "We don't associate the same way down here." Still after this awkward start both told a John tale, and the smaller man launched off into further yams. He was Harrison Stanfill, a war veteran with apparently an adequate pension; he knew a "gang of stories," and agreed to tell me more, but on return visits I found him steadily less cooperative. Once his blind friend deferred me from going upstairs to Stanfill's room, saying he was drunk, and when I returned next morning Stanfill protested that he had a clean record and asked me to leave him alone; nor could I allay his suspicions. The fact that no one around the hotel knew me, that I asked Stanfill for the details of his birth and occupations, and perhaps that illicit transactions were conducted in the hotel, which bore a curious air of mystery within its winding corridors, blunted this contact.

3. MISSISSIPPI

Mound Bayou
Only one all-Negro town can be found in Mississippi, Mound Bayou in Bolivar County, whose mayor holds a Harvard law degree. Hearing of Mound Bayou while collecting in Pine Bluff, Arkansas, I decided to return home through northern Mississippi, and visit this unusual community. On a scorching day in the summer's heat, July the first, 1953, I drove through the endless cotton fields of the Mississippi Delta, where clusters of straw-hatted Negroes chopped away at the weeds endangering the green plants—and swapped tales as they worked—until I reached the little town on the highway where eight hundred Negroes and no whites resided. For the night I had to return a few miles to Cleveland, and put up at a shabby hotel. A nineteen-year-old Negro bellhop took my suitcase into the elevator, and before we had reached the fifth floor Archie "Billy Jack" Tyler had told me two folktales, and agreed to accompany me to Mound Bayou the next morning. Bright and quick, an enthusiastic talker when he had the floor, but subdued and passive among his elders, Billy Jack proved a fine companion, and a far better informant than any I met in my short visit to Mound Bayou.

Born in Cleveland, February 10, 1934, Billy Jack gets his name from a black billy goat in the yard the day of his birth. As a matter of course he

45

chopped and picked cotton in the fields, where he heard many stories. "They tell them in different arrangements." For three years he worked in cafés and restaurants in Greenville, doing "commercial cooking." For another three years (1948-1951), he worked for a "hoodoo" in Cleveland, Dr. Toby George. "He sent me to the drugstore for Blue Seal vaseline, Sweet Spirits of Nitrate, and Epsom Salts, in large green bottles. Then he'd have me get five gallons of gasoline, for rubbing compound." Women would come to Dr. George foaming at the mouth, and he would heal them, and find their missing husbands, "just like he was an information bureau." He had studied at Algie, across from New Orleans, with Aunt Carolyn Dye, the famous fortune-teller. Next Billy Jack had come to the hotel, and now within the week he would join the Navy.

The following day we prospected in Mound Bayou, calling on the mayor, knocking on doors, and hanging around the stores. When I drove back to an air-conditioned restaurant in Cleveland for lunch, and revival, I left Billy Jack with a notebook and pencil, and on my return he had collected two full texts of European animal tales, and located a good hangout, the barbershop. There "jackleg" preachers—licensed to preach but lacking a church—sat around, none more impressively than the Reverend J. H. Lee. Ancient, portly, heavy-jowled, his voice thick and nimbly with age, he read a passage to me from the Seventh Book of Moses, the so-called Black Bible, which he carried in his pocket. Then he matched tales with Billy Jack. Watching the septuagenarian and the stripling exchange variants, I appreciated the tenacity of Southern Negro folk tradition, that embraces the aged and the young with so firm a hold.

The paralyzing heat flushed me out of Cleveland and Mound Bayou within twenty-four hours, but not until I had garnered twenty mementoes.

---

[5] *The Echo, A Magazine For The Aged And Dependent*, ed. Rev. Mrs. L. R. Toler (Pine Bluff, Ark., vol. VII, May 1953).

III THE ART OF NEGRO STORYTELLING

Inert and rigid when set in type, and usually placed in a grotesque dialect, the Negro folktale has lacked the appreciation due a skilled art form. Its style and structure reflect the Southern Negro culture in which storytelling plays a daily role, as a source of entertainment and channel of belief. Much charm and lyric humor lie in the chants, mimicry, whiny dialogue, rhymes, and bits of song that intersperse the narratives. The storyteller continually breaks into altered tones and rhythmic sounds, to reproduce the antiphony of preacher and congregation, the cries of birds and beasts, or the weird noises emanating from haunted places. When Brother Rabbit and the other animals converse, or the little girl calls for her mama, they speak in high-pitched, almost falsetto voices, not shrill but cadenced, which is how Negroes talk to each other when greeting at a distance or calling out across the street or irately admonishing a child, a kind of second speech that falls blurred and muffled on unfamiliar ears. Two principal sources for the repertoire _ of musical inflections and tonal sounds that Southern Negroes possess lie in the barnyard animals and forest creatures whom they daily perceive, and the Baptist revivals and services where preacher and congregation swell into communal melody. With uncanny reproduction the speaker rumbles like a bull, croaks like a frog, crows like a rooster, caws like a crow. Once, walking on the front lawn of the Smiths' home, I heard a throaty call close by me, and looked all around without discovering a fowl underfoot; smiling broadly, Mrs. Smith revealed herself as the rooster issuing his mating cry, and said she had thus teased hens in Mississippi and sent them scurrying for cover. A favorite Negro tale relates the conversation of the farmer's fowls on a Sunday when the preacher is coming for dinner. The preacher always eats chicken, and the fowls attempt to warn the hen when the farmer approaches. Each teller raises his voice in piercing mimicry of the rooster's bugling—"Is the preacher go-o-o-o-ne?"—and lowers it to capture, according to the variant, the guinea's mutter, the turkey's gobble, the goose's hiss, all adapted to like-sounding phrases. In a barber shop in Mound Bayou, Mississippi, I heard an old, portly "jackleg" preacher, Reverend J. H. Lee, his voice thick and nimbly with age, suddenly turn clear and sharp as he imitated the fowls with uncanny realism, adding one call new to me, the hen shrieking in panic, "Good God good God look *out*, good God good God look *out*"—telescoping the first five words and shrilling the last, with a feverish snap, in startling likeness of a fluttering hen's cackle.

A Negro Baptist revival at Pine Bluff, Arkansas, gave me unexpected insights into Negro storytelling. The revival meeting in itself constituted a rich experience: six preachers sitting in suits and ties, despite the 100° heat, on a small platform facing the members; three sobbing women on the mourners' bench beneath them; the guest preacher, up from Louisiana, a small, round, bald dynamo; flailing his arms, rubbing his face, and chanting his exhortation, based on the metaphor of fishing—the gospel is the hook, the church is the pole, repentance the bait, and eternal salvation the catch. As his chants expanded in volume and vigor, the other preachers and the congregation met his enthusiasm with equal fervor, echoing his terminal words, interposing holy expressions, shouting and "getting happy"; in between rounds the packed little church soared into song, spontaneously, without recourse to hymnals, filling the grubby wooden walls with rapturous spirituals. All this is an old story to students of Negro life, but its relevance to the Negro folktale needs stressing. The intoned prayer, the rhythmic cry, the chanted phrase, and the religious lyric become stock in trade of Southern Negroes, and their tales incorporate these possessions. In the many jokes about preachers, the chanted sermon and ecstatic outcry are manipulated for humorous effect, but their reproductions by the storyteller are perfectly genuine and convey a ready meaning to his audience. In Cleveland, Mississippi, I heard a simple anecdote from a nineteen-year-old hotel porter, Billy Jack Tyler, about two deacons who went to church after a long absence. One deacon went into his prayer, but couldn't "call" (recall) the names of the two persons he knew he must invoke; his friend reminded him they were the Lord and Christ. Billy Jack easily slipped into the familiar wordless chant of the intoned prayer, to make the point of his jest; few white men could tell that story.[6] Suggs switches from a deep boom to a treble shriek and back again in a breath, to portray a preacher and a shouting woman, and so conveys the electric excitement and antiphonal response of the revival, all in one voice.

Many Negro tales derive their best effects from these interpolated sounds and rhymes. Some, like the foregoing, depend on mimicry, while others are regular verses on which the plot may hinge. In one episode the Deer escapes from the Fox, who guards him within a stockade, by singing a song that captivates the Fox; he demands a repetition, and the Deer insists that the Fox lower the bars first, that he may come closer and hear better; eventually of course the Fox lowers the fence to where the Deer can jump over. As Suggs relates it, the Deer sings

Shoo lally shoo, shoo lally shoo,
I do this in the summertime,
I do this in the wintertime,
Mmmmh.

Variants give different verses, but the same nonsensical character prevails, and lends the humor to the story. Suggs recites the "rhyme" with a spirit that makes an otherwise ordinary narrative memorable.

One Old Marster anecdote, assimilated from British tradition, turns upon the sound of a crosscut saw in operation. Fed only soup by their mean Boss, the feeble workmen push the saw slowly and it sighs "Soo-ooup." Given a filling meal at the urging of the Boss's wife, they push the saw lustily, and it crackles, *"Bread—meat—and—pudding."* The raconteur drags out the "soup," and snaps forth the eatables in uncanny reproduction of a saw's slow and fast whizzing. In the little fable of the bee and the dirtdauber, which satirizes the know-it-all type of person, the dirtdauber resists the bee's instruction by whining, *"I knowww, I knowww, I knowww,"* in a self-assured drone.

Well-known European tales that contain these interspersions find their way onto Negro lips. Suggs delivers the Grimm plot of The Animals in Night Quarters with throaty imitations of the animals' cries that render most plausible the robber's retreat. In a hanted-house story John Courtney related to his family in Pine Bluff, Arkansas, an overhead voice warns the daring intruders, "I'm going to fall." After several recurrences the group hastily departs, save for their leader, John, who defies the thing to fall; it does, right on his skillet, sending meat and gravy on the floor and John out the door. The chief comedy in this little scene, thoroughly appreciated by colored folk who believe in hants and spirits, lies in the quavery treble Courtney employs to render the spook's voice, rising so high that the *l* in *fall* virtually disappears, and contrasting with Courtney's normally listless and ambling speech. A listener finds himself irresistibly mimicking the cry. Another story Courtney told has the Rabbit caught by the farmer and tied to a limb; as he rocks back and forth he intones, "Going to heaven in a swing-swing-swing." The Bear appears, is persuaded to take the Rabbit's place (hence Parsons calls this type "Take My Place"), and mis-sings, in a heavier voice, "Going to heaven in a deng-deng-deng." Attracted by the strange voice and refrain, the farmer comes back and seizes the Bear. Here again the chanted insert plays a key part in the story and in Courtney's rendition provides an almost hypnotic rhythm, the n's made heavily nasal and the phrase lilted to suggest the captive animal's rocking motion. Later on I heard his youngsters echoing the chant by itself.

These stories verge on the cante-fable, the form that combines narrative and song. The oft-told encounter of a preacher with a grizzly bear (O Lord, if you won't help me, please don't help that grizzly bear) hovers between a minstrel song, a cante-fable, and a tale, according to its deliverer. In the rhythmic account of Simon Fishing on Sunday, the lethal commands of the fish Simon caught are given in an eerie singsong. Occasionally tales overlap with toasties, the rhymed sentiments, usually scatological, so popular with Southern Negroes at convivial gatherings. Blackamore told the saga of cowboy Bill as a toastie and the ballad of Stagolee as a partially rhymed narrative, while Suggs gave the first as a tale and sang the second conventionally. These cases illustrate the close connections between Negro storytelling and metrical and musical forms of Negro folk expression.

Even the manufacture of noises and indescribable sounds distinguishes the Negro tale. In his story of the monkey who ran away with a train, Suggs realistically imitated an engine gathering steam; Mrs. Smith and Mrs. Richardson reproduced the commotion made by witches tormenting them, with sound effects that a radio technician would envy. Since many Negro narratives are told as true personal experiences, these accompaniments strengthen their plausibility and verisimilitude.

Idiomatic language provides additional sauce. The Southern Negro possesses a rich and zesty vocabulary, a striking sense of imagery, some special locutions, and a bold spirit for word usage—the whole forming an exhilarating oral style. "I can't seem to soople up," complained rheumatic Walter Winfrey. "I'd buck-prick my ears to get every word," Suggs declared. "It looks like it's going to fair up," said Grandma Leonard. Mrs. Smith referred to a turkey gobbler as "strut walking." Mrs. Richardson described a cow as "so mean she could kick the sweetening out of a gingersnap." "Are you twenty-five cents rich today?" sang out a young woman to a sharply-dressed buckaroo crossing in front of her barracks apartment. "Oh, I'm a dollar and a half rich," he called back.

Nature contributes bountifully to Negro metaphor. "Up North here people aren't near so friendly as down South," Mr. Smith was saying. "Why, they pass you on the road as if you was a tree." A simple, but an unusual, analogy. "I'd rather crawl up a possum holler than have a fuss," confided Mrs. Richardson, and another time explained she had come to Calvin from Chicago to "live near the earth, like the rabbit. I'd rather stay here and fry frogs." Certain expressions are standard usage: to "pass" for to die; "call" for bring to mind, name, or recall; "carry" for take by car or other transportation; "come on" for "come in." I have heard "impitate" for "imitate" more than once; Winfrey called one yam "The first stablish of money," meaning establishment; "tooth-dentist" cropped up in an Irishman joke. All these piquancies of speech do not constitute a primitive dialect, but a vivid and racy handling of the common tongue.

Negro storytellers not only fully utilize their oral resources but also gesticulate and even act out parts in exciting narratives. When the rabbit scoots away from the fox, or John runs from the Lord, the narrator slaps his hands sharply together, with the left sliding off the right palm in a forward direction—a manual trademark of the Negro raconteur. To indicate continuous running, rather than a sudden sharp spurt, he drops his hands to his sides, spreads the fingers, and wiggles his wrists in a sideways motion, thus suggesting steady movement. Sometimes the reciter gets to his feet and weaves, writhes, gestures, and groans, to simulate the preacher exhorting his flock, or a witch straddling her victim. These histrionics build up to a small performance, the tale verging onto a drama or farce, and the audience rolling with laughter, exclaiming, commenting, and otherwise appreciating the efforts of the star.

Minstrel entertainments, which the story vendors have watched or played in, influence them. Both Suggs and E. L. Smith acted in "minister" shows while in the South, Suggs in a traveling troupe that toured the country, Smith in a local group amusing the neighborhood. Throughout Suggs's reminiscences crop up references to "magikins," evangelists, daredevils, and similar breeds of showmen, whose electrified audiences repeat and re-enact their antics. When I turned on my machine to record Sarah Hall, the listless housewife suddenly rose from her seat, burst into a strange spiel, and pointed toward a comer of the ceiling; after I had somewhat recovered, she explained that she was merely reciting a barker's monologue for the recording. Another time a limber old fellow dropped in to her parlor and introduced himself as Johnnie Walker, onetime tapdancer extraordinary, who had traveled to Germany with Billy Kassin's minstrels, danced with the Ringling Brothers Circus, and managed his own show, which made him worth $35,000, until a girl friend in Des Moines blew it away. Then to prove his statements the sixty-six-year-old entertainer broke into a series of fast-breaking steps while Sarah Hall clapped time, and pulling me out into the yard, picked up a long stick and somersaulted it on his arm while he jigged; "Astaire learned that hat and stick trick from me," he declared. Tommy Carter, the Benton Harbor comedian, among his various pursuits had acted as radio announcer in a cotton-picking contest, played in a jazz band, and peddled talismans. A fast-talking jackknife of a man I met in New Bethel, Andrew W. Smith, "an old globe-trotter," recounted a checkered history during which he had played parts in the Mardi Gras and Rabbit Foot Minstrels (under the pseudonym of "Alabama Blossom"). Lacey Manier, celebrated in Inkster as a toastmaster, composed his own verses for the convivial ceremonies at which he officiated. Not all these entertainers proved top storytellers, and some good storytellers lacked any theatrical background, but in the vaudeville atmosphere surrounding Southern Negro community life, the talents of singers, dancers, musicians, raconteurs, actors, and clowns all had their chance to blossom and to cross-fertilize. Suggs, for instance, combined all these roles.

Practice and custom have sharpened the Southern Negro's storytelling aptitude, and given him an easy and relaxed delivery. The telling of old tales, rhymes, lies, jokes, riddles, and toasties becomes second nature, an integral part of social life and the daily round, not a gift for the few but a faculty possessed by many. Suggs thus describes the social context for story entertainment from his childhood in Mississippi.

> From Christmas to New Year's the people did no cooking, just visited each other and ate. The men had nothing to do on winter days but ride to town and get a jug of whiskey. People would go from house to house then—they wasn't self-conceited like they is now—and there was fiddling, singing, dancing, blowing horns. Every house would

have a spread, with whiskey, wine, cider. They'd have quilting bees, where they'd cover up a bashful boy and girl in a quilt; that would often break up their bashfulness and give them a starting point, to get talking to each other. Then there'd be a dance and a frolic. Older people would tell hant stories to the children wasn't big enough to dance. If it was something bad I'd scrooch up and try to get away, but listen anyway; if it was something good I'd buck-prick my ears to get every word. After all that they'd have a candy-pulling, with sorghum molasses.

Besides the congenial winter holidays, other opportunities for telling and listening to tales in the routine of Southern life are mentioned by informants. Teams of half a dozen or more workers picking and chopping cotton under the broiling sun lack all distraction save what their tongues provide, and here narrators find a willing audience. Every August in recent years Negroes drive into Michigan in battered cars bearing license plates from Louisiana, South Carolina, Arkansas, to pick the fruit harvests, and in the apple and cherry orchards Southern tale-tellers continue their practice of the cotton fields, and regale their Northern co-workers with the old-timeslavery humor. Country courting, oddly enough, provoked story-swapping, for couples out on the plantation lacking other diversions soft-talked each other with funny tales of foolish widows and silly girls seeking husbands. Both Suggs and Winfrey spoke of spinning yams when sawmilling in Arkansas and traveling with semi-pro baseball clubs through the South, and apparently wherever knots of good sports gathered. The chief deterrent against "lying" appears to have been the churches; one old blind man in Arkansas told me he had given up telling stories since he learned the price he would have to pay for them on Judgment Day. Yet the churches themselves contributed to the contents of traditional story with the buffoonery of preachers and deacons and the choral effects of sermons and services.

Moving among Southern Negro groups, in the North and in the South, the collector stumbles on his informants at all age levels, among both sexes, and in manifold occupations. Suggs, my outstanding contact, was sixty-five when I met him, and John Blackamore, another star, was thirty. In a barber shop in Mound Bayou, Mississippi, I heard nineteen-year-old Billy Jack Tyler exchange folkyarns with a septuagenarian preacher, Reverend. J. H.

Lee. Ten-year-old Effie Dean recited stories even more fluently than her mother. Education matters not; Reverend Altheimer, a graduate of the Negro college at Pine Bluff, had spent most of his eighty-odd years teaching and preaching, but recounted tales with utmost facility. In fact, a story carrier may turn up anywhere, unpredictably, in the Negro world. During a Saturday night dance at Ab's tavern in Calvin, I bought a beer for a young musician in the band at intermission; he seemed so unlikely a prospect I made no attempt to collect from him, but Jerry Moultrie asked me my business, and at my sheepish admission that I "collected stories," reacted with immediate enthusiasm and narrated a fine text of How the Buzzard Got his Bald Head, spilling it out hurriedly while the band waited impatiently. Twenty-one-year-old Jerry had grown up in East Chicago with Louisiana stories in his ears, brought north by his grandmother and great-grandmother. Such experiences affirm the pervasive force of folk narration in Southern Negro life, where folktales weave in and out of ordinary conversation.

If many Southern-born Negroes display a common gift for yarning, the conclusion by no means follows that they employ a common style. The themes, internal devices, gestures, phrases, and signature endings bear a uniform stamp, but over and beyond this homogeneity stands a considerable variation in individual delivery.

A collector who works over a period of time with superior storytellers comes to recognize their distinctive mannerisms, despite their common fund of traditions. While Suggs narrates with fire and gusto and great animation, Blackamore speaks in a dead flat monotone. Nevertheless Blackamore qualifies as a first-rate narrator, because of his uncanny memory and fullness of text. Where the inferior teller brings forth a truncated edition of the tale, reduced to the skeletal motifs, Blackamore fills out the narrative with circumstantial and minute detail, and marches to the signature with never a pause. His texts customarily run a thousand or more words, where an average raconteur may spin the same plot in a couple of hundred, and yet his rendition never seems forced or unduly expanded. For instance, a widely told little anecdote has one slave brag to another of "putting his hand under Old Missie's dress"; his friend tries it, with dire consequences; the braggart then explains that the dress was hanging on the clothesline. Customarily no more than this is given, but Blackamore fattens the simple jest into a plausible, realistic, and full-bodied adventure, taking fifteen or twenty minutes to relate. As penalty for his lack of inflection, the interspersed chants that often decorate the Negro tale are missing in his repertoire, and he even reduces a song like "Stagolee" to partially rhymed prose.

An idiosyncrasy that pleasantly marks Suggs's style appears in his comments and reflections upon the folktale he has just recited. After repeating it in an enthusiastic gush (a not uncommon trait), he frequently isolates the moral and applies it to a human situation. "The Farmer and the Snake," which ends in the betrayal and killing of the farmer by the snake he has kindly warmed in his bosom, reminded Suggs of a real-life villain who would always gain people's confidence and then destroy them. "The Bee and the Dirtdauber" led him to moralize on persons like the dirtdauber who think they know it all and refuse instruction. A natural entertainer, Suggs narrates with infectious spirit and verve, but with sober conviction too, on dark affairs. He projects himself wholeheartedly into the tale, neatly ordering his material into proper story form, often shifting from the third to the first person as he identifies himself with the chief character. In relating his encounter with a ghost train, his speech achieves a taut, tense quality that fully conveys his sense of nocturnal murk and mounting dread.

Walter Winfrey resembles John Blackamore in his lack of inflection and expressionless delivery. In his case a physical cause undoubtedly affects his style, for being badly crippled with arthritis he cannot gesture easily, and pain lurks in his voice. As with Blackamore, his external manner deceives, for he rolls off stories with assembly-line dispatch, but there the similarity ends; Blackamore is a master of the long tale, and Winfrey of the short. When collecting from Winfrey, I matched him stories, the stimulus he needs; he told me of having a recent contest with a white man, who finally acknowledged defeat after they had exchanged twenty-five or thirty jokes. This swapping or matching practice, under the speeded-up tempo of Northern life, demands relatively short jests, with punch-endings. (When Blackamore began dictating a long Rabbit narrative to me, his friends grew restless and bored, asked him to hurry up, and soon departed.) The twenty years that Winfrey has spent around Detroit, since leaving Arkansas, have altered his technique. Sitting around with other factory workers before the morning shift (they had to drive in early to get a parking space downtown), or during the lunch hour, he swapped yarns, but perforce they must be rapid-fire, hilarious, and mostly scatological. By contrast, Blackamore still retains the leisurely, countryside, all-night attitude of southern Missouri, where his circle used to narrate till three and four in the morning—but in the eight years since he left Missouri, he has told none of the old lies.

A range in storytelling styles greater than John and Julia Courtney exhibited would be hard to conceive. Slow-moving and cancer-ridden, John talks with seeming effort, dragging each word out (not a trait acquired from his illness, but inherited from his father, who speaks with equal labor), fumbling, repeating, interposing "y' know's" at every other phrase; and yet John holds his audience. He knows his texts faithfully and fully and, in spite of his crawling pace, pushes his way authoritatively through to the end, covering the ground with the painstaking fidelity of a Theodore Dreiser. This massive forward movement commands attention; John's stolid countenance renders the comic situations the more ludicrous; and his gift for the singsong rhyme and the eerie outcry arrestingly flavors his prose. Julia, his wife, talks as rapidly as John talks slowly, and one wonders how they manage to communicate. Determined-looking Julia spews out words with a machine-gun tempo but in a richly idiomatic phrasing. She admits uttering six words to the average speaker's one, and attributes this faculty to both sides of her family tree, one side specializing in quick hand gestures and the other in racing speech, with a double effect on her own output. When unexpectedly she began telling stories, to the surprise of her own husband, she demurred at my tedious note-taking, and said she couldn't talk slow enough for me to write her words down. We soon fell into a rhythm, however, as Julia crackled out one or two sentences, nursed her baby while I caught up, and then resumed her tale. She delivered a model text, clean and crisp with never a stumble or falter, the sentences neatly spaced and complete no matter what grammatical tangle seemed to threaten her fluency.

In the barber, Joe D. Heardley, the storyteller and the actor-comedian merge. The slightest joke he wrapped in extravagant theatrics, as he strutted and pranced around his hapless victim in the chair, deluging him and delighting the hangers-on with a steady volley of witticisms, quips, and retorts. Inevitably he employed the first person for exaggerative effect; the very first yam he gave me—a common windy about the mule who froze to death on seeing com pop in summer heat, thinking it was snowing—he rendered into an autobiographical saga of his trip from the deep South up to Michigan on muleback. Another time, standing on the sidewalk in front of his shop, he described a quarreling couple. Every time the husband slapped his fat wife she bounced back —and Joe bounced in dumb show; then the wife cut her man with a knife and he lit out a-running—and Joe slapped his hands cymbal-like, in the familiar gesture to indicate running, and underscored it by leaning forward slowly until it seemed he must topple. The jest by itself amounted to little, but the pantomime captivated the bystanders.

One final word needs to be said. Southern Negroes make not only good tellers but also good listeners. The family circle and social group hang avidly on the speaker's words, laugh delightedly at his comedy, and cluck sympathetically at his disasters. No cynical, bored, or blasé airs deter the narrator, who may always count on a pleased and responsive audience. Today of course the blare of radio and the gloom of television are drowning out and stifling the old storytelling ways. In Arkansas, Idell Moore heard many folktales from her father, with which she could now entrance her half dozen youngsters; instead they sit hypnotized before a television set, listening to the shrieks of Western badmen. Luckily, the contemporary collector can still observe the general traits and individual styles that make Negro storytelling a pleasure of life and indeed a delightful art.

---

6 I did hear a variant from the distinguished playwright Paul Green, who of course knows intimately Southern Negro lore.

IV THE HISTORY OF JAMES DOUGLAS SUGGS

In Europe, where folklore study rests on systematic and organized field collecting, storytellers with vast repertories do not astound the collector. In an illuminating essay on Scottish Gaelic folktales, Kenneth Jackson tells us of an Irish woman who yielded 375 stories, of which forty were long wonder tales; of a Lochaber man with five hundred shorter type anecdotes; of a single tale written down by the great Campbell of Islay that occupies eighty pages in print; of a West Kerry beggar who spent seven nights relating one narrative.[7] Alongside such feats the 175 assorted yarns and the score of songs given me by James Douglas Suggs may seem modest. But for the United States, lacking the medieval heritage of hero-traditions and Marchen, and the static peasant culture that still obtains in the Highlands, and much of the. Old World, this figure does startle. More than mere volume is involved, however, for Suggs narrates with art and relish, and his agile, retentive mind mirrors the ample folk traditions of the Southern Negro.

James Douglas Suggs was born March 10, 1887, in Kosciusko, Attala County, Mississippi, the second child and oldest boy of five children. All his grandparents grew up as slaves. He said: "I knew them as well as my own folks; they lived not far apart. Their Marster, old man Suggs [whose slaves of course bore his name], he treated 'em good. He let them make crops themselves, let them clear a few acres in the woods and plant com or cotton. He'd give them everything they made on it. They could work Saturday evenings and moonshiny nights, in the early part of the night. They stayed on there after freedom. They was raised up with the young Marsters and stayed with them as sharecroppers and tenants."

Like all my other Negro informants in Michigan, Suggs came from a mixed ancestry. He himself was very dark, but his father, who was half Indian, and one sister were light. Both his parents were born in Mississippi, his mother (Isabella Cottrell), in Artibashaw County (?) and his father in Goodman, where he worked as carpenter, janitor and handyman; in later life he turned preacher. Kosciusko, the county seat, contained five thousand people, mostly colored, and there Suggs went to school from his fifth to his fifteenth year, getting through the twelfth grade. "I went all the year round, and made two grades some years." Once he began steady work, Suggs entered a variety of occupations that took him into thirty-nine states. His first "public working job" was guard on a county prison farm at Itta Bena, Mississippi, in his twentieth year. In 1907 he joined the Rabbit Foot Minstrel Show and traveled from New Mexico to North Dakota, singing, dancing, and telling jokes in a troupe of twenty-eight Negro entertainers. He turned to professional baseball in 1908 and 1909, pitching and catching for the Sliding Delta team sponsored by a Negro friend of Theodore Roosevelt who owned a big farm near Indianola, Mississippi. The team played exhibitions in Greenville, Memphis, Helena, Vicksburg, and Little Rock. For three of the next four years Suggs worked out of Memphis as a brakeman for the I. C. (Illinois Central). "The men who were turned down were all dolled up; I was dressed for the job." He switched to a sand hog in 1912 while the Harland Bridge was building across the Mississippi River.

Returning to Mississippi he worked for a wealthy white planter, Dave Bishop, as cook and nurse. With Mr. and Mrs. Bishop he visited Quebec, Florida, Texas, Salt Lake City, and Newport News. The boss would give him money and he would go to the colored section. He voluntarily entered the army in September, 1917, fought in France with the Ninety-Second Illinois, a light infantry division, and was discharged in April, 1919. Next Suggs worked on a dredge boat around Carrothersville, Missouri, for the MacWilliam Drainage Company, which built ditches to drain the county of flood water. From 1920 to 1922 he cooked short orders in a "vanold" in the depot at Poplar Bluffs, Missouri, where he had previously visited a cousin. Crossing the line to Arkansas, he worked for a big oil man named Lattimore at Jonesboro, making mortar and cleaning his stores. In 1924 and 1925 he made molds in a steel foundry in St. Louis, and the two following years hung around Chicago with his brothers, "just spo'ting."

In 1928 he married, at the age of forty-two, a part Indian girl he had met in Bono, Arkansas. For the next dozen years he headquartered in Arkansas: farming, fishing, cooking in private homes and for hunting parties, and acting as handyman, "like a good old hunting dog." The hunting trips organized by wealthy doctors, rice growers, and syrup makers, which he accompanied as camp cook and general factotum, earned him up to $150 in ten days; Suggs, apparently a fixture and comedian on these excursions, cut off a hunter's shirttail when one missed a deer. On one such trip in 1939 he worked seventy-two hours straight without sleep, and then drank some wine, which affected his already high blood pressure; he blacked out, and spent four months in the hospital at Hot Springs. He now brought his family back to Chicago, where his brother ran a rooming house, and from 1940 to 1947 helped him rent flats. When his brother bought a home in Vandalia, a village of mixed population some five miles east of Cassopolis, the county seat of Cass County in southwestern Michigan, Suggs followed him, like many Chicago Negroes farming out into the countryside during the last three decades. After three years at Vandalia he shifted to the next township, Calvin, where I met him in 1952.

On subsequent visits, in June, September, and November, 1952, and February, March, July, and August, 1953, I recorded his stories and songs in notebooks and on tapes, finding him always an effortless and inexhaustible talker. In the summer of 1953 the Suggses moved to a smaller and even more derelict structure, on the other side of the Four Corners, a one-story affair with perhaps three rooms; they had to leave extra beds outside, and that so large a family lived and cooked in such quarters seemed physically impossible, especially during the winter months when they must be so closely confined. A well supplied water and gas lamps light. Actually, apart from the house, their situation had advantages over city living, since the children could see open fields and sky and breathe clean air. Mrs. Suggs appeared indeed *non compos mentis;* for all the tens of words her husband delivered to me, she scarcely vouchsafed a dozen. One time she called out to me, "Hey Mister," as I was leaving, greatly to my wonder; Suggs hushed her and I learned no more about the matter until my next visit when he replied to my query with his usual candor. The boys had been kidding his wife. They had told her that when Suggs said he was going to Cassopolis to make a recording with me, he was really playing around with a girl in town.

I give these details about Suggs's history and circumstances for the light they may throw on the human channels of folklore. Suggs rose supreme above his poverty and faced the world with indomitable good will. At sixty-five he had nothing to show materially for his varied life but a parcel of young mouths to feed, the price of his late and prolific marriage; he worked as a laborer for construction companies in South Bend, hitching rides since his own jalopy had finally gasped out, and when snow interrupted work, he drew compensation. Yet a smile, laugh, or joke always hid near his surface, and he once said to me: "I was born lucky. It's lucky if you are born with a veil over your face. Well, I've never had to go on relief." And he looked confidently at the field across the way, and talked of building on it next year. Well built, unwrinkled, pleasant featured, Suggs showed little trace of age and none of care; he exuded high spirits, as if all the world were a minstrel show, and he the chief performer. His expressive eyes, wide-breaking grin, and fluent, melodious tongue equipped him well for his self-appointed role. He joked with the boys, on the job or in the tavern, with wholehearted delight, and in the course of his varied career had soaked up a mass of fraternal jests and tales. A sober supernatural strain tempered his jocularity however, for he believed in spirits, hoodoos, and the dark powers of the universe, and regularly quoted Scripture to document their reality. Like other Southern Negroes I met in Michigan and Arkansas, he devoutly accepted the literal word of the Bible, and constantly recited, within his own vernacular, its miraculous passages.

Suggs's story repertoire falls for the most part into definite categories. The largest group, some twenty-three, deals with talking animals, followed by experiences (16), spirits and hants (15), assorted folktales (15), tall tales (15), Biblical and moral tales (14), preachers (13), hoodoo and fortune-telling (11), Old Marsters (10), humorous anecdotes (10), beliefs (9), Irishmen (5), colored man (5). (I omit from this count some narratives not strictly classifiable as folktales or folk history.) All these divisions reflect major patterns of Negro tradition in the United States, as indicated from the literature and from my own collecting. Except for the one text of "The Animals in Night Quarters" (Type 130), no Märchen with aristocratic characters occur. Some tales that seem intruders, like "The Devil's Daughter" (Type 313A), or "The Mermaid," or "The King of the Beasts Meeting Man" (Type 157), are nonetheless well established in Afroamerican storylore. Suggs faithfully represents his ethnocultural group, in the inclusion of American whoppers and Irish noodles, the limitation of wonder tales, the reinterpretation of Christian lore, the contrast of preacher jokes and spectral experiences, and the recognition accorded two tricksters, Mr. Rabbit in the animal cycle and the crafty slave in the Old Marster cycle.

In addition to his narratives, Suggs sang for me twenty-two traditional songs. These too display his range and versatility, covering spirituals, minstrel numbers, ballads, blues, and army songs. The texts and tunes are printed in *Folklore and Folk Music Archivist* (IX, Fall 1966).

What made Suggs an outstanding storyteller? The circumstances of his varied and mobile life clearly expanded his repertoire, by enlarging his experience and contacts. His own gregarious and congenial nature led him easily into social groups and friendly talk. He related tales with mnemonic authority and contagious enthusiasm, customarily repeating his narrative in a swift recap as soon as he finished it, with high excitement. Once having heard a story he never forgot it, so he claimed, and his narrative powers bore out the boast. Whatever he described, whether the technology of his jobs, the local color of Bible plays and election fights in the deep South, or actual folktales, he etched fully with myriad details and hues. He did not simply tell the story but acted it out and dressed it up with sounds, gestures, and tumbling words. Even in ordinary conversation his range of inflection and musical timbre enriched his speech, while certain vagaries of his vocabulary—"impitate" for imitate, "minister" for minstrel, "Sinus and Arts" for the School of Science and Arts on my letterhead—added to its flavor.

Happily Suggs proved as cooperative an informant as he was skilled a raconteur. He took considerable satisfaction in the visits and attention of the professor and talked freely to all his tavern cronies about our recording and dictating sessions. Several times he asked if anyone had ever told me as many stories as he had, and appeared greatly pleased to learn that he far outdistanced my other informants.

Two years passed after August, 1953, without my getting to Calvin. When I returned, it was to learn that Suggs had moved to South Bend the previous fall, to be near his work, and died there in March, 1955, as he entered his sixty-eighth year. He never lived to see the books of Negro folklore to which he contributed so substantially. It is consoling to know that the spirit and salt and kindly humor of Suggs will not completely vanish with his death.

---

[7] "The Folktale in Gaelic Scotland," in the *Proceedings of the Scottish Anthropological and Folklore Society*, IV (Edinburgh, 1952), p. 136.

Part Two
THE TALES

ANIMAL AND BIRD STORIES

Most persons immediately associate Negro tales with Brer Rabbit, and visualize a frizzy-haired benign old darky relating animal fables to a wide-eyed little white boy on the veranda of a majestic mansion. This picture, created by Joel Chandler Harris and his illustrator A. B. Frost and reinforced by imitators, contains some truth. Harris appreciated the fertility of Southern Negro storytelling, and in one preface describes an experience at a railroad station where he found himself ringed by competing Negro raconteurs. He recognized the folklore nature of his material, and points out some parallels. As a portrayer of United States Negro folk tradition Harris falls short in many ways however, principally by identifying the tradition with animal stories. His use of excessive dialect and his creation of Uncle Remus unfortunately placed Negro folklore in the nostalgic antebellum setting dear to Southern romancers like Thomas Nelson Page and Virginia Frazer Boyle, and continued the stereotype of the faithful retainer with his arch and droll mannerisms. Folklore science of the period regarded "primitive" peoples as childlike, ignorant, and amusingly superstitious, and so buttressed the literary picture of the old plantation with its happy darkies telling African nursery stories to white children. That African folktales did not concern only beasts, that in any case American Negro tales owed little to Africa and much to Europe and the New World, readers of Harris could never divine.

Nevertheless the forest brethren constitute one important theme in Negro fictions. Ber[8] Rabbit plays the common role of trickster—a perennial rascal around whom is strung an episodic cycle of deceptions and hoaxes—so popular throughout folklore. As one informant put it, "Rabbit always the schemey one." Whether the Rabbit represents an ego projection of the underdog Negro, who finds satisfaction in the little creature's discomfiture of the larger beasts and his breaking of cherished taboos imposed on the colored man (as some commentators would have it), one cannot tell from the narrators. They relish the wiles of Mr. Rabbit, but even Suggs the moralizer never attempted any racial identification of the hero.

The Tarbaby story, for all its fame, came my way rarely. Curiously the most popular animal narrative I heard, some eighteen times, has been only thrice reported among American Negroes. Brother Rabbit has entered most American versions of this tale, in a part just tailored for him, the sly weakling who introduces the king beast of the forest to man, and then scoots off while the lion, bear, or wolf gets badly shot up. Another popular rabbit adventure, the so-called Playing Godfather type, where the trickster leaves the animals to steal their butter, on the pretext that he must name his wife's new babies, turned up as frequently in the field as in the literature. These three representative instances indicate how the present field collection sometimes shows close identity with the known Negro repertoire, and sometimes offers startling surprises.

Such a surprise lies in the prominence of the buzzard as a folk character. An unpromising subject for children's books, the scavenger of the South nonetheless is a stock personality in the Negro bestiary; half a dozen widely known tales capitalize on his unorthodox eating habits and explain the baldness of his pate. Another popular personality is the parrot, a continuous favorite in Indo-European storylore.

One pattern of the Negro animal story departs from the woodland fraternity of the Rabbit, Bear, Fox, Terrapin, and Buzzard, and presents a simple fable involving two less familiar creatures. In these conflicts the slow inchworm outdoes the speedy "hoppergrass," the elephant turns the tables on the jackal, the crane finally pins the slippery eel, dirtdauber refuses to learn from the bee, the ox posthumously punishes the traitorous mule, who is whipped with rawhide whenever he balks.

From the barnyard, the fields, and the woods which formed their environment, Southern Negroes drew a fair portion of their story material. Why they neglected such familiar denizens as the coon and the possum in favor of the rabbit and the fox, and preferred the buzzard over the owl, remain teasing questions.

1 Who Ate up the Butter? (J. D. SUGGS)

This is Aarne-Thompson Type 15, "The Theft of Butter (Honey) by Playing Godfather," widely known among New World Negroes. I have other versions from Joe Booth, Sarah Hall, I dell Moore, James Shackleford, and Maria Summers (the last printed in Dorson, Pine Bluff, pp. 12-13). Texts and full notes are given by Parsons in Andros, pp. 1-2; Sea Islands, nos. 2-4, pp. 5-11; Antilles, no. 73, pp. 94-97. *Klippie gives five references, from the Hottentot, East African Cattle Area, Congo, and Western Sudan. Richard Smith, "Mr. Rabbit in Partners" pp. 220-224, follows the present text closely in having a jump contest to determine the thief, but not over a fire. Parsons, "Guildford," no. 46b, p. 193, has the fire jumping sequel, and refers to two Uncle Remus tales. This episode belongs under Motif K891, "Dupe tricked into jumping to his death." Other motifs are K372, "Playing Godfather" and K401.1, "Dupe's food eaten and then blame fastened on him." Crowley gives a number of Bahamian variants of "Theft of Butter" in* I Could Talk Old-Story Good.

Stith Thompson in The Folktale, *p. 221, discusses the wide distribution of Type 15.*

All the animals was farming a crop together. And they bought a pound of butter—they was in cahoots, all chipped in equally. So the next day they all goes to the field to work. All at once Brother Rabbit says, "Heya." All of them quits working, ask, "What is it, Brother Rabbit?"

"It's my wife, she's calling me, I ain't got time to fool with her." All of them together say, "Well you better go on, Brother Rabbit, and see what it is she wants." Off he goes to the house to see what his wife wants.

Twenty minutes he was back. They say, "What did your wife want, Brother Rabbit?" "Well she got a new baby up there." So they slapped Brother Rabbit on the back, said "Good, good. You named him yet?" "Yes, I named him Quarter Gone."

So they begin to work again. About thirty minutes more Brother Rabbit begins to holler again, "What do you want?" They say, "What was that, who you talking to?" "That was my wife, didn't you hear her calling?" "Well, you better go see what she wants." The Rabbit said, "I'm working, I haven't got time to fool with her." They said, "You'd better go on, Brother Rabbit."

So he goes on to the house to see what she wants. In about twenty more minutes he was back again. "What's the trouble this time, Brother Rabbit, what did your wife want?" "Same thing, another baby." They all said, "Good, good, what was it?" Said, "It was a boy." "What did you name him?" Said, "Oh, Half Gone." Said, "That sure is a pretty name." So he goes back hard to work.

After a while he hollers again, "Oooh, I ain't studying about you." They said, "What you hollering about, what you studying about, we ain't seed no one. Who was it?" "It was my wife." (She'd been calling him all morning.) "Well, why don't you go on Brother Rabbit, and see what she wants." "No, we'll never get nothing done if I just keep running to the house; no, I'm not going." The animals said, "That's all right, Brother Rabbit, it's only a little time, we don't mind, go on."

So Brother Rabbit goes on to the house. Well, he was there about forty minutes this time. "Brother Rabbit, what was your trouble this time?" "My wife had twins." "Good, good, good." They just rejoiced over it. "You'll have to set 'em up when we go to town this time." He said, "Well, the reason I was gone so long I was studying what to name those two twins so it would sound nearly alike." They asked, "What did you name them, Brother Rabbit?" They'd never heard tell of twins before, or of the rabbit having four. "Three Quarters Gone and All Gone." They insist on "Let's go see 'em." He says, "Well, we'll just work on till noon, then we'll have plenty of time, no need to hurry."

So he sent Brother Terrapin into the house to get some water. Well, he drank the water. Then he wanted a match, he wanted a smoke bad. So he said to Brother Deer, "Brother Terrapin is too slow, you run up there and bring those matches." Told Brother Fox, "You run on and drive the horses to the barn, we think we're going to plow this evening. We'll be home 'gainst you get there." So he taken off to drive the horses. When Brother Fox got out of sight good, Brother Rabbit said, "Well, we'll go." So they had to go slow, 'cause Brother Terrapin poked along, and they all walked together with him. When they got to the house, Brother Fox was sitting on the front porch waiting for them. He said, "Mens, I sure is hungry, let's wash up and get in the kitchen."

In a few seconds, they was all washed up and in the kitchen they'd go. Brother Rabbit was the first one in there; he says, "Well, where's the butter? The butter's all gone!" (Loud) The first one they accused was Brother Rabbit. "Remember when he came by the house to see about his wife and them babies?"

He says, "No, I didn't even think about the butter. Now listen, you remember more than me come to the house, Brother Terrapin and Brother Deer and Brother Fox, and I'd be afraid to 'cuse them, for I know I didn't and I wouldn't say they did. But I got a plan and we can soon find out who done it, I or him or whom."

They all agreed to hear about Brother Rabbit's plan—they was confused and mad and forgot about being hungry, and said, "His plan always did work."

Now Brother Rabbit told them, "We'll make a big log heap and set fire to it, and run and jump, and the one that falls in it, he ate the butter." So they made the log heap and put the fire in it. The fire begins to burn and smoke, smoke and burn. "All right, we're ready to jump."

They were all lined up. Brother Deer taken the first jump. Brother Rabbit said, "Well, Brother Terrapin, guess I better take the next one." He done jump. Terrapin was waiting for the wind to turn. He was so short he knew he couldn't jump far. The wind started blowing the smoke down to the ground, on both sides of the log heap. So Brother Terrapin said, "Well, I guess it's my jump." He ran around the heap and turned somersault on the other side. Brother Rabbit and Brother Deer were looking way up in the smoke to see the others coming over; they weren't looking low, and thought he had jumped over. They said, "Well, Brother Terrapin he made it."

So all the rest of them they jumped it clear, Brother Fox, and Brother Bear, and that made everybody on the other side. "Well, Brother Deer, it's your jump again." So the three they jump over again, and only Brother Bear and Brother Terrapin is left. Brother Terrapin says, "Step here, Brother Bear, before you jump." Said, "I hear you can jump high across that fire, cross your legs and pull your teat out and show it to 'em (his back teat), stop in space, and then jump from there onto the other side. I don't know if you can, I only heard it." Brother Bear says, "O, yes I can." So Brother Terrapin was glad he was making that deal, for he didn't know if the smoke would be in his favor going back.

The Bear says, "Stand back, Mr. Terrapin, let me jump first this time, you can see this." (*Deep, gruff*) The Bear backed further, further than ever to get speed up to stop and cross his legs. He calls out, "Here goes Brother Bear," and takes off. In the middle he tries to cross his leg, and down he went, into the fire. Brother Rabbit said, "Push the fire on him, push the fire on him." (*Excited*) "He's the one that eat the butter." So all of them go to the end, and begin to shove the chunks on Brother Bear. They all give Brother Rabbit credit for being the smart one to find the guilty fellow what eat the butter.

None of them ever thought Brother Bear was the only one never went to the house. Just like in a law case many men are convicted from showing evidence against them where there isn't any. They get a smart lawyer to show you was there when you wasn't there at all, trap you with his questions, get you convicted and behind the bars. Then they say, "He's a smart lawyer."

2 Who Ate up the Food? (JOHN BLACKAMORE)

This version of the preceding tale type (15) displays Blackamore's elaborately detailed style and modern touches (icebox, Cadillac). His text ends unusually in having the rabbit not simply throw guilt on the bear but also take over his job. Motif K401.1, "Dupe's food eaten and then blame fostered on him" is present here.

The Fox had a big plantation and the rest of the animals was working for him. This Fox he had them all chopping weeds out of the cornfield. So the Rabbit he gets tired and he wants to rip around and he thinks of some kind of excuse to get away. So the Fox had the Bear overseeing for him, and he was pretty tough on the Rabbit because he knew he was shiftless—he was lollipopping around and doing nothing all day. And so he finally got to a solution to get away. So he calls the Bear over and tells him he's going to have to take about an hour off. The Bear wants to know what for. So he tells the Bear that his wife is being conceived, that she is going to have some little ones.

So he looks around for some mischief to get into, after the Bear let him go. So finally an idea struck him. The Fox had gone into the city. He [the Rabbit] got all tired and hungry and everything, so the idea that he had was to go to the Fox's house. He goes over there and wasn't anyone home. So first thing he done was look in the icebox, found some fried chicken and fruits, so he ate that. So he cuts out into the shrubs and starts to lollipop some more, and then he notice that his hour was up. So when he gets back to the field everybody wants to know what he named the baby. So the first thing that came in his mind was all the food that was in the icebox, which he had just got a start on, with a piece of chicken and fruit, and he wanted to figure out a way to get back, so he said, "Number One Gone."

So he commenced to work again. So the more he worked the more he thought about that food he left in the icebox. So he gets another idea that rabbits have more than one baby at a time, eight or nine, so he calls the

Bear back again. So he tells the Bear, "It's about time, Mr. Bear." The Bear says "Time for what?" He tells him, time for his wife to have another baby. He let him know that a Rabbit have more than one. So the Bear let him go again. So he made a beeline for the icebox again. So when he gets there he starts on some ham the Fox had in his icebox. He eats all the ham the Fox had. So he cuts out again, and goes out to the field. So when he gets back to the field they want to know what he named the second one. So he tells him, "Number Two Gone." So he commenced to work again, and everybody was wondering why he named the children such odd names—Number One Gone, Number Two Gone—but still they couldn't figure it out. So he pulls grass about another hour maybe, and then he calls the Bear over for another leave of absence. So he makes another beeline for the icebox. When he gets there next time he eats up all the beef. (He can only hold so much each time.) So when he gets back they want to know what he named him this time. So he named this one "Half Gone."

So he commenced to work again about another half hour, and then he wants to take another leave of absence. The Bear let him go. So he makes another beeline for the icebox again. This time he drinks all the juices and all the milk that he can hold. So he goes back to the field. Everybody wants to know what he named this one. He named this one "Three Fourth Gone."

Old lady Squirrel wants to know how Mrs. Rabbit was getting along, wants to know she might need some lady help. So the Rabbit was afraid she'd find out she wasn't having no little ones, you know. So he tells her everything is under control, that she don't never have any trouble, that in fact she does it all the time. So he works a little while longer and then he wants another leave of absence. The Bear grants it to him. He goes back to the icebox again. So this time he drinks all the cream and eats all the cheese and butter. All the other stuff that he didn't like he puts in the garbage disposal. So he goes back to the field. Everybody wants to know what he named him this time. So he tells him, "Well, she's all th'ough, I named him 'All Gone.' "

So he got to work with ease after he ate up all the food and did all the mischieveness. So the Fox comes back from town about three-thirty in the afternoon, drives his big Cadillac out to the field, and wants to know what's been going on while he's been gone—somebody ate up all his food. So the Bear tells him, "Well everybody's been here but Brother Rabbit, but I don't think he had time to do it, for his wife is having some babies." So the Fox says, "Well I'll find out who done it." So he says, "When everybody get in camp tonight I'll find out who done it." So he has some of the workmen go out and kill a cow and barbecue it. So after it's barbecued everybody eats and eats so much and they is already exhausted so they went right in to sleep. So the Fox he builds a fire while everybody's laying in their sleep, and the reason why he build the fire is that he knows whoever ate the butter it would run out on him. He had about two pounds of butter in his icebox. So while he was sitting waiting to see who the butter was coming out of he went to sleep. So the Rabbit woke up, saw all his butter running out of him. So he gets up, and after he finds all the butter running out of him he sees what the Fox is trying to do, he built up the fire. So what he figured on doing was blowing it on the biggest one in the crowd 'cause he could eat the most. So he goes down to the pond and washes himself off, so the Fox couldn't see butter coming out of him. So when he comes back everybody was still asleep just like he left them, fire was still going. Picks up a small rock and th'ows it over against the Fox's face so he'd wake up, and then lays down with the rest of them.

So the Fox wakes up and he figures it's about time for him to examine them while they's asleep. And the Rabbit was the only one that left the field, so he examined him first. He was all dry and everything. So he still pretend to be asleep. The Fox say, "He's okay." Since the Bear accused the Rabbit he decided he was another likely suspect, so he goes over and inspects the Bear. So when he gets to the Bear he finds the butter where the Rabbit had rubbed it all on him, so he knows that he being the biggest one he must have ate it up.

So the Fox decided he going to get a shotgun while he still asleep, he going to kill the Bear. So when he goes up to the house to get the shotgun the Rabbit lay quiet until he see the Fox coming back from the house with the shotgun. So when he got almost within shooting distance he (the Rabbit) woke the Bear up—he wanted to see some running. He tells Brother Bear, "The Fox is going to kill you for eating up all his food." So the Bear he seems surprised, he didn't know what was happening, he wants to argue about it, you know. So the Rabbit tells him, "You better run." The Bear tells him he ain't got nothing to run for. The Rabbit tells him, "You just wait a minute, you'll have something to run for." So by that time the Fox saw the Bear standing up, so he thought he was trying to get away. So he let both barrels loose after him. So the Rabbit tells him, "Well Brother Bear, I guess you got something to run for." So the Bear cuts out through the thicket while the Fox was reloading. So the Fox started after him—the Bear and the Fox went off through the woods, the Fox was shooting at the Bear.

So the Rabbit he decided he'd tell the Fox he was going to help him catch the Bear, but instead he runs off and hides. So the Fox lost the Bear and quit chasing him. So the Rabbit he slowtails the Bear and catches up with him after the Fox had gone home. When he gets to the Bear he said, "I told you so, I told you the Fox was going to kill you for eating up all his food." So the Bear insisted that he didn't and the Rabbit tell him, "It don't make no difference, he going to kill you anyway, because he won't let you talk to him." So the Bear asked the Rabbit, what would he do. So the Rabbit said, "Well if I was you I'd go to some other part of the woods, because you can't live around here." So the Bear leaves.

So he goes back to the Fox's house. So the Fox is sitting on the porch with the gun across his lap, in case the Bear comes back and tries to softtalk him. (He wouldn't stand for no softtalk.) So he tells the Fox that he doesn't have anything to worry about no more. The Fox ask him why. So he tells him he caught the Bear and chased him, and he never will come back no more 'cause he chased him into some quicksand. So the Fox congratulated him and tell him he appreciated it very much. And he said, "Since you is a man of action, I'm going to need a new foreman." And since he so helpful he was going to appoint him for the position. So the last I heard of him he was still plantation foreman.

3 The Tar Baby (E. L. SMITH)

Another example of Type 15, "The Theft of Butter by Playing Godfather" but this time combined with Type 175, "The Tar baby and the Rabbit" (Motif K471). Parsons, Antilles, no. 24, pp. 48-51 gives 25 texts of Tarbaby, and in no. 25, pp. 51-52, cites 4 texts of the customary final episode, "Briar-patch Punishment for Rabbit" (Type 510A and Motif K581.2), also found below. I printed another Tar Baby variant from Julia Courtney in Pine Bluff, p. 17. A Hausa variant has the Spider say to the Tarbaby, "I'd like to suck your titty."

There was a Rabbit and a Fox. So they was having what they call a house-raisin'. An' the Rabbit was s'posed to be a doctor. And they had milk in the spring. An' this here Rabbit, every once in a while, he'd work a little bit, and he'd holler "Whooooooooooo." Fox said, "Who is that?" "Somebody callin' me." Says, "What they want?" "Oh I don't know, I ain't goin' to see." "Oh yes," says, "youse a doctor, you'd better go and see." So he went on down to the spring, and got in this milk, and drink some of it, come on back. And when he got back the Fox says, "Who is it, what was it?" Says, "Just Started."

All right, went on, worked a little bit, and directly he says, "Whoooooooo." "Who is it, who is that now?" "Somebody else callin' me. I ain't goin' this time." Fox says, "Yeah you go ahead," says, "you got to go, youse a doctor." He went on, down the spring, and drink up this milk, part of it, 'bout half of it, come back. Fox says, *"What his name?"* "Half Gone." [*Laughter*]

He went on back and worked a little bit, directly he said, "Whooooooooo." Says, "What is that now?" "Somebody else calling me." "Well, better go see." "No, I ain't going." "Yeah, you go ahead." So he went on down the spring and drink it all up, filled the jug with water. Kept on doing that till the Fox 'cided he would see what, who it was. He put him a tar baby down there.

So, Rabbit he come down there an' seed him sitting there, say, "What you doing here?" Tar baby didn't say nothin' to him. "Speak du'n ye, I'll knock you over." Tar baby just sit there, didn't say a word. He hauled off and slapped him with one foot. When he slapped him that foot stuck to him. He says, "Better turn me loose, I got another un here," says, "I'll kick you with this, I'll kick you over." So he kicked him with that foot and that un stuck. He says, "You better turn me loose," says, "I got another one here," says, "I'll hit ye, kick ye with hit," says, "I'll kick ye clear over." He kicked him with that un, and that un stuck. He says, "Better turn me loose," says, "I got a head here, if I'll butt ye, I'll butt ye to pieces." So he butted him, and his head stuck. There he was, couldn't get loose.

Fox he come down the spring, "Mhm, I knowed I'd get ye, I knowed you was the one drinking up my milk." He took him loose, started to the house with him. Says, "I don't know what hardly to do with you," says, "I'm going take ye to the house." Got up the road pretty good piece toward the house, an' there was a big thick briar patch there. He says, "I'm a good mind to throw you out there in them briars." Rabbit says, "Ohh Mr. Fox, please don't throw me out there in them briars." Says, "I'll get all scratched up and all tore up with them briars," says, "don't throw me out there." [*Plaintive*] "Yes I is, you *shut* up. Throw you right out there in the middle of 'em." After a while he took the Rabbit you know, and th'owed him over in the briar patch, and the old Rabbit kicked up his heels, said, "Ohh ho, here's where I want to be, here's where I was bred and bo'n anyhow."

4 *Stealing the Butter, Hiding in the Log* (JOHN COURTNEY)

This is a truncated version of Type 15 plus two additional episodes. The first is the "Fire Test," for which see Parsons, Sea Islands, no. 7, p. 14, and ante, tale 1, "Who Ate Up the Butter?" by J. D. Suggs, in which the Terrapin, not the Rabbit, fakes the jump. Richard Smith's variant, "Mr. Rabbit in Partners," similarly uses a jump test to determine the thief, but not over a fire ("Richard's Tales," recorded by John L. Sinclair, transcribed by Stella A. Sinclair, in Folk Travelers, TFSP XXV (1953), 220-224).

The second episode follows an independent tale, explaining how the Buzzard became bald, where the Buzzard traps the Rabbit or the Fox in a hollow tree; See post, "The Reason the Buzzard Is Got a Bald Head," by Sarah Hall, tale 24. The three narrators in Michigan whom I heard tell the buzzard tale, Sarah Hall, St. Elmo Bland, and J. D. Suggs, all recited the conversation between the captive and captor animals in singsong. Courtney's thinner text follows this device to the extent that the Rabbit answers in progressively weaker tones. Under Motif K714.3, "Dupe tricked into entering hollow tree," Thompson gives one reference, to Joel Chandler Harris, Nights with Uncle Remus, no. 14 ("Brother Terrapin deceives Brother Buzzard"). Actually the tale-analogue is in Harris, Told by Uncle Remus, no. 9, "Why the Turkey Buzzard Is Bald-Headed."

Brother Fox, Brother Bear and all of 'em was picking cotton. And they were all staying in the same house, and they'd buy their groceries together. So every evening they'd come in they'd go to the store. Brother Rabbit's money was kinda short, he wasn't making much that day 'cause he felt a little ill. So they was all going to book their money in and buy some butter. Brother Rabbit he didn't eat butter, and he was short. So they went on and bought them two pounds of butter. They all went to the field next morning. There they worked all the next day. They come in, Brother Rabbit was the first to go to bed. He'd catch them all sleeping; he'd get up and eat some butter. And next morning Brother Rabbit'd be up early smoking his cigar with his legs crossed.

And they were going on to the field and work that day. So when they come in they missed that butter. Say, "Who was eating that butter? We didn't eat all that butter!"

Brother Fox said, "We won't work tomorow, we'll have a test on the butter. One eat that butter we'll find him out."

So they built a great big fire next morning. And then Brother Buzzard he was going be the captain, the boss of it. Because practically everywhere he go he flew. So they got the fire built, a great big log heap fire. So Brother Buzzard says, "Okay, Brother Fox, you may be first." Brother Fox he backed up and he lit out—Woody, woody, woody. And he jumps, he jumps it clear. And he comes on back. Brother Buzzard says, "Okay, Brother Rabbit you're next." Brother Rabbit he backed up, pulled his derby off, and he hits it just as hard as he could go right toward the fire. And Brother Rabbit got close to the fire—Boody, boody, boody, boody—then whipped his belly agin the ground and run around the fire. And they thought they heard him hit the other side. Brother Buzzard say, "Okay, Brother Bear, you're next." So Brother Bear he backed up and he lit out. And he leaps right in the fire.

Brother Rabbit say, "Yeah, I told you Brother Bear eat that butter."

So Brother Bear walks on back close to Brother Rabbit, and he made a break at him, and it was a hollow log right down close to him. So Brother Rabbit run in that hollow log, wasn't but one way in. So Brother Bear fastened up the other end of that log with Brother Rabbit in. "I'll show you about tricking me." And they all went on and left Brother Rabbit in the log.

Next morning they went down to see about it.

"Brother Rabbit." [High]

"Hunh." [Loud]

"Oh let's go on back and forget about you." So they went on back and Brother Rabbit stayed in there. They went back to see him again. So they called him again, "Brother Rabbit."

"Hunh." [Weak]

He answered like he was nearly about gone. "O yes, nearly about got him." They went away and left him. So next morning would be the end of the week he'd been in there. "I know he'll be dead this morning." They went down to see about it.

"Brother Rabbit." [High]

Brother Rabbit wouldn't answer. He'd done study a trick on them.

"Brother Rabbit." Call him twice.

"Oh yeah, we got him." Brother Fox, Brother Bear they pulled that chunk out of the log. Brother Fox reached up in there to get Brother Rabbit. Out come Brother Rabbit, out by Brother Fox's hands.

"Oh yes, you son of bitches think you're smart, I can be your schoolteacher yet."

5 *The Bear Meets Trouble* (J. D. SUGGS)

I also have a version from E. L. Smith. South Carolina Folk Tales *gives a text, "Buddah Rabbit an Buddah Gatah," with the alligator as the sufferer, and seven Southern Negro references, pp. 3-4. A version is recorded in* Negro Folk Music of Alabama, *Vol. 1, Secular, Side 2, Band 6, "Brer Rabbit and the Alligators," told by Rich Amerson (*Ethnic Folkways Library, P 417 B*). See also the elaborate text in* Coyote Wisdom, *TFSP XIV (1938), 135-144, "Trubble, Brudder Alligator, Trubble," by E. A. McIlhenny (from Louisiana). One African reference, from the Ibo of Nigeria, is given under Motif K1055, "Dupe persuaded to get into grass in order to learn new dance. Grass set on fire." A Chinese reference is the only entry under Motif H1376.5, "Quest for trouble"*

Mr. Rabbit met Mr. Bear, and was telling him about having all kinds of trouble. If he make a bed he have trouble, and if he stay up at night there's trouble, and if he stay up or lay down in the day there's trouble. He had more trouble than anyone—the dogs and hawks in the day, and minks and owls at night.

Mr. Bear say, "What is trouble?" And the Rabbit said, "What, you ain't seen no trouble?" Mr. Bear been living in the middle of the swamp all the time, and had never been out.

So Mr. Rabbit said, "Come on out with me, and I'll show you trouble." So he gets him out to a big old sage field, and say, "Now you lay down here and go to sleep. And when you wake up you'll see trouble."

So Brother Bear he went out there and lay down. Brother Rabbit waits about three hours, to give him time to go to sleep. It was kinda cold out there, the wind was blowing. When Mr. Bear goes to sleep, Brother Rabbit takes him a torch and he fires the field all around, for about twenty acres, and he was right in the middle, Brother Bear was. The fire got to blowing and roaring, and whichever way the wind blow it would blow the smoke to him. Mr. Bear woke up and begins to sniff. He runs around, try to find a way out, but any way he runs he finds fire all around him.

Mr. Bear begins to holler, "Trouble, trouble." And Brother Rabbit say, "Now that's what I been telling you about, that's real trouble."

So he got burnt up trying to find out what trouble was.

6 *The Bear in the Mudhole* (J. D. SUGGS)

Parsons, Antilles, no. 48, p. 76, "His captor says a grace" (the A text, from Dominica) furnishes a full parallel. Usually the final episode appears independently, and is classified with Types 227 or 122, but Klipple correctly suggests the Motif K562.1, "Captive trickster persuades captor to pray before eating," giving a Hottentot provenience; Beckwith, Jamaica, no. 59b, "Saying Grace," p. 64, and Harris, Nights, no. 27, "Brother Fox says Grace," conform to this motif, and Harris pointed out its similarity to a Hottentot story (Nights, introduction, xxii).*

Well, Mr. Bear he was hungry. He goes gets in the mudhole and lays down flat on his back, to make them think that he was bogged up to his neck. He starts hollering, "Help, help, help." Mr. Rabbit looked around him and sees Mr. Bear in the mudhole.

"Mr. Rabbit can you help get me out, can you pull me out?" (*Plaintive*)

"No, I can't pull you out by myself, I'll run to get the boys." Mr. Rabbit gets Mr. Turtle, Mr. Terrapin, Mr. Possum, Mr. Coon, and Mr. Fox, and brings them all back.

Mr. Bear said, "Let me catch hold of your tail, Brother Rabbit."

Rabbit said, "No no, my tail is skinned. Brother Bear, catch hold of Brother Turtle's tail; Brother Turtle, catch hold of Brother Possum's tail— he's got a long tail and that will put him way out on the ground." (The possum ain't much of a swimmer.) "Mr. Possum, catch hold of Mr. Coon's tail; Mr. Coon, catch hold of Mr. Fox's tail. Well, we ready to go?" (Rabbit was the boss-man.) "*Haul away!* Hiya coming, Mr. Bear?"

"Oh, you moved me three or four inches."

"Well, let him rest a little—don't worry about that, Mr. Bear, we'll get you out. Okay, *ready to go! Haul away!* Feel yourself coming any, Mr. Bear?"

"Oh yeah, I come about three feet, but I'm stiff and sore through."

"Well, let the boys rest again—well git ye this time. Don't worry. We'll make it snappish and let's get him out this time, boys. *Haul away.*"

Well, they got him about five feet and he's out on the ground. Rabbit say, "How you feel, Mr. Bear?"

"Oh I feel sore and stiff from this mud—rub my legs a little bit. Oh that's good, rub my shoulders a little bit."

Brother Rabbit says, "We're going to get you so you're well in a day or two—you'll be well."

So when they rub his shoulders the Bear says, "Oh, rub my neck, that's where I been laying on it, it's so sore, rub my neck." When they got rubbing his neck he grabbed Mr. Rabbit. Brother Turtle he soaked down in the mud (he was a mudturtle). Brother Terrapin he went off to the woods and lay down side of a log—he was so slow he didn't wait till the Rabbit got through rubbing. Up jumped Mr. Rabbit, he went to running too. So Brother Bear caught Brother Rabbit.

Rabbit said, "Oh, you know if you say your prayers before you eat me you'll have something to eat all the time—that's what the Good Book says." Well, Mr. Bear shut his eyes and returned thanks. When he opened his eyes Brother Rabbit was gone.

7 *Rabbit and Bear Inside the Elephant* (MRS. L. R. TOLER)

Helen L. Flowers, A Classification of the Folktale of the West Indies by Types and Motifs (*Indiana University doctoral dissertation, 1952*), *describes an independent subtype of Type 676, "Open Sesame" for which she finds 22 variants in the West Indies (nos. 14-35). She comments, "Here the distinguishing feature is the use of the password to gain entrance into a living animal for the purpose of cutting meat from it" Flowers draws her material from Parsons, Antilles; see no. 26, "In Cow's Belly," pp. 52-56, for the 22 texts, and comparative references, to Louisiana, Canada, France, Portugal, and Africa. Flowers nos. 17, 22, 27, and 29, Parsons E, D, R, U (Guadaloupe, Dominica, St. Martin, Haiti) are closest to the present text, which has lost the magic password motif but otherwise follows the basic plot fully. In the four texts above, Rabbit and Zamba, Rabbit and Tiger, Jack and his greedy brother, and Bouqui and Malice all enter a cow. In Crowley's texts, Booky and Rabby enter the cow's belly (I Could Talk Old-Story Good, pp. 46-48, 92-93). The substitution of the elephant for the cow in the Toler text is curious. Ludwig Bemelmans in* Hotel Splendide *(New York, 1941) pp. 65-66, relates a Senegalese story of a Hare that jumps inside the Elephant's mouth, eats his bowels and heart, and escapes from his intestines. The Joel Chandler Harris version, in* Uncle Remus, His Songs and his Sayings, *no. 34, "The Sad Fate of Mr. Fox," follows the West Indies form in having the fox and the rabbit jump inside a cow, and in retaining the magic password, which is "Bookay," the name of the cow, and obviously a carryover from "Bouqui," the trickster in the Haiti texts (Parsons, p. 56). Harris has "maul" where Mrs. Toler has "melt" for the hiding place of the trickster's dupe, properly milt, or spleen. A text from Creoletown, La., has "Bookee" and "La Pain" (A. H. Fauset, "Negro Folk Tales from the South," JAF XL, 1927, no. 235, p. 242, "In the Cow's Belly").*

This story clearly has closer affinities with the Thumbling-Petit Poucet complex, where the tiny hero is swallowed by a cow (see Grimm no. 45, Thumbling as Journeyman") or even with Jonah and the whale, than with Open Sesame, to which it is linked only by one stray motif.

Mr. Bear and Mr. Rabbit were good friends. Mr. Rabbit came up one day with a bucket of lard. Mr. Bear wanted to know where he got it, he wanted some.

Mr. Rabbit said, "Oh, Mr. Lion and Mr. Elephant and all of 'em down there telling big tales. Mr. Elephant laughed so long and loud, opens his mouth so wide, I jump in, go and get me a bucket of fat, jump out before he can shut it."

Mr. Bear decided he could do the same things. So both of 'em went down with their buckets, sitting by the side of Mr. Elephant, waiting for him to laugh. Soon Mr. Elephant laughed, in jumped Mr. Rabbit, in jumped Mr. Bear, began tearing out the fat. Mr. Elephant closed in on 'em before they could get out.

Mr. Rabbit said, "He never done this before."

Mr. Bear said, "What we gonna do?"

"You go in the melt, I'll go in the bladder."

Pretty soon Mr. Elephant took sick and died. Then his friends begin to wonder what killed him so quickly, better have an examination. Had a meeting, decided to cut him open and see what his trouble was. They cut him open, first thing they come across was the bladder, and they threw it down the hill. When they threw it down it crushed.

Out jumped Mr. Rabbit, and hollered up to them, "Look out, don't throw your nasty mess down on me. What's the trouble up there?"

"Mr. Elephant's dead."

"What's the trouble?"

"Mr. Rabbit, we don't know."

Said, "Where's the melt?"

"We threw it down the hill."

Then Mr. Rabbit said, "Show it to me. All right, get you some switches every one of you. Beat on it till I tell you to stop."

Beat him into a jelly. Lifted the veil off it, found Mr. Bear in there dead."

Mr. Rabbit said, "That's what killed Mr. Elephant."

8 *Take My Place* (JOHN COURTNEY)

The popularity of this tale can be seen from the extensive references and many texts provided by Parsons, Antilles, no. 23, pp. 41-47, for "Substitute Victim (Take My Place!)." The key motif here, K842, "Dupe persuaded to take prisoner's place in the sack," appears in several international folktales with human characters, but has become entrenched in the American Negro animal cycle; Joel Chandler Harris uses the plot four times (Uncle Remus, His Songs and His Sayings, no. 23, "Mr. Rabbit and Mr. Bear," and no. 29, "Mr. Fox Gets into Serious Business"; Nights with Uncle Remus, no. 31, "In some Lady's Garden," and no. 32, "Brother Possum gets into Trouble"). These last two examples interestingly juxtapose two variants, one from Uncle Remus and one from African-born Daddy Jake, who claims he heard the tale differently. Uncle Remus philosophically comments, "One man, one tale; 'n'er man, 'n'er tale. Folks tell urn diffunt" (Nights with Uncle Remus, Boston and New York, 1883, p. 189).

Courtney has combined the substitute-victim story with a separate incident, the first Negro folktale I ever heard, from St. Elmo Bland (born in Mississippi) in Calvin, Michigan, in March, 1952. His text follows.

The Fox called the Buzzard, "Mr. Buzzard." [Very loud]

The Buzzard wouldn't answer.

Mr. Fox said, "I was just going to tell you where you could find some dead carr'on."

So the Buzzard slowly turned around and said, "Whu-u-u-t?"

The Fox told him where there was a young mule dead in the field (he was only asleep), and how to get him away. "Tie a rope around your head and around the coifs legs." The Fox tied the rope so, and tested the colt. Colt woke up, and started running. Fox began to laugh and call out, "Hold him, Mr. Buzzard, hold him."

Buzzard said, "How the devil can I hold him if my feet ain't touching the ground?" (Cf. *"Richard's Tales"* in Folk Travelers, pp. 241-242, *"Dead Colt Comes to Life"*; Motif K1047, *"The bear bites the horse's tail"*; Harris, Nights with Uncle Remus, no. 2, *"Brother Fox Catches Mr. Horse"*) See post, tale 28, *"Crow, Buzzard, and Mule."*

Once there was a Brother Rabbit and he'd found out where there was a big garden of greens. So he would go up every morning and he'd tell the little girl her father had said turn him in the garden, and at twelve o'clock turn him out. So he would make it his business to go there every morning and call the little girl. "Little girl, father said turn me in the garden, twelve o'clock come turn me out."

So the little girl said, "Okay." So they begin to miss those greens.

The girl's father say, "Somebody's eating these greens up around her. I can't tell where my greens is going to." So he asked the little girl.

She told him she said, "Father said Brother Rabbit come here every morning and turn me in the garden, and twelve o'clock turn me loose."

He say, "When he come today just turn him in, when twelve o'clock come just let him stay till I come."

So when twelve o'clock come Brother Rabbit called the little girl, "Little girl, oh little girl." Say "Little girl, twelve o'clock, turn me out. Dang-dong, dang-dong."

So up come the girl's father. "Brother Rabbit, what you doing in there?" Say, "Okay, I'll just fix you." Say, "I'll send you Brother Fox and Brother Bear." When Brother Fox and Brother Bear got there, girl's father say, "Brother Fox, who's been getting my greens?"

Brother Fox say, "I haven't had a mess of greens this year."

And Brother Bear say, "You know I've been away up north."

So he say, "Well that leaves it up to Brother Rabbit."

Brother Rabbit sitting there saying nothing, studying his way out. So he takes Brother Rabbit out there and tied him up to a great big old limb. And when he climbed down he left Brother Rabbit swinging. That's the way he was going to punish him. Brother Rabbit he swung and he swung and he swung, by the limb.

"I'm going to heaven in a swing-swing-swing.
I'm going to heaven in a swing-swing-swing."

Brother Fox and Brother Bear heard him singing. So Brother Fox told him, "Let's go up there, Brother Bear, and see about Brother Rabbit."

When Brother Fox and Brother Bear got there Brother Rabbit called, say, "Brother Bear, I haven't had a drink of water since that man tied me up here." Say, "You come up here and let me tie you up here until I can get a drink of water. I'll be right back." So Brother Bear let him tied him up there. But Brother Rabbit stayed so long till Brother Bear went to singing. Brother Bear couldn't think of the song Brother Rabbit was singing.

"I'm going to heaven in a dang-alang-alang.
I'm going to heaven in a dang-alang-alang."

And the girl's father heard Brother Bear singing. He knew that was a different voice. He was going back and see about that. So when he got there Brother Bear in the tree. And he said, "Brother Bear, what you doing up there?"

Brother Bear said, "Brother Rabbit got me to stay till he come back."

He said, "I'll fix you, taking Brother Rabbit's place." He took Brother Bear down and give him a good beating. Brother Rabbit done gone on home.

So Brother Bear he was crying and he gone down to the house and Brother Rabbit was sitting up on the porch, smoking a cigar with his legs crossed, his derby on. (He was a hard sport.) And Brother Bear he jumped at Brother Rabbit and missed him. Brother Rabbit told him, "I tell you what, I know just where we can get some meat at." So they went on down there. Brother Rabbit told Brother Bear, "There's a dead mule." Say, "Brother Bear, your tail's longer than ours, and heavier too, I'll just tie your tail to the mule's tail." When he got his tail tied, Brother Rabbit reached down and got a flail, and lammed the old mule in the side. So the mule jumped up and started running. And Brother Rabbit commenced to hollering, "Hold him Brother Bear, hold him." [High]

He said, "How in hell can I hold him with ne'er foot touching the ground?"

(That mule had his tail up and was knocking him with his hocks.)

9 Rabbit and Hedgehog (JULIA COURTNEY)

For the distribution of this tale see Type 1074, "Race"; Motif K11.1, "Race won by deception: relative helpers"; The Folktale, p. 196; Parsons, Antilles, no. 50, pp. 78-80, "Relay Race." A close text from Mary Richardson, who was raised in Tennessee and Mississippi, "Rabbit and Hogshead [sic] *have a Race," is in Dorson,* Negro Folktales in Michigan, *pp. 37-38. Cf. my "Negro Tales from Bolivar County, Mississippi," no. 2, "Tapin and the Deer," p. 106. May A. Klipple,* African Folktales with Foreign Analogues (*Indiana University doctoral dissertation, 1938, abstracted by Stith Thompson*) gives 38 references, seventeen coming from the East African cattle areas. Flowers, A Classification of the Folktale of the West Indies, *adds two African examples to Klipple, and cites 10 West Indies texts.*

Rabbit and Hedgehog lived 'jining farms. And every day the Rabbit would go down and make fun of the Hedgehog's babies. And he would tell them:

"Short leg long wit,
Long leg not a bit."

Every day he would come down and tell them that same thing:

"Short leg long wit,
Long leg not a bit."

So he made Old Lady Hedge mad. And so the Rabbit told the Hedge they'd have a race. (That's the way they had of evening up things.)

And that night Old Lady Hedge talked it over with her husband and daughter. And the next day Brother Rabbit came over to their home. Old Lady Hedge was ready the next morning, she and her daughter. They had a mile run. Old Lady Hedge got on one end, and she on the other.

So the Rabbit told the Hedge, "Are you ready?"

She said, "Yes."

So they begin running. And the Hedge went toddle toddle, and Brother Rabbit was so busy running, he didn't miss her when she stopped.

When he got near the other end, Old Lady Hedge's daughter raised up and said, "I'm here."

So the Rabbit said it wasn't dead fair. "We'll try it over."

So they started running again. And the little Hedge went toddle toddle. This time the Rabbit still didn't notice the Hedge toddle. When he got to the other end, Old Lady Hedge raised up, and said, "I'm here."

(He had to quit making fun then you know. Them legs is so slow the Rabbit couldn't see her when she stopped, she's so low down. A hedgehog is a short thing.)

10 Mr. Rabbit and Mr. Frog Make Mr. Fox and Mr. Bear Their Riding-Horses (JOHN COURTNEY)

Other variants were told me by Tobe Courtney and Mrs. L. R. Toler. The present text is unusual in having two riders and riding horses. This is Type 72, "Rabbit Rides Fox A-courting," and Motif K1241.1, "Trickster rides dupe horseback." See Parsons, Antilles, no. 47, pp. 73-76, "Riding-Horse." Klipple under Type 72 suggests Motif K1241.1, "Trickster rides dupe a-courting," and provides five African references. Martha W. Beckwith describes the story as "very common in Jamaica and presents no local variations from the form familiar in America" (Jamaica Anansi Stories, MAFLS XVII, 1924, p. 235, note to no. 3, "Tiger as Riding-horse," pp. 5-6). The Joel Chandler Harris version appears in Uncle Remus, His Songs and His Sayings, no. 6, "Mr. Rabbit Grossly Deceives Mr. Fox." This latter tale presents Brer Rabbit smoking like a "town man" in the same conception John Courtney gives in no. 8, above, "Take My Place," where he describes the Rabbit as a "hard sport."

Mr. Rabbit and Mr. Frog were courting two girls, and Mr. Bear and Mr. Fox were liking them too. Mr. Fox and Mr. Bear they had the best going, the girls cared most for them. So Brother Rabbit went down to Brother Frog's house, and built up a scheme to play on Brother Bear and Brother Fox. So they set a night that they were going to the girls' house, an off night from what Brother Bear and Brother Fox were courting. And so they went on a Friday night, and they told the girls, "Brother Fox and Brother Bear's our riding-horses. You're crazy about them boys but there ain't nothing to them."

So the girls says, "Oh no, I can't believe that."

So Brother Rabbit told them, says, "I'll prove it if you'll be my girl friend." And Brother Frog said he would too. So they set a night that they was going to prove it, in the following week. So that evening Brother Fox and Brother Bear come over to Brother Rabbit's house.

Brother Rabbit say, "You just the man I want to see." So Brother Rabbit say, "We ought to go to some extra girls' house tonight, we need some more girls." So they finally made it up and begin to get ready. They carried them a saddle apiece, Brother Rabbit and Brother Frog, and hid them by Brother Bear's girl friend's house. So they went on that night down to this extra girl's house. So they stayed there till nine o'clock. Brother Bear and Brother Fox they had to stay by their girl friend's house. So they all got ready and started out. Brother Rabbit took sick. Brother Rabbit was so sick, Brother Bear 'cided to try to tote him. So Brother Frog he had a bellyache. So that made him sick too.

So Brother Fox said, "Well we'll just tote them two guys up here and we'll stop over."

Brother Bear told them, says, "Crawl up on my back, Brother Rabbit, I'll tote ya." And Brother Fox told Brother Frog to crawl up. Both of them was so sick, he could get up there but he couldn't stay up there.

Brother Rabbit told him, says, "I just can't stay on your back. I gotta get something to hold to." Brother Rabbit told him, "I know what, I see the very thing I can hold to." [Excited] Brother Frog say the same thing. So Brother Rabbit say, "Here's some saddles here, here's the very thing we can hold on to." So they put the saddles on, and Brother Rabbit and him climbed up in the saddle. Both of 'em was so sick they couldn't hardly stay in the saddle.

And when they got to the girls' house, Brother Bear say, "Now you've got to get down, Brother Rabbit, at the steps. This is far as I can carry you."

So Brother Rabbit told him, says, "You take me to the top steps, we can make it." He had done put him a pair of spurs on he and Brother Frog. So when they got up to the top step, Brother Rabbit popped them spurs to Brother Bear. Brother Bear ran right on in his girl friend's door. Brother Rabbit said, "I told you Brother Bear was my riding horse."

Brother Frog said, "I told you Brother Fox was my riding horse."

11 *Why the Rabbit Has a Short Tail* (SARAH HALL)

The present text varies from the regular form of Type 2, Motif K1021, "The Tail-Fisher," in that the usually clever rabbit loses his tail, rather than the stupid bear. (I have a bear version from Newt Curry.) See also Motifs A2216.1, "Bear fishes through ice with tail; hence lacks tail"; A2378.4.1, "Why hare has short tail"; A2325.1, "Why rabbit has long ears." Harris, in Uncle Remus, His Songs and His Sayings, no. 25, *"How Mr. Rabbit Lost His Fine Bushy Tail" gives a variant close to Sarah Hall's, but without the long ears motif. In* Nights with Uncle Remus, no. 21, *"Why Brother Bear Has No Tail" the bear is tricked by the rabbit into sliding down a slippery rock, and so loses his appendage. Two other Southern Negro versions are listed under Motif K1021. In quite a different story, the fox burns his tail, and the rabbit charitably gives him his own long tail to replace it (Motif A2378.4.1; Smiley, JAF XXXII, 1919, no. 6, p. 361, "Wolfs Tail to the Hungry Orphan"). Stith Thompson cites the study of Kaarle Krohn demonstrating the thousand year life of the tale* (The Folktale, *pp. 119-120).*

Once upon a time Brother Rabbit had a long bushy tail. And every time he'd see Brother Fox he'd shake it at him and wave his tail in the Fox's face. Brother Fox studied and studied how to get even with the Rabbit. Well, he went to fishing and he had good luck. As he was coming home from fishing, the Rabbit run out and says, "Brother Fox, how did you catch all these fish?" (The Rabbit loves fish.) Brother Fox said to himself, "Now's my time to get even with the Rabbit." Out loud he said, "Any cold night, all you got to do is to go down to the creek and hang your tail in the water, and let it hang there from sundown to sunup the next morning, and you'll have more fish than you can pull out."

He meant that his tail would freeze in the ice. "All right," said Brother Rabbit, "I believe that I'll go fishing tonight." So he took with him a blanket, and his pole, and bait, and sit on a log with his tail in the water in the middle of the creek, all night long. It growed so cold, he began to shiver, and shiver, and he shiver. All night he set there and shuck and shiver. But he's thinking about the fish he's going to have in the morning. Late that morning the sun begin to rise, so the Rabbit tried to pull his fish. But his tail was froze too tight in the ice. He pulled and he pulled, but his tail stuck fast. The Rabbit begin to be afraid that the Man would come along and see him. So he thought he would call for help. "Help! Help! Help!"

Brother Owl heard Brother Rabbit. He says, "I wonder where Brother Rabbit's at. I heered him holler for help." So he flew over the creek, and there he seen Brother Rabbit sitting on a log. And he flew down to help Brother Rabbit. He caught a holt of his right ear and begin to pull. It grewed longer and longer. The Rabbit said, "Why don't you catch my left ear?" He caught hold of his left ear, and he began to pull. He pulled and pulled, but it grew longer. The Rabbit says, "Brother Owl, don't you see what you did! You pulled and pulled my ears until my best friend won't know me. Why don't you catch my tail?"

So the Owl grabbed a holt of his tail, and begin to pull. He pulled and pulled, and off went the Rabbit's tail. So the Rabbit been having long ears and short tail ever since from that day to this.

> I stepped on some tin and it bent,
> And I skated on away from there.

12 *Rabbit and Fox Go Fishing* (MARIA SUMMERS)

Two popular tales are joined here. For "Playing Dead Twice in the Road" see Parsons, Antilles, no. 9, pp. 29-31, who synopsizes West Indies texts, and her discussion in Folk-Lore, XXXV III (1917), 408-414, "The Provenience of Certain Negro Folk-Tales," where she attributes the migration of the tale to a comparable incident in "The Master Thief (Type 1525), transmitted by Portuguese traders to Gold Coast Negroes and thence to Southern slaves. I printed a variant from John Blackamore in "Negro Tales," Western Folklore, XIII (April 1954), 83-84, "The Rabbit, The Fox and the Bear: Playing Dead in the Road."*

The second episode is Type 2, Motif K1021, "The Tail-Fisher." A variant in which the rabbit tells the fox to fish with his feet in a bucket of water is in my "Negro Tales from Bolivar County, Mississippi" (Southern Folklore Quarterly, XIX, 1955), 105-106, no. 1, "Brer Rabbit an' Brer Fox" See also "Richards Tales," PTFS XXV, 1953, 233-235, Mr. Wolf Goes A-Fishing."

The Fox and the Rabbit was staying together, and so they went out fishing. The Rabbit was too lazy to fish so he run on ahead and lay down like he was dead. The Fox come along, say, "Here's one of Brother Rabbit's people. If I seen another one I'm going to lay my fish down and go back and tell Brother Rabbit." Rabbit jumps up and runs around and gets ahead of him again, lays down like he was dead. And the Fox laid his fish down and went back to tell Brother Rabbit. After he got out of sight Brother Rabbit jumped up and carried his fish home and was cooking 'em when Brother Fox come in. Brother Fox say, "Hey Brother Rabbit, where you get all these fish?"

"I caught 'em."

And the Fox say, "I had a string of fish and I saw some of your people dead, and I went back and I couldn't find either your people or the fish."

The Rabbit said, "I ain't got 'em. I went down to the creek and th'owed my tail in the creek, and every hair had a fish hanging to it. You better go try."

He went to the creek and the water friz around his tail, and he thought he had a lot of fish. Brother Rabbit come by and say, "Hey Brother Fox, how many fish you got?" He said he had so many that he couldn't pull 'em out. The Rabbit he listened.

"What's it?"

"It's that man yonder with his fox dogs."

"Pull, Brother Rabbit, pull."

The Rabbit he was grunting like he was pulling but he wasn't doing nothing. "Unh, unh." So he said he'd go get the ax and cut his [the Fox's] tail so he could get loose before the dogs get there. And so he cut the tail off, and the Rabbit said to the Fox, "Oh yes, you got a short tail like me."

(Looks like he oughta know the Rabbit couldn't th'ow his tail in the water and get those fish—he didn't have no tail. Looks like everything ignorant but the Rabbit.)

13 *Playing Dead in the Road* (J. D. SUGGS)

A variant of the previous tale (Type 1525). Rabbit's escape from the animals in the text below forms a second, separate episode, falling under the general motif K550, "Escape by false plea."

Ber Rabbit didn't like to fish. So Brother Bear come along, say, "Ber Rabbit, come along get your hunting pole let's go fishing."

Say, "No it's too hot, I don't like to fish."

So Mr. Bear he goes on down to the lake and commence to fish. Brother Rabbit he follows him down there but lays upon the hill in the shade watching him in the hot sun. Well about three o'clock Brother Bear had caught enough fish, decided he'd go home. He reached down in the water and pulled up this long string of fish, about three feet long. Brother Rabbit was up on the hill watching him. "Phew, I sure want some of them fish." So Brother Rabbit lit out back to the road, lay down acting like he was dead.

Brother Bear said, "Why here Mr. Rabbit dead." He retched [reached] down and felt Brother Rabbit—"Hm, he ain't been dead long, he's warm and just as fat as he can be." Says, "Aw I don't need him, I got plenty of fish." Just left him stretched there alongside the road. Lays him down, says, "Well, I'll go on home."

At that point Brother Rabbit jumped up, run around about fifty yards and lay down again by the side of the road. So Mr. Bear lays his fish down and feels Brother Rabbit. "Sure he good and fat, something must have hit him like it did Brother Rabbit back there, and he just as fat as he can be. Oh well, I'll just lay him right alongside the road so won't nothing run over him." He wasn't aiming to go back but he hated to see the meat destroyed. So he picked up his fish, went on. Same thing again. "Well here's another Rabbit—that makes three—big snowshoe rabbits." Says, "Well, I'll just lay my fish down here and go back and get the other two." (It was worthwhile now.) When he got back there was no rabbit there. He goes back and the fish and the rabbit are gone. Then he knows Brother Rabbit had tricked him.

So Brother Bear goes around and gets up the crowd, Mr. Wolf and Mr. Panter and Mr. Fox—Brother Rabbit had been tricking lots of people. They were going to fix him now sure enough. So Brother Rabbit had cooked his fish and was sitting down eating it. He looks out the window and seed them —so out the window he goes. Mr. Bear say, "Yon go Brother Rabbit, yon he go," and they all taken after him. Brother Fox and Brother Deer was gaining on him—they could catch him if he didn't go in a hole.

Brother Rabbit thought of another trick on them. He looked up and seen a tall cypress tree. He run to the tree and grabbed it and tell them to run quick, the world was falling. Say, "All of you run and hold it while I go get an ax to cut a prop and hold it." They look up and see the tree wiggling against the clouds, looked as if it was falling—the world done mashed it over—low clouds made it look like the world was falling. He going to get a prop to keep it up on that side. (I've seen it with the skyscrapers—it looks like it just weaving. Fellow never seen a skyscraper would think it was falling—"Looky yonder, building swaying.")

He run to get the ax and never did come back.

(Rabbit is a smart fellow—he'll stop dead in his track, let the dog run over him, then double back. You've got to use all the senses God gave you in this world.)

14 *The Rabbit and the Dog* (J. D. SUGGS)

This is a form of Type 62, "Peace among the Animals." An abbreviated variant I heard in Mound Bayou is in "Negro Tales from Bolivar County, Mississippi" no. 5, p. 107, "The Convention" from Rev. J. H. Lee. Walter Winfrey of Inkster, Michigan, also told me the story. Hurston, Mules and Men, has the tale, pp. 146-147, "What the Rabbit Learned." Stoddard has recorded a Gullah form on Record L46 A4, Booklet p. 11, "E Might Ober Run De Law." The Fox tells the Turkey about the new law that all creatures are friends, but then runs from the hounds; such long-legged devils might run over the law. Thompson has a Joel Chandler Harris reference to Motif A2494.4.4, "Enmity between dog and rabbit," but it belongs to a different plot.

Well the animals all met, and called a meeting at the hall. "We want every animal to meet, to get together and be as one." Mr. Bear was the moderator. So he gets up, he began to speak to them, "Now listen gentlemens, we wants to live peaceable, and we all'll be as one. Mr. Hound won't bother Mr. Rabbit, Mr. Panter won't bother Mr. Fox." Says, "Well you know who all has been enemies to each other."

Well all the animals had got in but Mr. Rabbit—he was kinda late. There was just one vacant seat next to Mr. Hound Dog. So he had to sit down by Mr. Hound Dog. Mr. Hound Dog had fleas on him and the mange awful bad. So the fleas begin to bite Mr. Hound, and the mange begin to eetch [itch] him. So he begin to retch [reach] up and want to scratch what's biting him. Mr. Rabbit he's superstitious. Mr. Rabbit he's scared. Up he jumped and began to run around in the hall.

Mr. Deer says, "Brother Moderator, we's here on business and Brother Rabbit keeps jumping around. Now I motions we fine him five dollars. We's here on business, we ain't got time for that." So they fine him five dollars. He pays his fine and goes back to his seat again.

Brother Bear says, "Now ladies and gentlemens, I'll start the p'ceedings where I left off at. We all must live together in harmony."

About that time the fleas begin to bite Brother Hound again, the mange begin to eetch. He go to scratching, up go Brother Rabbit again, running all around the hall.

Brother Bear say, "Order, Brother Rabbit, order, Brother Rabbit. We's here on business, we don't want this running around."

Brother Deer say, "Brother Moderator, I motion we fine him fifteen dollars—might keep him quiet." So he paid his fine, went back and taken his seat.

Brother Bear say, "Well I'll p'ceed again, on my subject." Says "Ladies and gentlemen, I'll p'ceed where I left off. We got to live together in harmony and peace with each other."

Fleas beginn to bite Brother Hound again, mange begin to eetch him, and he goes to scratch again. Rabbit superstitious, up he go again. He makes straight for the door this time—he going outa there. Brother Bulldog was the inner guard. He grabbed him and th'owed him back in there, said "Sit down and be still."

Mr. Deer says, "Mr. Moderator, we'll have to fine Brother Rabbit twenty-five dollars."

Brother Bear says, "It has been motioned and seconded that Brother Rabbit would pay the sum of twenty-five dollars for jumping up and running around in the time of business." Brother Bear say, "Are you ready for the question?"

Brother Rabbit say, "Not ready."

Brother Bear say, "Then state your unreadiness, Brother Rabbit."

"My unreadiness is, the way Brother Bulldog he grab people and th'ow 'em around, somebody going get hurt. I was only going out the door."

(Old Bulldog he's powerful you know, that's why they want him for the inner guard.) [Suggs hereupon went into a description of a bulldog grabbing a horse by the nose and throwing him.]

15 *The Deer Escapes from the Fox* (J. D. SUGGS)

This gives a nice twist to Motif K622, "Captive plays further and further from watchman and escapes" See the Southern Workman, *v. 26, no. 12 (Dec, 1897), p. 249, "The Rabbit and the Girl" (Alabama); Smith, "Mr. Rabbit in the Pea Patch," pp. 224-230 (which joins Tarbaby with the escape); Vann, "The Animals' Spring" pp. 172-177 (the closest text, with the deer as captive); Parsons, Antilles, no. 130, pp. 120-121, "The Escape," particularly texts D and E. Flowers gives examples from Andros Island, Antigua, Dominica, Jamaica, St. Croix.*

The Rabbit and the Fox had a pea-patch together. And the Deer would come at night and slip in and eat all he wanted. So they made a trap and caught the Deer. After they caught him they split rails and made a pen thirty-two feet high, and put him inside, and left Brother Fox to stay on watch to guard him. They was going to keep him there till executin' day. While Brother Fox was watching him the Deer began the song,

Shoo lally shoo, shoo lally shoo,
I do this in the summertime,
I do this in the wintertime—*mmmmh.*

Brother Fox said, "Sing that song again. I never did hear that song. Best song I ever did hear." "If you throw down one of those rails I'll sing it again." "Please sing that again, I've never heard a song like that." "No, I wouldn't sing that no more for nothing, not for nothing." The Fox he begged and begged, till the Deer said, "Well, I'll tell you what I will do—throw four more of those rails, and I'll sing it for you."

The Fox threw down the four, but the Deer wouldn't sing. He said, "Tell you what, you throw down ten more, so I can get real close to you, and lay my head in your bosom; it sounds real good then." So the Fox throwed down ten more. Then the Deer eases up to him and lays his head over on him. "Now sing," says the Fox.

Then the Deer jumped over the fence, knocked the Fox off, and called back to him, "My song is in the woods." When the Rabbit came back he executed the Fox for letting the Deer get away.

There's people just like that, these confidence men. You start talking to them, and draw all your money out of the bank, and give it to them before you know what's going on. Didn't you read in the papers about that old man, seventy years old, who confidented all those women out of their money?

There's a lesson in all those stories.

16 *Fox and Rabbit in the Well* (J. D. SUGGS)

Motif K651, 'Wolf descends into well in one bucket and rescues fox in the other," gives four American Negro references', including one from Joel Chandler Harris, Uncle Remus, His Songs and His Sayings, *no. 16, "Old Mr. Rabbit, He's a Good Fisherman." Suggs's text is close to Harris's, even to the mocking verse the rabbit sings to the fox as he passes him in the buckets; Harris's analogous lines are "Fer dis*

is de way de worril goes; Some goes up en some goes down." Type 32,
corresponding to the motif, gives only European references.

The Fox was after the Rabbit to kill him. So Ber Fox was about to catch Brother Rabbit. There was a well down in the flat between the two hills. It had two water buckets, one on each end of the rope. When you let one down, you'd be pulling one bucket of water up. Brother Rabbit jumped in the bucket was up. Down he went, the other bucket come up. The moon was shining right in the well. It looked like a round hoop of cheese. Ber Rabbit didn't know how he was goin' git back up after he was down there. He commenced hollering for Mr. Fox to come here quick.

Mr. Fox goes up to the well and looked down in there, says "What you want, Brother Rabbit?"

"See this big old hoop of cheese I got down in here?" Says "Man, it sure is good."

Ber Fox says, "How did you get down in there?"

Says "Git in that bucket up there," says "That's the way I come down." Mr. Fox jumped in that bucket was up, Brother Rabbit jumped in the one was down. Down goes Mr. Fox, up come Brother Rabbit. Brother Rabbit passed Brother Fox. "Hey Brother Fox, this the way the world goes, some going and some coming."

My sister'd been watching round that well and she left a bar of soap. I stepped on it, and I skated on back home.

17 The Elephant, the Lion, and the Monkey (JOHN BLACKAMORE)

The cycle of "toasts" or rhyming verses about "The Signifying Monkey" is treated by Abrahams, Jungle, pp. 136-157. To signify has the sense of to trick. Blackamore's prose text contains some rhymes. I have a verse form from Johnny Hampton. In the usual plot the monkey connives at getting two large animals to fight each other.

The Lion was supposed to be the king of the beasts, and the Monkey wasn't satisfied. He thought, well, maybe there was a lot of animals in the wood was more substantial than the Lion, so he thought he would get up a contest. So the next day he decided on the Lion and the Elephant. So he swung around through the trees until he found the Lion. Well, then he decided to go dig up the Elephant. But when he found the Elephant, the Elephant was eating his dinner. So the Monkey walked up to the Elephant and spoke to him. The Elephant didn't want to be bothered, told him to beat it. So the Monkey told him, "Well, you oughta be nice to me, for I know something you don't know." So the Elephant wanted to know what did he know that he didn't know, 'cause he figured he knew more than the Monkey.

So the Monkey say, told him, "Aw well, that's all right, you don't want to listen to me, you want to eat your dinner." So the Elephant insisted he tell him, you see, what he was talking about. So the Monkey say, "Oh, it's just that Lion again, talking about you and all your kin-peoples." Said, "I know you can't be friends. The way he talked about you is a doggone sin." So, he say, "Even talked about your mother, and your cousin, too. He talked all about your face." He says, "From the way he talked, you don't belong to no animal race." He says, "But I shouldn't be telling you this, for you-all's friends." He say, "I guess I better go on and let you all be. Of course this don't make no difference to me."

So he went on and got up in the tree, and watched the Elephant. So the Elephant went through the woods in a big rage looking for the Lion. The Lion was unaware that the Elephant was in a rage, so he asked him, "Where are you going this fine day?" At this time the Monkey was up in the tree above watching him. So the Elephant told the Lion, "You ain't got no use for me, how come you is trying to be so friendly?" So the Lion said, "Well, I don't understand what you mean." The Elephant grabbed the Lion up in the snout and th'owed him against the ground. Well, the Lion got mad then and charged the Elephant. Well, the Elephant caught him in the snout and th'owed him against the ground again. So he almost broke the Lion's back. So he couldn't charge no more, right then. So the Elephant charged on through the woods, for he figured the Lion had enough. So after the Elephant got on out of sight, the Monkey started grinning on top of the tree. And the Lion looked up and he saw him, he saw this Monkey grinning. The Lion say, "Well, I see what's going on now." The Monkey say, "There you's laying up there with your side all caved in, your back hip out of place, saying that the Elephant don't belong in no animal race." Say, "Your eyes all bloodshot, got the nosebleed, even your rear need a couple of stitches. You call yourself the King of the Beasts." Say, "Now, ain't you bitching?"

The Monkey was up on the limb, he was so happy prancing around, jumping from limb to limb, his tail slipped and he hit the ground. The Lion jumped up and jumped on him with all four feet. He said, "I'll teach you how to signify, getting me all beat." So the Monkey got scared, and trying to figure a way out. So he told the Lion, say, "If you let me up like a man should, I'll get up and kick your rear all over these woods." The old Lion was so surprised that he let him up. So the Monkey he run on up the tree. He say, "Now, I'm up here so you can't get me. I'm gonna tell everybody in the jungle if I live that you're not King of the Beasts, the Elephant is."

I step on a piece of tin, the tin bent,
And that's the way the story went.

18 *King Beast of the Forest Meets Man*

Sixteen variants of this seldom reported Negro tale that I collected in Michigan appear in my article, "King Beast of the Forest Meets Man" Southern Folklore Quarterly, XVII (1953), 118-128. Walter Winfrey gave me three distinct versions, and John Blackamore and Newton Curry each two. I printed two Arkansas texts in Pine Bluff, *35-36. The lion, bear, panther, buzzard, and alligator all run afoul of man.*

This is Type 157, "Learning to Fear Men"; Motif J17, "Animal learns through experience to fear men"; Grimm no. 72, "The Wolf and the Man"; Bolte and Políka, II, 96-100. United States Southern Negro texts appear in Faulkner, World of Fun Records S-253-B, "Brer Bear Meets A Man" (title inadvertently omitted from the record imprint); Fauset, "South," Animal Tales no. 38, p. 243, "Are You Man?"; Hurston, "How the Lion Met the King of the World," pp. 171-174; Johnson, "Lion Looks for Man," p. 145. Harris, Nights, has two accounts of the lion meeting man: no. 7, "Mr. Lion Hunts for Mr. Man," told by Uncle Remus, but this is Type 38, "Claw in Split Tree"; and no. 57, "Mr. Lion's Sad Predicament" told by the African Daddy Jake, in which man shoots the lion severely, but without the lion first seeing a little boy and an old man. Beckwith has a Jamaica text, "Man is Stronger," pp. 67-68, in which the Tiger at first mistakes Mr. Ram-Goat for man. Parsons under the same title, Antilles, no. 64, pp. 90-91, gives a basically different story.

Bolte and Polívka have references for most of the European countries, but African examples are scarce; Klipple gives only one, from the Western Sudan. African texts can be found in W. H. I. Bleek, Reynard the Fox in South Africa *(London, 1864), no. 23, p. 47 [Hottentot]; Zeitschrift für Ethnologie, XL (1908), 918 [Hausa]; S. W. Koelle, African Native Literature (London, 1854), pp. 177-179*

[Kanuri]. Thompson in The Folktale, *p. 289, lists but one example apiece of African and American Indian borrowings of Type 157.*
In some Southern Negro variants, the Colored Man comes to replace plain Man, and demonstrates his power with a match in place of a gun.

a *The Lion and the Rabbit* (NEWTON CURRY)

This Lion moved out from where he was, things were dull, so he found a new place, where there was a ledge of rock facing east. And early in the mornings he'd get out there and roar, "Me and My God." All the small animals got scared, and were afraid to go out and get something to eat. They got pretty hungry, so they got together and held a conference to see who should go and ask this fellow to move. The Rabbit being one of the fastest and quickest dodgers, was chosen to be the one to go and visit this fellow the Lion. Well, the Rabbit gets up on the ledge above him where he could talk to him and convince him that he should go back where he came from. So he told the Rabbit he's not going to take orders from nobody, for he's King of the Forest. So he asked him if he'd ever met Man, for Man's King too, he said. So while he's there talking he sees Man on the other side of the ravine; he had his gun you know. The Rabbit had ducked the man. He tells the Lion, "That's Man. He's King too." The Lion let out a roar, "Me and My God." This fellow saw him, and he was in good range, so he showered right down on him. He shot him full in the face. He turned to run in his cave, and he shot him behind.

Nothing more was heard of him for several days. Finally Rabbit was detailed to go over and see what happened. So Rabbit went over and old Lion was just able to get around—he was out there sunning himself. Rabbit said, "Well, Brother Lion, how are you?" "Well I'm just able to git around, that's all. That fellow you called Man, he lightened in my face and thundered in my behind, and I'm just able to get out to sun myself."

After that happened old Lion would roar, "Man, me and my God."

b *The Bear and the Rabbit* (J. D. SUGGS)

Mr. Rabbit and Mr. Bear met one day, and got to discussin' 'bout different things in the world. Mr. Bear said he'd been all over the world. He'd seen everything but Man. "They tell me about Man, and I wants to see him." Brother Rabbit says, "Why I can show you a Man. Come on and go with me up here this side o' the road." They set down. After awhile along come a boy, about eight years old. Mr. Bear looks up. "Say, is that Man comin' yonder?" Brother Rabbit looks up, sees him. "Why no, that's going to be Man. But be patient, Man will be along directly." Brother Bear was so anxious to see them he kept his eyes on the road all the time. "Say Mr. Rabbit, that's Man comin' yonder." Brother Rabbit looked up, he seen an old man comin' on a stick, about eighty years old. Says, "No, no, that used to be Man. He's got a walkin' stick. But be patient. Man'll be along directly." Brother Bear keeps his eyes on the road. Brother Rabbit looks back the other way, the east end of the road. Says, "There comes Man, that's Man comin' down the road." Brother Bear straightens up and looks. "Now that's Man, go out and meet him." He's twenty-one years old and has a gun on his shoulder.

Off to the thicket Mr. Rabbit ran, down to the road and off to the woods. Mr. Bear walks down the road and stands up on his two legs, right in the middle of the road. Young man, off his shoulder come the gun, let the bear have both barrels, boom, boom. Down went Mr. Bear on all four'ses legs. Into the thicket he went, where Brother Rabbit was. "Say, I seen Man. He had a rail on his shoulder, he take it down and pointed at me, it lightened at one end, and it thundered at tother end. Look, it just filled me full of splinters all over." Said Mr. Rabbit, "Well you've met Man and you've seen what he is."

(You take a bad man, he beats up on a little boy or an old man, but when he meets a real man, he gets beat up.)

c *The Lion and the Cowboy* (WALTER WINFREY)

The Fox was beat up by a Lion. And he wanted to get even with the Lion. He was laying down by the side of the road, and he saw a cowboy come along riding a horse. He had a 45 on his right side, he had a 45 on his left side, and he had a 45 Winchester across his saddle. Then the Fox crawled off and met this Lion, and asked him, had he ever seen a Man. So the Lion told him no. If he did see one he would roll his hair over his head and jump to him and tear him to pieces.

"Okay," the Fox said. "You come with me in the morning and I'll show you a Man." So he placed this Lion in the middle of the road, and he laid beside the bushes. The cowboy rode up the road and the Lion saw the cowboy. He rolled his hair up over his head and made for the cowboy. The cowboy took his 45 from the left side and shot the Lion in the left side. The Lion grabbed a handful of leaves and stuck it on the wound. The cowboy drawed the gun from the right side, and hit the Lion in the right side. That turned the Lion—he wheeled and run. There was a hill he had to go up and over, and as he was going over the top, the cowboy shot him with the 45 Winchester.

He just made it to his den. When the Fox came by, he was laying there grunting and aching with pain. The Fox asked him, innocently, "What's the matter? Did you see the Man?" Lion said, "Yes. He pulled out something and throwed it and hit me in the left side. And I grabbed some leaves and stuck it on my left side, and made towards him. He throwed something with his right hand and hit me on the right side. And I wheeled and run." And he says, "You know that little hill I have to go over? Just as I went over that hill he throwed up something and it said *Sshow*. And my tail flew up, going over the hill, and he cut me a brand-new ass."

d *The Alligator, the Whale, and the Colored Man* (ANDREW SMITH)

The Whale had never saw Man. So Alligator was going to show him a Colored Man. He said that Colored Man was a bitch with his ass. So the first thing they saw was a have-been, an old man fishing on the bank. They swimmed on down the lake, and next thing they saw was a little boy. Whale asks Alligator, "Is that Man?" "No, that's a gonner-be." They swim on down a little further, finally they saw Man. He was on the back end of a boat. Whale he swimmed on back ("Man's a mess, he kills things"), he left Alligator there.

Alligator began to tackle the Man and the boat. The gas tank had just busted on the boat, and the Man was fixing to smoke. He took out a match, scratched his ass, ht the cigarette, and threw the match into the water. It blew up the gas, and knocked the Whale clean out of the water. He goes back to meet Brother Alligator and tells him, "Man is a bitch. He retch up in his pocket, and got him a cigarette, which you call thunder, and retch up in his pocket and got him a match, which you call lightning. And he rubbed it against his ass, and threw it in the water, and set the world on fire."

e *The Alligator and the Slave* (JOHN BLACKAMORE)

The Alligator was cooling out in the surface of the bayou one day enjoying the scenery. Some boatloads of oil came in from the Mississippi River. (The dock is up in the bayou off the river, because it's still water.) So whiles he was looking the boat docked and a bunch of slaves started unloading the boat. These slaves had two-wheeled trucks, hand trucks. So one of the slaves rolled his truck almost into the other guy, and he exclaimed, "Watch where you going, nigger!" So the Alligator said, "So that's what he is. I seen a whole lot of those guys and I just now found out what he is." (That's what the Master called them and they thought that's what they really was—all they knowed was what their Master had told them.) So the slaves they'd seen the Master smoke, and one of them had stolen a pack of tobacco and some matches; Master didn't allow them to smoke. So the Alligator goes back down to the bottom and asks his wife, did she ever see a nigger. She told him no. So he asked her to come on up to the surface and he'd show her one. So she goes on up with him. When they reached the top he showed her all the slaves pushing the barrels and things around.

In the meantime one of the drumheads spilled oil on top of the water. So one of the slaves got away from the crowd where he could be alone to take him a smoke. So they saw him take out his tobacco and make him a cigaroot. Strikes a match on the seat of his pants, and lights his cigarette, throws the match onto the water. The match caught the oil on top of the water, and the fire spread across the surface. He gets over to the Alligator, and the Alligator tells his wife, "Come on, let's go on down below." When they gets down the Alligator asked his wife, "Well honey, did you see them niggers?" She said "Yes honey, I saw them. That nigger's a bitch. He strikes his ass and set the world on fire."

19 The Rat in the Whiskey (BEULAH TATE)

Reported only from Negro informants. See Bacon and Parsons, no. 32, p. 279, "In Liquor"; Parsons, Sea Islands, no. 65, p. 75, "Man in Liquor"; Brewer, Worser Days, 100-101, "The Mountain Rat Who Outwitted the Cat." This probably belongs under Motif K611, "Escape by putting captor off guard," and falls close to the escape motifs of the sixth and fifteenth stories. The tale was also told me by William Smith and Al Simmons.

The Rat fell in a barrel of whiskey, and when the Cat come by he asks him, "Please help me out." "Will you let me eat you if I help you out?" "Sure." The Cat pulls the Rat out and the Rat says, "Please let me dry by the fire before you eat me. I won't eat good if I'm wet." The Cat sets him by the fire and puts his paw on him. And he turns him over to dry him. But he falls asleep by the fire, and the Rat he's near his hole, and he runs into it. The Cat wakes up and sees him, and says, "Mr. Rat, didn't you promise you'd let me eat you?" He says, "Don't you know a man will say anything when he's in his whiskey."

(You know when a man gets all teed up with whiskey he'll say anything —I used to feel all big when I got lit up.)

20 *Elephant and Jackal* (HAROLD LEE)

> *For a close variant, "Jackal and the Camel," see my "Negro Tales of Mary Richardson," no. 6, p. 9. Klipple,* African Folktales with Foreign Analogues, *gives one example from Madagascar of Motif J2137.6, "Camel and ass together captured because of ass's singing." In the African story the dog barks to retaliate on the crocodile.*

It was actually India, but I put it in Louisiana. That's the center point for ribbon cane. So they'd ate all the vegetation on one side of the river, and the Jackal wanted to go to the other side, but he couldn't swim. So the Elephant could swim, and the Jackal begged him to carry him over to the other side. Elephant say, "If I carry you over there will you promise to be quiet, so the farmers don't hear me?" The Jackal promised, so he kneeled down for the Jackal to jump on his back. Away they swim. Got over, start eating. Jackal got full. Elephant was still eating, he started to holler. Farmers came and beat the Elephant real good. The Elephant said, "Mr. Jackal, you promised not to holler."

Said, "After I eat with a full stomach I. just got to holler, Mr. Elephant."

Several trips the Jackal did the same thing, made the Elephant get a good whipping. So the Elephant waited till he got in the deepest part of the stream. So he started turning over in the water. The Jackal said, "Mr. Elephant, why are you turning over? I can't swim."

"After I have a full stomach I've got to take a bath."

21 *Bullfrog and Terrapin* (SALLY COURTNEY)

This suggests the Aesopic fable of Motif J995.1, "Frog tries in vain to be as big as ox." Cf. Ray B. Browne, "Negro Folktales from Alabama," Southern Folklore Quarterly, XVIII (June 1954), no. 12, p. 134, "The Frog that Wanted to be Big" Klipple gives five African examples of this motif. A text given me in Calvin, Michigan, "The Frogs and the Elephant," combines the fable and the present incident. The mother frog bursts in trying to emulate the elephant. Next day the elephant steps on the baby frog at the creek. "Am I very heavy?" "No, not so heavy, but you're so hard on my eyes" ("Negro Tales of Mary Richardson," Midwest Folklore, VI, 1956, no. 5, p.

Mr. Bullfrog and Mr. Terrapin was having a race. One went one road, the other went this one, and at the forks of the road they was going to meet up. The bullfrog jumped in a rut, and a truck come along over him, and busted both eyes. Along came Mr. Terrapin, crawling.

"Well Mr. Bullfrog, you *made* it?"

He said, "Yes I made it, mighty hardest."

Says, "What's the matter with your eyes?"

Says, "Oh, just a little straining on them."

(The terrapin didn't have sense enough to know the bullfrog hop faster than he could crawl.)

22 The Farmer and the Snake (J. D. SUGGS)

This is one formulation of Type 155, "The Ungrateful Serpent Returned to Captivity" (Motif J1172.3). Four groups of variants discussed by Waldemar Liungman in Varifrån Kommer Våra Sagor *(Djursholm, 1952), pp. 36-38, are summarized by Archer Taylor in his review in JAF, LXVII (1954), 93-94. Customarily the ungrateful animal is restored to its original situation by a third creature called in as judge; I have such a text from Iola Palmer of Niles; compare Dean Faulkner, S-252-A, "Bre'r Possum and the Big Snake," and Harris, Nights, no. 46, pp. 281-287, "Brother Wolf Still in Trouble." Liungman recognizes the variants in which the snake is the deceiver as the most important complex.*

Farmer's out early breaking his land in February, he wants to get good subsoil. Well, he's plowing along, and he plowed up Mr. Snake, a great big one. Mr. Snake was in a quirl where he'd quirled up for the winter, you know; he was cold and stiff. Farmer stopped and looked at him, says, "Well

I declare, here's Mr. Snake this time of year." Mr. Snake says, "I'm cold, I'm about froze to death. See how stiff I am, I can't even move. Mr. Farmer, would you put me in your bosom and let me warm up a bit? I'm cold." Farmer says, "Noooo. You'se a snake, I can't fool with you, you might bite." He said, "No, I wouldn't bite you for nothing in the world. Do you reckon I'd bite you after you warm me up?" He talked so pitiful Mr. Farmer decided he'll warm him in his bosom. So he stoops down to pick up Mr. Snake, and puts him in his bosom. Well, he tells his horses, "Git up," gets his plow, and goes back to work.

About nine o'clock he unbuttoned his shirt, looked down in his bosom. "How do you feel, Mr. Snake?" Mr. Snake says, "I feel pretty good, I'm warming up considerably." He buttoned his shirt up, goes on and plows till about ten-thirty. Unbuttoned his bosom, looked at it, says, "How do you feel, Mr. Snake?" "Oh, I'm feeling pretty good. Ain't you feeling me moving around? I can move now." The farmer says, "Yes, I'm glad you feeling better, feeling warm." Well, he plows till about fifteen minutes to twelve. He said, "Well, I'll go down to the other end and put Mr. Snake down." He could feel him moving around quite spirited like, so he didn't bother to unbutton his bosom at all. After a while when he got near the other end, he was going to take him out and go on to dinner. He kinda looked down and the snake done stuck his head out and was looking right in his face and sticking out his tongue. (A snake wants to fight then, you know, when he sticks out his tongue.) Farmer says, "Now, Mr. Snake, you said you wasn't going to bite me; you said after I warmed you up you wouldn't bite me." Snake says, "You know I'm a snake, Mr. Farmer." "Yes, but you said you wouldn't bite me." Mr. Snake said, "Now you know, Mr. Farmer, I'm s'posed to bite you."

So he bit the farmer in the face. The farmer goes home, tells his wife how he carried Mr. Snake in his bosom and got him good and warm; then Mr. Snake bit him. Said, "Don't care what a snake says, don't never take one in your bosom to warm him up. For when he gits warm he will bite." In the end Mr. Fanner lay down and died.

(Now you know there's people will confidence you just like that snake. Like Dan Sprowell. He was the terriblest rogue, and just as pleasant to look at, and a good worker. Dan was from Goodman, Mississippi, in Attala County. As a boy he began stealing onion sets from stores, put them in his pocket. The laws caught him, and sent him to the pen. He chopped cotton so fast they made him a trusty in three weeks, and he walked out—changed states. He worked for my Uncle Jack Suggs after he got out, for just his keep. One day my Uncle was going to Memphis on an excursion. While he was gone Dan pressed the clothes of the boys and the girls and took them all. He stole a horse and buggy in Water Valley, worth about $175, and was driving some girls around, and they arrested him and was carrying him back for a trial, when a gang took him to lynch him. They was going off a piece, and Dan knocked down the fellow with the lantern and made a lunge out in the woods. They fired at a man's height and he was crawling off on his all fours, so he got away.

They arrested him for stripping a woman's clothes line. The judge asked him, "Have you even been in the Penitentiary?" "Yes." "How long?" "Three weeks." "How long were you sentenced for?" "Three years." The judge said, "I sentence you to six years of hard labor." But in three weeks he was out again.

Yeah, he was crooked as a barrel of scales. He'd steal his own hat off his hoe, just to keep in practice. And as fine-looking a young man as you ever seen. He just loved to steal, and he'd sell for nothing. And he didn't drink either. Anybody'd fall for him. He was a snake. You put him in your bosom and he'd bite you.)

23 The Quail and the Rabbit (SILAS ALTHEIMER)

The Quail and the Rabbit were out hunting fruit. The Rabbit would run from place to place, but the Quail would fly. So finally the Quail found a patch where there were ripe peaches and ripe canteloupe and ripe watermelons and ripe plums and a field of ripe peas nearby, all of which the Quail liked, especially the peas. But he didn't want the Rabbit to share in it. So the Quail rose and flew in the direction the Rabbit went until she saw the Rabbit, then she fell to the earth, and ran all around, shuffling her wings, and fall down and roll. The Rabbit said, "Mr. Quail, what's the matter?"

And the Quail shuffled her wings and rolled around and said, "Mr. Rabbit, we'd better leave here, and run as hard as we can. I went down that way and a great big man met me. He beat me half to death. I wouldn't have gotten away had I not flown."

And so the Quail began to run a little bit and fly, run a Utile bit and fly, and the Rabbit ran too, and he carried the Rabbit in the opposite direction. After getting the Rabbit considerably away the Quail got some of his friend quails and flew back to the orchard and peafield, where they feasted on peas and ripe plums.

So that's one time Mr. Rabbit was beaten.

24 The Reason the Buzzard Is Got a Bald Head (SARAH HALL)

Although Motif A2317.3 gives "Why buzzard is bald," for a Negro reference one looks to A2317.11, "Why john-crow has bald head" (Beckwith no. 47, pp. 56-57). Flowers gives four texts under this motif, all Jamaican. Still these do not correspond to United States Negro tales of the buzzard becoming bald, with their chanted conversation between the buzzard and his captive. See Backus, "North Carolina," pp. 288-289, "How Come Mr. Buzzard to Have a Bald Head"; Fauset, "South," pp. 218-219, Animal Tales no. 4, "Buzzard Traps Rabbit in a Hollow Stump" (and compare no. 2, pp. 216-217, "Rabbit Fools Buzzard" for the musical dialogue); Fortier, no. 6, p. 23, "Corn-pair Lapin et Madame Carencro"; Southern Workman, v. 26, no. 12 (Dec. 1897), p. 249, "The Rabbit and the Busard" (Alabama); ibid., v. 33, no. 1 (Jan. 1904), p. 49, "Why the Buzzard has a Red Head" (Alabama). Harris" elaborated tale, "Why the Turkey Buzzard is Bald-Headed" (Told by Uncle Remus, no. 9), presents a normal rather than cryptic conversational exchange between the buzzard and the captive rabbit. I have other cante-fable texts from St. Elmo Bland and J. D. Suggs, the latter printed in Pine Bluff, pp. 158-160.

Once upon a time the Buzzard and the Crow went out on a trip, and when they got out a ways they run upon a Fox, and the Fox j'ined in with 'em. And they walked on and walked on. And they got hungry. They come to an old hollow tree. The Buzzard said, "Brother Fox, I believe you'll find something to eat in that holler." So the Fox went up into the holler to see what he could find. He got up inside and the Buzzard commenced to chunk blocks in there to stop the hole up.

Brother Fox called, "Brother Buzzard, what you doing? It's getting mighty dark up here." (*Plaintive*) Said, "Oh, I'm just fixing you a footway" (so he could come down). That kept on and kept on, getting darker and darker. "Brother Buzzard, getting mighty dark." "Oh, just wait, I'm fixing you a footway." By and by the Fox come down to the hole to get out. Buzzard flew away. The next day the Buzzard came back.

Da-tum, da-tum, da-tum, dey,

I been sailing three or four days.
The Fox in the hole says
Da-tum, da-tum, da-tum, dey,
I been starving three or four days.
So the Buzzard flew off saying "No, I ain't quite got him." He stayed off three or four days longer. So he came back again.
Da-tum, da-tum, da-tum, dey,
I been sailing three or four days.
The Fox said, low this time
Da-tum, da-tum, da-tum, dey,
I been starving three or four days.
Buzzard said, "Oh I near about got him. I'll have him next time I come back."
So he stayed off three or four days longer. So the next three or four days the Buzzard come back.
Da-tum, da-tum, da-tum, dey,
I been sailing three or four days.
Fox didn't answer.
Old Buzzard said, "Oh yes, I got him, I got him, he ain't said nothing, I got him."
He begins to unchunk the hole. When he got the chunks all out he stuck his head in there. The Fox grabbed him by the head and pulled all the feathers off him. That's the reason the Buzzard got a bald head today.
'Bout that time I stepped on a piece of tin, and it bent, and I skated on away from there.

25 The Bear and the Buzzard (TOBE COURTNEY)

Ordinarily this yarn of a man holding a hear around a tree falls within the Old Marster and John cycle. See Brewer, "John Tales" pp. 92-93, "John, McGruder, and the Bear in the Cornfield"; Hurston, pp. 100-101, "Massa and the Bear"; and post, tale 61, "John, the Bear and the Patteroll."

The incident of the previous tale telling how the buzzard became bald has been neatly added.

I don't know just who it was tied the Bear, but I think it started like this. There was two mens in the woods hunting. Well they was a good little piece apart. So the Bear was coming out of the cornfield. So the man was sitting down on a log, and the bear slipped up on him, he was 'bout half asleep you know, had been hunting all night. And he commenced hollering for the other fellow was out there with him. And he run round a tree (now look at me). The bear tried to catch him, and this was a pretty good man, he jumped behind the tree. And the bear was reaching at him, and he caught the bear's foot, both of 'em. And he holding the bear and hollering for his friend in the woods, the other man. And when the other man come he say, "Now you hold him, and I'm going to tie him."

Well when the other fellow got hold of him, he so weak and tired he sat down and said, "Now when you've hold him as long as I have, then I'll tie him." Finally he decided he'd get up and tie him you know, and they left him out there. They wouldn't kill him, they left him tied.

So Mr. Buzzard he flew around, till the Bear got weak you know. He found out where his meal was at. So finally one day he flew down at him. And when he flew down on him, the bear hit him with his foot, and knocked that patch of hair outa his head. He knocked him kind of crazy and he flew backwards into a tree, and knocked off the rest of that patch. And he been bald-headed ever since.

26 *Why the Buzzard Went South* (JEFFERSON HAIRE)

The idea of the buzzard waiting on the salvation of the Lord occurs in a separate tale, where the impatient hawk kills himself diving after a bird, and the buzzard eats the hawk. I have texts of this form from E. L. Smith and Sam Wilder, and see South Carolina Folk Tales, *p. 7, "Buzzard an Hawk" and references; Browne no. 10, pp. 133-134, "The Hawk and the Buzzard"; Faulkner S-251-B, "Bre'r Turkey Buzzard Waits for Dinner." Variants of the buzzard's trip North were given me by Tommy Carter, Louis Edwards, Mary Richardson, Andrew W. Smith, and Walter Winfrey. The Southern buzzard may visit the eagle, the sparrow, or his cousin the Northern buzzard; Winfrey has the Southern sparrow visit the Northern sparrow. Always the buzzard gets disgusted in his quest for food. A related version appears in Fauset, "South," Animal Tales no. 3, pp. 217-218, "Where They Throw Away the Oranges" (two texts and a fragment), in which the buzzard and the rabbit trick each other by singing, "I'm goin' where they th'ow away oranges."*

The Buzzard was visiting his friend the Seagull. The Seagull was showing him the surroundings and the Buzzard wanted to see how he lived. He told him, "We boys here, we hustle." You know he hustles for a living, but the Buzzard he waits for something to die. The Buzzard says, "We waits on the salvation." (He meant they wait till something dies.) The first thing that happened to him in his favor was that a cow died when the train hit her. And then he said, "That's a good meal now, there's where I can get a good meal." But being just fresh killed it didn't have the odor to suit him. He gone off to wait until it smelt bad. And when he returned he found that the section hands had buried the cow. Then he says, "Now I'm going down to the sunny South, where they never buries the dead."

That's why the Buzzard is down South—he wants to go where he can be lazy—he don't like to work. That's like some people who don't care to hustle or work, they love to stay where they can get a muskrat or pawpaws.

27 The Buzzard Goes to Europe (J. D. SUGGS)

This is a unique modernization of the previous variant. Suggs served overseas in the First World War, when the tale was no doubt adapted to the new situation.

The Buzzard heard that they was killing people so fast in Europe, in the first war, thousands and thousands a day, that they didn't have time to bury them. And so he went around and told all the Buzzards the news. And they got together and were going to have an express (like the crane express from the United States to the Mediterranean to get fish; more small fish there and easier to catch).

They begin to sing,
I'm going where the living don't bury the dead.
And the little ones say,
Lord, Lord, Lord,
We're going where the living don't bury the dead.
So they flew off on their way to Europe. It was true that they weren't burying them, but they was burning them up. So the Buzzards gets back in the flock again, getting ready to leave from there.
And they sing
I'm going back to where people throw away something sometimes.
And the little one he repleats [sic] the same thing, and he says
Lord, Lord, Lord,

We're going back to where people throw away something sometime.
(People are like that, they hear about something good somewhere, and they got a good job already, making $2.25 an hour in St. Louis; but they goes to the other place, and find it's only paying $1.00 an hour, and then they want to come back.)

28 Crow, Buzzard, and Mule (JOHN BLACKAMORE)

Variants were given me by Moses Armstrong and Charles Brown. Fauset, "South," Animal Tales no. 34, pp. 241-242, "Try him! Try him!!," gives two texts from Alabama. I gave this episode from St. Elmo Bland in the headnote to "Take My Place" ante, tale 8. As might be expected, the motif of the baldheaded buzzard sometimes intrudes here; when the buzzard "tries" the mule in the rear, the mule clamps his buttocks around the buzzard's head, and the buzzard pulls all the feathers off his head trying to get away. Mary Richardson and Carl Williams told it that way.

The Crow and the Buzzard was sailing around the sky one day looking for food. Both of them liked dead meat, but this Crow he likes it fresh. But he's scary, you know. So the Buzzard he goes by the smell, he don't like anything till it stinks. Well, they came on a mule laying out there in the sun. The Crow he didn't want to tackle this mule because he wasn't dead, you see, he couldn't smell him, so he puts the Buzzard up to going down. So the Buzzard goes down and circles over, and saw his eyes open—a mule always sleeps with his eyes open. (And when he dies his eyes still be open.)

So he goes back up and tells the Crow, "Well I can't smell him but his eyes are open. I wonder is he dead." Then the Buzzard went on down and lit on the mule's back and walked up to his head, and the mule didn't move. He walked around and tried to peck him in his eye; the mule flopped his ear and knocked the Buzzard on the ground, and he flew away—the mule still lay there.

So, he tells the Crow again, "He looks like he's dead but I don't believe he's dead." The Crow still says, "Try him." So he goes back down and lights on his head again, tries to peck him in the eye. The mule flopped him again with his ear. The Buzzard took off again. So he gits back up there and tells the Crow what happened again. "Every time I go to peck him in the eye he hits me in the ass."

Crow tells him, "He can't be asleep with his eyes open. There's only one thing left for you to do." Buzzard wanted to know what that was. Told him, "You go down there and hit him in *his* ass."

So the Buzzard cuts on back again, lights on the mule's side, and walks on back to the rear. Mule had his tail laying stretched out. Buzzard reared his head way back and give him a good sock. And this mule drew his tail in and caught the Buzzard's head, between his tail and his ass. Mule jumped up and started running around the barnyard—still had the Buzzard's head under his tail. Crow he flies down and sits on the high fence post, and watches. Every time the mule would pass the Crow would holler, "Try *him*." (That's all he can say.) The Crow hollers until the mule run himself to death with the Buzzard's head under his tail. So the Crow ate up the mule and the Buzzard too.

29 *Lazy Buzzard* (J. D. SUGGS)

Type 81: In winter the hare says, "If it were warm, I should build a house," but in summer he says, "Last winter passed satisfactorily" Baughman gives twenty references scattered from Maine to Texas, two of which are Southern Negro, for the Arkansas traveler form of this notion, about repairing the roof in the rain. For the buzzard form see Jones, "Buh Tukrey Buzzud an de Rain" no 2, p. 4; Parsons, Sea Islands, "Dilatory Buzzard" no. 42, p. 56; Smiley no. 38, p. 374, "Dilatory Buzzard"

Mr. Crane called to Mr. Buzzard, "Why don't you build a house, Mr. Buzzard?" He said, "What do a man need with a house? Look how nice and cool this wind is blowing." Buzzard was sitting in the shade, wings apart to let the air through, just resting easy. That morning early it begin to thunder, lightning, and rain. Buzzard begin to get wet. "Well the next sunshiny day I'm going to build me a house." So the next morning the sun was bright and pretty and the wind was blowing like it did the day before. Said "Shaw, what do a man need with a house now?"

30 *Straighten Up and Fly Right* (JOHN BLACKAMORE)

The closest parallel appears in Harris's rare book, Daddy Jake, "How the Terrapin Was Taught to Fly" pp. 90-93. The rabbit and the fox bet who can ascend the highest; when the rabbit plans to mount on the buzzard, the fox bribes the bird to fly out of the country; the rabbit stops the buzzard by biting him under his wing. The first part of the story (pp. 86-90) contains a well-known tale, in which the buzzard teaches the terrapin how to fly, but not how to land. I have a text of this from Jimmy Williams; see Fauset, "South," no. 7, p. 269, "Lighting Is Hell" (Irishman tries to imitate buzzard flying); Parsons, Sea Islands, no 84, pp. 92-93, "Landing Is Hell" (the same); Puckett, pp. 94-50 (rabbit and buzzard).

Do you know where the title of the song "Straighten Up and Fly Right" comes from—the song by Nat King Cole?

One day the Buzzard was sailing around the sky looking for food. He hadn't found none, when he spied a Rabbit looking for a cool place to rest, in the midday sun. So he decided he'd try to get him. So he lights down beside the Rabbit, and spoke to him. Asked him how was he doing. Rabbit says he's pretty hot. Buzzard tells him it's cooler up where he came from, and suggested the Rabbit go for a ride. The Rabbit didn't know what to think about that: "It's closer to the sun and should be hotter up there." But since Buzzard looked so rested and cool, finally he accepts. He gets on the Buzzard's back, and they sail around up in the sky. When he thought the Rabbit felt all cool and comfortable, Buzzard assures him they are going to make a landing. Down he roars, about a hundred feet straight down in a power dive, and then zooms back up. And the Rabbit falls off. So he had the Rabbit for lunch.

Next day when he's looking for food, he sees a Squirrel. So he comes down and lights beside the Squirrel, asks him how did he feel. Squirrel told him he's pretty hot. Buzzard says, "It's cool where I come from. Why don't you take a ride with me?" Since the Squirrel had been accustomed to the trees being cooler up high, he accepted; he figured it would be cooler the higher up he got. So they went sailing way on up. And the Buzzard gave him time to cool off. By the way, a small Monkey was in the top of the tree, watching the Buzzard play his trick on the Squirrel. When the Buzzard gets the Squirrel cooled off, he takes another power dive, and goes right back up, so the Squirrel falls off his back. And he eats the Squirrel for dinner.

Next day the Monkey watches the Buzzard. When he sees him coming, he gits out where the Buzzard can see him, and pretends to be hot. Buzzard lights down beside him, says "Good day," and asks him how he feels. So the Monkey tells him the sun is burning him up, and he wishes he knew

where there was a cool place. Buzzard tells him it's cool where he came from, and asks him to take a ride with him. The Monkey accepts. So they sails around. When he figured the Monkey had got all cooled off, the Buzzard started to make another power dive. But the Monkey wraps his tail around the Buzzard's neck. "Let go, you're choking me." "Then straighten up and fly right. You won't have no Monkey for dinner today."
The buzzard took the monkey for a ride in the air.
The monkey thought that everything was on the square.
The buzzard tried to throw the monkey off his back.
The monkey grabbed his neck and said,
"Now listen Jack,
"Straighten up and fly right."

31 Belling the Buzzard (MARY RICHARDSON)

Randolph in We Always Lie to Strangers (*New York, 1951*), *pp. 260-261, mentions the belled buzzard as a tradition strongly credited in the Ozarks. He cites Ira W. Ford,* Traditional Music of America (*New York, 1940*), *pp. 187-188, "The Belled Buzzard", a gloomy legend of a hoodoo buzzard, known by his tinkling bell, whose coming always brought typhoid fever or other calamity in his wake. A fiddle tune (p. 60), accompanies the story, the fiddler plucking a string to simulate the sound of the bell. An earlier account can be found in Charles M. Skinner,* American Myths and Legends (*Philadelphia & London, 1903*), *I, 274-275, "The Belled Buzzard," localized in Roxbury Mills, Maryland.*

My father belled a buzzard way back in slavery time. He told us that. Him and some more boys were in the woods one Sunday, and they found a buzzard's nest. And they 'cided they'd go to the house and get one of the little turkey bells—kind of like a breakfast bell, little bitty old bell. And so they crawled up in the old hollow log and pulled the buzzard out. (They had a nasty job.) And took this bell and tied the bell to the buzzard's neck. Then they turned him loose. The buzzard was setting on some eggs, and the bell made her leave the nest. I reckon it drove her crazy. She flew from North Carolina to South Carolina. And the people heard the buzzard and saw him, and it was such a 'stonishing thing to see a buzzard with a bell on, they put it in the papers. That's how my father knowed that that buzzard had gone so far.

32 Bee and Dirtdauber (J. D. SUGGS)

Rarely collected. See Smiley, no. 9, p. 362, "Dirtdauber" (from Virginia), where the hornet or yellow-jacket tries to instruct the dirtdauber. This is Type 236, "The Thrush Teaches the Doves (etc.) to Build Small Nests," not reported outside Europe.

A dirtdauber is just like a wasp but he's black. Some of 'em are brown. He makes up mud in his mouth in a little ball, and holds it with his two front legs, then he carries it and sticks it up in any dry place that has a hole in it—a house, a bam, a fence. He makes him a house out of it, like a honeycomb.

When he's getting the mud together he goes "Myennnn." And when he's building his house he goes "Myennnn." He won't sting you without you catch him; he favors a wasp.

Mr. Dirtdauber went over to Mr. Bee's house to take dinner one day. Mr. Bee had some good old sweet honey for dinner. Dirtdauber says, "Say, Mr. Bee, where did you get this at?" Mr. Bee said, "I made it." "I sure wisht I could make that." Mr. Bee told him, "Be over here early in the morning before daylight, and come and go with me; I'll show you how to make this honey."

So the next morning Mr. Dirtdauber's there on time. Off they goes to the mudhole, 'bout a mile through the woods, where Mr. Bee gets his water. So the Bee lit right on the edge, and begin to suck him a little water. Mr. Dirtdauber, he begins to ball up mud, and tells Mr. Bee, "I know, I know, I know." (*Chanted*)

So he flies back to the Bee's house, and begins to stick on his mud. He worked days and days, and built him a comb. When he got it finished, there was no honey in the cells. Said, "I know what I'll do. I'll just lay my eggs in the back end, then I'll put a little thin coat of dirt between them and the food." (That was his storehouse.) Next he puts spiders, little bitty insects, in there and seals it up. Then the eggs hatch worms, and they eat the spiders till they're strong enough to bust out and care for theirselves. He never did learn how to make honey, and never did go back to the Bee's house.

(People's the same way. They won't wait to let you tell them—"Oh, I know, I know." Then they have a failure and put it on you. Won't wait for you to be learning them.)

33 The Preacher and the Guinea (J. D. SUGGS)

Variants of this popular Southern Negro tale were told me by Tobe Courtney, Lee Curtis, Sarah Hall, J. H. Lee, Mary Richardson, James Shackleford, Al Simmons, E. L. Smith, Beulah Tate, and Walter Winfrey. Of these I have printed three texts, in "Negro Tales from Bolivar County, Mississippi," no. 6, pp. 107-108; "Negro Tales of Mary Richardson," no. 8, pp. 10-11; and Pine Bluff, p. 38. Baughman lists this as X459.2*(b), "Fowls hide when preacher comes to visit," and gives one reference, "The Preacher's Dinner" no. 19, pp. 226-227, in "Folklore from St. Helena, South Carolina" In Botkin, Burden, "What the Fowl Said" p. 24, a Yankee replaces the dreaded preacher. Fowls speaking in other contexts can be found in Botkin, Burden, "Barnyard Talk," p. 24; Cox, "How the Birds Talk," pp. 109-118; The Frank C. Brown Collection, I, pp. 634-635, "What the Guinea Hen Says"; Parsons, Antilles, no. 359, pp. 326-327, "Cockcrow" and no, 361, p. 327, "Animal Cries," the A text (from Nevis); Parsons, Sea Islands, no. 128, p. 119, "Guinea-Hen Call." I have two unusual variations, from Henry Phillips, "Chicken Thief" where the fowls address a hen robber, and Suggs, "Fowls at the Crap Game," in Pine Bluff, pp. 170-171, in which the fowls shoot craps to see who will be killed for the preacher's dinner.

Well, the preacher came home with the brother from church for Sunday dinner. So the goose he runs up under the house, the guinea he stayed out in the yard, the hen and the rooster they took out in the woods—but they had to jump on a fence before they got to the woods.

Rooster's crowing, he says, "The preacher go-o-ne?" (*High*)

The guinea says, "Not yet, not yet." (*Tightly*)

Old goose says, "Ssssh, ssssh."

That time the old man stepped round the house with a shotgun and let go, "Boom," and shot the hen. Old rooster jumped off the fence and down through the woods he went.

Guinea was saying, "No more than I expected, no more than I expected." (*Tightly*)

And the preacher had him his hen. (The preacher always wants chicken —mighty few of them want goose or duck or turkey. It's custom; a boy says, "If I grow up and be a preacher I'll eat chicken," and his mind sets that way.)

34 The Poll Parrot

An extensive cycle of Negro stories revolves around a poll parrot who in slavery times spies on the slaves for Old Marster and in more recent times reports misdeeds of the colored maid to Old Miss. Besides the five stories that follow I have variants from Tommy Carter, Lacy Manier, Mary Richardson, Willie Sewall, and E. L. Smith in Michigan and Silas J. Altheimer, Edna Nelson, and Maria Summers in Arkansas. The common thread and comic element of these eleven texts and their analogues is the punishment of the parrot and the parrot's reaction.

a The Poll Parrot, the Hawk, and Jim (JAMES SHACKLEFORD)

A close variant form has the hawk carry off and kill the parrot while Jim watches: Altheimer's text; Halpert no. 263, "Just A-Ridin' "; and from England, Sidney O. Addy, Household Tales with other Traditional Remains *(London and Sheffield, 1895), pp. 12-13, "The Hawk and the Parrot." The present tale includes Motif J551.5, "Magpie tells a man that his wife has eaten an eel." (He has his feathers plucked out for tattling and thinks a bald man has also tattled.)*

Old Marster had a poll parrot, and this poll parrot would watch Jim and tell his Marster what Jim would do. One day while out in the field watching Jim a hawk caught him. And he thought within himself he was taking a ride. So he said to Jim, "I'm riding, Jim." And Jim told him to ride on. So the hawk took the poll parrot out in the woods and began to peck and pull the feathers out of his head, trying to kill him to eat him. The poll parrot began to call, "Help, help, Jim." But Jim wouldn't go. So finally Jim's Marster made him go and run the hawk away. This excited the poll parrot and made a Christian out of him.

His Marster was the pastor of a church, and so he made the poll parrot an usher in it. And one night they had a big gathering and the poll parrot begin to seat the people. When they had most all been seated, two old baldheaded gentlemen came in. The poll looked at them and said, "You two fellows must have been hawk-riding. Have those special seats."

b *Polly Tells on the Slaves*

Back in slavery days Old Marster and his wife would go to town to shop. And the slaves'd take the time to have a big party—there was so much food it wouldn't be missed. They would cook cakes and pies and potatoes and kill chickens and bring out their fiddle and dance. But no matter how they pledged themselves to secrecy, Old Marster would know all about it when he came back. And then one day one of the maids who worked in the house heard the poll parrot reviewing all the things they had done at the last party.

"Pass the 'tater pie."

"Gimme another piece a chicken."

"This is good cake."

"Are you going to dance now, are you going to dance now?" [*Croaky*]

"Swing your partner."

(They go off—they lose interest in the conversation.)

So they knew how the Marster knowed about them— Polly had told them. They had gradually stopped the parties, and Marster thought soon it would stop altogether. Next time Marster went to town they draped a black cloth over his head and put him under the washpot. When Marster came back he asked Polly what she'd seen.

"Polly don't know. Poor Polly been in hell all day." (Darkness is her idea of hell.)

c *Poll Parrots and Biscuits* (JOHNNY HAMPTON)

For the theme of the parrot's punishment see Motif J2211.2, "Why the sow was muddy," which refers to Johannes Pauli, Schimpf und Ernst *(2 vols., Berlin, 1924), ed. Johannes Bolte, no, 669. Stanley Robe gives a text in his "Basque Tales from Eastern Oregon,"* Western Folklore, *XII (1953), 154-155, and in note 3 refers to thirteenth-century Persian, fourteenth-century French, and sixteenth-century German variants, two modern Mexican texts of his own collecting, and a bibliography of the motif in Otto Schutte,* Zeitschrift des Vereins für Volkskunde, *XIII (1903), 94. American examples appear in Boggs, "North Carolina," no. 8, p. 294, "The Parrot Eats the Bread"; Botkin,* Burden, *7, "Polly Parrot."*

This is one of the most popular forms of the Negro parrot jest, punctuated by the key phrase, "Hot biscuits burn your ass."

Once Old Marster and Old Missus went away and left their cook and parrot at home. They didn't allow the cook to eat much; so she decided she would cook some biscuits and eat them while they were gone. Just as she begins to eat, Old Marster and Miss done come home. So she placed the biscuit under the cushion of the rocking chair. Old Missus was fixing to set down. Poll parrot cried, "Oh no, Miss, don't sit down, 'cause hot biscuits will burn your ass." So Old Missus found the biscuit under the cushion, and whipped the cook.

Next time Old Marster and Old Miss went away, the cook said: "I know how to get even with the parrot. I'll cook some corn bread and give it to him." When the parrot ate the corn bread, it made him constipated. And when he got ready to go outside, it kind of tore him up behind. He went out in the weeds. Long came a boar hog. Parrot said, "Poor swine, your rear end is tore up just like mine."

d *Poll Parrots and Hens* (A. J. KING)

A white informant in Fayetteville, Arkansas, Mrs. Dagmar Fondoble, also told me a case of the parrot treading hens. The master plucks the parrot, and has him usher people to a party; seeing two bald men, he says, "Oh, you bald-headed chicken-chasers will have to get on the piano with me" Cf. the (a) text.

Marster had quite a few poll parrots in among his slaves, to watch them if they were doing anything wrong. So the parrots began treading the hens, and the slaves told on them.

And the wife was crazy about working jigsaw puzzles, and she would even crack the eggs and put the shells back together on the shelf. And she had to go away to visit her daughter, who was the belle of the community. And while she was away the husband decided he would cook breakfast. He began to crack the eggs, and didn't anything come out the shells. So he just rushed to the parrots and said, "I told you to stop treading those hens, and the least you can do is use a prophylactic."

e *The Parrot and the Woodman* (GRACE BEDFORD)

This actually happened in Pine Bluff. The woodman would come around with his load of wood, and the parrot would call, "Wood, wood. Drive around to the back and throw it off."

This one lady had installed gas, and while she was out the parrot called the woodman. He drove around to the back and threw his wood off and went back to the front to collect. He knocked and knocked, then went next door to find out where the people were. The parrot said it again, and he saw it again. He was going to wring its neck, when the lady came home and paid him.

[8] The contraction of "Brother" in the storyteller's vernacular cannot be exactly rendered, but "Ber" or "Buh" comes closer than "Brer."

OLD MARSTER AND JOHN

Folktale interpreters who see the Rabbit as the psychic symbol of Negro resentment against the white man cannot know of the crafty slave named John. Seldom printed, the spate of stories involving John and his Old Marster provides the most engaging theme in American Negro lore. In all his volumes of animal fictions, Joel Chandler Harris includes only one example, and apparently never understood the cycle to which it belonged. Yet trickster John directly expressed and illuminates the plantation Negro character. No allegoric or symbolic creation, he is a generic figure representing the ante-bellum slave who enjoyed some measure of favoritism and familiarity with his owner.

The narratives[9] about Old Marster (sometimes called Old Boss, the post-bellum title of the white employer) reflect the physical circumstances of slavery life, and mirror the mixed attitudes held by the bondsman toward the planter. John often engages in petty thefts and duplicities, which Old Marster anticipates and exposes, in an amicable spirit; each knows the other, and feints and thrusts for the good-humored victory. Actually Old Marsa relishes the cunning of his prize hand, boasts about his fortunetelling ability to neighbor planters, and stakes a heavy wager on John's powers. Master and slave thus enter into uneasy partnership, for John must win the contest (as he does by a ruse or luck) or incur disfavor. An opposite tendency sets the oppressive slaveowner and his discontented chattel sharply against each other, in the relationship described by the historian John Hope Franklin. Slaves steal from the big house, shirk their work, run away when they can, and murder white men, while the planter scorns his ignorant hands and punishes them with whippings and death on slight provocation. Some narratives suggest this harsh and lethal conflict.

The Old Marster cycle portrays the realities of plantation life with often surprising detail. In the variants that deal with a fight between two strong slaves on neighboring plantations, the plots hinge on an institutional feature of slavery, the selection by the planter of a husky hand for breeding purposes and general strongarm duty.

Seemingly these unified and highly localized Old Marster tales grew on Southern soil from American Negro experience, but actually they come from the ends of the earth. By the mysterious selective process of folklore, jousts between masters and servants recounted centuries ago in Europe or West Africa have found their way into slave traditions. Thus a contemporary English collector points out the frequency of humorous folktales about masters and hired men in Westmorland County, where farmers engage in much seasonal hiring, and two plots fit smoothly into the analogous master-slave situation of the Old South. From India comes the wonderful tale of the Sorcerer's Apprentice, with its magical transformation combat between the wizard and his pupil, to surface in Michigan in a unique text brilliantly adjusted to Negro slave life, with Old Marster out-hoodooing John at each successive step. The stark narrative of "The Talking Bones" would appear a direct outgrowth of the plantation system, perhaps even based on an actual killing of a too talkative slave who told Old Marster he had seen skeletons in the woods close by—but Negro Africans relate the same event. Some years ago scholars became interested in the "Mak" story, an episode in the Towneley plays of the fifteenth century, where a shepherd hides a stolen sheep in a cradle and conceals his theft by pretending it is a baby. Evidence proved this little dramatic scene to be a recurrent folktale with several literary appearances; not surprisingly it turns up as one of John's escapades. Only Estonia yet records "The Flattering Foreman," a yes-man finally exposed by his boss when he echoes a ridiculous suggestion; Winfrey tells not a close but an exact parallel. In the most popular Old Marster yarn, John saves his skin with an inadvertent pun —"You've caught the old coon at last"—that enables him to guess a raccoon is hidden under a pot; throughout the West Indies and Europe a charlatan diviner named "Crab" or "Cricket" performs an identical feat. A tale with extraordinary vogue among white people in Europe and America deals with thieves dividing their spoil in a cemetery, whom passers-by mistake for God and the Devil counting souls; sure enough this event gets attached to Old Marster and John. The tricky-slave cycle has absorbed pertinent tales from remote reaches of time and space.

I JOHN AS DECEIVER AND ROGUE

35 *Coon in the Box* (JOHN BLACKAMORE)

Other versions of this best known of all Old Marster stories were told me by Ray Brooks (who alone had Blackamore's twist of the coon inside three boxes), Tommy Carter, Carrie Eaton, Bill Franklin (slave guesses both coon and fox), E. L. Smith, J. D. Suggs. Usually it is told as a brief anecdote. New World Negro and other references and seven West Indies texts are given by Parsons, Antilles, no. 285, pp. 282-284, "False Diviner." Baughman shows the American Negro absorption of this tale with nine out of ten Southern Negro references, the tenth being California Portuguese, under Type 1641, "Doctor Know-All." Add Hurston, pp. 111-112, "The Fortune Teller"; Southern Workman, v. 23, no. 12 (*Dec. 1894*), p. 209; Abrahams, Jungle, pp. 222-224, "The Coon in the Box." *Flowers lists examples from Antigua, Dominica, Grenada, Guadeloupe, Haiti, Jamaica (2), Martinique, Puerto Rico (8), St. Kitts, St. Lucia, St. Martin, Trinidad. Klipple gives a text from the East African Cattle Area. The major motif for the tale is K1956, "Sham wise man."*

Only the third episode of the complex, "The Covered Dish," carries into Negro tradition. (The motif cross-reference in the Type-Index is Motif N688, "What is in the dish: 'Poor Crab'.") In the type analysis, the pun on the hidden animal involves Crab, Cricket, or Rat; in Grimm 98 it is Krebs (Crabb); Parsons and Flowers report Cricket as commonest, rarely Fox. But all the United States Negro texts hinge on the colloquial sense of "coon." Randolph gives a Coon form in the white tradition, Devil's Pretty Daughter, *133-135, "Second Sight."* W. A. Clouston points out a close parallel with the Grimm version from the Sanskrit of the Katha Sarit Sagara, *in which the lucky impostor saves himself with a play on frog in the pitcher* (Popular Tales and Fictions, New York, 1887, II, 425-426).

Once upon a time there was a Boss had a servant on his farm, kind of a handyman. Every night this handyman, Jack, would go down to the Boss's house and listen while he ate supper, so he'd know what Boss was going to do the next day. One night when Old Boss was eating supper he told his wife he was going to plow the west forty acres the following day. After Jack heard that he goes home to bed; next morning he gets up earlier than usual, and gets the tractor out and hooks up the plow. When Old Boss came out Jack was all ready to go. So he said, "Well Jack, we're going to plow the west forty acres today." He said, "Yes, Boss, I know, I got the rig all set up." Well, Old Boss didn't think much about it. He gets on his horse and goes in there and shows Jack how he wants him to plow it up.

So the next night when Boss sits down to eat his supper Jack goes on down to his favorite spot where he could hear everything. He heard his Old Boss tell his wife that he was going to round up all the livestock for shipping. Next day Jack gets up early, and gets the Boss's horse ready that he always rides when he rounds up the livestock. When Boss comes out later, he starts to tell Jack what he's got on the program. Jack cuts him off and says, "Yes, Boss, I know, we're going to round up the livestock this morning. I got your horse all saddled and ready to go." So Boss says, "Jack, what puzzles me is, every morning when I get up you tell me what I'm going to do before I tell you." And he wants to know what's happening, how did Jack know what he's gonna do. Jack says, "Well I don't know, I just knows." So Boss says, "Well, something funny going on." Jack says "Maybe so, but I know."

So they goes on to round up the livestock, and at the end of the day Boss sits down at the supper table again. And Jack takes the same position at the window, so he can hear everything that's talked about. Boss tells his wife about he's going to clean out the stable the next day, to use the waste to fertilize the fields. So the next morning Jack was out in the stables cleaning 'em out, before Old Boss was up. Boss eats breakfast and he goes on out to the barn, sees Jack busy working. So he asks Jack, "How did you know I wanted the stables cleaned out today?" Jack says, "That's all right, I knowed you wanted to get it cleaned out so I went and got it started so I could hurry up and get the job done." So Boss says, "Yes, that's right, but what puzzles me is how a nigger like you can figure out what I'm going to do every day before I tell you." He says, "Well that's all right Boss, I know everything." So Old Boss shook his head and walks on up. So that night he was still puzzled at suppertime. Jack was still at the window. He listened to what his Boss was talking about. Old Boss told his wife, "Well this handyman we got around here, he's the smartest one I ever seen. Every morning I go out to tell him what to do he's already done it or he's telling me what we are going to do. And I don't know what to do about it."

So he was going up to the council next night, where the landlords have their meeting every Wednesday night to discuss their crops and problems. When Old Boss comes out of the house to go to the meeting, Jack had his rig all ready. Old Boss says, "Well thank you, Jack." And Jack says, "I hope you have a good time at the meeting, Boss." So Old Boss went on down to the meeting and he was telling the other landlords about this smart nigger he had down at his place. All the other councilmens laughed at him. But it didn't tickle Old Boss. He says, "You guys think I'm joking, but that's the truth." So one smart aleck he jumped up and said, "There ain't no nigger that smart." Everybody laughs again. So Old Boss got peeved. He says, "Well, all you crackers think it's so damn funny; I'll bet money on my nigger, 'cause he knows everything." Everybody begins to get quiet then, except this smart aleck. He says, "Well Jim, since you think so much of your nigger, I got $ 100,000 to say that I can outsmart your nigger." Old Boss called the bet. He said, "Now any of you other crackers in here think that's so funny and want to bet, I'll cover you too." So everybody kicks in with $100,000 apiece. When the total was counted up the bet run over a million dollars. So this Carver—that was the smart aleck—he says, "Well, you can expect us down tomorrow about two o'clock, and we'll have something your nigger can't tell us about."

Old Boss went home. Old Jack was still up waiting, so he could find what's going to happen tomorrow. Old Boss went into his bedroom, and he sat down side of the bed and he commenced to telling his wife what he was doing. And he said he was going to give a big barbecue the next day, so he needed to have food and drinks ready for the crowd when they come on down. Then he went on to bed.

Next morning old Jack was still sleeping when Old Boss got up. He was making himself scarce. He knowed they had some kind of a trick for him; he didn't want Old Boss to think he was so smart any more. So Old Boss rapped on the door, said, "Jack, get up, it's day." He says, "Coming, Boss." Old Boss walks on off and went on back in the house. And Jack was so used to Old Boss getting up and he being ready for him ahead of time, he begins to prepare for the party, without the Boss even telling him. When Old Boss come out, he says, "That's right, Jack, that's right. We're going to have a big party this afternoon, and I got a lot of money bet on you." Jack wanted to know then what for he had his money bet. So Old Boss said, "Well you know—you're trying to kid me that you don't know."

When the crowd had all of them gathered around they called Jack. Jack came around slowly. Old Boss said, "Come on up, Jack, come on up, don't be bashful." So Mr. Carter, the smart aleck, he says, "Well darky, they tell me you're pretty smart around here." So Jack says, "Aw, I wouldn't say that." Old Boss says, "Oh he's just trying to be modest." Then Old Boss said to Jack, "Didn't you tell me the other day that you know everything?" So Jack stretches his head and says, "Yes, that's right," rather slowly, scared to call the Boss a liar. So Mr. Carter says, "All right, let's get down to business, we got a lot of money bet on this. And I want you to tell us what it is, 'cause if you don't, I'm going to have your head tomorrow." Then Carter he called Jim over to tell him what the surprise was, before Jack would tell them. Carter told Jim it was a box in a box in a box in that box, and in the small box was a coon. And why they had him in so many boxes was so that Jack couldn't hear the coon scratch.

And then Jack started scratching his head and trying to tell them what was in the box, although he didn't really know. So Carter asked him again, "Well Jack, what do you say is in the box?" Jack started repeating what Carter had said. He says, "In the box, in the box, in the box." And he decided that he didn't know in his mind what, so he just scratched his head and said, "You got the old coon at last." (He was using that as an expression.)

So Old Boss grabbed him and shook his hand and said "Thanks, Jack, thanks, that's just what it is, a coon in them boxes."

36 Efan and the Panter (J. D. SUGGS)

This story resembles the preceding one in the lucky extrication of the clever slave from his predicament, but has not been previously reported in the Old Marster cycle. Comparable incidents can be found under Motif K1951, "Sham warrior," particularly the Grimms's story of The Brave Tailor (Type 1640 and Motif K731, "Wild boar captured in church"; Bolte and Polívka, I, 148ff). Clouston cites the Kashmir sham hero's lucky killing of an elephant and a tiger (Popular Tales and Fictions, I, 152-154).

Efan told Ole Marster he could catch most anything, he didn't care how bad it was. All he wanted to do was get close enough to it to get hold of it. So one night he's coming in, carrying his long club with him (they didn't allow slaves to carry knives), and he sees something squat, he thought it was a dog. So he let go his club and he broke its neck. When he walked up and struck a match, he seen it was a panter; he grabbed it, and went in the wagon with him to the Old Marster's house. "Here, Old Marster, *open the door,* open the door." "What you want, Efan?" (*Loudly*) "I've got a live

123

panter here." "Don't you bring no live panter in here, don't bring him in here." (*Loud*) "Well, I told you I could catch anything live—all I wanted to do was to get close enough to it. So, I'll just kill him then, if you don't want him live. Come out and look, I killed him now." Old Marster ran outdoors then, felt him and the panter was just as warm as he could be. "Well, Efan, you sure can do what you say you can."

He told Mr. Smith about Efan catching that live panter and bringing him home. Mr. Smith said, "Nooo, he ain't caught no live panter." "I'll bet you if you could get one and put him in some place, Efan'll go in and bring him out." "What will you bet?" "I'll bet you that last four hundred acres down next to the creek, against six thousand, he'll do it." "Okay, we'll set next Saturday week. Bring Efan over to my place for business."

Saturday week Old Marster carried Efan over. There was a great crowd there, womens and childrens and mens, to see Efan going in and catch the live panter. "Okay everything's ready, unlock the door." Efan says, "Slam the door quick as soon as I get in." In goes Efan, the door slams. They heard a rumbling in there—a-running round and round. Efan was running from the panter as hard as he could. Old Marster said, "Efan's after him, he'll ketch him." 'Bout that time Efan run over the end of a plank, and it flew up just in front of the panter's face. (In those days the boards weren't nailed, and a green board would fly up if you stepped on it.) He saw the hole and he dug his head in it. And Efan was running so fast he caught up with him and stepped on the plank before he could stop. So then he stayed there, and pressed on the plank till he broke the panter's neck. Efan grabbed the panter and hollered, "Open the door, I got him." "No, don't open that door, there's womens and childrens out here, he'll kill them, don't open that door." Efan says, "Well, I'll kill him then, but I thought you wanted me to bring him out alive so you could see I had him."

In about five seconds Efan said, "Open the door, I got him, I got him dead." So out come Efan dragging the panter, twelve feet long from the tip of his nose to the end of his tail.

37 *The Swimming Contest* (LULU POWELL)

Type 1612, "The Contest in Swimming"; Motif K1761, "Bluff: provisions for the swimming match" Parsons, Antilles, no. 286, pp. 284-285, "Bluffing Swimmer," gives six references, including one from West Africa but only one American Negro, and five texts; four have the stowaway incident present in Lulu Powell's tale but lacking in the Type Index. Her texts are also listed in Flowers. Brewer gives a variant with the stowaway in Humorous Folk Tales, pp. 3-4, "The Faithful Slave," apparently from the same source as Parsons above ("Folklore from St. Helena, South Carolina," no. 16, p. 225, "The Swimmer," two texts). Harry Oster has recorded an elaborate text from Louisiana.

This I never heard anywhere in my life before, except from this friend of mine, and it was the biggest lie I ever heard. Will Gray—he was married to my stepsister—told me that fifty years ago. How we laughed!

This master freed his slaves, but one slave didn't want to leave. The master and his wife were leaving on a ship—probably for the Old Country, since they were going away from this country. So the slave stowed away, and when they got nearly to land he began to call out, "Oh, Massie George, oh, Massie George." At first it sounded faint, and then it kept getting louder. They said, "That must be John," but they couldn't believe it. He slipped out and began swimming toward the boat. So they pulled him aboard, all dripping, and asked him how he got there. "Well, I swim all the way here; I wasn't going to let you leave me."

So he went along with them, and his master was bragging about how he had the best swimmer in the world. There was a white swimmer parading around, and they made a date with him to have a contest. The day of the contest he was waiting on the beach, until finally the colored man came, puffing and making a lot of noise, with a cookstove and provisions on his back. He said, "Where's that white fellow who's goin' to swim with me?" (in a big voice). The white man said, "Here I am" (in a little voice). John said, "Man, ain't you carrying nothing to eat with you?" He answered "No." "Well, you'd better, for I'm a-fixing to stay." The white man ran away.

38 The Fight

There is a resemblance here to Motif K1711, "Ogre made to believe small hero is large: overawed," in the category of "Deception Through Bluffing" (K1700-1799), and also to Motif K1951, "Sham Warrior" (see "Efan and the Panter"). The theme of "Wagers on Wives, Husbands, or Servants" common in the Old Marster tales, belongs under Motif N10. Overawing the giant by pretending to throw a heavy object across the ocean or up to heaven is well known. Baughman inserts this into the Motif-Index at K18.1.2, "Throwing contest; trickster addresses Angel Gabriel or St. Peter, warns him to get out of way of missile trickster is about to throw," and gives four Southern references, two Negro and two white. Fauset, "South," Fairy Tales no. 6, p. 250, "The Strong One," has the hero bluff giants by saying he will throw a big spike maul into northern Ireland (Motif K18.1). Brewer, "Juneteenth," pp. 50-51, "Experts with the sling" follows my texts in the idea of a strong-slave contest. Hurston, pp. 197-198, "Strength Test between Jack and the Devil," moves toward the Samson-Satan subtype (see post, tale 135, "Samson and the Anvil").

a (JOE D. HEARDLEY)

There was two plantation owners, and they each had a bad man. They met each other in the road and they was sitting on their horses talking about the hands they had on the farm. And one said he had the baddest man. Other said his man was the baddest, could whip everybody. So they was going to have a fight, and bet their plantation against the other plantation—Coker against Brian Dewies (that was down in Mississippi). All the hands and the sharecroppers went in with the bet, and whichever badman win, his master takes over.

They set the fight for Saturday evening. Coker's bad man was a little bitty fellow. Brian's was a big burly cat, like a mule. Coker's man told him, "Boss, you go saddle up your best saddle horse you got there." (He was supposed to saddle the horse, but now he's giving the orders, 'cause the Boss got his stake up, his home, plantation, money, everything.) "And git the shovel and go down and dig his grave, out there where we're going to fight, 'cause I'm going to kill him. I'll be down soon as I take a bath, and shave, and get my shoes shined. Hitch the horse out there, and comb his mane." (He was particular—he done take over now.) He come down with a red handkerchief tied round his neck, and a starched and iron overall suit. People was there by the thousands, come to see the fight. (That's the farmer's day, Saturday —everybody comes to town.)

He gets there fifteen minutes late. The big fellow was in training with a thousand pound maul, throwing it up a quarter of a mile, a half a mile up in the air. Then he'd dig down about four feet to get it out of the ground. He was pulling the trees up, four foot through the butt, and throwing them outside to get the ring cleared off.

The little fellow tells his Boss, "Have you dug his grave yet?" He said, "No." Tells him, "Start digging right now, 'cause I'm going to kill him." He pulls his coat off, he's going to work out a little before the fight. He reaches out and gets the maul; he can't lift it. So he yells up to the sky, "Saint Peter, move over, and tell Sister Mary to move out the way, and move baby Jesus."

So this big fellow said, "It's a little too rough around here for me."

b (SILAS ALTHEIMER)

For the strong man throwing a horse and his rider over the wall, see my Jonathan Draws the Long Bow *(Cambridge, 1946), p. 126 and n. 14 (told on George Washington Briggs), and Thomas F. Waters, Ipswich in the Massachusetts Bay Colony (2 vols., Ipswich, Mass., 1905-7), vol. 1, p. 242 (told on Jonathan Wise).*

Two men had slaves, one named Mike and the other Peter. And they often met and discussed the strength of their slaves, how they were giants and so forth. Finally they made a bet on them, and all their friends made bets. So they appointed a day to fight in the town square. But they built an enclosure in the town square, so all the people could see them fight to a finish. On the day set a great crowd gathered. One man had come in and seeing the enclosure, but not knowing it was the place for the fight, he carried his horse on in the enclosure and hitched him. So when Mike and Peter went inside, the first thing Mike did was go to the horse that was saddled and pick him up and lifted him over the fence.

When Peter saw that he said, "No fight."

c (CHARLES BROWN)

The only close text of this form is in Brewer, Worser Days, *pp. 108-110, "Big John and Little John," in which Little John kisses his master's wife and kicks his master in the seat of the pants.*

You take in the South, they always have one strong colored guy on all the plantations. He's given a lot of consideration by the boss—usually he be foreman. Can put two or three of the others in his back pocket.

So one plantation owner said to the other, "My colored guy can whip your guy." The other boss said, "I'll be damned if he can." So they signed up for a fight, them two farm owners. And so each man went and told the tough colored guy on his place that he got a fight coming up. Each tough guy went off to himself thinking, "I can't whip that bastard." Jim said, "I can't whip John," and John said, "I can't whip Jim." But back in slavery times you can't back out. So they set a date for the fight.

So the boss said to each colored guy, "What do you want for the fight? What are you going to wear?" Jim he thought he'd make a display to frighten John. He asks his boss to make a link chain, about four feet long, with an iron stake at the end of it, to drive into the ground, and to put an iron ring in his nose. And he'll be scratching and licking up dirt when John comes, like a bull, and running back and forward on the chain. And his boss would be trying to keep him quiet. "Steady, steady there, Jim, whoa, just a few minutes."

When John's boss asked him what he wanted, he said, "Just give me Old Puss to ride down to the battling ground." He was quiet-like, tough but quiet. He was slow riding down—he almost like to be late, and forfeit the bet. That was a great big day, a holiday, people from twenty miles around was there in their horse and buggy and ox teams. So when he was late, his Missus got worried, and as soon as he came riding down she went over to him. John saw Jim on the chain and he was studying how to scare him, he was already scared himself. He's thinking fast, working his brain. When his Missus come over, he knew she would say something pretty flip. So he thinks: the minute she opens her mouth, I'll slap her. Missus said, "What kept you? Why you so late?" (*Very rough*) John he slapped her face. Jim pulled up the stake and ran, sold out, forfeited the fight.

So the loser, Jim's master, had to pay off John's boss the three or four thousand dollars they'd put in a bag. Still, John's boss got mad about his wife being slapped. He asked John, "What was the idea slapping my wife?" "Well, Jim knowed if I slapped a white woman I'd a killed him, so he run."

39 *Big Feet Contest* (A. J. KING)

During slavery time the Old Marsters would get together and brag which of their slaves had the largest feet. And one of the slave Marsters said, "My slave's feet are larger than yours."

And the other said, "No, my slave's feet are longer than yours."

So the other slaveowner says, "Give me proof that your slave's feet are larger than mine."

So this was his proof. He says, "Whenever I buy shoes for my slaves, they come in separate boxes, and they send a pair of oars with them."

So the other slaveowner gave his proof. Said, "You know the five hundred acres I own? You know those field mice was on those five hundred acres?" Says, "John was plowing at one end of the five hundred acres, and I hollered, 'Field mouse.' And John raised his foot. And I said, 'Did you get him, John?'

"And he said, 'Yes, if he's anywhere in the field.' "

40 *Old Marster Takes a Trip* (WALTER WINFREY)

See Fauset, "South," Old Marster Stories no. 5, pp. 266-267, "Master Gone to Philanewyork"; Smiley no. 8, p. 362, "Master Disguised." I also have texts from Ray Brooks and Katy Pointer, who has the slaves sing, "Massie's gone to Philly-me-jinks, Going to be gone three long weeks." The idea of the clever slave changing his square dance call appears in a separate tale; he has been calling the dancers to swing a fat white girl to him; after his Master whips him, he call to them to swing her away from him. Beulah Tate gave me this text, and see Fauset, "South," Animal Tales no. 17, p. 226, "Rabbit at the Party." Hurston, "How the Negroes Got Their Freedom," pp. 112-114, combines the present plot with no. 54, where John tricks Marster at the praying tree.

Old Marster had this main fellow on his farm he put his confidence in, John. Old Marster told him he was going away on a trip, and he'd be gone for three weeks. He packed his bags and left. So when John figgered Old Marster had left, he goes around and invites all of the friends and all of the hands that was on the farm. And he kills up a couple of sheeps, a couple of hogs, bakes a gang of cakes, and told them, "We're going to have a big flangdang." When the company begin to pour in they start a regular old barn dance. And John was calling the sets:

All over there come over here,
All over here go over there,
Won't that be gitting t-h-e-r-e.

After a while his wife discovered Old Boss had come in. Old Boss had got him a partner and started to dance. He'd smutted his face, and when he began to dance he sweats, and when he sweat you could see white streaks on his face. So John's wife says, "John, I believe that's Old Boss done come in." John tells her, "Go on old lady, go on; you don't know what you talking about; I'll haul off and knock a brain outa you." But as Old Boss danced and sweat his skin showed up more and more, and John discovered too it was Old Boss. So John said, "Wait a minute, I got something to tell you all:

> You all get outa here the best way you can,
> 'Cause I'm going out the chimley."

41 *Baby in the Crib* (E. L. SMITH)

This is the Mak story from the Second Shepherd's Play in the Towneley Cycle (see The Towneley Plays, *Early English Text Society, Extra Series No. 71, 1897, repr. 1925, pp. 116ff., and pp. xxxi-xxxiv for a parallel two centuries later in the ballad of Archie Armstrong's Aith). Baughman adds to Motif K406.2, "Stolen sheep dressed as baby in cradle," seven references from Southern states, two being Negro. For a related variant, see post, tale 78, "The Hog and the Colored Man," which also employs the general motif K406, "Stolen animal disguised as person so that thief may escape detection." Randolph and Halpert discuss American texts in their notes, pp. 173-174 to Randolph's tale, "The Baby in the Cradle," in* The Devil's Pretty Daughter, *pp. 19-20. These texts come from Arkansas, Georgia, North Carolina, South Carolina, and Texas.*

A popular Negro variation of this episode has the thief profess surprise when his alleged possums prove to be pigs or chickens. I have texts from Newton Curry, Johnny Hampton, and Walter Winfrey, and see Botkin, Burden, pp. 3-4, "It was a Possum A While Ago"; Brewer, "John Tales," pp. 81-83, "How the Boss-man Found Out John Was Taking His Chickens"; Brewer, "Juneteenth," pp. 11-12, "Possum in the Pot"; Smith, "Possums Turn to Pigs," pp. 251-252. In Christensen, pp. 94-100, "Br'er Rabbit an' Br'er Wolf Plant Pertater an' Hunt Honey," bricks change to bread and sand to honey. I have a text of bricks turning to potatoes from Wash Cockrell.

John stole a pig from Old Marsa. He was on his way home with him and his Old Marsa seen him. After John got home he looked out and seen his Old Marsa coming down to the house. So he put this pig in a cradle they used to rock the babies in in them days (some people called them cribs), and he covered him up. When his Old Marster come in John was sitting there rocking him.

Old Marster says, "What's the matter with the baby, John?" "The baby got the measles." "I want to see him." John said, "Well you can't; the doctor said if you uncover him the measles will go back in on him and kill him." So his Old Marster said, "It doesn't matter; I want to see him, John." He reached down to uncover him.

John said, "If that baby is turned to a pig now, don't blame me."

42 John Steals a Pig and a Sheep (RAY BROOKS)

In contributing "Analogues to the Mak Story," Thomas B. Stroup gives a close variant to the present text, from Fletcher, North Carolina, with a preacher rather than John being the pig thief (JAF XLVII, 1934, pp. 380-381). In spite of his attempt to vary the reading "under the bed" to "in the bed" for the pig's hiding place, I see this as a quite separate tale. In other tales John sings altered words to get himself out of a scrape (see ante, tale 40, "Old Marster Takes a Trip"), but this device plays no part in the Mak story; the disguise motif, and the oath to eat what is in the cradle, play no part in the present plot.

Another variant appears in Bacon and Parsons, no. 60, p. 294, "Saving Hog" (Florida), where the stolen hog is pushed under the bed and revealed when the cat drags out a large piece of fresh pork.

The second incident falls under Motif J1390, "Retorts concerning thefts." In Brewer, "John Tales," pp. 84-85, John caught by the Colonel in the sheep pen yells out, "Ah ain't gonna let no daw-gone sheep butt me to death."

Old Marster had some sheep, and a fellow named John living on the place, a tenant there, he got hungry and he stole the meat from Old Boss. Then he got tired of the sheep meat and stole him a pig. Old Marster come down night after he stole the pig, to get him to play a piece on the banjo. Old Marster knocked on the door, when John had just got through putting the pig away. So Old Marster come in and say, "Play me a piece on the banjo." John started to pick a piece on the banjo; while he's playing he looked around and sees a pig's foot sticking out, so he sings, "Push that pig's foot further back under the bed." (He was talking to his wife.)

When he got tired of that pig meat he turned around and killed him another sheep. So he went back down to the barn and told Old Marster, "Another sheep dead, can't I have him?" Old Marster give him that sheep and he took that one home and ate it up. That made two that Old Marster had given him, so Old Marster got a watch out for him. John killed another one and went and told Old Marster again that a sheep had died. Old Marster told him, "You killed that sheep. What did you kill my sheep for?" John says, "Old Marster, I'll tell you; I won't let nobody's sheep bite me."

43 *The Yearling* (WILLIAM BROWN LEE)

This tale too can be placed under Motif J1390, "Retorts concerning thefts," although J1260, "Repartee based on church or clergy" also applies.

In the old days the only things the slaves got good to eat is what they stole. Old Marster lost a yea'ling, and some of the preacher's members knowed its whereabouts. So Old Marster told him to preach the hell out of the congregation that Sunday, so that whosomever stole the yea'ling would confess having it.

The preacher got up and pernounced to the crowd: "Some of you have stole Old Marster's yea'ling. So the best thing to do is to go to Old Marster and confess that you stole the yea'ling. And get it off right now. Because if you don't, Judgment Day, the man that stole the Master's yea'ling will be there. Old Marster will be there too, the yea'ling will be there too—the yea'ling will be *staring* you in the face."

John gets up and says to the preacher, "Mr. Preacher, I understand you to say, Judgment Day, the man that stole Old Marster's yea'ling will be there, Old Marster will be there, the yea'ling will be there, yea'ling will be *staring* you in the face."

Preacher says, "That's right."

John replied then, "Let Old Marster git his yea'ling on Judgment Day—that'll be time enough."

44 *Hog Jowls* (J. D. SUGGS)

A further example of Motif J1390, "Retorts concerning thefts" For eating hog jowls and black-eyed peas on New Year's Day to bring good luck, see Puckett, pp. 350-351.

Ol' Bill he was an awful fellow, he'd steal hogs. It happened that another fellow saw Bill stealing and went and told Old Marster. Old Marster he goes down there the next morning. Says, "Say Bill, come here. What did you steal my hog for last night? No need deny it, because I seen you."

"Well Old Marster, I'll tell the truth, I did steal one, I will admit that, but that's all I ever stole." "Well, where's it at?" "It's in the cellar under my house there." "Well, by your telling the truth, I'm going to let you keep that hog; I'm going to give you that hog. I'm just going to look at it, to see how big a hog it is."

Old Marster goes down in the cellar. He sees a big pile of fresh meat right over by the door, and keeps finding little hunks all around, and he throws them on the pile. It looked like Bill had about five hundred pounds of meat. "Say, Bill, I thought you didn't steal but one hog. Here's about five hundred pounds of jolls [jowls]."

"Well, I'll tell you the truth, Boss, I didn't steal but one; it's just that I like jowl meat so good I cut the whole hog up into jowls."

(Jowls are mostly for seasoning. They go right up to the jawbone. The marrow is good for the mumps. I don't like them myself because they've got kernels. You eat jowls and black-eyed peas the first of January, for luck. Colored people do that all over. My wife was taught that if they kill a hog in the fall of the year, they shouldn't sell the head, but keep it for jowls.)

II OLD MARSTER GETS THE BETTER OF JOHN

45 *The Mojo* (ABRAHAM TAYLOR)

A unique tale in Southern Negro tradition. This is a fine adaptation of the transformation combat, which appears in Type 325, "The Magician and his Pupil" episode IV b, and Motif D615, "Transformation combat." The little known Child ballad no. 44, "The Twa Magicians" recounts a transformation contest between a blacksmith and a maid; in verse ten they take the shapes of a greyhound and a hare; in the end she changes to a silken plaid, "Stretched upon a bed, And he became a green covering, And gained her maidenhead." This theme has worldwide distribution and appears in the myths of the Egyptians (Horus and Seth), the Greeks (Heracles and Achelous), the Finns (Lemminkainen and Pohjolainen); there are stirring instances in the Mabinogion and in the Second Kalendar's Tale in the Arabian Nights. N. M. Penzer gives many references in his note on "The 'Magical Conflict' Motif," in The Ocean of Story, III (London, 1925), pp. 203-205. An extended discussion of the Magical

Conflict cycle can be found in W. A. Clouston, Popular Tales and Fictions *(New York, 1887), 1, 413-439. One Negro version given by Beckwith from Jamaica contains metamorphoses to a pigeon-hawk and a fowl-hawk (no. 120, pp. 153-154, "The Boy and his Master"). Stith Thompson mentions a Portuguese Negro recovery of Type 325 brought to Massachusetts from the Cape Verde Islands, and indicates its origin in India, in* The Folktale, *p. 69.*

There was always the time when the white man been ahead of the colored man. In slavery times John had done got to a place where the Marster whipped him all the time. Someone told him, "Get you a mojo, it'll get you out of that whipping, won't nobody whip you then."

John went down to the corner of the Boss-man's farm, where the mojo-man stayed, and asked him what he had. The mojo-man said, "I got a pretty good one and a very good one and a damn good one." The colored fellow asked him, "What can the pretty good one do?" "I'll tell you what it can do. It can turn you to a rabbit, and it can turn you to a quail, and after that it can turn you to a snake." So John said he'd take it.

Next morning John sleeps late. About nine o'clock the white man comes after him, calls him: "John, come on, get up there and go to work. Plow the taters and milk the cow and then you can go back home—it's Sunday morning." John says to him, "Get on out from my door, don't say nothing to me. Ain't gonna do nothing." Boss-man says, "Don't you know who this is? It's your Boss." "Yes, I know—I'm not working for you any more." "All right, John, just wait till I go home; I'm coming back and whip you."

White man went back and got his pistol, and told his wife, "John is sassy, he won't do nothing I tell him, I'm gonna whip him." He goes back to John, and calls, "John, get up there." John yells out, "Go on away from that door and quit worrying me. I told you once, I ain't going to work."

Well, then the white man he falls against the door and broke it open. And John said to his mojo, "Skip-skip-skip-skip." He turned to a rabbit, and run slap out the door by Old Marster. And he's a running son of a gun, that rabbit was. Boss-man says to his mojo, "I'll turn to a greyhound." You know that greyhound got running so fast his paws were just reaching the grass under the rabbit's feet.

Then John thinks, "I got to get away from here." He turns to a quail. And he begins sailing fast through the air —he really thought he was going. But the Boss-man says, "I will turn to a chicken hawk." That chicken hawk sails through the sky like a bullet, and catches right up to that quail.

Then John says, "Well, I'm going to turn to a snake." He hit the ground and begin to crawl; that old snake was natchally getting on his way. Boss-man says, "I'll turn to a stick and I'll beat your ass."

46 *Marster Paying off John* (MOSES ARMSTRONG)

A variant is in Dorson, Pine Bluff, p. 58, "Lazy John." See Hurston, pp. 125-126, "You Think I'm Gointer Pay You But I Ain't." The Southern Workman for October 1897 (Vol. 26, No. 10), p. 210, has a tale of the slave who steals his master's potatoes, and serves them to his disguised master, saying "I call dese tings blowindites" Next morning his master invites him to have some cowhide lashes, and repeats Sam's phrase. Joe Thomas told me a close variant, where Old Marster repeats the phrase, "Forty-five last night, and forty-five tonight; some call 'em blowhards, but I call 'em sweethearts"; Sam says to his wife, "Martha, somebody been talking." See Bacon and Parsons, no. 56, pp. 292-293, "Sweet-Potatoes."

Marster told John to go cut some wood, and he'd pay him by the rick. So John went off into the woods with his ax, and started hitting a snag with the back of his ax, so it sounded as if he were cutting. And he was saying, "You think I'm cutting but I ain't, you think I'm cutting but I ain't."

But all the time Old Marster is in the woods looking at John. When payday come, John went after his pay. Marster rattled his money in his hand and told him, "You think I'm going to pay you but I ain't."

47 *Efan Prays* (J. D. SUGGS)

Suggs here joins two popular Negro tales of John praying and finding his prayers answered too rapidly for comfort. Baughman lists the first as Motif J217.01.1., "Trickster overhears man praying for death to take him," and supplies references, chiefly Negro, from seven states. The two usual forms the story takes place John at the praying tree, where Old Marster or boys he has sent there answer his prayer, or in his quarters, where Old Marster comes as God. In either spot John prays for death for himself, or for the white folks. To Baughman's references add, for the praying tree, Botkin, Burden, p. 40, "Josh and the Lord"; Hurston, pp. 120-121, "Kill the White Folks"; for God knocking at the door, or dropping a brick on John at home or in church, add Brewer, Humorous Folktales, pp. 39-40, "Uncle Si's Prayer"; Fauset, Nova Scotia, no. 141, p. 93 (3 texts), "Only in Fun"; Harris, Friends, no. 4, "Death and the Negro Man"; Hurston, pp. 96-99, "Ole Massa and John who Wanted to go to Heaven"; Parsons, Antilles, no. 340, p. 321, "God Comes" (two texts, from Saint Kitts and Saint Croix). See also Halpert, nos. 233 and 264, "Lord Can't You Take A Joke," and "Running From The Lord" and notes.

A combination of the two episodes, as in Suggs' version, appears in Fred W. Allsopp, Folklore of Romantic Arkansas (2 vols., The Grolier Society, 1931), II, 175.

I have versions of the praying-tree form from Ruby Booth, Carrie Eaton, and Abraham Taylor, and of the God-at-the-door form from Lee Curtis, Effie Dean, Carrie Eaton, and Mary Richardson.

Efan was supposed to be at a great big plantation in Tennessee. He'd get hisself in a jam and he'd scheme out somehow.

Old Marster was cruel on him and beat him every day. So Efan would go down into the apple tree at night after dark and pray to the Lord to come take him away, for Old Marster was so hard on him. "I'm tired staying here and taking these beatings." John passed by and heard him; so he told Old Marster about Efan praying to go to heaven. Next night Old Marster slipped down there before Efan and climbed in the tree. He began to pray again, "Lord, come get me, for Old Marster is beating me." Old Marster said: "All right, Efan, I'll be after you tomorrow night at eight o'clock. Be here and I'll take you to heaven."

Efan went back home and told his wife, "Dinah, I'm leaving you tomorrow night." "Efan, is you going to carry me with you?" "No, but I'll make arrangements and come back after you."

Next night at eight sharp Efan was there. Old Marster is hid up in his tree, and he's letting down a rope with a loop in it. "Efan, I'm here to carry you to heaven tonight. Just stick your head in the loop." Efan puts his head in, and Old Marster begins to draw the rope up. And Efan starts to choke. "Wait, Lord, you're choking me. Let me down." So Old Marster he let the rope slack. Efan got his head out the rope and ran home. "Dinah, if the Lord comes and ax for me, tell him I ain't in." "All right Efan, I'll tell him."

In a few minutes Old Marster was there wrapped up in a sheet. He's singing out, "*Ooooh, Efan.*" Dinah goes to the door and says, "Efan ain't here." "Well, Dinah," the Lord tells her, "you'll do just as well." Dinah turns around to Efan: "You'd better come out'n from under that bed; you hadn't oughter told the Lord to come out after you."

Efan went out the back door. Old Marster heard him go out and he tuck out after him. Dinah said, "Lord, you just wants to quit. You can't catch Efan, 'cause he's barefooted."

Well then Efan decided to change his mode of praying. He said, "Dinah, we going to pray to the Lord to kill all the white folks and leave all the niggers. You know he answered my prayer once, and come after me." So every night they would pray to the Lord, "Kill all the white folks and leave all the niggers."

In those days they didn't have no lock on the door, and they'd leave it open till they were ready to go to bed, then turn the latch to keep it from blowing—people didn't rob or murder in them days. Well, John passed by and heard them praying. So he told Old Marster that Efan was praying to kill all the white men and leave all the niggers.

Old Marster put his sheet around him, and goes down to Efan's house. Efan and Dinah were on their knees. Efan was praying, "Oh, Lord, please kill all the white folks and leave all the niggers." Old Marster had his ax-handle in his hand—he whaled Efan alongside the head with it. Efan fell over, and looked up at him, and said, "Oh, Lord, don't you know a white man from a nigger?"

48 *Planting Salt* (WALTER WINFREY)

This is an identical replica of Type 1574*, Motif K1637, "Flattering foreman tricked by his master" reported only from Estonia.

He was one of them smart guys y'know. Anything Mahster wanted to know he'd tell him. So he says, "Old Mahster, I'd like to go out tonight. How about letting me go?"

"No, you'd better stay here tonight; I got lots of work laid out for you."

Next morning when Old Mahster got up he says, "John, you ketch the mule over there, and saddle up my horse." So they gets on the horse and mule, and rides around over the farm, which has quite a bit of vacant land, till they come to a small empty place of about ten acres. So he says, "John, suppose we plant some peas here, do you think they'll grow?" "Oh, yes,

137

they'll come up." Old Mahster stood there and looked around, he's thinking it over, and so he asks, "How about planting some com in that space over there?" John says, "Oh that would be fine." "Now John, since you know everything," he says, "if we plant some salt in that spot over there, do you think it'll grow?" John says, "Yes, Mahster, I was just thinking about that."

49 *Dividing Souls* (A. J. KING)

Two well-known tales are cleverly intertwined here. The story of the passerby who thinks he hears the Lord and the Devil counting souls in the graveyard enjoys extraordinary vogue; Vance Randolph says he knows fifty persons in the Ozarks who can tell it (Who Blowed Up the Church House?, p. 204). *Stith Thompson comments on its European and American popularity, in* The Folktale, *p. 214, and provides references under Type 1791 and Motif X424, "The Sexton Carries the Parson." In United States Negro texts the slave houseboy sometimes carries his crippled Old Marster down to the graveyard, who in fright runs home under his own power; thus see the variants by E. L. Smith in my "A Negro Storytelling Session on Tape," pp. 205-206, and by John Blackamore, "Old Boss Wants into Heaven," post, tale 58. (Grimm no. 59, "Frederick and Catherine," concludes with a similar incident.) A text without the lame listener motif appears in my "Negro Tales from Bolivar County, Mississippi," from Billy Jack Tyler, p. 111, "Counting Souls." Many other variants have been told me. The second incident present here is discussed in the note to the following tale.*

During the period of slavery time Old Marster always kept one slave that would keep him posted on the others, so that he would know how to deal with them when they got unruly. So this slave was walking around in the moonlight one night. And he heard a noise coming from the cemetery. And it was two slaves counting apples, which they had stole from Old Marster's orchard. They couldn't count, so they were exchanging 'em. "You take dis un and I'll take dat un. Dis un's yours and dat un's mine."

So this slave hear them, and he listened, and he ran back to Old Marster. And running he fell over a skeleton head, and he spoke to the skeleton head. "What you doing here?"

And the skeleton head said, "Same thing got me here will get you here."

So he told Old Marster when he got to the house that the Devil and the Good Lord was in the cemetery counting out souls. "Dis un's yours and dat un's mine, dis un's yours and dat un's mine."

Old Marster didn't believe him, but he went with him to the cemetery. And Old Marster told him, said, "Now if the Devil and the Good Lord ain't counting out souls, I'm going to cut your head off."

Sure enough the slaves had gone and Old Marster didn't hear anything, and he cut John's head off. Then John's head fell beside the skeleton head. Then the head turned over and said, "I told you something that got me here would get you here. You talk too much."

(That's one my daddy would tell us when we were talking too much.)

50 *Talking Bones* (BEULAH TATE)

I have other texts from Adelle Leonard and Iola Palmer. Baughman mentions five Negro variants for Motif B210.2, "Talking animal or object refuses to talk on demand. Discoverer is unable to prove his claims; is beaten" citing Herbert Halpert's notes, pp. 179-180, to the title story in Vance Randolph, The Talking Turtle And Other Ozark Folk Tales *(New York, 1957). African versions involve both the talking bones and the talking turtle; see W. H. Barker and Cecilia Sinclair,* West African Folk-Tales *(London, 1917), no. 21, pp. 119-121, "The Hunter and the Tortoise"; Leo Frobenius and Douglas C. Fox,* African Genesis *(New York, 1937), pp. 161-163, "The Talking Skull" (Nupe). The Motif-Index gives one reference, to the Ibo of Nigeria, under E632.1, "Speaking bones of murdered person reveal murder."*

This tale brings to mind the disclosure of the murdered child by a singing bird or green flies or the like, in Type 720, "My Mother Slew Me; My Father Ate Me," widespread among New World Negroes. (See the version, post, tale 119, "Eating the Baby")

They used to carry the slaves out in the woods and leave them there, if they killed them—just like dead animals. There wasn't any burying then. It used to be a secret, between one plantation and another, when they beat up their hands and carried them off.

So John was walking out in the woods and seed a skeleton. He says: "This looks like a human. I wonder what he's doing out here." And the skeleton said, "Tongue is the cause of my being here." So John ran back to Old Marster and said, "The skeleton at the edge of the woods is talking." Old Marster didn't believe him and went to see. And a great many people came too. They said, "Make the bones talk." But the skeleton wouldn't talk.

So they beat John to death, and left him there. And then the bones talked. They said, "Tongue brought us here, and tongue brought you here."

51 *Talking Turtle* (JULIA COURTNEY)

A variant of the preceding tale and its Motif B210.2, with a talking turtle in place of the talking bones.

Every day John had to tote water from the bayou, and every time he'd go to the bayou he would start fussin'. "I'm tired of toting water every day." The next day he went to the bayou and he repeated the same thing (you know just like you repeat the same thing). So last one day John went to the bayou, the turtle was sitting on a log.

Turtle raised up and looked at him, and told John, "Black man, you talk too much."

So John didn't want to think the turtle was talking. He went back to the bayou, got another bucketful of water. The turtle told him the same thing. John throwed the buckets down, took and run to the house, and called Old Marster, and told him the turtle was down there talking. And so Old Marster didn't want to go because he didn't believe it. But John kept telling him the turtle was talking. So finally Old Boss 'cided he could go. But he told John if the turtle didn't talk he was going to give him a good beating. So they all went on down to the bayou, and when they got down to the bayou the turtle was sitting on a log with his head back halfway in his shell.

And so John told the turtle, "Tell Old Marster what you told me." So John begged the turtle to talk. So the turtle still didn't say anything. So Old Marster taken him back to the house, and give him a good beating, and made him git his buckets, and keep totin' water.

When John got back down to the bayou, the turtle had his head sticking up. John dipped up his water, and the turtle raised up and told him, says, "Black man, didn't I tell you you talked too much?"

52 *The Talking Mule* (JOHN BLACKAMORE)

This is a good example of Blackamore's highly individual storytelling style, whereby he elaborates a well known simple plot (presented in the three preceding tales) into a circumstantial narrative.

One day on the Fourth of July, John's Boss-man called him down to the house, told him to hook up old George that morning, and go down and plow up five acres of new-ground. Because the day being the Fourth of July, John didn't want to work, he wanted to take off. So he asks his Boss: "Do I have to work today? I'd like to take today off, being the Fourth of July; I'd like to go to town." And so Boss told him, "No, that five acres got to be done today; it might be raining tomorrow and we got to get that corn in."

So John say, "Oh well, all right." So he hooked old George up to the plow, went on down to the five acres of newground and begin to plow. So he plowed about a couple of hours. George, the mule, he stopped and says, "Oh I sure am tired," then started off again. John looked all around, he didn't see nobody; so he kept following the mule. Then George started talking to hisself again. He said, "Ain't it awful, us poor mules and all the niggers have to work all the time, and the white man gets all the money. Don't never get any rest. All we get to eat is beans and hay."

So old John he told George, "Whoa." Looked all around to see who it was talking. He didn't see nobody; so he hit the mule in the side with a rope, told him to git up. The mule started up again. George said, "I get tired of working all the time, don't you, John?" John told him, "Whoa." He still didn't see nobody. So he thought to hisself, well there ain't nobody here but me and George. So he asked George, "George, was that you talking to me?" George says, "Yes, I asked you don't you get tired of working all the time?"

John took off to the house running. When he got to the farmhouse he was just about out of breath. So Old Boss asked him, "John, what's wrong with you?" John says, "Ain't nothing wrong with me; it's George. He's out there talking." Boss says, "Now, John, you know a mule can't talk. I told you you couldn't have the day off; why don't you give up and go on back and plow the five acres."

But John says, "No, sir, Boss; if you want those five acres plowed, you'll have to go and plow it yourself, new-ground or old ground." So the Boss begins to feel sorry for him, figures he's out of his head, and talks soft to him, "Aw, come on, John, tell Boss what did George say to you?" "Well, Boss, I can't tell you that; you don't believe me nohow." "Oh, yes, I do, come on now, what did he say?" John tells then, "Oh he just say he's getting damn tired of working all the time, and you getting all the money, and all the good food. He don't ever get any rest, all he gets to eat is hay."

Boss says, "Oh, John, that's just your imagination. You go on back down there and start plowing. I'll be on down in a few minutes. The day's about half gone and you ain't even got started." So John went on down in the field, hit George in the side with the plow line, told him to get up.

George told him, "Yes, you went telling on me to the Boss; you going to get enough of that one of these days." He says, "Yes, you talk too much. And it will get you in a lot of trouble."

So John told George, "Oh, come on, George, I don't want to tell about your talking to the Boss, I wants to get this five acres of newground plowed." George started on off pulling the plow, made three or four rounds, and said, "I sure am tired."

Off John started to the house again. On the way he met Old Boss coming out to the field. So Old Boss asked him what's wrong this time. John says, "Same thing, George is still talking." Old Boss got a little warm, he thought John was kidding him, see. So he says, "You come on back, John, and if that mule don't talk to me I'm going to hang you tomorrow." (He figured he'd scare John to go to work.) So he and John walked on back to where George was, still hooked to the plow. And the Boss told George to get up.

Mule walked on off and Boss plowed him a furrow or two. Then he says, "See that, John? You go ahead and finish this five acres, 'cause I'm getting tired of fooling with you."

So John says, "Well, you doing all right with him, you keep on, 'cause I ain't going to plow George no more." That made Boss hot, John talking to him like that. But he says, "All right, just take George on to the barn and turn him loose, you can have the rest of the day off." So John took George on down to the barn and unhitched him, and gave him his hay and water.

He was still disturbed about his Boss not believing him; he had never lied to his Boss. So he decided to go on up to the house and eavesdrop, to see what his Boss was talking about at dinner. When he got to the window he heard the Boss telling his wife about him, that John was losing his mind, he was going crazy. "We'll have to take him out and shoot him." (That's what they did with mules and slaves, so they wouldn't waste no time with them.)

Well he didn't know what to do, that hit him pretty hard, he being loyal to his Boss and all, and all of a sudden his Boss don't believe him. So he moseyed on back to the barn where the mule was. When he sit down on the manger where George was eating his dinner, George told him, "See, I told you you talk too much. I could have told you Old Boss would never have believed it, about what I said, but you never gave me no time."

John didn't say nothing. So George the mule said, "Oh, well, I guess you'll be better off than I am."

53 Master's Gone to Philly-Me-York (SILAS ALTHEIMER)

For variants of the present tale, see Fauset, "South," pp. 266-267, "Master Gone to Philanewyork"; Hurston, Mules, pp. 112-113; Portia Smiley, "Folk-Lore from Virginia, South Carolina, Georgia, Alabama, and Florida," JAF XXXII (1919), no. 8, p. 362, "Master Disguised"; and ante, "Old Marster Takes a Trip," tale 40, from Walter Winfrey, in which John at least avoids chastisement. I have another variant from Katy Pointer of Mecosta, Michigan, in which the partying slaves sing, "Massie's gone to Philly-me-jinks, going to be gone three long weeks." They throw chicken bones to a ragged white man, their disguised master, who is amused and does not reveal himself.

Slave named John was in the confidence of his Master, a trusty. John did everything, melted out the rations to his slaves—Master didn't use a slave-driver—John kept his accounts, in his head. He couldn't read or write, but he had a wonderful memory. So his Master would often go away on a big trip, would stay sometimes as much as a month. And so his Master was finally warned by some of his neighbors that John didn't always behave as he ought, that he often had frolics with the neighboring Negroes when his Master was away. So his Master resolved to find out if John was betraying his trust. He and his wife and daughter feigned to go to New York on a visit. And so John as usual barbecued his pork, barbecued a lamb, or calf, or kid, whatever he could get his hands on, and sent a runner to tell his friends on neighboring plantations to come to a big dance, a big barbecue.

The slaves all dressed in their best, came in early that night to the frolic. So the dance began in the danceroom in the big house. John always stayed in the big house to take care of things. And of course the dance would be carried on by his comrades while he would be out superintending the tables, having the food placed on. And so after John get things arranged so and eating could begin, he'd go in and observe the dance hisself.

In the meantime his Master had slipped in in disguise, his hand blackened, his face blackened, and a cap on his head. And so while his Master was observing all this he went in and began to shout:

"Joy yourself, joy yourself,
Master's gone to Philly-Me-York."

Then Master disappeared and took the soot off his hands and his face. When he returned John was patting and stamping and hollering:

"Joy yourself, joy yourself,
Master's gone to Philly-Me-York."

And when he came out again he saw his Master, and recognized him fully. And as a matter of course his feathers fell, and the slaves fell out of the windows, and that broke up the party, and John was left on his knees begging his Master's forgiveness.

III JOHN GETS THE BETTER OF OLD MARSTER

54 *Old Boss and John at the Praying Tree* (TOMMY CARTER)

This reverses the usual situation at the praying tree in which Marster fools John. Compare the sham miracles given under Motif K1971, "Man behind statue (tree) speaks and pretends to be God (spirit)," although none of the examples given involve an accomplice. In Brewer, "John Tales/' pp. 96-97, "How McGrudefs Prayer Was Answered" John plays the Lord and drops six dollars to McGruder, who pockets them and says he'll find the other four elsewhere.

This also happened back in the old days too. It was one year on a plantation when crops were bad. There wasn't enough food for all the slave hands, no flour at all; all they had to eat was fatback and cornbread. John and his buddy was the only slickers on the farm. They would have two kinds of meat in the house, all the lard they could use, plenty flour and plenty sugar, biscuits every morning for breakfast. (They was rogues.) The Boss kept a-missing meat, but they was too slick for him to catch 'em at it.

Every morning, he'd ask John, "How you getting along over there with your family?" John said, "Well, I'm doing all right, Old Marster. (*High-pitched, whiny*) I'm fair's a middling and spick as a ham, coffee in the kittle, bread on the fire, if that ain't living I hope I die."

The Old Boss checked on John. And he saw his hams and lard and biscuits all laid up in John's place. (In those days people branded their hams with their own name.) He said, "John, I can see why you're living so high. You got all my hams and things up there." "Oh, no," John told him, "those ain't none of your ham, Boss. God give me them ham. God is good, just like you, and God been looking out for me, because I pray every night."

Boss said, "I'm still going to kill you John, because I know that's my meat."

Old John was real slick. He asked his Marster, "Tonight meet me at the old 'simmon tree. I'm going to show you God is good to me. I'm going to have some of your same ham, some of your same lard, and some of your same flour."

So that night about eight o'clock (it was dark by then in the winter), John went for his partner. They get everything all set up in the tree before John goes for Old Boss. They go out to the tree. Old Boss brings along his double-barreled shotgun, and he tells John, "Now if you don't get my flour and stuff, just like you said you would, you will never leave this tree."

So John gets down on his knees and begins to pray. "Now, Lord, I never axed you for nothing that I didn't get. You know Old Marster here is about to kill me, thinking I'm stealing. Not a child of yours would steal, would he, Lord?" He says, "Now I'm going to pat on this tree three times. And I want you to rain down persimmons." John patted on the tree three times and his partner shook down all the persimmons all over Old Boss. Boss shakes himself and says, "John, Old Boss is so good to you, why don't you have God send my meat down?"

John said, "Don't get impatient; I'm going to talk to him a little while longer for you." So John prayed, "Now Lord, you know me and I know you. Throw me down one of Old Boss's hams with his same brand on it."

Just at that time the ham hit down on top of Old Boss's head. Old Boss grabbed the ham, and said, "John, I spec you better not pray no more." (Old Boss done got scared.) But John kept on praying and the flour fell. Old Boss told John, "Come on John, don't pray no more." "I just want to show you I'm a child of God," John tells him, and he prays again. "Send me down a sack of Old Boss's sugar, the same weight and the same name like on all his sacks."

"John, if you pray any more no telling what might happen to us," Boss said. "I'll give you a forty-acre farm and a team of mules if you just don't pray no more." John didn't pay no attention; he prayed some more. "Now God, I want you to do me a personal favor. That's to hop down out of the tree and horsewhip the hell out of Old Boss." So his buddy jumped out with a white sheet and laid it on Old Boss.

Boss said, "You see what you gone done, John; you got God down on me. From now on you can go free."

55 *A Dime for the Sack* (HARRISON STANFILL)

Another praying-tree story in which John comes out on top of Old Marster. Cf. Hurston, pp. 112-114, "How the Negroes Got Their Freedom," where the Philly-Me-York tale is joined with that of John and his accomplice in the praying tree. Motif J1473.1, "The 999 gold pieces;' furnishes the trick here.

Old Boss had all kinds of confidence in John, and said that anything he asked Jesus for he'd sent it to him. John had been a favorite around for a while and Boss was going to give him $100 for his holiday. And he called John in and asked him, "John, you go on down and pray the Lord to send you $100 for your holiday, and if he send that, I'll have all kinds of confidence in you." So Boss-man sacked up $99.90 and gave it to two of his little boys. So they saw John going down to the tree that evening and they went along ahead of him and climbed the tree.

John got on his knees and said, "O Lord, I'm praying to you to have a brilliant Christmas, I wants $100." No quicker said than done, the little boys dropped a sack of dough alongside of John. John grabbed the sack and got off his knees and went hopping off to the house and said, "Master I got it, I got it."

So Master said, "You sure, John, you got it?"

"Yes Master, I got it."

"Well now, pour it out on the counter and see how much you got." So John couldn't count but $99.90. "So you can see John, you only got $99.90."

"That okay Boss, he did what he said he did, but he charged me a dime for the sack."

56 *Eating Further up the Hog* (J. D. SUGGS)

The title phrase enjoys a proverbial currency in rural farming areas. Lulu Powell also gave me a text she had heard from Albert Reese, minister of the First Baptist Church in Vandalia. "Mr. Reese is not an educated man, but he has a lot of good horse sense—he's from the South." A variant from Rev. Mrs. C. R. Toler is printed post, tale 184, as a protest tale.

Old Marster killed about forty or fifty hogs every year. He had Sambo to help him. When he was ready to pay him off he said, "Sambo, here's your pig head, and pig feet, and pig ears." Sambo said, "Thank you, boss."

So Sambo killed hogs for about five years that way. That's what he got for his pay. Then Sambo moved on back of the place and got himself three hogs. Old Marster didn't even know he had a hog. Next winter at hog-killing time Old Marster went down after Sam. Old Marster called, "Sambo." Sambo came to the door— "Yessir." Says, "Be down to the house early in the morning. I want to kill hogs—be there about five-thirty." Sambo asks, "Well Old Marster, what you paying?" "I'll pay you like I always did. I'll give you the head, and all the ears, and all the pig feet, and all the tails."

Sambo said, "Well, Old Marster, I can't because I'm eating further up the hog than that now. I got three hogs of my own now; I eat spareribs, back bone, pork chops, middling, and everything else. I eat further up the hog now."

So Old Marster didn't ask him to kill no more hogs.

57 *The Mean Boss* (DOROTHY FOWLER)

Baughman lists under Motif J1341.11, "Hired men sing of displeasure with food; change song when food is improved (cante fable)" seven references, for Cumberland, Westmorland, Yorkshire, Minnesota, New York, and North Carolina; the last is Negro. In his valuable article, "Some Humorous English Folk-Tales; Part 2, Tales not included by Aarne and Thompson" (Folklore, XLIX [1938], 227-286), Edward M. Wilson places his Westmorland text, "The Hungry Mowers" (pp. 279-280) under a category called Tales of Masters and Men. He comments that these are "frequent in Westmorland, where the farms are small and the unmarried farm servant always lives in the farmhouse and usually eats at the same table with his master." This situation of course offers some comparison with Old Marster and his house servant John.

The Negro text in The Frank C. Brown Collection, *I, p. 701, "Meat and Bread and Pudding Too" is very close to the present. Both differ markedly from the English and American white versions discussed in Herbert Halpert, "The Cante Fable in Decay,"* Southern Folklore Quarterly, *V (Sept. 1941), 193-194.*

A Finnish proverb has the servant at the loom go fast when she does her own work, "ittellenittellen-ittellen" (for-me-for-me-for-me), and slowly when she works for her mistress, "ta-loo-hin, ta-loo-hin, ta-loo-hin" (for the house, for the house). Etela-Pohjanmaan Sananparsia (Porvoo, Helsinki, 1938), p. 39, no. 558.

This happened way back in your great-grandmother's time, in St. Louis, Missouri. She was one hundred and four when she passed away.

There was a real rich landowner who had some laborers sawing wood for him. Every day for lunch he would give those woodsmen only soup for dinner. And while they be sawing the wood, sawing down trees, the saw would say,

SO–O–OUP, SO–O–OUP, SO–O–OUP. (*Slow, thin, and reedy*)

So the landowner's wife told him he would get more work out of his men if he would give them better food. The next day she fixed dinner and gave them bread, meat and pie, or pudding, that's what it was. And when they went back to work this time, the saw would say,

BREAD–MEAT–AND–PUDDING–TOO,

BREAD–MEAT–AND–PUDDING–TOO. (*Fast and snappy*)

58 *Old Boss Wants into Heaven* (JOHN BLACKAMORE)

The second half of this narrative embodies one of the most popular folktales in United States white and Negro tradition, Dividing Souls. See ante, tale 49. The American form differs from the European as reported in the Type- and Motif-Index (Type 1791, "The Sex-ton Carries the Parson," Motif X424, "The Devil in the Cemetery"), where thieves in the cemetery mistake the sexton for a companion who has stolen a sheep, and ask "Is he fat?" The sexton who is carrying the gouty parson answers, "Fat or lean, here he is." In the commonest American form the sheep-stealing allusion disappears; the two boys dividing nuts, apples, or ears of corn, "One for you, one for me," finally allude to the two they left at the gate. In some Negro versions, as in Blackamore's, the tale is adapted to the Old Marster cycle, and falls closer to the European type, in having a house slave carry his crippled Marster down to the cemetery; when the white man hears God and the Devil counting souls, he outruns the slave home. Blackamore has combined this plot with a separate, unreported episode, turning on Old Marster's literal interpretation of a Scriptural text (Motif J2470, "Metaphors literally interpreted"). Dividing Souls was told me by more Negro informants in Michigan and Arkansas than any other tale.

For comparative references see the extensive notes by Herbert Halpert to two versions in Randolph, Church House, "The Devil in the Graveyard" and "Dividing Up the Dead," on pp. 188-189, 204-205. An interesting historical and comparative analysis by Hazel Harrod appears in "A Tale of Two Thieves," The Sky Is My Tipi, ed. M. C. Boatright, PTFS XXII (1949), pp. 207-214. The author traces the tale back to a late sixth-century Latin text, and compares twenty-two American variants.

Old Boss he was a big plantation owner, but he was paralyzed and he couldn't even walk. So every time he was ready to move he'd call Mac up, to carry him around on his back and push him around in his wheel chair. This was back in slavery times, and Mac was his servant, his slave. Old Boss had a whole lot of slaves working for him, but Mac was the main attraction.

Every time the Boss had Mac carry him on his back, Mac figured he was being done wrong, since Boss had a wheel chair. He got to talking to himself about it out loud: "O Lord, these days ain't going to be much longer; God almighty going to call us all in." Then he wouldn't have to carry Old Boss around no more, 'cause he'd be flying around with angels in heaven, and Old Boss'd be down in hell burning with brimstone. Quite a few times the Boss heard him say it; so finally he asked him what did he mean by that remark.

Mac tells him, "You-all know what the Good Book says?" So the Boss says: "What do you mean by that? If anybody's going to Heaven I'm going, because I got all the money I can use, I got a lot of land, I got all the slaves I want to work the land, so I got everything I need to get to Heaven."

"That's just how come you ain't going to Heaven," Mac answers. "The Good Book says so." But Old Boss he really thought because he had all the land and all the money and all the slaves he was fixed straight, that was all he needed. Mac was kind of afraid to speak up any more, being a slave, you know. He just said, "That's all right Boss, you'll see," and kind of walked off from him.

Old Boss couldn't sleep that night. He tried to brush it off his mind but it kept coming on back to him, what Mac had told him. Finally he decided that Mac didn't know what he was talking about, that he was an ignorant slave and didn't know no more than what he (Old Boss) said: "I'll give you a forty-acre farm and a team of mules, if you accept about what work to do." Finally he went on to sleep. Early next morning Mac gets up and starts about his chores. Boss heard him singing.

Soon I will be up in Heaven with the angels,
Having a good time enjoying eternal life.

So that thought kind of hit Old Boss again—he wanted to know how could a slave go to heaven, and he himself being rich and going to hell. That kind of lay on his mind all day. That was Saturday. Sunday morning Mac gets up singing another song. He got on his clean overalls, and a clean shirt, and he gave himself a shave with one of the Boss's old razors—he was barefooted even on Sunday, but he was still happy; he was going to church. The song he was singing was:

I'm going to the mourning bench this morning,
And praise my master up above.

Boss knew they had a church, but he'd never heard a song like that before; so he got curious. He gets his wheel chair, and kind of sneaks on down to the church where they were having the meeting. So when he got there service had already begun. The preacher is up in the pulpit asking did anybody want anything explained to them. Mac raised his hand to let the preacher know he had a question. So he told him about his discussion with Old Boss. Since he could not read, he asked the preacher to explain it to him. The preacher gets his textbook, and gives Mac the book and the chapter and the verse, and then he read it to him. (Some of them could read and some of 'em could not.) So he read, "It's easier for a camel to go through the eye of a needle than it is for a rich man to go to Heaven." (In the meantime Old Boss is outside the window listening, taking it all in.) So he says, "Sisters and Brothers, there only two places to go after you die, and that is Heaven or Hell. And since Old Boss can't go to Heaven, there's no other place for him to go but to Hell."

Old Boss heard enough then. He wheels his chair on back home, he sets down on the porch, and calls his wife to bring him the Bible. He remembered the book and the chapter and the verse and he wanted to see if they knew what they were talking about. When he turns to the page, he found there in big red letters just what the preacher had read. That kind of worried him; he felt uneasy all day Sunday. Mac was away so he couldn't talk to him. Night came; still no Mac. So he decided to set up and wait for him.

On the way home from church Mac had to pass a graveyard. This being Sunday night, a couple of fellows had gone into Old Boss's cornfield and had stole a sack of corn. They went in to get two sacks of corn, but when they heard Mac coming they thought it might be Old Boss, and jumped over the fence into the graveyard. In getting over the fence they dropped a couple of ears. Mac heard them and that kind of scared him, because he thought they was hants, and so he hid behind a big tombstone.

One of the fellows said, "Well, since we didn't get but one sackful we're going to have to divide it." Mac didn't know what they were talking about, so he sat and listened. The two fellows started counting the corn. They figured they didn't have time to count all the ears together and then separate them; so they started counting off, "One for you, and one for me." And they kept that up for quite a while.

Mac said, "O Lord, Judgment Day done come. I better go tell the Boss." So he struck out to running. When he gets to the house Old Boss is sitting on the porch smoking his pipe uneasily. Boss was glad to see Mac, and kind of scared for him too, 'cause he was running so hard. Before he could ask Mac how to get to Heaven, Mac fell upon the porch, almost out of breath. "I told you Judgment Day would be soon here; I sure told you!"

Old Boss says: "Well calm yourself. Tell me what this is all about." Mac tells him, "God and the Devil is down there in the graveyard separating the souls." Old Boss doesn't believe it. "Well, that couldn't be true, you know you're just lying." So Mac tells him, "Well if you think I am lying, I'll take you down there and prove it to you."

So he carries Old Boss down to the graveyard on his back. When Old Boss gets there he hears him counting, "One for you and one for me." So he wants to get a closer look; he wants to see what God and the Devil look like. It was dark out there, and the two fellows had moved around to the other side of the fence, where they'd dropped the corn. But when Old Boss gets around there he can't make out who it was because each of them had a great white cotton sack; that was all he could see, that cotton sack. Mac says, "See Boss, I told you so, they're down there sacking up souls." So one of the guys said, "Well, one for you and one for me." T'other pointed over to the fence where they had dropped the two ears, and he said, "There's two over there by the fence—you can have the big one and I'll take the little one."

Old Boss didn't want to hear no more. Mac was scared too. In fact Mac was too scared to move; he froze there in his tracks for a minute. Since Mac wasn't moving fast enough to carry Old Boss, Old Boss jumped down and run. And Mac looked around to see what had happened to Old Boss. Old Boss was out of sight. He figured 'cause Old Boss couldn't walk they must have sacked him up. So Mac run for Old Boss's house to tell Old Missy what happened. When he gets to the house he falls on the porch again, calling Old Missy.

Old Boss come out, without his wheel chair. Mac went to tell him what had happened to Old Boss. Then he realized it was Old Boss he was talking to. He froze again, so Old Boss asked him, "What happened after you left?" Mac told him, and asked Old Boss what happened to him. Boss said, "Well, you weren't moving fast enough; so I decided I'd come on without you." And he's been walking ever since.

Then Old Boss gave all his slaves an equal share in his kingdom that he had already built. He didn't want to get caught in that predicament no more.

59 *John Outspells Master* (BERTHA WHITE)

The same idea is presented in Hurston, Mules and Men, pp. 62-63, "How to Write a Letter."

It's about John and his Boss in slavery. John was very smart. Boss liked to show him off because he was a good speller. His master had company one day. He said, "John, come and spell some for us." John took his seat. He called John several little simple words. John spelled all he called. John finally got tired of his Master's entertaining.

And he said, "Master, you spell some now. Let me try you."

Master says, "All right John, I can spell anything you call."

Then John says, "All right, stand up, Master." He says, "Spell tstststschtsch."

"John, what you take me for, a fool?"

John says, "Yessir Master, take your seat."

60 *Planting Corn* (J. D. SUGGS)

Talley, Negro Folk Rhymes, *p. 208, "How to Plant and Cultivate Seeds," has the following verse that matches Suggs' anecdote:*
Plant: One fer de blackbird
Two fer de crow,
Three fer de jaybird
And fo' fer to grow.
Old Marster told John, "I want you to go out and plant com for me this morning." So John planted all day. That night when he went back in Old Marster asked him, "John, did you get that com planted right?" John says, "Yes, Old Marster, I know I did." Old Marster knew John couldn't count; so he asked him, "How do you know?" John says, "I know I planted it right because I planted two grains for the blackbirds, two for the crow, two for the cutworms, and two of 'em for to grow."

(The blackbirds they're going to get it when you first plant it, if it isn't deep enough. If it turns cool weather when the shoots first come up, the cutworms will cut them down. The crow he'll pull them up when they first stick up out of the ground. So that left two in the hill, a good start of corn.)

61 *John, The Bear and the Patteroll* (J. D. SUGGS)

In Hurston, Mules and Men, pp. 100-101, "Massa and the Bear" John persuades his Massa to grab the bear's tail he has held all night. In Brewer, "John Tales," pp. 92-93, "John McGruder, and the Bear in the Cornfield," John has his friend McGruder seize one of the bear's paws. In both of these texts John mistakes a bear for a thief in his Marster's cornfield. Amos Cross gives a related story where Sam throws the bear over his shoulder and brings him back to Massie, but runs into the house and shuts the door when he sees the thief is a bear. See also ante, tale 25, "The Bear and the Buzzard" from Tobe Courtney.

John had been out late that night, and as he was coming in a bear got at him. So he ran and ran till he got to a big tree and the bear was about to catch him. He run around the tree and the bear run after him trying to catch him. He was trying to reach on both sides, and John grabbed him by each paw and held him right to the tree. Bear turned around on his left hand to bite him, John'd yank his right hand. When he turned to the right, John'd yank his left one, and make him look round the other way. So he hollered for the patteroll to come here, he had a bear. (Patterolls was whites who make a living whipping the poor slaves if they was out without a pass— it was the only way they could make a living in slavery times.)

So the patteroll didn't come that night, but next morning he come with a shotgun, just down the hill. John says: "Don't shoot him. I'm going to give you the hide; let me shoot him. There's a certain way you have to shoot him. My Marster gets $500 for them hides—let me shoot him." "O.K." John says. "Well, catch hold of the paw over here, get both of 'em now, and yank both of 'em to the tree—I'll fix him then."

The patteroll catches the bear's paws, and John starts to walk off with the gun. Patteroll says, "Ain't you going to shoot him, John, ain't you going to shoot him?" John says, "I'm just going off to the right distance to shoot for the hide." Patteroll calls, "You better come get him—come get him." John keeps walking. "You better yank that bear, man." "Come get him, he's trying to bite me." (*High, excited*) John just walks on: "You'd better yank that bear—I yanked him all night; surely you can yank him till dinner."

62 *Charlie and Pat* (MRS. E. L. SMITH)

This belongs in the general category, Motif M341, "Death Prophesied." A variant, "The Talking Mule," is in "Folklore from St. Helena, South Carolina," pp. 225-226; the abuse of the animal and death of the owner are present, but the prophecy is missing, suggested however in the variant in note 1, p. 226. Curiously four variants are reported in Helen Creighton, Folklore of Lunenburg County, Nova Scotia *(Ottawa, 1950), no. 46, p. 18, "Oxen." Angelo de Gubernatis* Zoological Mythology *(2 vols., New York & London, 1872), vol. I, p. 258n, summarizes the present tale, and gives two German references.*

The two mules, Charlie and Pat, were talking in the bam. Charlie says to Pat: "We're working so hard, working so hard. What are we going to do tomorrow?" Pat says, "Well, it's nearly the end. Tomorrow we're going to haul Old Marster to the cemetery."

Sam, who was out in the barn, heard 'em talking, and ran to the house and told Old Marsa. "Pat and Charlie are talking; they say they're working so hard—and tomorrow they're going to haul you to the cemetery." Old Marsa wouldn't believe it. Sam says, "Come down to the bam and hear for yourself." Old Marsa says, "If you're telling a lie, I'll take all your clothes off and put a mule-hide on you."

So he went down to the barn, and when he got near there he could hear something talking. He peeped through the crack and looked in their mouths, and heard Charlie say to Pat, "We're working so hard, so hard." And Pat says, "Well, it's about over; tomorrow we haul Old Marster to the cemetery." Marster jumped up and ran for the house, jumped over the fence, got his foot caught in the paling, fell, and broke his neck.

So old Missie had to get him ready, because they didn't keep him out then like they do now (they didn't embalm you). Next day Pat and Charlie hauled him to the cemetery.

63 *Old Marster Eats Crow* (JEFF ALEXANDER)

Motif Q478, "Frightful meal as punishment," is present here. Billy Jack Tyler told me an analogue in Cleveland, Mississippi, where Old Marster declares he would whip John if he had his pistol; on hearing this John threatens him (see Dorson, "Bolivar County," no. 8, pp. 108-109, "John Whips Old Master").

John was hunting on Old Marster's place, shooting squirrels, and Old Marster caught him, and told him not to shoot there any more. "You can keep the two squirrels you got but don't be caught down here no more." John goes out the next morning and shoots a crow. Old Marster went down that morning and caught him, and asked John to let him see the gun. John gave him the gun, and then Marster told him to let him see the shell. And Old Marster put the shell in the gun. Then he backed off from John, pointing the gun, and told John to pick the feathers off the crow, halfway down. "Now start at his head, John, and eat the crow up to where you stopped picking the feathers at." When John finished eating, Marster gave him the gun back and throwed him the crow. Then he told John to go on and not let him be caught there no more.

John turned around and started off, and got a little piece away. Then he stopped and turned and called Old Marster. Old Marster said, "What you want, John?" John pointed the gun and says, "Lookee here, Old Marster," and throwed Old Marster the half a crow. "I want you to start at his ass and eat all the way, and don't let a feather fly from your mouth."

IV JOHN AS FOOL

64 *The Flower Bed of Eve* (ANDREW SMITH)

This tale has only twice been reported in United States Negro tradition, by Hurston, pp. 109-110, "The First Colored Man in Massa's House," and Brewer, Worser Days, pp. 62-64, "The Intelligent Slave." I have good variants from Tommy Carter (shoes—creeping creeturs; bed—flower bed of eve; fire—evaporation; cat—four-legged runner; road—dusty beaters; barn—Hightime Mountain); Sherman Jones (bed—flower bed of ease; stove—steamolater; shoes—walking gators; cat—speedfast; road—dusty beatem; haystack—Yonder mountains); and Philip Kennedy, a former student of mine who learned it at second remove from a Negro in Southport, N. C.

The Type-Index does not recognize this tale, and Baughman suggests inserting it as 1833 E, but it properly belongs by itself. An excellent assembling and analysis of British variants by Kenneth Jackson and Edward Wilson has appeared in Folklore, XLVII (1936), 190-202, "The Barn is Burning." See also the note by Wilson in ibid., XLIX (1938), 192. They report nearly a hundred versions known to them, and enumerate eleven examples from England, three from Wales, six from Ireland, and two from the United States. The authors distinguish two main types: I involving a farmer and his servant; and II a priest and a young scholar. They see the original home of the jest, whose first printed appearance is 1479, as Germany; all the German texts conform to Type I. So do the six American Negro versions, which reveal a close identity.

This boy had been working for Old Marster for years. One day he told him, "Old Marster, I'm going to take a trip." So he went over to Detroit, and stayed there three or four months till he got in bad. So he decided to go back and visit Old Boss; got back there long about dusk dark. Old Boss was sitting round the fireplace. When John walked in, he said, "Hi Boss; just thought I'd walk back to see how you was getting along." Boss said, "Did you have a good time in Detroit?" "Oh, I had a fine time. I don't know whether I want to stay on." So the Boss said, "You gonna work for me?" "I'll stay a couple of days and think it over."

The Boss told him, "Things have really changed since you been around here. You see that fire over there?" John says, "Sure, I got warm before it many times." The Boss said, "That ain't no fire. That's fleam of flobberation." John says, "Well suh, you is changing things around." Boss said, "That ain't nothing at all. See that thing down there under your feet?"

John says, "Yeah. That's an old cat." "No, that ain't no cat. That's a bald-headed simmon." John says, "You is gitting on the ball." Boss said: "That ain't nothin at all. Come into my room. See that thing sitting over there in the corner." "That is your old bed, Boss." "No, that ain't no bed. That's the Flower Bed of Eve. You see that sitting down alongside the bed?" "Them's your shoes." Boss said, "No, them ain't no shoes. Them is my bootleg crackers. Look what's hanging up side the wall." John said, "O Boss, you still got that old hat?" He said: "That ain't no hat, John. That's the World's Fair." Then he said, "Let's go down to the barn." They start off. "You remember walking down this old road?" John said, "I've wore it out." Boss said, "This ain't no road." "What is it, Boss?" "This is a dusty beater." They went on down into the bam. John says, "Boss, you sure is got a lot of hay." He said, "John, that ain't no hay." "What is it then?" "Well, that's the Hightop Mountain." John says, "Well then, Boss, you really have changed things around, I'm telling you. You really is on the ball."

He decides to stay now. Boss says, "All right, John, you come down in the morning and make me a fleam of flobberation."

While he's making the fleam of flobberation, the cat tried to be friendly and brush up against John, but he scratched him. John got mad and throwed him in the fire. The cat ran out the door and run down the road to the barn and set it on fire. John ran in to wake up Old Boss. He shuck him and shuck him and shuck him. In loud distress he said, "Boss, Boss, Boss, wake up out of your Flower Bed of Eve, put on your bootleg crackers, get your World's Fair, 'cause the baldhead simmon have caught on a fleam o' flobberation and gone out the shelter and hit the dusty beater, gone down to the Hightop Mountain and set it on a fleam of flobberation.

The Boss asks, "What is you talking about?" John tells him, "Git up out of your damn bed, and put on your damn shoes 'cause the damn cat have caught on fire, and gone down the damn road down to that damn haystack and set it on fire." And the Boss whizzed out of there.

65 *Efan and the Dumplings* (J. D. SUGGS)

Efan told Old Marster he could eat more dumplings than anybody. So Old Marster made the bet.

Mr. Johnson said, "No, I got a man could eat more than he can."

Said, "Okay we'll have a contest."

Efan said, "Put on me about twenty gallons of dumplings. Said, "I don't want no bread, we'se just betting on eating dumplings."

So him and Sam begin to eat. When Sam had eaten about five gallons, he quit. Said, "Sho, I thought you was going to eat some dumplings."

So Efan said, "I'll clean the pot." Well, Old Marster gets the money, wins the bet.

So Efan goes home, lies down. "Phew, my stomach hurt." He say, "I feel like I got a cramp. Get a horse and carry me to the doctor." Efan go all the way "Mmh, mmh" [*sound of distress*].

When he gets to the doctor, doctor says, "Come in, Efan, come in. What seems to be the trouble?"

"Oh Doc, gimme something quick."

So doctor begin to give Efan medicine and shots. After a while doctor says, "Open your mouth, Efan." So Efan opened his mouth, doctor looks in. Says "Great Sho, you got the dumplings, I can see them."

(They were right up level with his th'oat. No medicine couldn't go down, so he died.)

66 *John Praying* (HARRISON STANFILL)

In this variant of John at the praying-tree, little boys rather than Old Marster trick him, as in "Efan Prays" from J. D. Suggs, ante, tale 47.

This old Boss-man said he was going to whip John within an inch of his life on Wednesday night. John started praying every day from Sunday to Wednesday. On Wednesday evening that was his last prayer. He told him, "Lord, I been praying every day since Sunday and you've never failed me. I want you to take me away this evening." The boys heard the prayer and they went down and climbed the tree with a ladder rope. So when John made his final prayer that night he said, "Lord I got to go, because I've only got fifteen minutes before my execution."

So they said, "Okay John, you'll have to come by way of the rope because my chariot is broke."

He said, "All right, Lord, let it down, I'm willing to go any way you carry me."

Little boys up in the tree put down the rope, said, "John, put your head in this loop." So they commenced tightening on the rope, and he commenced praying fast.

"O Lord, didn't you say you know everything? Well, don't you know damn well you choking me?"

67 Watching the Pot

Herbert Halpert notes to a text in Folktales and Legends from the New Jersey Pines: A Collection and a Study (2 vols., Indiana University doctoral dissertation, 1947), "Something in the Pot" (vol. II, no. 162, p. 653) eleven references, one each from Texas, Illinois and Newfoundland, two from the West Indies, and six from England. Baughman assigns Motif J1813.8 to the incident. The variant by Maria Summers is close to that in "Richard's Tales," pp. 243-245, "Sheep-Head Dumplings" Halpert remarks, "It is interesting to note that several collectors have thought this a purely local story."

a Hoghead and Peas (A. J. KING)

During the period of slavery Old Marster always kept a little boy to watch the pot on the stove while the family attended church. So when they went away to church this Sunday they had a new boy, so they told him, "When all the peas go to the bottom, the dinner is done. So you watch the peas, John."

So the little boy start playing and forgot about the peas. So when he did take a look the peas had all gone to the bottom, and the hoghead mouth had opened. And two or three peas passing across the mouth. All he knew he was going to get a good beating if all them peas were gone. So he lit out for church. When he got to church he ran in with both hands up and mouth open, calling, "Oh Marster, oh Marster. That hoghead done ate all those peas and got his mouth open trying to catch them two or three bubbling round on top."

b Sheephead and Dumplings (MARIA SUMMERS)

The little boy's mother was at the church, and she told them to notice the meat in the pot. And the little boy saw it boiling over so, he thought it was the sheephead. Along them times people made dumplings to meat. And the little boy went to the church to tell his mother; she becked her hand for him to go back.

He told her, "You needn't to wink, you needn't to blink, 'cause the sheephead at home knocking all the dumplings out the pot."

(She might had some meat there and he thought she had dumplings in the pot, and the water boiling over was the dumplings jumping out the pot.)

68 *John and the Tigercat* (HARRISON STANFILL)

This falls under the general motif J1750, "One animal mistaken for another."

In olden times Old Boss liked to hunt. He had one of his Negroes his name was John, so he was a great fur-hunter, hunt for coons and such. At last one night they went out and John put the wrong thing up a tree—happened to be a wildcat. So John went up the tree to bring him down, like all the other little animals he went up after, like coons and possums. John went up, and the wildcat went up too, till he seen he couldn't go no further.

So he decided he'd come on back down. When he got down the tigercat would slide around. So he slid around enough to tear John's butt with his paws. So John let the tigercat alone and slid down the tree to meet his boss. Boss asked him what the trouble was.

He said, "I got one up the tree."

"Why didn't you bring him down?"

So John told him, "No, you'll have to shoot that son-of-a-bitch, he carries a razor."

69 *John's Courtship* (JULIA COURTNEY)

This unusual John tale makes use of Motif J2266, "The bungling speaker."

John's Boss-man had a boy, and he and John was long together. His Boss-man's boy would go see his girl reg'larly. Late one night John went to see his girl, and the next day he was out in the field plowing. So the boy went down in the field where John was. So John got to the end of the road he [the boy] said, "Hi John. What do you say when you see your girl?" (That's what he asked John.)

And John said, "We just play." See John was shamed to tell him what they were talking about. So John axed the boy, "You said you went to see your girl friend last night." Said, "What did you tell your girl friend last night?"

The boy said, "I talked co'tship."

John axed him, "What is co'tship?"

He says, "Man, when I went to my girl's house last night, you know what I told her?"

John said, "No."

He said, "Well I told my girl, 'Good mo'ning.' (Said) 'Now, sit down.' And I told her, 'Your eyes look like dove eyes. Your cheeks look like a blood red rose. Your teeth look like pearl. Your breath smell like the best thing in the world. And I'm good mind to kiss you.'" So he kissed her.

So that evening commenced to getting late. John had learnt something to tell his girl friend. John couldn't wait till the sun go down hardly. He went to the lot, put his mules in the lot, and went running home. Took him a good hot bath, put his clean clothes on, and lit out to his girl's house in the biggest kind of hurry. John had waited so long till he done forgot what the boy told him. But he didn't think he had. John went on in his girl's house. Before she could get a chance to rest his hat he said, "Hi."

She said, "Hi." [*Sweetly*]

John couldn't sit down before he started to talking. He says "Yo' eyes look like dove eyes. Your cheeks look like a blood red rose." He say, "Your teeth look like garden rakes. Your breath smell like burnt garlic." Then John drawed his hand back and said, "I'm good mind to slap the hell out of you."

That's what he told her. And he hit her. And she quit him.

(That was told in cou'tship. That's a cou'tship story. People couldn't party out in the country like they could in town.)

---

[9] These may be in cante-fable form, "spoken semi-rhythmically or sung over a guitar accompaniment," according to Harry Oster, who has recorded some first-rate texts from blues singers.

COLORED MAN AND WHITE MAN

While John the trickster typifies the plantation slave, a less fully developed figure speaks for all the colored people. He goes by the name simply of "colored man," and chiefly associates with other generic characters—the white man, the Jew, the Mexican, the Chinaman—who usually overtop him. Often in these small jests the tragedy of the Negro is explained in a comic Genesis, which finds him arriving late, or failing to solicit, at the Lord's distribution of gifts. One special offshoot of Colored Man's mishaps relates his entrance into the white man's heaven, where he carries on boisterously until his wings are clipped. Sometimes the anecdotes pivot around pervasive cultural traits, such as the Southern Negro's anticipation of payday and frolicking in town on Saturday, or the cooperation between white and colored people in contrast to their resentments among themselves. Suggs says simply, "All nationalities work against each other."

This jokelore can be matched in other groups, from Jews to Indians, who find ironic laughter in their own minority position.

70 *Colored Man, Jew, and White Man*

a (TOMMY CARTER)

Many variations deal with the theme of God's gifts to the races. I have two texts with a Chinaman, from Nat Brooks and Walter Winfrey, and another with the Jew from Julia Cofield. Compare Fauset, "South." V, no. 18, "Nothing for the Negro"; Brewer, Brazos, 86-87, "Little Jim Lacey's Desires" (Boss-man asks for greedy Negro's address). In Brewer, Brazos, 88-89, "Good Friday in Hell," the Jew has only nine instead of the needed ten dollars to get out of hell; the Mexican is broke; but the colored man offers to pay the Devil eleven dollars on Sunday. A. A. Mazique in Pine Bluff, Arkansas, told me the one about the Jew putting the check in the coffin.

Sometimes the first apportionment of jobs is connected with a race between the white man and the colored man for bundles; the big bundle, which the colored man wins, contains heavy work tools. Thompson calls this motif A1671.1, "Why the Negro works," and refers to Davis, 244; see also The Frank C. Brown Collection, *I, 633, and* Hurston, Mules and Men, *102. Willie Sewall's text has a ham as second prize, and a book and pencil as first; the colored man overruns the first prizes and grabs the ham, and with the pad and pencil the white man charges him.*

Idell Moore tells of the Mexican vendor shouting a big spiel for "Hot Tamales" at the top of his voice, and the Jewish vendor quietly saying "Same thing."

Once there was a colored boy, a Jew, and a plain white man. They all were debating on the best thing through life. So they decided to take the conflict to God. God says, "Gen'mens, as you all wish, I would like to help you all." Then God tells them, "Anything you ax, I'll give it to you. Just come back tomorrow at noon."

Next day at noon they all come back. God had a small package, a medium package, and a large package. He says: "I'm going grant you gen'mens all three of these packages. Whatever you all wish, is apt to be in these packages." First thing the Negro run and got the biggest package on the shelf. The white man got the next largest package and the Jew said, "Veil, there's nothing left—I'll take the little bitty package and be thankful." Negro he was just boasting: "I know God thinks more of me than he do of you. See how big my package is and how little yours is!" Oh, he just couldn't wait to tear into his package. When he tore it open out stepped a great big mule, with a brand-new plow. And a note on the plow said, "For the rest of your days you shall be a farmer."

So he went back to God and said, "God, you didn't treat me fair." God told him: "If you hadn't been so doggish trying to git everything you see at one time you might a got some money too. Don't you know good things come in small packages, you fool?"

The Jew got money, and the white man got wits of knowledge.

b (TOMMY CARTER)

Once a blessing was given out in Heaven. There was a Jew, a white man, and a Negro man there, and God was going to bless 'em all, give 'em all something they could live by. First he axed the white man what he would rather have most in life. He said, "Common Knowledge." He axed the colored man what would he want. He told God he wanted all the money he could spend, all the cigars he could smoke, a new Cadillac, and a pretty woman. Last he axed the Jew fellow what would he have. He said, "Just give me Sam's address and I'll get all I need."

c (JOHN BLACKAMORE)

A colored man, a Jew, and a white man go in to the merchant to get a suit of clothes. The white man was first on the list. He goes in and the merchant tells him how much the suit of clothes costs, $35.00. The white man reaches in his pocket and pays him off.

So the next come in was the Jew. The man tells him the price of the suit of clothes, which is $35.00. So the Jew he kind of scratches his head and says, "Vell, I couldn't do that—too much money." The merchant says: "What do you mean, too much money? Just what would you pay for a suit of clothes like that?" "Vell, I'll tell you what, I'll give you $34.98." So he buys that, and then sees another garment the merchant has that he wants to buy, a cap. The price on it was $3.00. The Jew says, "I like this, but that's too much money." So the merchant wanted to know what would he pay for a cap like that. So he said, "Oh about $2.79." Well, he got his package and walks on out.

In comes this colored fellow. He sees the same suit of clothes. So he likes it too. He wants to buy it. The man tells him it's $35.00. When the merchant gets it all wrapped up and ready to go, the colored man tells him to put it on the bill. He says, "I'll pay you Saturday if the Lord spares me and nothing happens."

(He was going to drink up the money that he had in his pocket, quit his job and go on the bum, and the merchant never would get his money.)

d (BEN JONES)

Cf. the preceding variant from John Blackamore and Brewer, The Word on the Brazos, *pp. 88-89, "Good Friday in Hell" (the Jew tries to bargain the Devil down from the ten dollar fee, and the Negro offers to pay eleven dollars the coming Saturday). A racy text with colored man outwitting the Devil is in Abrahams, pp. 217-218, "Irishman, Jew, Colored Man."*

The white man, Jew and colored man died and went to hell. And the Devil he had so many souls he was crowded out, and he told them if they would give him five dollars apiece, they could go back to yonder world. So the white man he give him five dollars and left. So he came on back, and when the people seen him they said, "We thought you three fellows had died and gone to hell together."

"Yes but it was so crowded the Devil said we could give him five dollars and come on back."

They wanted to know where the other two fellows were.

"When I left the Jew was offering him $4.98 and the colored man said he would pay him on Saturday."

e (WALTER WINFREY)

There were four fellows, the Jew, I-talian, a white man, and a colored man. They was all four buddies. So they were sitting down talking one day, and this colored fellow says, "Let's make a pot; the first one dies gets five dollars apiece to carry him across Jordan."

Well, in about a couple of months this I-talian died. So the colored fellow told them, "Boss, let's go and give our I-talian friend this five dollars." The Jew says, "B'jesus, how can we give him the five dollars; he's dead and in the box." So the white fellow says, "Oh, that's easy, just follow me and I'll show you what to do about it."

So they line up and go in. The white fellow taken out his billfold, pulled five dollars out, and dropped it in the box. So the colored man he was next; he taken his billfold out, and drops five dollars in the box. And the Jew he was last. He reached out and got the ten dollars was dropped in the box, and wrote the I-talian a check for fifteen.

71 *White Minister and Sam* (T. V. MINOTT)

A related idea appears in the jest about "No Preacher in Heaven" told me by Ben Jones in Gethsemane, Arkansas, where a young couple killed on their way to get married can't get wed in Heaven, because no

165

preacher has been admitted for twenty-five years. See Type 1738, Motif X438, "The dream: all parsons in hell."

There was a colored man who was quite religious around town. So the white reverend asked him to attend his church as a publicity stunt; it would attract a lot of people, since they hadn't seen a colored man before. He said that, although his church never had colored people, they had the privilege of coming. The church was packed that Sunday, but Sam didn't appear.

On the following Monday the minister met Sam on the street and told him of the large attendance that they had, and asked why didn't he show up. Sam said: "I had a dream the night before, and saw Christ, and I told Christ of the invitation. Then Christ said to me that he had been trying to get in that same church for fifty years, and they wouldn't allow him in. For that reason I had to change my mind, you understand. Since Christ could not get in there I didn't think that was a fit place to go to."

72 *Why the Negro Has Kinky Hair*

a (NEWTON CURRY)

There is no motif number for this trait, although A1661.2 gives "Why the white man has short hair." "Why the Negro is Black" in Harris, Uncle Remus, His Songs and His Sayings, no. 33, explains the kinky hair of the Negroes as due to their getting last to the pond; the other peoples had used up the water to un-kink their hair.

In the beginning nobody had any hair. So they called all the peoples together to beautify them and give them hair. While they were getting ready to issue it, they had a big watermelon party. When they issued the call that the hair was ready, the colored people didn't come. They wanted to finish the watermelon. The other people, Chinese and Japs and whites, put the hair on and smoothed it down. (All the other peoples have smooth hair.) Then they issued a second call to the colored people. The only hair that was left was what the other people didn't want—they had stepped on it. [Gesture of twisting foot into the ground.] So the colored people had to put on kinky hair.

b (J. D. SUGGS)

Irvis gives two tales, pp. 173, 174, which explain why the Negro is black, and has big feet.

When the Lord was makin' 'em, he made the colored man big and strong, and he told 'em, "Now go look in the glass and see how you look." He [colored man] started walkin' on off, leaving him. Says "Wait, y'ain't got no hair yet."

So he retch over and grabbed 'em some kinky hair.

Lord said, "No, reach over and get you some of that good hair."

So he said, "This all right, I'm going to keep it cut off anyway." He was in too big a hurry and he thought he looked all right without the hair.

So now most older colored persons keep their hair cut off. The whites look funny with their hair cut off—it stands up straight like porc'pine.

73 *Colored Man and the Mexican* (JOHN BLACKAMORE)

This is Type 1700, Motif J2496, " 'I don't Know' thought to be a person's name." A striking parallel from the Accra people in the African Gold Coast occurs in "Honourable Minu," West African Folk-Tales, collected and arranged by W. H. Barker and Cecilia Sinclair (London, 1917), no. 17, pp. 95-96; and reproduced in Harold Courlander and George Herzog, The Cow-Tail Switch and Other West African Stories (New York, 1947), pp. 59-64, as "Younde Goes to Town" (and recorded by Courlander in the LP record, "Folk Tales from West Africa" Folkways Records, New York, FP 103). An Akim man from the country visits the city of Accra whose people speak Ga, and reply to all his questions "Minu," meaning "I don't understand you." He returns to his village thinking that Minu owns all the property in Accra.

In a variant from Iola Palmer, the Mexican tells the colored man, "Lord-a-mejesusfethamechrist me no savvy," and the colored man thinks Savvy owns all the houses on the street.

The colored man and the Mexican were hoboing on the same train. This Mexican couldn't talk English. So they rode and rode and rode, and the colored fellow got kind of lonesome, he wanted to talk some, and he got hungry too. So he decided he was going to talk about some food. He says, "Boss, I sure am hungry." The Mexican didn't say nothing. So by that time they were passing a real swell farmhouse, with many acres of wheat. The colored fellow says, "That sure is a beautiful farm; I wonder who owns it."

He looks at the Mexican as if he was asking a question directly to him. The Mexican says, "Me no sabe."

So they rode on. The Mexican didn't say no more; so this colored fellow decided to try again to get him to talk some. By that time they were passing another farm. So he spoke up again, "That's another beautiful farm; I wonder who owns it." Looks at the Mexican again. Then this Mexican says, "Me no sabe." This colored fellow thought to himself, "Ah, wise guy."

So he waits patiently till they gets to another farmhouse and says, "What a beautiful farmhouse this is. It is even beautifuler than the others." And he looks up into the sky, he's so sure what the Mexican is going to say. And the Mexican says again, "Me no sabe." So he gets mad then, he hauls off and slaps this Mexican. And when he slaps him, this Mexican says, "Quilla, quilla" (that's "quit" in Spanish). So this colored fellow he says, "I know good and goddamn well Mr. Sabbie don't own all these beautiful farms around here."

74 *Colored Man in Heaven* (TOMMY CARTER)

Although popular with my informants, this tale has rarely been reported; see Smiley no. 16, p. 365, "Zip! Zip!" for an inferior text. William Alexander Percy, Lanterns on the Levee (*New York, 1941*), *pp. 292-293, sets down a variant told him by his Negro servant in Mississippi. The colored angel does a loop-the-loop to impress a good-looking lady sitting on a cloud. I have good variants from Nannie Demby, Lacy Manier, Marvin Rice, Mary Richardson, Mrs. Smith, and J. D. Suggs. Sometimes the colored man sneaks into heaven by carrying in his Marster's bag (Baughman: K2371.1, "Heaven entered by a trick").*

Mary Richardson told as true an account of a colored woman from the country who became so excited at seeing a store decorated for Christmas she commenced slapping her hands, jumping on the counter, grabbing their ribbons, and shouting, "Lord, is this Heaven, and am I here?" until she was put in jail for damaging the goods.

There was onct a colored fellow was in Heaven. At that time he was the only one. God had taken him away from down here and placed him in Heaven. The angels were feasting off milk and honey, and flying around in their golden wings, but he felt lonely, and like most colored peoples do in a strange place, he goes around looking for a friend. He had a friend down here running home brew in a liquor still; so he comes down, sits around all that day, and wouldn't drink nothing. The pearly gates were closed at six o'clock. He made it that day.

God told him, "You stay away from down there in that old sinful world. You going be drinking that old home brew and that old rotgutten liquor." He says, "No, God, I ain't going to do that, 'cause I like it up here."

Next morning bright and early he flew on back down here. His friend coached him on to taking a taste of the whiskey. "That tastes good," he says. The old Devil was in his other partner, who kept saying, "Drink as much as you can, just as much as you want." The colored fellow was just fool enough to drink too much. So at six o'clock he didn't show up. About seven-thirty he made it here. He's beating on the pearly gates, holl'ing, talking loud, "Let me in here before I tear the gates down." The angels rushed to him, to make him be quiet. He said, "Don't hush-hush me, 'cause I know my rights." ("Yes, whiskey and beer done give them to him"—Mrs. Marvin Rice.[10]) "Tell God I want to see him. I just want to talk to him and let him know how I feel."

God told him to go to sleep; he'd see him the first thing in the morning. "I can't wait. I want to tell you what happened. I been down in the sinful world and got high as a kite." So the next morning God called a meeting. Colored man was in the front line. "Don't remember nothing," he said; "don't know nothin' about nothin'." God told him, "Well, you went down in that sinful world yesterday, dranken up all that rotgut whiskey, chased it down with that home brew, and you don't know nothing about it! You wanted to talk to me last night, but I'm going to talk to you today. If you go back down there again, I'm going to take the wings, and cast you out of Heaven; there'll be sins on you for the rest of your days." "No, God, I ain't going no more."

Just as soon as the gates were opened, colored angel stole some of the pearls from up there, and come back down to see his friend. "Say, man, pour me half a pint of that whiskey, half a gallon of that home brew. I'm so mad at God I don't know what to do." His partner said, "What went wrong up there, man?" "Oh, wasn't I mad last night when I got up there! Some of that little stuff I drank yesterday must have spilled on my wings. You know I hate the sight of folks anyhow. Set me up another half a pint of that stuff. Here's a few little things I brought you from Heaven. Don't you think this pearl is worth two pints of whiskey? Well I'll pick up the half gallon of home brew on the way back up there."

Drank the two pints of whiskey down, goes out in the street and has a fight, gits knocked down and breaks his wings, goes back to the place to pick up his half gallon of home brew, jumps on his buddy 'cause he didn't have no more whiskey, started back to Heaven way before time because he'd gotten high. Gets back there and tells God, "God, I guess you'd better take your wings" (they was all broke and dragging when he got there) "because you give 'em to the wrong feller. But you know one thing, God, I was a flying black bastard while I did have them."

75 *Jake in Heaven* (J. D. SUGGS)

Suggs heard this tale from his cousin, Ike Shaw, also from Mississippi, but who had lived in Vandalia, Michigan, next to Calvin, for twenty-four years. This is a personalized form of the "Colored Man in Heaven" theme, also using Motif K2371.1.

Well Old Marster he told us if we would be good we would all go to heaven. Be obedient unto him like his father's slave was unto him—they all went to heaven. So week later Jake decided he was going on up first. Well he went up to heaven and knocks on the door.

Saint Peter come to the door. Say "Who is that?"

"Jake."

Say "Wait a minute, Jake." Says "I got to see if your name on the book." In a couple of minutes he's back. Says "No, no such name as that on the book." So he closed the door in Jake's face and Jake going on back home. He's awful heartbroken with his head down because he couldn't get into heaven.

So when he'd walked about six miles he met his Marster with a great big heavy suitcase and a small briefcase in his hand. Jake said, "Hello Marster, where you going?"

"I'm going to heaven, Jake. Here take this suitcase. I want you to go back and carry it for me."

Jake was so glad, he said, "Yes sir, Marster, I'll carry it, yessir." In a couple of hours he was at the door. Old Marster knocks.

Says "Who is that?"

"This is Old Man Craft from Shaw, Mississippi."

St. Peter said, "Come right in, Mr. Craft, right over this table here is where you sign up."

Jake, when he turned around to go signing up, dropped the suitcase and [*gesture to indicate speed*] through the door to Heaven he went. Rafel and Gabel taken right after him. Down the golden streets Jake went, crost a sea of glass, Rafel and Gabel right after him.

The Lord said, "Let him alone, he'll break up all the furniture up here." [*Loud*]

Mr. Craft he rushes right in, up to the altar where they had Jake. Says "He's a good worker, he's a good worker at home. If you got anything that he can do I'll be glad if you give him a job."

Said "Well, we have the moon to put out every night, and the sun to take in. And then we have the sun to put out and the moon to take in—that's all he'll have to do."

So he made a trade with Gabel, if all his servants be good he give them a job, of hanging out all the stars and taking them in. So that was the way the colored man first got to Heaven, by being good, and the colored man been going ever since.

(So that made whole lots of them got a job up there. Like the fellow who said, "How many stars are there up there?" And the other one answered, "Eleven billion, seven hundred and eighty-two thousand, eight hundred and fifty-one, and if you don't believe it go and count it for yourself.")

76 *Nicodemus from Detroit* (J. D. SUGGS)

This tale belongs to the large cycle of stories about departed souls confronting Saint Peter in heaven, as in Type 1738, "The Dream: All Parsons in Hell." Suggs characteristically illustrates from real life the folk-tale he has just told.

Well, Nicodemus went up to the Golden Gate and knocked. Saint Peter was the doorkeeper—you had to see him to get registered. So he walks up to the door and he knocks. Saint Peter says, "Who is you?"

Says "Nicodemus from South Bend."

"Wait a minute." Looks over his record. Said "No, there ain't no such name as that from South Bend."

So he goes on off a little piece. He got to studying. Goes back and knocks on the door again. Saint Peter come to the door. Says "Who is you?"

Says "Nicodemus."

171

Says "Where are you from?"

Says "Chicago."

Says "Wait a minute." Saint Peter goes in looks over the register. Says "No, there's no such name as that from Chicago here."

Nicodemus begin to get worried bad, he don't know what to do. Said to himself, "I'll make one more try." Goes back and knocks on the door again. Feeling awfully downhearted then, he was.

Saint Peter come to the door. Says "Who is you? What's your name?"

Says "Nicodemus."

Says "Where are you from?"

"Detroit."

He shuts the door, says "Wait a minute." He goes in looks over the register—comes back and throws the door wide open. Says "Come right in Nicodemus, for you are the first Negro ever come to heaven from Detroit."

(That was his native home. I know a colored fellow did that from Clarksdale, Mississippi. He had his leg broke, and they had him laid on his back in a plaster cast in the station ready to be shipped out, in Ioway or Nebraska —he'd put that down on his card. About five minutes before the train come in—he was a section hand, knew the train times—he commenced to hollering, "I want to go home, I want to go home."

They told him, "Well, you're going home. We're going to send you home." They had a pass for him. Finally they got mad and stopped pitying him, and asked him, "Well, where is your home at?"

He said, "Dublin." It was just five miles away from there, could have pushed him down in a pushcart.

Lots of people around here won't own they're from Arkansas, or Georgia. Say they was raised in Chicago.)

77 *The Monkey and the Colored Man* (J. D. SUGGS)

Irvis has a similar text, pp. 170-171, where the monkey plays the part of a beggar and is run over by a Negro who takes away his dime. The monkey then says, "Our race won't do." Suggs brings me into his moralizing comment here, to show that the white man proves a better friend to the Negro than one of his own race.

Well, the monkey you know he'd been working hard, and he come to town and he got tired and set down right on the intersection. And along come a great big fellow in a Cadillac. He drove around him. Here come along a fellow in a Rocket 8. And he drove around him. Here come one in a Studebaker, going to turn to his right. Here come along a colored fellow in a Model T Ford. It was hitting and missing—"Spit, bang, boow." It runs square over the monkey and knocked him over and knocked his hip out of place—he could just barely hobble over to the curb. He set down on the side of the curb, and his wound was hurting. He shook his head, and he said,

"My peoples, my peoples won't do."

(Anywhere you go colored people will tell you, we do each other more harm than anyone. Like when I told this colored fellow about you, on the job. He was a mud-maker, getting $2.10 an hour. I was getting $2.00, so he went and told the foreman, 'cause he thought I was getting superior, saying you would write my stories.

A white fellow will pick up a colored fellow, but not a white fellow. And a colored fellow will pick up a white fellow. All nationalities work against each other.)

78 The Hog and the Colored Man (JOHNNY HAMPTON)

Motif K406, "Stolen animal disguised as person so that thief may escape detection." The present type-variant should follow right after Motif K406.1 and Type 1525*, "Stolen sheep dressed as person sitting at helm of boat." Other texts were given me by Tommy Carter, Willie Sewall, and Walter Winfrey; the hog is alleged to be a sick brother, a sick grandmother, or a drunk friend. Carter swears the police in Wilson, Arkansas, arrested the thieves who had clothed the hog in a bonnet and dress; he attended the trial, at which they were sentenced for five to eight years.

One time there was a colored guy running a cafe, and he sold out all of his meat one day, when he had a large crowd of peoples. And they was steady asking for barbecue. He went to get some meat, and all the stores were closed. And so he said: "I know what I will do. I will get my Winchester and a blanket, and drive to where there's some hogs always in the road, and will kill me one."

So off he went, and sure enough a big hog came across the road. He said, "No, I won't shoot the hog; I will put this Cadillac in low gear and run over him right quick. And no one will hear me." So he ran over the hog and put him in the back seat of his car, and put the blanket over everything but his head. By being in a hurry coming back to town he ran the light, and the cops chased him and caught him at the next light. Axed him where was he going in such a hurry. He said, "Officer, I have a sick brother in the back of the car." The officer said, "Okay," and looked in the car and shook his head. He said, "Go on, but if you ever run another light in this town I will put you under the jailhouse."

As the colored fellow started the car, the cop said, "Just a minute," and he looked again. He said, "Go ahead, but tell your brother he is the blackest and the ugliest bastard I ever saw. Tell him he has a mouth just like a damn hog."

79 *Saturday Night and the Colored Man*

This story derives its point from reality. Geleva Grice in driving me around Pine Bluff and Altheimer Saturday afternoon particularly wanted me to see the great clusters of country Negroes come to town, to congregate and relax. The idea that the Negro wage-earner lives from Saturday to Saturday, when he gets his pay check, appears in earlier tales in this chapter.

a (A. A. MAZIQUE)

Fellow was working on Saturday in a furniture store, and the boss had some deliveries he just had to get out that night. And he offered to pay him time and a halt to do the work. John said, "Any other day but I just can't do it tonight." Then he offered him double time. John said he still couldn't do it tonight—any other night but tonight.

"Well John, what's wrong with tonight, that it's different from any other night?"

"Well Boss, if you could be a nigger one Saturday night you'd never want to be a white man any more."

b (E. M. MOORE)

The O. H. Harden Furniture Company of McGeehee, Arkansas, were working practically all Negroes, and they had very competent help. They got in a carload of furniture. The car came in on a Saturday morning. (This happened in 1937.) They wanted to get the car unloaded that Saturday to save the demurrage on it. Mr. Harden asked his workers if they would work that Saturday and Saturday night. If so they could unload that car and save this demurrage. So one man that had worked for that company twenty years told him he'd work that Saturday, but he wouldn't work that Saturday night. Mr. Hardin wanted to know why he couldn't work Saturday night.

Said, "I just have to go out on Saturday night."

He said, "Well tell me, what is it you people do on Saturday night?"

"Well I don't know, but if you would get out and be a nigger one Saturday night, you never would want to be a white man again."

80 *Our Father* (DAN HOLMES)

Colored man was hungry, he asked for something to eat. But the white man was religious and he attempted to teach him the Lord's prayer. He said, "Say 'Our Father.' "

But the colored man said, "You-all's father."

The white man said, "Why don't you say 'Our Father'?"

"Well, the word Our would mean your father and my father and that would make us brothers."

The white man says, "That's right." (He hadn't thought of it that way.)

Colored man said, "Well, give me a bigger sandwich then and don't make it look like you-all's father."

---

10 The landlord's wife, who was sitting on the porch with us.

HOODOOS AND TWO-HEADS

No very clear line distinguishes the natural from the supernatural in Negro storytelling. Any such division must be made by the collector or editor, for the outright violence of white masters and the arcane poisons of colored sorcerers seem comparable phenomena to their victims. Many Southern Negroes believe in hoodooing, and can describe its dread effects with personal examples. Usually some grudge-bearer hies to a reputed "two-head" and purchases the evil dose or trick that, placed near or in the dwelling of the victim, brings on suffering and death. Sometimes the malefactor possesses hoodoo power in his own right. The afflicted individual, finally recognizing the diabolical nature of the symptoms, in panic seeks out a counter-charmer who can discover the trick, and even retaliate on the enemy. Most cases involve love triangles, with the jealous party acting against the lucky rival—who is also the narrator. Never does the jilted spell-buyer divulge these proceedings.

A curious dual attitude surrounds hoodooism. Suggs, who completely accepts the Mississippi Negro's belief in darker powers, still can explain how a two-head with a little sleight-of-hand pretends to cut lizards from a patient's belly. By pure chance I met such an "occultist," as he called himself, in Benton Harbor, a dark hollow-faced old man standing composedly on a street corner, who bore the name Timotheus Verona Minott. He told me "How the Turtle got his Form," saying he had heard the tale forty years before from gypsies in the West Indies. "I was born in Kingston, Jamaica, but my mother came from Madras, India." Hindu, Portuguese, German and Jamaican blood mingled in his veins. Minott did not mention any Negro strain, but obviously was a Maroon, the Jamaican blend of European, Asiatic, and Negro. He claimed to speak five languages, and to have traveled widely as an interpreter on Cook's tours. Naturally such talents made a splendid background for a two-headed consultant. My young friends, John Blackamore and Joe Booth, discussed Minott with shrewd insight, and attributed his successful divinations to advance information, clever deduction, and the law of averages. Yet Blackamore himself firmly believed in two-heads, and confided to me the accurate prophecy of impending accident given him by an old codger hanging around the fruit market.

A colored lady in Pine Bluff, Arkansas, rocking with laughter, revealed the technique of a former housemate who had set up as a fortuneteller. Her white partner, who owned a large insurance business downtown, recommended his clients to the fortuneteller, and then phoned her in advance to describe their circumstances. Unknown callers she sized up from their appearance, and tried several likely guesses as to their troubles—they had dreamed of treasure, had lost jewelry, were looking for their mate—until they acquiesced in surprise. Convinced of her power, they accepted with confidence her recommendations.

Although "two-head" designates any person with esoteric gifts, the Southern Negro speaks of three separate kinds. The hoodoo doctor diagnoses and treats diseases caused by hoodoo evil. The fortuneteller, like renowned Aunt Caroline Dye of Newport, Arkansas, prophesies the future, and locates lost persons and property. The healer cures natural ailments that baffle doctors through his secret arts. Some of the most graphic stories told by Negroes involve these two-headed practitioners.[11]

81 *A'ntie's Swollen Feet* (MRS. E. L. SMITH)

The following two selections are transcribed directly from a tape recording.

"Reptilian Complications" are described by Puckett, pp. 253-255, who indicates the common belief among Southern Negroes of snakes, lizards, toads, and other creatures being hoodooed into their insides. See, for example, Drums and Shadows, *p. 43: the speaker claims to have felt a snake running through her, which the hoodooer grabbed and took away; Hyatt no. 9580: a hoodoo doctor extracts a lizard and beetle bug from the arm of the feller's uncle; Hyatt no. 9553: a spider is driven from the invalid's nose; Hyatt no. 9180: the feller's father suffers from a lizard under the skin.*

Mr. Dorson: Will you tell us what you were saying the other time, Mrs. Smith, about how your aunt had to go to the hoodoo woman, in Okolona, Mississippi. How does that go?

Mrs. Smith: Well, it came a little red spot on her feet, and it just eetched [itched] her so bad, and she scratched it and scratched it, and it commenced a-swelling. It just swell, swell, and every place she would touch on her she would swell up, and then she would scratch it. She would put her hands on her jaw, and her head would all swell up, and her hands all swole up. And the spots would just eetch her and eetch her.

So she'd been to the different doctors, and they'd give her medicine, and she didn't seem to get no better. She was going to try another, and her youngest son was taking her down, and on the way they met an old neighbor friend of theirs, riding a mule. When he seed her, head all swelled up, feets all swelled up, setting in her little buggy, he called her, "Sister 'Melie, what's the matter with you, Sister 'Melie?"

So she said, "Well, I don't know, Brother Jerry, I don't know what's the matter with me." And then she began to tell him how it started, and the doctors she had been to, and no one had did her no good. So he said, "Sister 'Melie, you been hoodooed; somebody done hoodooed you." "Well, my husband wouldn't believe that." Brother Jerry told her, "You need to go down to see this old hoodoo woman." (He called her name, Aunt Dinah, I think.) A'ntie said, "My husband wouldn't let me go." "Well, you better get there and get to her *quick*, 'cause you ain't going to last long."

She asked him, "Would you go by my house and get my husband to let me go?" He said, "Yes, you turn round and go back." So he went on home with her. And her husband was happened to be at home; so Brother Jerry told him, "Bud, you better send Sister 'Melie to this hoodoo woman, 'cause she's in bad shape, and she ain't going to last long if you don't do something." "All right." They convinced him to let her go.

So this oldest son of hers, which was about twelve years old, he drove the buggy and horse and carried her down there. And when they got to this woman's house—she lived in Aberdeen, Mississippi—she wasn't home, but her daughter was there, and she told A'ntie to come in, and she fixed a place on a couch she had there, and let her lay down. And first she looked up in a wardrobe. (They didn't have closets in the home then; so you made this great big old something with long glass doors —some of 'em is very pretty.) And they had a quart bottle in there with what looked kinda like tea made up with wine, and she gave A'ntie a drink of that, a dose of it. And A'ntie got a little ease and just went right on to sleep.

Then this woman turned something in that wardrobe; a little old something she turned, and said, "Well, Mama will be here pretty soon, 'cause she's looking in this direction." Pretty soon her mother come in, and she looked at A'ntie, and told her, "Yes, you in a bad shape, but I can do something for you." So she got some stuff and 'nointed her with it. Then she gets right out in the middle of the floor, in front of A'ntie, and *wheeled* around—just *turned* around on her heel—and she turned *so fast*, she just kept a-wheeling until you couldn't tell what it was. And when she stopped turning it was a big old turkey gobbler. It said "Puht, puht," and so he went on in the kitchen, went on through the house, strut walking, and pretty soon this natural woman came on back. And she give A'ntie some medicine to take, and told her, "Now you *go home*, and about four feet from the bed, outside the door, you dig down about two feet in the ground, and you're going to dig up something. And when you dig up whatever you dig up, you put it in a bottle and bring it to me. Then I'll fix the person that hurt you."

And so A'ntie said she did. She went home and laid out about four feet from her bed, and she begin to dig. And she dug and finally she dug into a little old rag, and cut into it, and a lot of little old wood lice commenced to running out. So it come into her mind maybe that's what she was supposed to get, so she picks up nine off these little old wood lice and puts them in a bottle, and carried them to A'nt Dinah, the hoodoo woman. She said, "Well, if you hadn't tore this rag I'd have gotten every one of them lice, and fixed it so the person did this to you would be dead pretty soon. But you're going to get well."

And she taken the lice and fixed them, and A'ntie began to go down. Her feet went down, her head went down, and she got normal. That was way back there, let me see, about nineteen—oh—eight, I imagine, and she lived here till—I don't whether it was the first of the year A'ntie died, or was it the fall?

Mr. Smith: Last fall, wasn't it?

Mrs. Smith: See how long she lived, since she's got over it. And they said this woman what cured her was one of the *witches*, and could really turn. Now that's a very true story, 'cause I talked with A'ntie many a time after she got over with it.

Mr. D.: Have you ever heard of anything like that, Mrs. Richardson?

Mrs. Mary Richardson: Sure, I heard of witches. I've heard of people's getting poisoned. I have a grandma just went crazy.

Mr. D.: How did that happen?

82 *Grandma Goes Crazy* (MRS. MARY RICHARDSON)

Baughman reports ninety-one English and American examples of Motif G263.4, "Witch causes sickness" Puckett, pp. 294-296, provides data on "Finding the Hand."

Mrs. Richardson: Well, my grandmother went down to see her son's wife one day, and said, "Bea, why don't you patch your husband's pants? Let me show you how to put a patch on there so it won't pucker." And Bea got mad with the mother-in-law for going down there, bossing her around in her house. Her own mother was said to be an old cunjer, and give Bea a dose of little rags, to put in grandma's bedtick (a feather mattress, sewed up all the way around).

So my grandmother took a spell, and crawled up the wall, and set a-straddle of the j'ice. In them old log houses the ceiling wasn't hid; the j'ices wasn't covered; they went from wall to wall. My grandmother set up there, and sang, and my Daddy took me down to see her, 'cause they all thought she was going to die. And she sung a little old song about

> The old grey horse
> Come out the wilderness,
> Come out the wilderness.

Just a crazy song. I was thrilled. They put pants on her, she clung so, clung like a *wreck*, just anywhere, all over the house. So they decided she was poisoned, or hoodooed. (Some object I didn't never believe in. They can put poison in you, but I didn't believe nobody could plant nothing for me to step over, or lay on, and it would take effect.)

So there was a old hoodoo man, a little white man, told my Daddy: "You go on back home, and she'll be resting pretty good when you get there. The first somebody comes there, that's the one fixed the dose and give it to her. Don't let nobody in that house till I get there." And sure enough, my grandma had dozed off to sleep, Papa said, when he got there. So the hoodoo man come, and they waited, and who was the first one that come to the house? You riddle.

Mrs. Smith: I wouldn't know.

Mrs. R.: It was her son.

Mrs. S.: Yes!

Mrs. R.: Her son! His wife fixed up the dose, give it to her husband; he took it down to his mother's house and put it in the comer of the bed mattress—and she slept on it till she done lost her mind. I call her crazy. And the brothers wanted to kill him—my Daddy, and my Uncle Zeke, and Uncle Benny, and Uncle Jake—they wanted to kill him, because he'd put the dose in their mother's bedtick, to please his wife. The old hoodoo found it, and took it off her, and she come normal, and act like a woman that had some sense.

83 *The Dry Birth* (MARY RICHARDSON)

George Lyman Kittredge gives examples of burying bottles with urine of the bewitched, to throw the spell back on the witch and cause strangury (Witchcraft in Old and New England, *Cambridge, 1928, pp. 102-103*). *Hyatt, no. 9153, says that if one wets in a bottle containing a person's hair and photo, that person cannot wet until he dies.*

This is an old hoodoo tale but it's true, too true to be a story. I was living on King and Annison's place, out from Clarksdale, Mississippi, and I was cleaning off the yard, digging the grass off, under the steps. And I dug up a little skillet, a little round skillet, with three legs to it. And under that skillet was a half pint bottle, corked up good and tight, and looked like clear water inside. I opened it and smelled it, and it didn't smell like whiskey.

Well, I wanted a little skillet to cook on the fireplace; so I carried that in, and throwed the bottle out in the yard, in the weeds—I thought it might have been some old poison medicine in it. Mrs. Balmo, who lived next door to me, come to my pump to get some water. I said, "Look here, what a pretty little skillet I found under the bottom step, buried level, and the skillet turned over a bottle." She said, "That was Nora's skillet; she used to stay here." But she was more interested in the bottle than in the skillet. She went out in the weeds and found it, and carried it to the doctor, and had it tested. And do you know what she told me that was? It was the dead woman's water.

Mrs. Balmo told me there was a man and wife living in my house, before me, and the man took in a sweetheart. The sweetheart put Nora's urine in the bottle, and set the bottle under the steps, 'cause she wanted the husband—and she got him too. Nora stepping over the bottle dried up her bladder, till there was no water. She couldn't pass water; and her baby couldn't pass either. The doctor announced it was a dry birth, and Nora couldn't deliver. And she and the baby both died.

84 *How a Hoodoo Doctor Works* (J. D. SUGGS)

*See Puckett, pp. 302-304, "Reptiles Removed." On p. 299 he writes,
"The king root of the forest is called 'High John, the Conqueror.' "
Suggs uses the phrase "John the Conquer."*

Years back they call it conju'ing; nowadays they call it hoodoo.

Uncle John was the great hoodoo doctor in the Deep South of slavery times. Well, Uncle Bill's daughter Hannah got sick, so they sent for Uncle John the doctor. He came and examined her, and he told her that she'd been conju'ed. Someone had put lizards in her, and they were alive. "But I'll be back on the morrow, and I'U get the lizards outa her." So the news spread like wildfire, that the doc would be back on the morrow to get the lizards out of Uncle Bill's daughter.

Uncle John always carried a greasy sack across his shoulder with a strap on the side, which was his medicine kit. So he goes through the woods, till he finds him a weed they calls a butterfly weed. So he pulls it up and gets the root and puts it in his sack. Then he looked off to his right—there was a bush where John the Conquer growed up. He pulls that up too and gets the root of it in the sack. So he walks a little piece further, down to the edge of the water where it was damp, sees a log, and turns it over. "Here's what I'm looking for." He finds that was a lizard about four inches long and had four legs. He was shiny and spotted. So he wraps him up in paper and drops him in the sack. Now this lizard is not poisonous and will not bite; he's awful harmless, and Doc knew it.

The girl was screaming, and hollering that she could feel something crawling in her stomach. The peoples had gathered excited around the bed. In walked Doc, stepping quick and lively. "Git two cups quick as you can, put water in 'em, get 'em hot." He yet keeps his sack on his back, he never takes it off—as doctors do now, you know. Men begin to cut wood to start the fire. The women begin to put on the water. Doc he reaches in his sack; he drops the butterfly root in one cup of hot boiling water, drops the John the Conquer in the next one. In a few minutes they were both boiling. "Now I'll have to put everyone out the room except the mother and father—it's too exciting for you all to see."

He pours a big cup of butterfly root tea and gives it to her. She begins to scream, "Oh, Doc, I wants to heave, I wants to heave." He said: "Hold her head, rub her neck, be sure you got your hand rubbing right back of her neck. Grandma, you rub her leg, just rub her leg right on the muscle; you ain't got time to look nowhere else but just where I told you to look at." Whiles they were holding her head, he eased his hand in the sack, gets a lizard, and dropped him in the bucket she was heaving into. He says, "Let her legs go, and run and get me a cup of John de Conquer right quick." Hannah's mother ran and got the tea. "Here it is, Doc." Doc says to Hannah, "Drink her down, drink her down."

After she had dranken it down, he told her, "I think I got that lizard." She got easy. Doc said, "Let the peoples in now. I think I got that lizard. I don't know, but I think I got it." So the peoples come in all excited to look at the girl; she was at ease laying there quiet. They were really astonished. Doc says, "Hand me that stick there; I think I got that lizard—I don't know but I think I have." So he begins to stir the bucket with the stick. Then the lizard starts to move. He says: "Oh, yes I got it; here it is. Now bring me a pan and some cold water. I wants to be sure what it is." So they ran and brought him the water and the pan. "One of you hand me another stick over there." So they hand him another stick. That made him have two. So he reached down in the bucket, and begins to stir again. The lizard begins to move. Doc grabbed him with the two sticks, lifted up the lizard and put him into the pan of clear water.

Everybody was excited: "It's a ground lizard, it's a ground lizard." Doc says, "Give me a rag." He reaches in the pan with his hand and get: the lizard, rolls it up in the rag and puts it in the sack. Says: "I'll fix the hoodoo that did her this work. He'll never conjure no one else." So, Mary she was well from that day on.

But she was only bilious.

(In the South there was lots of malaria—in Louisiana, Mississippi, Texas, Florida, all through the lowlands—from the damp warm climate. People get bilious, and spit as green as grass. From a doctor the treatment would take a long time, six or eight weeks. But Uncle John gave her the butterfly root to make her throw up, and John the Conquer to make her stop. They sell that stuff in New York now.)

85 *Bugs in the Stomach* (JOHN DAVIS TATE)

Puckett, pp. 249-252, "Reptiles in the Body," describes the snake dust that turns into snakes or insects inside the hoodooed person. Botkin, Burden, pp. 33-34, "Hoodoo," gives a case of a two-head who took wiggle tails out of a sick person by drawing blood into horns placed over incisions on the skin. In Hyatt nos. 9381 and 9408, a jealous husband puts a frog in his wife's throat, and a jealous wife puts lizards inside her husband.

When I was living with my second wife in Portersville, Missouri, she took ill with the stomach-ache, and couldn't nobody fix her up. Finally we went to see a hoodoo woman in Blithesville, Arkansas, that people kept telling us to see. She gave Beulah some little old medicine, looked green as grass, from a bottle about three inches high. Beulah heaved in about five minutes, and up come a lot of little bugs. I bet there was about a thousand bugs in the pan. They had been put in a bottle of pop that Beulah drank.

The two-head told her, "I'm not going to cure you like other doctors." Then she made Beulah take the gunpowder out of a black shell, mix it with water, and drink it down. Beulah's never been bothered since.

She told us it was my first wife who put the bugs in Beulah's stomach, and she wouldn't live long. The hoodoo woman had never seen her, you know—we were from a different state—but she knew just how it was done. She said that if you want to hoodoo someone, you take a lizard or a frog and let them dry out, and crumble them into pieces, put them into the person's food or drink, and they'll grow into worms or tadpoles inside of you.

I never believed in hoodoo till we saw that two-head in Arkansas. She told me all the money I had in my pocket, all the things I had said before I came. Now I don't question nothing no more.

86 The Curse of an Ex-Husband (SARAH HALL)

Puckett, pp. 244-245, speaks of the use of a person's photograph placed under dripping water or hung upside down to inflict headache, death, or insanity. Compare Hyatt no. 9153, mentioned in "The Dry Birth," ante, tale 83.

William Brown Lee was my husband. That house where you met him, the other side of Town Line Road, I bought that house at Sodus for one hundred dollars, and had it moved here for seventy-five. And then he'd never do any work, just lay around, and buy light bread and peanut butter for hisself and eat it in front of us. And during the winter he'd make his children carry his mess outside, he'd do it in the house, just too lazy to go out. And call me names! I birthed his baby fighting him.

He had my boy put in the reformatory in Lansing, and my daughter Odessa in the Adrian reform school. She was going to school and had a baby; so they took her and put her in prison, said she was too young to have a baby. She was fourteen, and lots younger girls around here had babies. Brown Lee gave my two youngest children, seven and eight, to his daughter, and she's living with another man; they go out and play pokina at night, and leave the young ones fastened at home. When the church at Benton Harbor was going to help me, Brown Lee stopped them, and called me a whore.

Year before last two of my kids, Barbara and Effie Dean here, were playing around his house, and they found some stuff in a bottle in the toilet. He'd put a piece of my bloomers and skirt and some roots and something like water, but red, in the bottle. That was to hoodoo me. The kids brought it back and poured it out. But it killed my father and my uncle.

Papa came down from Muskegon, and offered me a home with him, after I broke up with Brown Lee. Brown Lee told my papa he'd never see my face alive again. My father went back to Muskegon to build our house, and died in less than three months. My uncle, Cole Young in Benton Harbor, came out to visit me, and Brown Lee said, "You'll never see his damn face again." My uncle died a month later, loving his wife. Then William Brown Lee told me, "You'll be the next one to be buried."

And ever since I been having fits.

87 *Why My Nose Is Squashed* (MARY RICHARDSON)

Puckett, pp. 275-276, says that dust from a powdered rattlesnake is used in hoodoo to cause blindness and insanity. See Hyatt no. 9167, for rattlesnake powder that breeds snakes inside a person; and no. 9258, for frog powder that blinds the victim when placed under his hat band.

I got a dose of that hoodoo stuff. It all started on the Fourth of July, 1881, on Richmond Plantation, three miles from Clarksdale, Mississippi. We had just moved in March, from Tennessee. (My father read in the paper where Mississippi land was so rich you didn't have to manure it; so he sold out and emigrated.) Our neighbor, Mrs. Smith, who lived in the next house about a hundred yards away, liked my elder brother, Jesse. Jesse used to take the mule up to the white folks' lot, or barn—Mr. Richmond had over two hundred head of stock. And on the way he would stop by her house and talk with her; she'd ask him questions. If Mr. Smith was at home she wouldn't stop him. Jesse was about eighteen, and she was a young woman. My mother told him, "If you want to go courting go up to the quarters where the young girls are—stop standing around talking with that man's wife." She told him she's going to take a stick and break his neck if he don't quit talking with that woman.

So after that Jesse changed his route, and went across the field to the lot, instead of passing her house. That made Mrs. Smith mad. She didn't have no words about it; she asked the boy why he quit coming around, and he told her, "It's my mama made me quit coming." So that's what made Mrs. Smith mad with my mother.

White people had a knack of giving all their labor a free picnic on the Fourth of July. That was the system in that country. Mrs. Smith went, but my father didn't approve of picnics—and besides we all had chills. We were taking the climate of the country, the doctor said. So nobody from our home went. Mrs. Smith brought back the barbecue; she pretended she was so kind, and made us a present of three or four pounds of barbecue. My mother wouldn't let us eat it, and when Mrs. Smith left she throwed it away, out in the weeds. We could have used it—we didn't have any chickens or pigs or milk or butter—nothing but what we bought.

Next thing she gave was a half of a baked cake, cooked on a skillet on a fireplace. (Only rich people had stoves then.) My mother throwed that in the bushes, at the edge of the woods.

Then Mrs. Smith got mad (the hoodoo woman told us later), and decided to give someone else some trouble, because my mother was so smart. She planned mother would have a sick child to trouble with, the balance of her life. One day she was at our house visiting, and said to me, "Mary, if you run back over home and look on the bureau, and bring my snuffbox, I'll go to town Saturday and bring you something pretty." I was only seven then; I didn't monkey with that hoodoo business, so I ran over and got it and brought it back.

On Saturday she gave me a yard of ribbon to make a bow for my hair— deep blue—and a little white handkerchief with red flowers around the border. I put the ribbon in a bowl of starch to make it stiff, because it was slazey cotton ribbon; it wasn't silk or it could have stood up. The starch must have killed the poison, or it would have eaten my neck till it met my nose, and my head fell off; she'd a got me. When I took the ribbon out of the starch it was faded, just a light blue. But I didn't do anything to the handkerchief, just used it till it got dirty.

That was in August when she done give me the gift. In September little pimples begin to break out, on my nose. It just spreaded, and couldn't be cured. My parents began to carry me to different doctors, to find out what the trouble was. Some said it was cancer, some said it was poison ivy, and some said it was scarflow. [I asked what scarflow was.] There comes a knot on you wherever it breaks out; there comes a rising and it busts and flows; it's oncurable. Some people say it's bad blood. But none couldn't cure what I had. The bone in my nose was eat out; that bridge is plumb gone. I reckon colored folks has big noses anyhow, but that's the reason mine is so flat. I was scorned by children and grown people too. Other children wouldn't play with me. Nobody would drink behind me, out of the same cup, for 'fraid they would get it. But it wasn't catching.

Have you ever seen a rattlesnake? They live to be thirty, forty years old, and get about as thick through as that coffee can, and eight to ten feet long. And the rattlers grows on the tip end of the tail. I've busted them open with a stick and examined them good. The inside is just like snuff, dry and dusty. They say if it gets in your eyes it puts your eyes out. Mrs. Smith had put some of that powder in the handkerchief.

My pimples had scabs on them, and when I broke them off there were seeds inside, and that rattlesnake dust. But no blood—they didn't bleed, there's no blood in a rattlesnake's tail, only meat and rattles. It saps the blood outa the flesh, a rattlesnake's rattle does.

But the doctors didn't know that; they weren't dealing in hoodoo stuff.

Seven years later a friend told my mother she thought there was a woman could cure me, if she could get me to her. This woman lived in Dogwood, about fifteen miles from us. We drove there with a horse and buggy. She was a heavy-set, dark woman. She said she'd been waiting for us for three days. But we'd never met her. She told us everything that had happened about the family, how many children my mother had, how the business started, how many dopes Mrs. Smith had tried to give. She made up some medicine that cured me like you see. She said that Mrs. Smith's grandfather was two-headed, and she was getting that dope fixed up from him. She asked my mother, "Do you want me to put the stuff on her, or on a dog, or on a tree?" When she took it off, it seems she had to put it on something. My mother told her, "Put it on a tree; don't put it on nothing alive."

One thing in the medicine was cockleburs boiled in sweet milk. I took a tablespoonful of it three times a day. And the other mess I don't know what it was. She gave mama three kinds of medicine. And the scabs dried up and shed off, and my nose become well.

Mrs. Smith died seven or eight years after. She died cussing! The neighbors told me so. They couldn't hold her in the bed. She did so many evil things until she couldn't face death in peace.

People in those days called them smart ones hoodoos and cunjers. They call 'em mediums now. This hoodoo told us that Mrs. Smith had fixed the handkerchief up with rattlesnake dust. You see I didn't wash the handkerchief like I did the ribbon.

Now that's a true story. But it was a mystery to me how she could tell us all that about ourselves. And ain't nobody told her—we lived too far away.

88 *Triangle in Chicago* (MRS. E. L. SMITH)

A discussion of "Negro Love Charms" is given by Puckett, pp. 264-266. Hurston, under "To Keep Your Husband Home," has "Tie a sock in a knot and hide it under a rug and it will keep your husband home" ("Hoodoo in America" p. 378). See also idem, "Love, pp. 371-373. Hyatt no. 9486 says, "If you want to keep the desire of your husband, take a white cord string and tie nine knots in it and wear that next to your body."

A neighbor of mine in Chicago had a nicely furnished apartment and plenty of money, but no boy friend. She had a girl friend in Morgan Park, Mrs. Williams, who had a husband and two boy friends. And she promised my neighbor (her name was Carter) to give her one of her boy friends. She told Miss Carter, "Take this pair of his socks and put them under your carpet in two different places, with the feet turned in toward the house, away from the street; this piece of cloth slip under the mattress in the bedroom, on his side of the bed; tie a cotton string with nine knots in it around your waist, and sew it to this little bitty bag with needle and thread —wear it close to your meat so it won't lose off."

Then Mrs. Williams introduced this boy friend to Miss Carter, and he fell in love with her right away. He gave her all kinds of presents, turned over his pay check to her (he was a Pullman porter), and finally married her. He never went back to his first girl friend. Well, Mrs. Williams lost her other boy friend, and she wanted this one back, asked her girl friend to return him. "You know I only loaned him to you." "But we're married now." Mrs. Williams goes down to the station and meets her old boy friend when he comes in on the Pullman. She asks him, "How come you don't come around and see me no more?" He tells her, "Oh, I'm busy, tied up." She keeps after him, till he tells her: "You and me are done weaned from each other. I got a wife now." "Yes, but she hoodooed you into getting married. That was no real marriage." And Mrs. Williams tells him about the socks, and the cloth under the mattress, and the bag his wife wore next to her meat.

He couldn't believe it. But when he went home and looked under the carpet and the mattress, he found the socks and the cloth like his old girl friend had said. He burnt up all the stuff, and moved right out of the house.

When Miss Carter found out her girl friend had told on her, and made her lose her husband, she was mad as could be, and went to the hoodoo woman to get even. The hoodoo gave her some yellow powder, and told her to sprinkle it in the cracks of the sidewalk, on the street by Mrs. Williams' house, so she would have to walk over it every day. Well, in a few weeks Mrs. Williams took to bed, with night sweats. I seed her once in Morgan Park, two or three months later, when I went there looking for work; she knew the white people around, and used to arrange for jobs, cooking, washing, housework. I'd met her once before, at my neighbor's—she was a little, light, brown-skinned woman. She lay in bed with the sweat all over her, and big balls of water would hop off her face, big as tennis balls, and she'd sit up and scream, "Help me, help me!" She died not long after, sweated to death.

89 *Seven Diseases at Once* (MRS. JOHNNY BAKER)

Motif Z71.5 is "Formulistic number: seven," and see also under Seven in Thompson's volume 6 for instances of seven as a magic number in folk traditions.

A woman rooming in our house in Muskegon had seven different diseases at the same time. It was the first time in my life I saw a person bleed from the eyes and ears. She had heart trouble too and couldn't walk; so we had to carry her to the lavatory. Each time we carried her out she got worse; later we found out her enemy had buried things in the house when they built an extension onto it, and her passing over them made her sicker.

She went to I don't know how many doctors, and finally my mother and sister took her to Grand Rapids to this hoodoo doctor.

He told her that a certain person had buried seven things in the house belonging to her. And if she hadn't come to see him in seven months she would have died. She had to pay him seven hundred bucks. In seven weeks she was perfectly well, after we dug up the seven things.

She was going with another woman's husband, you see, though she had a daughter as old as this woman. So that woman hoodooed her. That was really true. She's okay now; I saw her about three years ago, and she didn't have any after-effects.

90 *Cured by a Medium* (LULU POWELL)

Puckett's section on "The Power of Faith," pp. 300-302, is relevant here.

I never believed in this hoodooism business, but my husband did. He made me go to the hoodoo woman the time I took sick so bad, in Indiana, about forty years ago.

We'd gone to a social at the Baptist church in Terre Haute. There was a fish fry, and then we gave a play; it was what we called the Old Maids' Convention—we all wore bustles and hoops and wigs. And after that I got on the train for Lafayette, to visit my sister, Mrs. Taylor [Carrie Taylor Eaton—see p. 20]. The next morning, Sunday, I had awful cramps; I was all bent over, and sweating. My father gave me red pepper tea; he believed in that. It fixed me for a while, but the spell came back again on Thursday; so he called the doctor, who said it was acute indigestion. When I went back to Terre Haute I saw another doctor, Dr. Cabell, and he said it was a fibroid tumor, and I had to be operated on. I was all ready to go to the hospital. But my husband sent for the hoodoo woman. He had been to her for treatments himself.

The hoodoo doctor's name was Young, but the spirit she talked with was Dr. McCoy. I don't believe in such things, but I heard a rushing like wind, like in a Punch and Judy show; and it seemed like I just couldn't stay home, I had to go, go, go. Jack, my husband, said he heard something like two boards clapping together, and he said that it was the spirit coming. The hoodoo woman talked with Dr. McCoy; I couldn't see her, but I heard a jabbering. And Dr. McCoy told her I was poisoned at the fish fry by a widow, Mrs. Poston, who was interested in my husband. Mrs. Poston had waited on me, and given me a fish sandwich.

Then the hoodoo bathed me in my own urine, soaked her hands in the bowl of urine, rubbed them over me, and wrung them out, and at the same time she mumbled something. The rest that was left in the bowl she whipped with seven thorns, like whipping a cake, and buried in the ground. Of course she put something else in it, but what I don't know.

It took me three or four months to kind of get together. I was all skin and bones. But she cured me, and I never went to the hospital. It's all Satan's work, this witchcraft. Don't think the Devil isn't smart; he can do everything like God but create; the Devil can even imitate Christ coming like an angel of light. That widow and her partner were Devil's agents. You know the Bible says any time people do witchcraft they should be put to death.

91 *The Spirit Defeats the Devil* (MRS. E. L. SMITH)

The blend of hoodoo and Christian notions represented here is treated by Puckett under "Religion and Conjure" pp. 565-567. In Hyatt, no. 9164, a hoodooed woman finds salt under the carpet and a conjure bag in the hem of her dress.

I was hoodooed in Chicago in 1933. I felt it in my feet first—it drove me crazy. It was worst in the bathroom so I couldn't go in there hardly. So I prayed, and the Spirit told me to smoke cigars; I never smoked before. I smoked nineteen. I'd smoke one each evening all the way down, and feel relaxed. Then I found three little wiggling straws under the pnoleum [linoleum] in the bathroom, and burnt them in the fire. We laid the pnoleum down around the stool and there was a crack there; so I looked underneath and found them, near the face bowl. I didn't feel as bad after that, but it still bothered me. The Spirit told me to quit stepping over the crack between the blocks in the sidewalk near the corner. (I lived in the middle of the block.) It didn't bother me as much, but I still wasn't free of it. The enemy could double the dose on you, if they'd see you getting better. They laid it down in those two places. I had an idea who it was, 'cause I seed them in my dream. The power of the Lord helped me, because I was praying all the time. If I hadn't been converted and knowed the Lord, the Devil would have overpowered me. People just hated to see me prosper, I guess.

Maybe one is the ringleader, but he has cooperators, when they lay down the stuff. If you give yourself in the hands of Satan, you learn how to do this; and you can tell others, and tell them where to put it, and they'll pay you. If it doesn't work he'll come and lay it down himself.

In my dream I drank the water in a spring and felt healed. There was a tall brown man who led me to the spring. And it came to pass, natu'ly, that we found this house here in Calvin, with the spring at the back, and whenever I get sick I take four swallows, and say, "In the name of the Father, the Son, and the Holy Ghost" three times. It helps for awhile, and then I have to drink some more. Other people get healed too—from sickness, complaints, cancer maybe. There was one man, a barber, had no strength, been to all the doctors; his wife carried the water back for him in a jar three or four times, and he is strong as ever now. The water in that spring comes from the Lord, and it can cure anything caused by the Devil.

92 *Death by Constipation* (MRS. JOHNNY BAKER)

See Puckett, pp. 255-256, "Lockin' de Bowels," where he says, "Another common bit of Negro conjuration is the 'locking of the bowels,' by plugging some of a person's excreta into a tree." Putting the monthly rags, or locks of a person's hair, in a tree kills that person (Hyatt, nos. 9148-9151).

This is true, I know, because it happened in my home. When our family moved to Muskegon, we had an open coal bin, and somebody stole the coal and wood one night and messed all over the bin. It was awful; I know because I went out to get the coal that morning. It looked as if he'd emptied a toilet in it. We asked the hoodoo man could he tell us who did that, and he said he'd fix the person. He took a nail with some of the bowel movement on it and drove it into a tree. "As long as that nail's in the tree, the thief's bowels can't move."

In a couple of days a fellow showed up at the hospital, and the doctors were working on him for constipation. When my mother heard that, she said he had been punished enough, and went around looking on every tree for that nail. She told the hoodoo man not to do that in the first place. But she never found the tree, because the Conservation Department had found a disease going around from the bark of trees—impetigo it was—and they had cut it down. So we couldn't get the nail out, and the thief died in the hospital.

93 *Becoming a Two-Head* (MARY RICHARDSON)

I heard my father say there was a man was teaching another man how to be a hoodoo. He told him, "Throw nine grains of corn in the creek before sunrise; then go back the ninth morning and wish your soul was as far in hell as the water was that hit the grains of corn."

And the devil then would come and teach him how to be a hoodoo. The devil would tell him anything he wanted to know, how to make poison, and drive people crazy.

That's the way hoodoos come about, they tell me; they learn it from the Devil.

94 *Testing to Be a Two-Head* (SILAS ALTHEIMER)

Tobe Courtney also told me about the two-head test. "I heard a fellow say once he paid twenty-five dollars to take that test. He had to go through a house with a big hallway, and rooms on each side. And every room had different things in it, different performances, fearful looking animals. He said if you weren't a mighty brave man you wouldn't go through. . . . After that, tricks he wanted to work, he could work them."

My stepfather told me this. He could tell them all night. His name was Frank Tallbert. That was in Calhoun County. He knew this two-headed man. A man wanted to be two-headed hisself. And so he went to his house and offered him money, to give him knowledge so he would be two-headed. (Two-headed really means two minds.) So he told him he couldn't stand it. "You couldn't stand to be made a two-headed man." He told him he could, he could stand it.

So the first thing the two-headed man did was to make this dinner table walk all around the room and leap from one end of the room to the other. And then he made the chairs chase each other around the table, the whole set of half a dozen.

So he sent him down by a worm fence, and when he leaned against it the fence fell down. And when he scraped himself up the fence would build itself up again. He endured that all right. And all the horses in the pasture came up and neighed, and they would kick and run. And he still stood his ground. And then the wild foxes came—many of them in that section—and barked and barked. And he stood still, determined to be two-headed.

Next a large rattlesnake came and crawled through the fence where he was, and shook his rattles, striking at him as he passed. He got out of the way. (That was the old man sending all those things to test him out.)

Next all the worm fences were surrounding him, and building themselves up, and falling, and building themselves up. And he got scared, and ran and went back to the house. The two-head told him he couldn't be a two-headed man, because he couldn't stand all the tests and trials that was put on him.

(That's purely imaginative, you can see how their imagination works. My stepfather said he knew the man who could do that. I think that's the way the man learned, by standing the test under some other man. My step-father'd tell me that when I was a little boy, and I'd listen big-eyed till I was afraid to go to bed.)

95 *The Healer* (WILL TODD)

This type of unlicensed practitioner is skillfully described by Vance Randolph in his chapter on "The Power Doctors," in Ozark Superstitions (*New York, 1947*), *pp. 121-161. In the index to* Drums and Shadows, *"Root and Witch Doctors" are personally named.*

My oldest son had two ruptures, my wife had "varicoose" veins, and I had a hernia. We heard about this man and wife, the Cages, who lived six miles below Allegan, and could cure just with the hands. We drove down Route 131 and then cut across, and stopped at a gas station to ask the way. Before I could say anything the station man said, "I know who you're after," and gave me the directions. So many people were always asking him for the Cages, you see.

There was a big row of cars in the yard at the Cages', and a white fellow sitting in his car called me over. He asked me why I'd come, and then told me what the Cages had done for him. He said he worked out of Kalamazoo as an engineer, and a freight car had stopped on his thigh. They were going to amputate it at the hospital, but he wouldn't let them! He told a friend not to let them cut it off, that he'd rather die with it on. It was always sore and 'noyed him bad, and he dropped to 130 pounds. Then he started the treatment, and in three months he weighed 185, before breakfast. "Look at me now."

The engineer hadn't no faith in the Cages hisself be-for the treatments, and only went 'cause his wife had gone, for a stiff-necked left shoulder. She'd had an operation for kidney stones left her that way, and she was always jawing at him if he drove over fifteen miles an hour, because it jarred her so. After the first treatment they were driving home, going forty-five, and she didn't complain; so he asked, "Why aren't you chewing the rag at me?" And he turned around and saw she was moving her head natu'al.

The first time we went Mrs. Cage treated my wife, and she got out and around the next morning. So I went back with my son. Mr. Cage wasn't there that time either. He worked five days a week going to California as a porter; they said he was even better than her. She was a good, portly looking young woman, about thirty, light colored. I told her my son wanted a treatment, and she put her hands over his head and ran them down to his feet, three times. Then she said to me, "You better have a treatment too." I said, "There's nothing wrong with me." She knew different though. So she gave me the same treatment, and when her hands reached level with the hernia, it felt like fire, though she didn't put her hands on me. I never been bothered since, nor my son.

The engineer was going to give the Cages five hundred dollars, but they wouldn't take anything. So I left money on the table.

96 *My Uncle and the Two-Headed* (J. D. SUGGS)

The present episode shows the two-head in the role of fortuneteller, as in Suggs' story of Aunt Carolyn Dye.

My Uncle Jack Suggs was-cou'tin' a lady, Mary, in Shaw, Mississippi. She got in a fight with another woman he'd been seeing, Francis, who was in the family way, and cut her across the stomach with a knife. So to keep her from being arrested he took Francis and skipped off to New Orleans with her, to see the two-headed. She told him to stay there seven days, and after the seven days he could go back. And the lady that had cut, she [Mary] would come to his house and beg her [Francis'] pardon-ness.

My uncle asked her, "What is your charges?"

She said, "Twenty-five bucks. But you don't have to pay that now. Whensomever she come, as I've said, and beg her pardness, you can send me the twenty-five dollars—which I know you will."

It happened just that way—Mary came and apologized to Francis.

97 *Aunt Carolyn Dye* (J. D. SUGGS)

There is an anecdote about Aunt Carolyn Dye and her marvelous fortunetelling powers in Botkin, Burden, p. *49, "The Stolen Colt."*

Everybody in Arkansas knew Aunt Carolyn Dye. She was a fortuneteller in Newport, Arkansas. I didn't believe in it and I never went to her. But I seen people she told their past to, just by looking in your hand.

Johnny Johnson, a white feller, told me about this. He had a friend, John Doyle, who lost his mules, and they went to Aunt Carolyn to find out where the mules were. Johnson said, "Aw, she can't do nothing, she can't tell no fortune." And so before they got to town, in the suburbs, he hid seventy-five cents under a log, to see if she could tell where he'd hid it, and what was under the log. So when they gets there, Doyle wanted Aunt Carolyn to tell where his mules was at. She asked to look in his hand. She told him, "Go to that big canebrake north of this house, about two miles and a half, and you'll find your mules." Then Aunt Carolyn turned to Johnny and said: "I won't tell you anything. When you go back get that seventy-five cents you hid under the log."

Johnny told his buddy he was aiming to ax her he'd lost some money along the road and where could he find it. But she didn't give him time. He told me that himself.

She was an old lady, maybe seventy-eight years old, when I knew her. She died year before last, when she was ninety. Aunt Carolyn ran a big hotel, for colored and white too, and never charged; just took whatever they gave her.

There was a song, "Yellow Dog Blues," had a part about her.

I'm going to Newport to see Aunt Carolyn Dye
For she's a fortunetelling woman, she never told a lie.

98 The Feather-Breasted Man (J. D. SUGGS)

Relevant here is Puckett, pp. 213-214, "Credulity of the Hoodoo-doctors"

In Poplar Bluff, Missouri, a fellow had set up as a hoodoo. A man named Alf Pack, who hauled garbage from one hotel to another, heard about how this hoodoo man was beating the people out of their money. So he asked one of the fellows to arrange for the hoodoo to meet him at Sixth Street about nine o'clock in the evening.

Lights were a long ways apart; it was a hilly town, and this place he picked out was in the dark. When Pack gets there he whistles, "Is that you?"

The hoodoo says: "Yes. I recognized who you was before you spoke." (Pack was standing in the electrict light.) So Pack tells him: "I'm kind of a little two-head hoodoo too. I'm not like other men. Other men got hair on their chest—I'm a feather-breast man. Did you ever see one?" The hoodoo says, "No." Pack says, "Just feel here." The hoodoo feels in Pack's breast, gives a loud squall, "Woow," and let out to run, and nobody heard from him in Poplar Bluff from that day to this.

Pack had put some chicken feathers on his breast with mucilage, and make 'em stick out, like they was growing.

99 My Uncle's Mojo (J. D. SUGGS)

Puckett, p. 19, conjectures "mojo" in the sense of charm or amulet to be African in origin, and gives a photograph of an informant wearing a mojo, opp. p. 385. An informant in Drums and Shadows, *p. 55, did a thriving business in "Mystic Mojo Love Sachet," a commercial product; and see the index under "hand" an equivalent term. For an Old Marster story employing this term, see ante, tale 45, "The Mojo."*

Henry Bates, he was the mojo man in Goodman, Mississippi. He told my uncle Chase he would give him a hand, and he could go to the store and anything he axed for, the merchant would let him have it. Cost him five dollars. So he paid him, and old man Bates gives him the hand, a little piece of red flannel sewed up in a bag. And then he gave him some root to chew, told him to spit it around the merchant. So he goes to the store, puts a big chew of it in his mouth, and he spit right towards him, nearly on his foot. So he moved a little, and Chase he spit over there again. He [the merchant] said, "I been moving and moving and you just keep spitting on me. You keep doing it I'll take one of my ax handles and beat hell out of you."

Didn't stay in town long, he was going back to get his five dollars from that mojo man. He went right on over to his house, called him out, said "Looka here old Nigger, you're gonna pay me my five dollars. I'd like to got the devil beat out of me with an axhandle." So he gave the hand back and got his money.

My cousin opened one and found in it some gravel and cotton seeds and coal cinders beat up. The hoodoo man told him he was hoodooed, but the doctor cured him of rheumatism.

100 *Two Hoodoos* (J. D. SUGGS)

Motif D1719.1, "Contest in magic," applies here.

Two hoodoos was arguing about who had the most power. One threw his coat down, and said, "Catch a fire and bum up." It catched fire and started burning.

The second took his coat off and threw it over the other'n, said "Rain down water and put it out." The rain came down and put it out, and though there'd been a big blaze it wasn't burned bigger than a dollar.

(Like if you had a big fire and called to Cass and the fire department came and put it out without anything burning. There's something in the Bible like that too. . . . [story of Elijah]).

101 *Bloodstopping* (WILL TODD)

This belief is not often mentioned by Negroes. Botkin, Burden, p. 27, has an example of an old colored man stopping the blood on a badly cut mule. For white bloodstoppers in the United States, see my Bloodstoppers and Bearwalkers (*Cambridge, Mass., 1952*), *ch. 7, and Vance Randolph,* Ozark Superstitions (*New York, 1947*), *pp. 122ff.*

Bloodstopping? I can stop the blood. An old man, just about ready to leave, Charlie Barr, gave me the prayer. He lost his power right after. I seen him use it on a horse bursting with blood; he dried her up, without touching her.

George Whitney's cow had its toenail just about off, and she was bleeding bad. When I heard about it, I asked for a Bible, and went out to see the cow. A young fellow out there was laughing when he seen me come with the Bible. He asked me if I wanted the cow, and I said no. He stopped laughing when the blood stopped running.

Joe Hiles came out to my place, six miles from Remus, to get a doctor for his nephew. (I was the only one around had a car.) His nephew had the measles, and was bleeding to death. I told him, "No, if the boy is bleeding like you said, he'll be dead before we can get to the doctor." I asked Joe his nephew's name, and treated him. Then we drove out there, pretty near a mile. The boy was lying in bed with a bunch of rags this high, but he wasn't bleeding no more. We asked Joe's sister when did the blood stop. She said, "Just about the time Joe got out to my place."

You got to have their name in full, and know where they're bleeding, before you can treat them. He was bleeding in the lung. The funny thing was, three of us treated him, me, my wife and George Norman, who was at the house when Joe came. And none of us knew the other was treating. Each thought he'd stopped the blood.

There's lots of people can do that, you see. You just treats, and the Lord heals.

---

[11] Puckett discusses hoodoo, two-head and equivalent terms, pp. 200-201. A good collection of eighteen true hoodoo cases is Zora N. Hurston, "Conjure Stories," pp. 400–411, in her article, "Hoodoo in America," JAF XLIV (1931). Much information can be found in *Drums and Shadows*, indexed under "Conjure," particularly the subdivisions "Doctors" and "Victims." Three sections in Hyatt under "Hoodoo and Witchcraft" are rich in Negro examples: "Methods of Doing Evil," "In Love and Marriage," "Protective Measures, Removing the Spell," pp. 462-545.

SPIRITS AND HANTS

Hoodoo necromancy forms but one channel between the physical and the invisible worlds that Southern Negroes regard as equally real. Spirits and spooks, ghosts and hants, pass back and forth, sometimes visible, sometimes merely audible, perhaps lifelike and again in shapeless or deceptive guises. A baby born with a caul over its head or a ghost-lobe in its ear[12] will always see spirits, while any meddler can run afoul of a hant.

Spirits may alarm the beholder who finds his kinsfolk evaporating before his eyes, but they never commit an injury. "I believe in spirits 'cause I seen them," says Suggs. "I guess they can't hurt you, like shadows." Then, as so often in esoteric matters, he cited Scripture to illustrate and document the point. After Christ rose from the dead, the disciples mistook him for a spirit crossing the water. ("Spirits can't cross water; you never see a spirit crossing a bridge.") To convince them, Christ told Peter to take his hand and walk on the water too, and feel his flesh and bones. But Christ didn't deny there were bloodless spirits, and obviously, as their mistake shows, the disciples believed in spirits. So why shouldn't I? asks Suggs.

The spirit of a living person is a "token" of his death. "There's a spirit that's in a live person," Mary Richardson explains, "and looks just like him. And when he dies he changes his clothes. When a person is going to leave you, you can see his spirit, or hear him call you, and maybe you answer it. I've had my name called, and answered, and run to the door, and look and see nobody. I'd lose someone in the family, or a friend or a neighbor, pretty soon." Spirits speak for the past as well as the future dead, and may take unlikely shapes. Suggs used to see "a great big old dog" sitting on an embankment in Bono, Arkansas; he hit at it with a water bucket, and it went right through the dog. The animal hung around the overgrown Jackson trail just where the Yankees had killed old man Cook; different people saw it, and in different forms, like a cat, or a rooster a foot and a half high.

Sometimes a spirit of the already dead returns with a definite purpose. A stringy young fellow from Calvin, Clayton Copley, part Indian, Irish, and Negro, and born with a caul to boot, saw a dead man, two weeks in the ground, walk toward him. He wore his burial suit—a blue suit with a white shirt, and white socks with blue thread, no shoes, and a rose in his buttonhole. The spirit merely walked in to the church where Copley was sweeping out rubbish, then turned and walked out the front door back to the cemetery—but Clayton got the point and left off courting the dead man's wife.

These uneasy and tortured spirits belong with conventional ghosts. The term "hant" covers all malevolent and inexplicable sights and sounds. Primarily hants protect buried treasure and linger about ghoulish death spots.

Guiding spirits frequently inform living persons of hidden riches. The buried-treasure obsession of so many Southern Negroes builds upon historical fact. Wealthy planters did inter their wealth in the ground, during the War between the States, and penniless freedmen would naturally dream of finding these riches. They dreamed literally, and in their dream-visions a spirit described the location of the cache. While Tobe Courtney was sitting on his front porch in Pine Bluff, Arkansas, his son John ambled over from next door, and told Tobe of a recent dream in which two spirits had conducted him to a treasure spot. John recounted its exact features—the pecan orchard, the pump, the path by the farmhouse—and then invoked his father's help, because he had driven all around the county without finding the locale. Tobe placed it instantly, in the vicinity of a certain farm, and the eyes of father and son lighted up pleasurably. I asked John what he would do now. Next time a rodeo came to town, and all the folks had gone to see it, John said, he would drive over to the farmhouse and start digging. He and Tobe then related other treasure quests they had attempted, usually attributing their failure to tardy arrival or the duplicity of a colleague.

Besides dreams and spirits, the treasure hunt involves two further items of folklore, the use of special treasure-finding equipment, and the encounter with hants that guard the gold. An elaborate and precise ritual governs the unearthing of buried wealth.

102 *Hants at Dusk* (MRS. MARY RICHARDSON AND MRS. E. L. SMITH)

A fine assortment of Negro hant experiences can be found in Drums and Shadows. *See the index under "Ghosts" and "Ghosts or spirit stories." Other examples are in Botkin,* Burden, *pp. 39-48, "Hants";* Emmons, *pp. 121-128, "Hants";* The Frank C. Brown Collection, *I, pp. 669-689 "Ghosts and Hants" (mixed white and Negro); Puckett, pp. 116-118, "Negro 'Ha'nts.' "*

Botkin, Burden, p. 35, "I Know It Was A Sign," is an account of a slave who saw the shape of his Old Master, and knew he was going to die. Baughman gives an elaborate breakdown under E442.4.4, "Revenant in female dress," but while he cites female revenants in white and black rustling silk dresses and other colors, he does not have examples of mixed colors. Nor does he mention a revenant in human form with a cow's head, although he has many instances of revenants in animal shapes.

Mr. Dorson: Do you know any stories about hants, or a hanted house? (*They giggle*) They always tell stories about that.

Mrs. Richardson: Oh, Lord have mercy, my people used to sit down and tell them things until I was 'fraid to go to bed. I was afraid of the dark, and the shadow under the bed scairt me so I'd run and *jump* up in the bed. I used to say I never would tell my kids them kind of stories. Made a monkey out of me.

Mr. D.: Did you ever see a hant?

Mrs. R.: Yeah, I sure have.

Mr. D.: Where was that?

Mrs. R.: Aw, once the cow was late coming up, and my grandma told me and my cousin to go out and milk that cow. She was a mean old cow; she'd kick all the time. We had to put her in a stall and tie her foot to a post, she'd kick out at everything so. We'd say she could kick the sweetening out of a gingersnap, if it was possible. (*Laughter*)

That old cow—her name was Nell—come up there that night about, oh, after it was good dark. The moon was shining, and just as we set the gate open for the cow to come in the pen where we was going to milk her, I saw a woman coming down the road. The road run besides the wire fence, between the fence row and the bayou— Hopsam Bayou. I caught eye on her, and she was up the fence row. Now this ain't no *joke*. She had on a black skirt and a white waist and a white bonnet, just as slick, and her clothes rattled like they was full of starch. Oh, she was just tippy.

So I didn't put the prop behind the gate. My cousin looked at me and wondered how come I didn't help her prop that gate up. Then she sees the woman too. When the woman got to about one post of the gate the *cow* saw her, and the *calf* saw her, and they begin to blow— Hoooh. And I lit out, I left and ran 'cross the lot, jumped over the fence, and when I got over my cousin fell on me. I looked up, there was the woman come in the gate where we didn't fasten it and come 'cross the lot, and standing there waiting for us to get up. Lord, if we didn't make it to the house! (*Giggles*)

We made such a to-do over it until we disturbed everybody that was on the porch. My grandmother and my uncle come on out to help us milk the cow, and we told them we saw a woman coming down the road 'side the fence. And they told us, "Oh, there ain't such a thing as a hant; that wasn't nothing but a wire fence post you saw the shadow of, in the bayou."

But, child, I know that was a hant.

Mrs. Smith: Yeah, there's hants all right.

Mrs. R.: I know that was something.

Mrs. S.: I remember I seen one. Oh, I guess I imagine I was around about twelve. My mother had been visiting a woman that was real low sick, and toward evening she sent me home, with two sisters of the sick woman. So we went over to our house, and had to pass right by the church and the cemetery. (They always had the cemetery right there at the church.) It wasn't sundown when I went over, and when we come back the sun had just gone down but it wasn't dark. Out there in the cemetery we seed something, looked like somebody bent over. Directly she straightened up, and this woman had on a black skirt and a red-looking waist. And Rosie—she was the youngest one—she said, "Oh look, yon's Mama." Her mother was dead, you see. And I stopped and looked, and there was a woman with a *cowhead* on, a great big old cowhead, and horns; she come walking on to us. So we knew then that the low sick sister was going to die—at least we believed it.

As the woman came a-stepping fast we lit out to running, do-own that road, oh, my, we was *flying*. She come right to the edge of the woods, but she didn't come down the road in the dust; I guess there was too much dust for her. We was sure making dust. And when we got back to Mama and the sick woman's people, all out of breath, we called Mama to the door and told her. And they just got a little sad then, because they figured that this woman was surely going to die. Naturally they believed us, 'cause we was truthful children, and we really seed this. I could tell that for the truth if it was the last word I was going to say. I seed that woman with a cowhead on, sure.

Mrs. R.: A mighty bad head to carry to Jesus, in my estimation.

103 *Tobe Courtney Has a Bad Evening* (TOBE COURTNEY)

Baughman lists 28 English and American references under E422.4.4(a) "Female revenant in white clothing"

When I was a young man, about sixteen, seventeen years old, living in Collins, I went to a dance. And long about nine, ten o'clock I reckon, fellow came in with a Winchester and broke it up, shot 'em up, and folks flew. I was the only one stayed in there, after everyone got out, bartender and everyone, and I filled up my pockets with cakes and candies and apples. And I coming up the railroad by myself, and I just eating to beat ya. And I got way up in a barpit (high banks along a railroad), and I heard a racket. I thought it was some of the boys trying to scare me, and I commenced cussing. And closer I got, I saw kind of a whirlwind, leaves and dust around, and something inside like a bell going "Loopty-loop, loopty-loop." And my hair got so tight, it stood up straight on my head, and I done some running—if ever you saw a little old dark man running, that was me. I run till I get to the station, and I had to stay there and rest.

Then along come another man, riding a mule, a friend of mine. And we went on down through the tanyard together, about a mile from town. And that's where I saw the natchal spirit, that white girl. And I knowed she was dead. And she was just as natchal as I looking at you. She was just as if walking back to her home place. That was a solid spirit.

She was Seefie Courtney. They was white Courtneys, they raised my father. And long in slavery times people went in under Marster's name. We grew up together. She'd been dead about two year—was about twenty-one, I reckon. The other fellow run off, he knowed it was a hant. But I stood there and looked at her till I saw who it was—I'd done run enough that night. She just kept on going back to her home house. If Dave Sanders was living today he could tell you the same thing.

She came on from behind that tree and kept on walking to her father's house. That's why I tell folks there's hants, there's spirits. Dressed in a long white robe, and holding that up in one hand. Maybe come back to visit her father or mother, either one.

104 *The Hotel Room in Greenville* (J. D. SUGGS)

Relevant here is Baughman's Motif E337.1.1, "Murder sounds heard just as they must have happened at time of death."

In 1910 I was passing through Greenville on my way to Vicksburg. I played ball then, and wanted to gamble going down the Mississippi River—

the train was too fast. It come to my mind a fellow killed his sweetheart in a colored hotel in Greenville. He axed her for fifty cents, goes uptown and buys him a box of 32 cartridges and a pistol, and he came back and went in their room—it was the No. 2 room. And when he shot her (he was jealous), lots of people rushed in the room, and the polices. He locked up the room. The wall was only nine feet high; it had been part of a store, and the piano set by the side of the door in the hall. The laws would get on the piano trying to get into the room, and he would pump them as they come over. He shot six polices—he killed everyone he shot. Then he got excited and ran out the back. Some civilian shot him with a shotgun, paralyzed his arm, and grabbed his pistol. The fellow ran in the toilet. And about twenty minutes after he was in there he come out with his hands up, he was bleeding so. The laws locked him up in jail. They were going to mob him that night. Nobody knows who called the governor, James K. Vardaman, but he sent troops there, the first troops ever to go to the rescue of a colored man in the South. They took him to Jackson. He was tried and hung. That was in 1905.

I'd read it in the paper, but I didn't know that the place where it happened was the first hotel I came to, half a block from the depot. A fellow named Solomon run it. I axed did they have a room. The landlord said, "Yes." I axed what was the price. "A dollar for a room with someone else and a dollar and a half for a room by yourself." I said I wanted a room by myself. The girl working there kept looking at me, and I didn't catch what she was trying to say. I was awful tired. I'd played ball for three days at Mound Bayou. The landlord showed me the room. It was about nine o'clock.

What aroused me, I heard some hollering, like it was way in the low end of the building. I laid there and I wondered what was going on. I thought they must be killing someone. And after awhile it stopped. Then it started again, commenced getting nearer and nearer. Well, it got so close, I grabbed my hand razor—it went like it was in the next room—I drawed the razor back and looked for it to come over. When I stood up it hushed, but every time I sat on the bed I heard it. I was scared there till four o'clock, till my legs and arms plumb gave out. I was afraid to light the light, for he'd see me. About four o'clock the girl came through and lit the light up front so she could cook. I gets right out the bed by the time the light clicked on.

"Good morning, Miss," I says. "What was all that trouble and hollerin' going on down the lower end last night?" She said, "I ain't heard nothing, never heard a thing." "It was just like somebody was killing people down there—it kept getting lower and lower, closer and closer." And she looked at me and smiled. She said, "Oh, that was right there in the room where you was at! Didn't you see me trying to give you the nod, shaking my head at you." I says, "Yes." She said, "That's where that fellow killed those six polices—that was right there in the room where you was at. There ain't nobody can stay in there. I couldn't a told you that or I'd a lost my job—landlord woulda fired me."

She asked me what I wanted for breakfast. I said, "Not anything but a cup of coffee." I was too sleepy to eat; I done stood up practically all night long. So I left and went to Vicksburg.

That's the scaredest I ever been in my life and yet never seen nothing. If I'm telling a tale I hope I fall a corpse.

105 *The Ghost Train* (J. D. SUGGS)

This falls under Motif E535.4, "Phantom railway train," for which Baughman has three American examples. In "The Ghosts of New York: An Analytical Study," Louis C. Jones reports only one ghost train out of 460 items of ghostlore—presumably Lincoln's funeral train (JAF, LVII, 1944, p. 244).

I was braking out of Memphis on the Y and M V (Yazoo and Mississippi Valley) in 1913, in July. We were heading back to Memphis from Cleveland, and were called out about eleven-thirty at night. We got orders to meet 777 at Shelby. It would be in sidings. When we'd a got about six miles from town that night, I was riding three cars back from the engine. We were making about thirty-five miles an hour traveling. All in a sudden the engineer plied the air brakes. Then he bio wed the signal for the brakesman to go ahead of the train and look out on the main line—one short and three long whistles was the signal. I comes down off the boxcar; I carries my white lantern in my hand. As I ran by the engine, the fireman handed me the red lantern. That's to flag trains with and let 'em know there's danger ahead, to stop. The engineer threw the lever in reverse and commenced backing up—choo, choo, choo. I runs up the track about two hundred yards around the curve where there's another straight track. In a few minutes the engineer backed out of sight. I seed no lights on the engine.

It was gone about two hours and a half. After awhile the engine rolls back in sight. I gets up and stands in the middle of the track with the red light so he could see where he dropped me off at. He brings the engine to slow, about fifteen miles an hour. I goes on up in the cab, sets my red lantern down in the corner. Then the engine begin to pick up speed again. The conductor, B. F. Edwards, setting on the seat right behind the engineer, says: "Come here, Suggs. What did you see while I was gone? See a train?" I said, "Sir, I hain't seen nothing but these two lights, the red and the white one, while you been gone." He said, "When Mr. Moten (the engineer) brought the engine to a dead stop and blew the flag outa here, remember that?" I said, "Yes, sir." He said: "We seen an engine working steam within three hundred yards of us. We thought we'd overlooked orders and had met 777 on the main line." I says, "Is that the truth, Mr. Ben?" He says, "Yes, didn't we, Mr. Moten?" Then he calls the fireboy over. He said, "Tell Suggs what we seen." And he told the same thing that they told—they seen it working steam within three hundred yards of us.

So Mr. Ben reaches in his pocket, hands me the whole order and told me to read it over again. So I read it. We was to meet the 777 at Shelby. So I hands it back to him. Then he tells me they'd backed up to Cleveland and wired ahead to Shelby to see whether the 777 was yet there. And he showed me the new orders—the 777 was in the hole, and we was running two and a half hours late. I begin to shake when he tells me that. I goes on the fireman's side and take the second seat, and I hung my head out the window, a thinking to myself.

And I says: "Supposing I seen that engine and they all gone!! It woulda slowed down and come easing up to me. I would have caught the engine then to climb up to tell the engineer to look out for Engine 647; she's backing up to Cleveland. I'd a retched for it, and there wouldn't a been no train." And I just sat up there and cried and cried; I ain't seen nothing but I just got scared, thinking of being there alone twelve miles from town. And sure enough when we got to Shelby the 777 was in the siding.

Several engineers had reported they had seen mystery lights, but that was the first time a train had ever been seen. It was said that about twelve or fourteen years before, a train had been wrecked there and had killed a fireman and an engineer.

106 *Haunted House in New Orleans* (SILAS ALTHEIMER)

Jeanne de Lavigne in Ghost Stories of Old New Orleans (*New York and Toronto, 1946*) *elaborates two score spectral legends based presumably on reports such as the present text. In "The Haunted*

House of the Rue Royale" (pp. 248-258) *a wealthy French lady sadistically tortures her slaves, whose shrieks thereafter echo through the mansion for more than a century. The applicable motif in Baughman is E337.1.1(o), "Cries of persons executed innocently"*

Professor Perkins told me this in 1929. He was principal of sixty teachers.

The story was that a lady of French origin, of French descent, visited often in Paris and Mobile and in New Orleans. So on one occasion she came and found her mother dead. She decided however that some of her slaves had killed her mother. In spite of their protest of innocence, she believed they had perpetrated the act. So she called the trusted slaves, especially her coachman, to put to death her slaves, to make them divulge the death of her mother. To the last they denied it. She killed thirteen. People would hear their screams and groaning, and never saw her slaves again. When some of the slaves informed the citizens what was taking place, and the citizens were preparing to punish her, she took all her money, and had her trusted coachman fly to Mobile with her. From Mobile she fled to Paris, and never returned.

The house stands today, and is known as the haunted house. It is said that people still hear cries and groans in the house, so no one dares to live there or to take possession of the property.

My friend, a graduate of Alcorn, carried me there, in the daytime. I wouldn't go in the nighttime, not under those circumstances.

107 *Willie Sees a Hant* (J. D. SUGGS)

This is an instance of the transmission of ghost experiences from whites to Negroes. The pertinent motif in Baughman is E338.1(fa), "Ghost walks in bedroom, disturbing occupants."

A white fellow in Bono, Arkansas, told me this, in 1924. He and his wife moved to a house was supposed to be hanted. His name was Willie, hers was Gert; he was about thirty, she was about forty-nine, near old enough to be his mother. She smoked a pipe and hunted with him—he was a hunter and trapper. He said, "Oh there ain't no such thing as a hant." The day they moved in they put up two beds, one in one room, one in the other'n. So they got to fussing and he got mad, and went in the other room. She was trying to get him to go in the bed with her.

He laid in the bed about an hour. The light was out, but a little moon was shining through the window, just enough to discern somebody. Said he seen a woman coming through the door from his wife's bedroom, with a nightgown on. So he thought he'd ease out there and grab her, to scare her, 'cause he thought she'd done got scared and was coming in to bed with him. When he reached her to grab her, his hands 'd just go round and come together [gesture], and she'd be standing in another place. Well, he made five or six dives at her, commenced to jumping and knocking over chairs— he just knowed it was her and he was trying to catch her. So the last big dive he made at her was over the trunk, and he bruised hisself pretty bad.

She was in the next room laughing; she thought he was cutting up trying to scare her. He said, "What are you laughing about?" He thought he was going to catch her any minute. She asked, "What are you doing keeping all that fuss in there?" He said, "Ain't this you in here I'm trying to ketch?" She said, "No, that's what I'm laughing about; you trying to scare me to make me come in there." Out of the room he went and jumped in the bed with his wife then. He said both of 'em was so scared, they just hugged each other; if one let go the other'd hang on. Though it was wintertime the sweat was just pouring off them. They left there the next day, he said.

Nobody that went in that house didn't stay there long.

108 *The Hobo and the Spirit* (J. D. SUGGS)

Another instance of white to Negro passage of spectral experiences. Motif E321, "Dead husband's friendly return" applies.

This is one my brother heard from a white fellow in Willis, Ohio. He was an old fire-builder in the round house, and when there's no fire to build they go in the shack and talk. The white fellow came there as a hobo, married, and stayed on. One day in the shack he told how he first come to Willis.

He said he got off of a freight train in Willis one night —it was raining bad—and he was going on through the yard. Someone spoke to him, "It's a bad night tonight." He looked and there was a man, dressed in a slicker and rain hat. The man asked: "You got anywhere to stay tonight? You can come home stay with me the night." "Okay, thanks." So the man with the slicker walked off and he just followed him. Neither one spoke; not a word was said. They went about two blocks after they got out of the yard, come to a house and walk up to the porch. The stranger told him to go in. So he walks in.

There was a lady with three chilluns in the house. He sits there five or ten minutes or more. No one come in. Finally he told her, "There's a gentleman brought me here, but he went on around the house, and told me to come in." She says, "Oh, that was my husband." He began to feel all right and good then. She fixed supper for him, and he ate it all up. She told him: "My husband often does that, brings people here. He got killed up there in the yard six years ago. And if it's raining or snowing, a bad night, he'll bring a hobo here."

He stayed but he couldn't hardly sleep; he lay awake all night. But the wife didn't think nothing about the whole thing; she expected it.

109 *Spirit of the Orchard* (SILAS ALTHEIMER)

A haunted orchard that frightens off a thief is in A, M. Bacon and E. C. Parsons, "Folk-Lore from Elizabeth City County, Virginia" JAF XXXV (1922), no. 49, p. 289, "Haunted House" The closest motif in Baughman, although not fully fitting the present case, is E293.1(b), in which a ghost frightens off apple stealers.

Mrs. Lou Cooper, my uncle's wife, a large stout woman, told this as a true ghost story, in Cleveland County, Arkansas, 1877. A slaveowner named Box had died in the big farmhouse—Box's place—and my stepfather rented the place and stayed there one year, made a crop. Good land, but he didn't stay there but one year. I used to hear something walking—tap, tap, tap on the floor, like a chicken, come right up to the bed.

The thing that brought the matter to a head was my aunt coming to the field one day to get fruit. We had a large orchard, ten acres or more (forty acres fenced in, and half of it was in fruit). And he'd let people come and get the fruit without charge, apples, peaches, plums. But four white Indian peach trees, big ones, he had marked with a string for family use, and told them not to take those. She said as soon as she pulled the fruit she heard this loud groaning at the house. She pulled half a dozen or more of those large peaches and put them in the bottom of her basket. She took the basket and went on to the plum orchard. He had it fenced off so the hogs wouldn't get in. The groaning stopped at the house. But as soon as she put the basket down the plums began to rain down. I never have seen such an orchard; the trees were so thick they just overlapped. (Box made his slaves put them out; sometimes you got two different kinds of apples off one tree.) She didn't know how she got out of there; she heard the groaning up above in the tree, and the basket was filled (so that looks like the spirits had action). She didn't come to herself till she was a quarter of a mile from the house (the orchard was back and east of the house) going home, and she never did come back. She was almost frightened to death when she got home. She told that because she was almost out of her wits.

We moved away the next year.

110 *The Fune Car* (MRS. E. L. SMITH)

Present here are Motifs E272, "Road-ghosts," and E275, "Ghost haunts place of great accident or misfortune."

In '34, we were driving from Chicago to look at our place in Calvin here. It was dark, 'cause I remember the cars had their lights on. My youngest daughter was with me, and my son-in-law who's here now, and his wife. And a black fune [funeral] car came along the same side of the road, and it met us—and ours went up twenty-five or fifty feet in the air. And I said, "Son." And he said, "Mother." And I said, "Lavora." And she said, "Mother." And I said, "Elizabeth." And she said, "Mother." And I said, "What was that?" And they said, "I don't know."

Now that's true. It might have been the spirits of some people who had been killed on that road just at that very minute. It looked as if it was going right into us. And then it looked as if we went over it. We all saw it. Elizabeth was only eleven, and she saw it. I said, "Maybe somebody had an accident just that same time, one year or two years or five years before, and we had the feeling of it." If it was just one of us they might say it was a vision or imagination, but all of us saw it.

111 *Return of My Mother from the Dead* (MARY RICHARDSON)

Motifs E323.1, "Dead mother returns to see baby," E421.3, "Luminous ghosts," and E422.4.4(a), "Female revenant in white clothing," appear here.

Yes, I've seen dead people come back. I saw my mother when I was eleven. She had died and left a little baby boy. The next morning after birthing it she died about nine o'clock. The fourth day after, I was laying down in bed—it was about ten o'clock. I had put the baby's nightclothes on, and gave it its milk bottle and laid it on my arm, just like I'd seen mother do it. There wasn't nothing burning but a little tin lamp, and I had blowed it, and that made the house dark.

Then mother came in and looked at the mantelpiece, as if she was looking for some medicine. Her robe she had on—you could call it a dress but it reached the floor—was so white it lit up the house just like as if I had the lamp on. That's what made me look, to see what it was lit up the house so bright. Her back was to me, but I could tell her shape. It scared me so I hollered like something was killing me, and got out and into the bed with my grandmother and my little cousin—I just slided right down between them, like a rat. Soon as I hollered the light went out. I reckon she discovered she had frightened me to death.

Mother come back after that baby. It died the next day. It got to foaming at the mouth and couldn't take its little bottle. My grandmother told me it was dying.

Grandma saw the light as it went out. She told me it was her Annie come back to see about the baby. Mother knew we couldn't raise it—it was too much of a burden to us that year; I didn't have no experience. Wasn't nobody to take care of it but me and my daddy.

You don't hardly never see a spirit's face. You know him by his voice or his shape or by what he's doing; he does what he was in the custom of doing before he died. I've seen several spirits, but sleeping or awake, I never saw one in the face.

112 *A Dream of Mother* (MARY RICHARDSON)

Motif V511.1, "Visions of Heaven." Puckett comments on dreams, passim; he quotes an informant, p. 570, as saying that "You can tell the location of a dead person's soul by a dream of that person . . . if you see him in a pleasant state his abode is in heaven." Compare in English white tradition "A Dream of Heaven" by a girl, in Sidney O. Addy, Household Tales with Other Traditional Remains *(London & Sheffield, 1895), pp. 14-15.*

I never saw my mother that way again, but I saw her in a dream. She was at a long table, near across the room, white as the drippings of snow, and what they put on it glittered just like the snow does when the sun shines on it, like it had little diamonds in it. And what they were dipping off the stove, serving it in plates, foamed like a plate of good heavy soapsuds, just bubbled, like cream. I recognized my mother; she was marching about that table in her long white robe. All the people had extra long dresses. Everything in that room was white, even the floor, wasn't nothing dirty in it. I didn't know a soul there, only my mother, and she didn't pay me no attention—that's what grieved me so. I just stood in the door and looked at them, until I left her; I wanted to taste that white cream, but no one didn't ask me to have a spoonful.

I figured it was because I was a sinner. I wasn't worthy of eating what they had. About two years after, when I was around sixteen, I became converted, at the New Hope Baptist Church in Clarksdale, Mississippi. But I never had the dream again.

113 *My Conversion* (MARY RICHARDSON)

Motif V510, "Religious visions" and Puckett, pp. 540-542, "Negro visions," fit here.

"How did you become converted?"

Well, I prayed, and went to church, and one day the Spirit got hold of me. I was in a path traveling, and I came to a mountain. And I climbed up on top of that hill. My holt broke and I slid back, rolled back down. I climbed up again, and it happened the same way. Then a voice spoke to me and said, "Why don't you pray?" And I prayed, while I rolled down there. And I got up, and He opened the door and walked with me through that house. It was a house instead of a hill I was trying to get over. And whiles we walked through the house He told me: "I'm too wide, you can't go round me. I'm too deep, you can't go under me. And I'm too high, you can't go over me. If you come up any other way except by me, you come as a thief and a robber. Lie, and the truth is not in you." And He picked me up, and took off my shoes, and carried me up, up on a mountain. And He stood out in the air and told me my sins were forgiven and my soul was set free.

114 *The Spirit and the Treasure* (KATY POINTER)

Buried treasure revealed by spirits in dreams or visions constitutes a large section of Negro belief tales, although Baughman gives only two Negro references under the numerous English and American examples of E371.4*, "Ghost of man returns to point out buried treasure" and identifies none for N531, "Treasure discovered through dream," or N511.1.8, "Treasure buried in chest. . . ." and N511.1.9, "Treasure *buried under tree.* " *The* Southern Workman *commented, "The ghost in Negro folklore is a being that is often misunderstood. If he is met with courage he rewards those who speak to him, as he is in many cases the guardian of concealed treasure. The two stories here given .. . are alike in showing this characteristic"* (v. 27, no. 3, March 1898, p. 57).

You know the Southern people are very superstitious. My friend from Georgia, Carrie Dunbar, told me of a family lived close to her, who had a cow and a bunch of hens and a little strip of land. The husband was going to market the next morning and he told her to get the butter and eggs ready. He wanted to make an early start, I suppose to get home early. And she got up and got his breakfast and got him started early. Then after he went she laid down—it was too early to go out to the barn and milk the cow and feed the chickens. And she heard a thunder. And she looked up, she raised up on her elbow—she thought it was going to rain and her husband would get wet. And she saw this big man covered with fish scales, standing by her bed. He spoke to her, and told her not to be afraid, that there was a pot of money buried under the hearth, and he showed her the flat stone. "Take that stone up and dig." (We had a flat stone hearth like that in Essex County, Canady, where I was born. My father, he was from the South; he built us a stick chimney and a stone hearth.) It thundered again, and the man disappeared.

She got up and went out, stayed outdoors most all day, fed the chickens, milked the cow. Her husband came back in the evening, and she told him about the man and the pot of money buried under the hearth. He told her she'd been asleep and dreamed that. She said, no, she hadn't been asleep. Then she worried him until finally he did dig down under that stone. (If she'd been asleep it would have passed like a dream, you know.) He dug under the stone, just to satisfy her curiosity, and found the pot, and it was all filled with silver, black silver. Carrie told me she'd had some of it, from change in buying her groceries.

They bought 'em a little farm, and a big span of black mules. (They was great for mules in the South, I heard my father tell it.) He could plant what he pleased and it was his.

At that time of the Rebellion them rich planters buried these treasures and then the heirs got to living away, and the houses fell to rock and ruin. When the Northern armies was coming, you see, they'd take possession of the plantations, kill the stock and cattle, just take everything. So the planters buried their money and their solid silver.

Carrie used to tell me that while she was peeling apples.

115 *Buried Treasure and Hants* (MARY RICHARDSON)

Many Negro treasure tales deal realistically with actual searches. Folklore elements intrude in such notions as the fireballs that irresistibly lead to the money (Motif N532, "Light indicates hidden treasure"), the fearsome creatures that descend on the diggers (N553.5), the taboo against talking while the chest is being lifted (N553.2), the ghosts that guard the treasure (N576), and the highly prized apparatus necessary to locate the treasure. These motifs appear in the narratives told me by John and Tobe Courtney, Dorothy Fowler, Sarah Hall, Sarah Jackson, and J. D. Suggs. Sarah Jackson says the fifteenth of the month is the best time to hunt, day or night (N555, "Time favorable for unearthing treasure"), and that you must stay away from your wife twelve days before setting out (a sub-motif of N553.1, "Tabu: incontinence while treasure is being raised"). A good typical example is in The Frank C. Brown Collection, I, pp. 694-697, *"Uncle Bill Digs for Money." A useful discussion with two case stories appeared in the* Southern Workman, v. 27, no. 10 (Oct. 1898), pp. 209-210, *"Searching for Hidden Treasure."*

There was a jackleg[13] preacher rented forty acres of land on what was called the old Key place. This was three miles out of Friar's Point, in Mississippi. His name was Paul Chillus. He had him two horses, and he decided he was going to make the crop with those horses. So he had planted his cotton and he was plowing around it. And he hired another man's wife to help his wife chop some cotton. His plow struck something in the ground like a rock, and the horses got scared of the noise, and tried to run away. So after he got 'em quieted down, they went to see what his plow struck, it rang so, made such a noise. And he saw a square chist, an iron chist looked like a suitcase, but it was made out of iron, or steel.

So he decided it was money in the chist. He just scraped the top of it with his plow. Then he told his wife, "We'll come back tonight and dig it up." About a little before sundown he got his shovel, spade, and Bible, and him and his wife went back to where his plow struck this chist. He sang a hymn —some old familiar church hymn—and prayed a prayer and read a verse in the Bible. Then he started to dig around, digging the dirt off'n the top of this chist. And when he got the top clear, then he went to digging around the sides.

He told us, "Something come across the cotton patch —whooooo—like a whirlwind." His wife squatted down, and covered the lantern to keep the light from going out. (They had a lantern to see to dig the hole down.)

The next thing he saw was a black dog come trotting up to the hole he was digging in. The dog jarred the earth as it was traveling 'cross and come by the hole and looked in. Still he wouldn't quit; he said them things was trying to run him away from the hole, and make him go in the house, but he was 'termined to get the chist up before he left, to see what was in it.

The next thing came was a bull, come 'cross the field, and as he breathed, sparks of fire come out of each nostril—"Huh, huh."

By that time his wife was getting very frightened. So they decided to let the hole alone till tomorrow night. They went to the house, and a few minutes after they had got there and was sitting down on the porch, six men came to the gate of the yard and walked up to the steps. They had on black robes, and they asked him, "Paul, I heard you found a hidden treasure." Paul says, "Wasn't no hidden treasures I know of. The horses plowed up a hornet's nest and tried to run off." But they didn't believe what he said, because this woman that he hired had went home and told her husband, "You know, Paul found a treasure in the field this afternoon," So he got on his mule and rode uptown to Friar's Point, and told the white folks that Paul had found some money but it was too heavy, he couldn't dig it up.

So that's why them six white men in the black robes came there and asked him where was that treasure he found. They went on through his yard and down into the field with flashlights, until they found the hole where he had dug, trying to get the treasure up. So they got it up, and prized that treasure out of the ground. (No hants didn't get after them—nobody's scared of hants but colored folks.) They had about thirty or forty yards to carry it before they got to the fence at the end of the field where the road run. And they put the box on the back of a buggy, and it was so heavy it broke one of the wheels off the buggy, so it wouldn't roll.

So the gang stayed there and one went back to town and got a two-horse wagon, with two mules hitched to it, and took it uptown. The wagon held up and they carried the chist in. They busted it open and counted the money, and then wrote the colored man a letter, and brought it down there the next night or two, and put it under the bottom step of his doorstep, with an old double-barreled Dunger [Derringer?] pistol—don't shoot but two times. In the letter, they told him to hush his mouth, there wasn't but $30,000 in the chist, and some notes, and business papers. And if he didn't hush his mouth about what he found, he'd get what was in that pistol. He hushed too.

The people that got the chist, they knowed who lived there and who owned that place, and that Mr. Key buried it there, back in slavery times. They say it's a sin to bury money, and so the hants watch over it. (*Mr. Richardson:* They kill a cat or a dog and bury it.) No, if anybody helps to bury it, they kills him and buries him with it, so he won't tell, and that makes the money hanted.

116 *Treasure Dream* (JOHN COURTNEY)

Spirits that lead Negroes to treasure and Hants that frighten them off also appear in "The Haint's Treasure," in Tennessee Folklore Society Bulletin, *XIX (Sept. 1953), p. 66. A ghost in a haunted house discloses the whereabouts of treasure, but the digger quits because of the cold, in Harry M. Hyatt,* Folk-Lore from Adams County, Illinois *(New York, 1935), no. 10470, p. 610. Familiar motifs here are E291.1, "Person burying treasure kills person to supply guardian ghost" and E371.4*, "Ghost of man returns to point out buried treasure"*

I lived in a place there was a horseshoe over every door, right off Altheimer, to stop the spirit. I seed it every night. He was a heavyset man, about my size now, a white fellow, an I'shman. My wife and I used to see him, we was just young married then. He'd be at the north side of the cedar tree, outside my yard by my woodpile. And he'd just stand there and vanish away, on down to the ground.

Then one night he came to me in a vision, and he gave it to me then. He had a colored man with him, a spare-made fellow. He knocked and he come in and I asked him what he want. And he told me, some money, at the spot where I'd seen him. I never did see him but once again. I used to hear that when they was two travel like that, they'd kill one—the colored fellow— and he'd be the one to watch. The white man owned the money.

My wife's uncle and I 'tempted to get it one night, but as soon as we put shovel in the earth, that's when they would 'pear up. They looked just like buffalo cows, big cows like in Texas, fearful looking; they come up in the shape of those, big horns, eyes big as a teacup.

So I told a white feller about it. I told him I wouldn't go near the place, but I'd show him where it was: three feet north of the root of the tree. After I showed him the spot I backed off, and I heard a noise, and I seed it just as he did, just as soon as he put the shovel in the earth. And I beat him back to the car. I figured that was what was going to happen. He offered me five dollars to go back and pick up his instrument; it cost him $1,000—it was a locator. He said I could make five dollars and I said I wasn't going to make anything except tracks.

(One night after I came from church, I was getting ready to move, and he 'peared up at that place.)

117 *Another Treasure Dream* (JOHN COURTNEY)

About three months ago I had a vision. There was a man, unknown colored man (kind of favored Ben King a little bit), and a boy who'd been killed twenty-one, twenty-two years ago—he got stabbed with a knife, they got into him on the corner here. They came up to the gate here, and called me—"John."

Seemed like I knowed them. I said, "Come on in."

He said, "I'm so tired and worried, I been getting around."

I said, "I been tired too, I been working a little bit today."

He came in and sat down on the side of the bed. His name was Luke. I kinda turned my head one side when I seed him, 'cause I knew where he was supposed to be. This other fellow said, "I got something for you."

I said, "Something for me?"

I just got up and slipped my pants on, zipped them up. They went on out the door, and we got on over the fence, and come on down to the road, and saw an orchard over on the left, a puccawn [pecan] grove, and a pump sitting right on the edge of the puccawn grove. The road was coming from the highway to the house; in the vision I was living in the house. He went to this place, right by the pump, and looked like he just raked it over, and I saw four bushels of money, in a great big oldtime pot, a round pot, deep. And he give me all that.

That whole family's died out. He said he didn't have anybody to leave it to. (They's passed you see.) I wish I knew where that was. I been all over the county looking for it.

[Tobe Courtney says the place is on highway 65 leading up to Mr. Phillips' house.]

218

When there's a big holiday or rodeo and the people's on the west side of town, I'm going out there.

118 *The Horse and the Money* (SARAH "AUNT JIM" JACKSON)

Puckett has a good deal to say about signs; see pp. 451-452 for prophetic signs connected with the feet, arms, and face. Sarah Jackson is rich in signs and in the taboos regarding treasure search. Negro midwives in Georgia are described by Marie Campbell in Folks Do Get Born *(New York, 1943).*

When I lived in my home house in Camden, Arkansas, my husband would go away at night carrying people to town or different places, and left me alone. I went to the well to draw water and I heard a "Buckity-buckity-buck." And being a mid-doctor, I thought someone was coming for me. And I said, "Wait till I carry my water into the house and I'll see what you want." Then when I drew the bucket up I wouldn't see nobody. Happened 'bout six or seven times. It would always ride away. My husband thought it was someone trying to scare me, and after a while he wouldn't leave me.

You see, I'd have to get my 'quipment ready, my uniform, before I could go help with the baby. When somebody was coming for me, my flesh on my arm would jump, if I had to go a short distance. If it was ten or twenty miles, the flesh on my leg would jump, like a leaf on a tree. I'd have a sign if the baby would be born before I'd git there; the flesh on my breast would shake. If it wouldn't be born, the flesh on my stomach would shake.

After the sign, someone always came in a car or a buggy or a truck, and they'd say, "I've come for you." Lots of times I'd have my uniform on, my doctor bag packed, 'cause I could tell if they was going to be needing me in a hurry. (Everybody has a sign, but not many people know how to read it.)

But when the horse came, I had no sign. Then my mother come to me one evening in a dream and shook me like (my mother's passed), and said, "Jim, I come to you in the form of a horse." She said, "I have something to give you that will do your lifetime, even to your generation; you wouldn't have to worry any more." Then she disappeared. But the horse didn't come again, because I didn't stay there long; I come to Lansing. The horse would have taken me to where my mother had buried her money.

After I been here three months my mother come to me again and told me to come back. But I didn't want to take the bus back home; two days and a night was too long. So I wrote my sister Beatrice, "Don't tell nobody, but

I'll be home when I can." Then my mother came and told me it was too late. Some people in Camden were digging for money, and they saw the tops of my mother's jars. And they were so happy they talked. "Here it is, boys." You can't talk, you know, until you get something under the chest, so it don't slip away. So my mother told them, "No, you can't have it, that belongs to Jim." The people digging they ran away, but next morning a boy came and dug it up.

It was too bad, after my mother saved it for me and my daughter.

119 *Eating the Baby* (SARAH HALL)

This is an international folktale, Type 720, "My Mother Slew Me; My Father Ate Me," plentifully reported from American Negroes. Baughman cites twenty-two American examples, two-thirds being Negro. Flowers gives three West Indies references from Parsons, Antilles, no. 126, p. 118, "Murderous Mother." Roberts, no. 27a-c, offers three variants. Randolph has a text "Pennywinkle! Pennywinkle!" in Who Blowed Up the Church House?, *pp. 53-54, with a note on British examples by Herbert Halpert, p. 195. Thompson speaks of its oral currency and cante-fable characteristic, in* The Folktale, *p. 116.*

One can readily appreciate the popularity of Type 720 among Southern Negroes, containing as it does the idea of a murder revealed supernaturally.

Well, once upon a time it was a woman and she had two chilluns. Her husband went hunting and he caught a big coon. He told her to cook this coon good and tender. She cooked the coon and, as she was cooking it, she was eating it. So when the coon were done he were done twice, he were done cooked and done ate up.

Then she begin to think what was she going to tell her husband become of the coon. All at once she thought of what to do. She says, "Oh, well, I believe I'll kill this baby and cook him in place of the coon." So she kilt the baby and cooked it. When her husband come in she set the table and put the baby on it. The green flies was singing around, "My mama killed me." The old man begin to eat. The green flies kept singing:

My mama kilt me,
My papa ate me,
My sister going bury my bones.

The old lady said, "Shoo fly, shoo." But the flies sung again:
    My mama kilt me,
    My papa ate me,
    My sister going bury my bones.
And then he said, "Where's that baby at?" The old lady said, "She's in the cradle." Dad looked in the cradle and the baby was gone. And then Dad cut the mother's head off.
    About that time I stepped on some tin,
    And I skated on away from there.

---

[12] A "ghost-lobe" is a hole in the lobe of the ear. An informant of Puckett says you can punch such a hole in your own ear to see ghosts (*Folk Beliefs of the Southern Negro*, 139).

[13] That means one who is licensed but not ordained."—*Mary Richardson*.

WITCHES AND MERMAIDS

Hants contain an element of humor since they cause persons to run pell-mell in highly undignified fashion, but there is nothing remotely funny about witches. Where a hant intimidates through comic frightfulness, but never actually harms, the witch comes to close and paralyzing grips with her victim. Sometimes the terms witch and hoodoo or conjer are used interchangeably to indicate spiteful women possessed of dark powers, but hoodoo ideas derive from the West Indies and West Africa, while witch beliefs follow closely the traditional English concepts. Witches ride the hapless, change their shapes, fly through the air, and are driven off and captured by time-honored methods. The most popular means of catching the witch is to salt and pepper her discarded skin; the pepper bums her raw flesh, and when she returns from evil-doing, she cannot put her skin back on. Often the witch is exposed accidentally, after a mischievous cat's claw is severed, and some neighbor woman appears minus a finger. These two episodes become generalized folktales, but are still occasionally told as local happenings, by Mary Richardson for instance, who says her grandmother cut the cat's paw, back in North Carolina. No one hearing the Smiths and Mrs. Richardson discuss their own encounters with witches (a conversation I was able to tape record) could doubt their sincerity. In their excitement they simulated all kinds of eerie noises, the stertorous breathing of the witch-rider, the solid squish when the witch plopped on the floor, the anguished cries of a child in torment.

Where witches appear, their master, the Devil, usually lurks close by. Mrs. Smith avers that the Devil "can tell you wonders." Suggs said: "I don't believe in no dead traveling; but there is something else you see, the Devil's imps, the spirits of the Devil. They can come in any shape or form they want to." Then he went on to remark how "Luceefus" tried to tempt Christ on the mountain in the likeness of a king, and to seduce Eve in the garden, in the guise of a serpent. "All witchcraft is from the Devil—miracles, hyp'tizing, seeing things. That always has been, and is going on today." Once in a while Satan turns up yet at his old tricks. An acquaintance of Mrs.

Smith who went fishing on Sunday caught a curious monster, "with great red eyes, and long hair, and a black face, and sharp pointed ears, and it had horns reaching out." He hollered to his partner, "John come here, I've caught the Devil!" In a tense collision with the Devil which Mrs. Richardson described (see tale 137), he assumed three shapes while on her trail. Baptist Christianity helps perpetuate this literal acceptance of a prowling Devil, flanked by an army of imps and witches.

Southern Negroes believe too that mermaids exist, as a species of underwater witch. They describe their ways in a consistent pattern not previously reported in the United States and differing substantially from European mermaid lore. Suggs verifies the story by pointing out that the modern use of lipstick derives from mermaids, who are always pictured with bright red lips, while "fifty years ago, or even forty-nine years, you never see a woman wear lipstick." Once I heard Mr. Smith question mildly how a mermaid could function, with her half-human, half-piscatorial torso; but his wife turned on him so sharply that he collapsed into good-natured submission, murmuring, "It's too deep for me." Most tellers place the mermaid's home in mid-Atlantic, but Sarah Hall localizes it near the mouth of the Mississippi, while Sarah Jackson actually saw the mermaid's hole by the bank of the Alabama River.

120 *Witch-Riding* (MR. & MRS. E. L. SMITH and MARY RICHARDSON)

Baughman lists English and American white examples under Motif G241.2, "Witch rides on person." Puckett has sections on "Ridden by Witches," pp. 151-153; "Driving Off and Capturing Witches," pp. 154-156; and "The Counting Instinct," pp. 163-165. The Frank C. Brown Collection, *I, gives four texts, pp. 649-650, "Ridden by Witches"* South Carolina Folk Tales *has "Witched" and "Hag Duh Ride Me," pp. 92, 93-96. "Rode by Witches" is in* Bundle of Troubles, *pp. 87-90. Numerous accounts of witch-riding are reported in* Drums and Shadows, *pp. 6, 16, 24, 34, 44-45, 59-60, 95-96, 108. Hyatt no. 9249 has the witch ride old master. A good discussion is in the* Southern Workman, *v. 23, no. 2 (Feb. 1894), pp. 26-27, "Hags and Their Ways," and "The Conquest of a Hag."*

Talk of witch-riding and other witch evil almost always leads into a discussion of means to ward off or catch witches. The informants in Drums and Shadows *speak of laying a broom across the door, sulphur* around the house, a knife or a Bible under the pillow, salt on the bedcover (4, 20, 24, 57). A North Carolina Negro spread brown straws around the house (Brown Collection, I, p. 650). A witch must pick up mustard seed lying before the door, but since she can't hold over ten she keeps dropping and recounting them till morning (Hurston, "Hoodoo in America," p. 394). Break a needle, stick the point in the eye, and in the morning the witch will be found with her big toe in the eye (Annah R. Watson, "Comparative Afro-American Folk-Lore," The International Folk-Lore Congress of the World's Columbian Exposition, ed. Helen W. Bassett and Frederick Starr, Chicago, 1895, 335). A horseshoe over the door makes a witch traverse the road covered by the horse, until day comes; pins placed in the seat of a chair will impale the skin of the witch and prevent her from slipping it off in order to ride the sleeper (Mary W. Minor, "How To Keep Off Witches [as related by a Negro]," JAF II, 1895, 76).

Sifters are frequently mentioned as instruments for catching the witch. Suggs told me a case similar to that of Mrs. Smith's. The sifters are placed in different positions in the house. If a sifter is laid face down before the door, the witch will be found in the morning as a ball of white smoke (Puckett, pp. 150-151). Or, since she cannot count over five, and must stop to count the holes (ibid., p. 163), she jumps through the last hole (Mary W. Minor, p. 76). Hang the sifter over the keyhole, and the witch counts until daybreak (South Carolina Folk Tales, p. 77). A fork thrust through the sieve impales the witch, and next day an old woman dies of "misery in the breast" (Fanny D. Bergen, "Two Negro Witch-Stories," JAF XII, 1899, 145-146). Hanging a bottle half full of water, with nine new needles stuck into new cork suspended half an inch above it, on the outer bed post, will also enable one to trap the witch, when she begins counting the needles (Southern Workman, v. 23, no. 3 [March 1894], pp. 46-47). Placing a table fork back of your pillow with the tines upward will impale the hag when she throws her bridle reins over your head; throw them over hers, then she will turn to a horse, which you must ride to a blacksmith and have shod (idem, v. 24, no. 3, March, 1895, "Hag Lore," p. 49).

Mr. Smith: Well, I had a witch or something ride me once. I don't know what the deuce it was. I heard it before day in the morning.

Mr. Dorson: A witch was riding you?

Mr. S.: Yeah, I heard it when it come in the house. I was awake.

Mr. D.: Really?

Mr. S.: It come up on the bed, and I could feel it when it pressed the bed—me and another fellow was in the bed together. And it got up on me, and I couldn't say a word. I lay flat on my back, and I commenced a-twisting this a-way, and a-whining in my sleep—"ennh, ennh, ennh"—and this boy ketched me. And I heard the thing when it hit the floor, 'bout like a big rat —*bip*—and out the door it went; you could hear it go on out. I said, "You better go, you devil you." (*Laughter*) It was about four o'clock in the morning. That's true.

Mrs. Richardson: Mr. Smith, I know you ain't joking. Because listen, I laid down one day at twelve o'clock. My husband had went to carry the mule to the lot while I cooked dinner. I had some time; so I said, "Well, I'll take a little nap." I laid down, and begun to read one of those birthday almanacs, you know—I was interested in reading. It looked like a shadow come over my eyes, but I wasn't asleep. And I saw a woman come in the door. Both the doors were open—I lived in a httle old two-room house—and I was layin 'cross the bed. And she walked in and she stepped straddle of me and she got on me, and she just started doing this a-way, "Runh-runh-runh-runh." And she shook me till I said, "Well Lord, I know I'm going to die." I give up to die. Then I heard her when she hit the floor—*vlop*. She got off a me and walked right out the door.

Mr. S.: And I heard that thing just as natural.

Mrs. R.: And that was *twelve o'clock* in the day—didn't look like I went to sleep; I hadn't had time to go to sleep; she just overshadowed me.

Mr. S.: Well, I heard my grandfather tell it—

Mrs. R.: Rode me till I was *drunk*.

Mr. S.: He said that back in slavery times, there was a woman they called a "Mammy Rye," and the boys all teased her. She was a witch. And you'd hear her coming—zip—zip—zip. They'd say, "Where you going, Mammy Rye?" She says, "Mm boy, you better git going; I'll give you devil before day in the morning." Granddad said one would have to stay awake while the others slept; that was the only way they could get to go to sleep. I heard him tell that more times than a little.

Mrs. S.: Wasn't there no way they could move, to git out of her way?

Mr. S.: Well, they stayed there, you see.

225

Mrs. S.: They're trying to get rid of all those witches now. When we first moved here some witches tried their best to run us away from here. Yes, there's witches.

Mrs. R.: I thought that was way back yonder in slavery times. I didn't think there was nothing like that now.

Mrs. S.: Yes, there is. They tried their best to run us away from here. Come in here in all kinds of forms.

Mr. D.: You mean in Calvin here?

Mrs. S.: I mean in this house here.

Mr. D.: Right in this house?

Mrs. S.: Yes. Yessir, right in this house there was somebody. I don't know whether they're dead now or not, but they done quit coming here. (*Sighing*) Witches jumped on me, and they used to bother the children. (I had the grandchildren here when I was little.) Witches were terrible trying to run us away from here.

Mr. S.: My grandson'd wake up way in the night and he'd holler and cry.

Mrs. S.: Sometimes before he'd ever wake up.

Mr. S.: He'd holler and cry, "Old horse going to eat me up; old horse got his mouth open; he's going to bite me." When he first started, we thought, you know, it was 'cause he was just carrying on so much devilment in the daytime. But he kept a-doing that till finally we had to go git him and put him in bed with us. Then he'd get all right. That was right upstairs.

Mrs. S.: Before he'd go to sleep he'd see it. He'd say, "Mommy, here come that old horse; here he comes, Mama; look at him with his mouth open; Mama, grab me, grab me. (*High, squeaky*) And I'd take him up and say, "Oh, he ain't going to eat you"—'cause I know what a feeling it is when you're scared.

Mr. S.: I thought to start with it was just devilment you know, but we found out different than that.

Mrs. S.: Sometimes I'd be sitting up there sewing, and I'd see a woman come up the stairs and step over into the other room. And I looked and said, "Who's there?" Pretty soon Charles, the youngest boy, come walking up natural. And I thought he was teasing me, and said, "Charles, wasn't that you in the room just now?" And he said, "No, Mama, you know I just come in."

Mr. S.: Well, I heard Joe Kratoff say, he set right out here at this big cherry tree and saw a woman come along here one evening, just about dusk dark good, and she wasn't natural. She wasn't a natural woman. And he went on up the road, and he wanted to turn around and come back, to see.

Mrs. S.: In the daytime I used to see a woman, had on a little old kinda reddish dress, about the color of this lamp. She come across that bridge, and just be walking alone, till she would get right even by my mailbox, and then she would just go *out*, just disappear.

And we used to hear something in the basement, big as a man, just like "Whoopdidee, whoopdidee, whoop-didee, whoopdidee, whoopdidee, whoopdidee." And I taken a flashlight down there and looked, but you wouldn't see a thing. They tried their best to run us out of here, but I just kept praying, and put out salt, and put up horseshoes. . .

Mr. S.: They claim making new steps and sech things as that. . .

Mrs. S.: And burn red pepper. . .

Mr. S.: That'll keep them from coming round and bothering you—witches and things.

Mrs. S.: Do what?

Mr. S.: Put new steps and things to your house. We just fixed some more steps out there and they finally quit bothering us here.

Mrs. S.: Yes, there's still some of them things is still—still existing, I guess.

Mr. S.: The same Devil then as now.

Mrs. S.: But it's just different people the Devil can have power with to do things. Now if you let the Devil talk to you, he can tell you wonders. I don't let him talk with me; I just makes him *git*. Don't never have a conversation with him.

Mr. D.: How does putting in new steps stop all that?

Mr. S.: I don't know; I've just hearn people say that. I don't know whether it's true or not.

Mrs. S.: They don't like to come over new lumber—new things anyway. And some say if you get a piece of pine board, and put it down in your floor, they won't come over that.

Mrs. R.: Well, I heard folks say, take a broom and lay it in the door and they won't walk over the broom. They'll sit there all night counting the straws in the broom. And when day comes you'll see them look like a little jug. Ain't you seen foxfire?

Mrs. S.: Uhhuh.

Mrs. R.: Well, I heard people say they look just like foxfire.

Mrs. S.: Well, I'll tell you what I started to tell a while ago. When I was, oh, 'bout ten, eleven years old, I was working with some white people. And this man, about a nicest white man as I ever want to see, was telling me, "Did you know, Zee, a witch rode me last night?" (He used to call me Zee, wouldn't say Leozie; his girl was named Vera, and he called her Vee and me Zee.) He said, "Look here, how I got my hair turned." He was redhead. We were always taught that redheaded people was the meanest men there was; so I said, "Maybe it's 'cause you're so mean." But he said, "You know, a witch just rode me last night, rode me, rode me, rode me, and rode me, until I just couldn't sleep."

Well, you know way back then they had those great, big, round sifters, to sift out your flour meal—thisaway.

Mrs. R.: Pitty-patty.

Mrs. S.: "Mr. Sparks," I said, "Mama say, if you take this sifter, and put some salt on it, a handful of salt, and turn it bottom side upwards, you'll catch that witch. And the next morning when you wake up, the witch will be there." And, oh, he used to just laugh, and take me up on his lap.

So this night when I come down (I always came to tell everyone goodnight before I went home, 'cause it wasn't so far, I could run all the way), he told me: "Hon, Zee, come early in the morning. We're going to have that witch, 'cause I'm going to throw the sifter down tonight." And he said, "Zee, I want you to git me a big handful of salt and put it down at my bed, and bring that sifter and turn it down." So I did. I put a big heapful of that kind of coarse, heavy salt down, and then they taken that big old sifter and turned it down, when he got into bed.

The next morning I woke up early. "I'm just going down to Sparks' dim early this morning, going to catch the witch." And when I got down there they hadn't awoke; so I knocked on the door. One of the boys sleeping in the other room, long about my age, he opened the door. They was always so tickled when I come early; we'd have a row! (*Whispers*) "I say, Ivy, let's go and see Daddy catch the witch."

So we eased in there and looked, and man! you know we seed a spider 'bout as big as my hand. And I said, "Hi, Mr. Sparks." And he said, "What's the matter?" I said, "You done caught the witch."

He hopped up and looked, and you know, that old spider's legs had got down in the wire of that sifter and had swole underneath, and on top, and he couldn't pull them out. And he was the biggest spider you ever seed in your life, and he had a big wide mouth, 'bout an inch wide, and he was making his mouth like this [*grimace*], and he looked like he had two lips. (*Loud and excited*) Now that is just as true as we look at each other, and if Mr. Sparks was living he could tell you. We caught that big old spider in the sifter; so I said, "I guess that old witch had turned and turned and that's the last thing he could turn to." And so the spider was the witch.

They taken him outdoors and put some kerosene on some straw and the sifter over it and burned him up, and threw the sifter away.

121 *Plagued by Witch* (SALLY COURTNEY)

Seems like it was a little bitty woman in a black skirt and a white waist and a white rag on her head, and she'd git up on me and just walk on me from my feets up, up to my head. She'd just smother me kind of, and I was trying to talk, till I got hold of her, and throw her over behind the chifrobe. Then I wakened up, and got up and sit up on side of the bed.

I sent for old Mrs. Long, midwife, lived about as far from here as Gray's Motel. She'd been doing that way for several nights. I said, "Why don't you quit 'noying me?" I said, "Every night you come down here and get on me."

She said, "Daughter, I ain't been on you."

I said, "Well yes you sure do, every night I throw you over behind that chifrobe."

She told me, "Take that baby out from the bed and it won't bother you."

After that I took the baby outa the bed and it didn't bother me no more, till I put it back in. Then it came in the form of a little bitty boy. He got up on top of me and held his arms out, and wanted me to tote him. So I picked him up and toted him and then I put him down. And then the hounds got after him and run him on off. And that's the last I ever saw him.

They just 'peared up all at once and got behind him. He was running from them. I carried him off to keep him from bothering me.

She told me, "He just come in the form of me," told me not to be scared. She was a friend of ours, a neighbor, died in '30.

(Tobe Courtney: They just shorten your breath—hah, hah, hah—until it looks like you can't wake up, until you do wake up. Sometimes I just tetch her [Sally] and she wake right up. Some people say you can put a horseshoe over the door can stop them.)

122 *The Witch Store Robber* (MARY RICHARDSON)

Baughman tabulates twenty-three instances of Motif G242.7, "Mistakes made by person traveling with witches. Person watches witches preparing to fly through the air. He imitates their actions and words and flies with them. . . ." Roberts no. 35 gives three tales from the white mountain tradition of eastern Kentucky, about flying witches, of which the A text, pp. 106-108 in his South from Hell-fer-Sartin, *is very close to Mrs. Richardson's, and bears the same title. There are Negro variants in Bacon and Parsons, "Folk-lore from Elizabeth City County, Virginia" no. 45, pp. 286-287, "The Six Witches," and note 1, p. 287; Parsons, "Tales from Maryland and Pennsylvania," pp. 209-210, second version of no. 2, "Out of Her Skin"; Parsons, "Folk-Lore of the Cherokee of Robeson County, North Carolina,"* JAF XXXII *(1919), 391-392 (the informant protests too much, "There is no Negro blood in us Indians"). Randolph's text, "Slipping Through the Keyhole," in* The Devil's Pretty Daughter, *pp. 47-49, has the flying boy land in bed with a schoolmarm; Halpert gives full notes for the witch imitator, pp. 182-184.*

Now this was told for the truth. (Folks used to sit around and tell about hants and witches till I was 'fraid to go to bed. I'd run jump up in the bed so hard the slats ud fall out.)

This widder lived in a house herself with her two children, two little boys. It was an old log house with a dirt chimley. (Them chimleys were made out of sticks and mud daubed on them, so the back was built up slanting side them sticks.) She would lay a bottle of grease up the chimley, and at night she'd ramble and steal for her living, after the kids had gone to bed. She was a witch. She gets her bottle of grease, and greases herself from her head to her heels. And while she's greasing, she says,

> Over the thick and th'ough the thin
> Way I go in the win'.

(That meant she could fly over the thick bushes, and walk through the thin places.)

After she greased she flew through the keyhole, like a shadow (she still has her shape but has no bones in her), and flies to the store. And when she got to the store, she went inside through that keyhole. She went to getting down from the shelves what she wanted to eat. Now when she piled her groceries on the counter, that she was going to take home—monkeyjunk I calls it, crackers and cookies—her little boy walked in. She said, very surprised, "How did you get here?" He told her he greased himself like she did, till he got all swizzled up, and could go through the keyhole. So she give him a cooky, and he was eating it, and he cried out, "Lord God, Mama, ain't this good?" And she told him, "Don't call the Lord's name." And out the keyhole she went; she just lit out before she turned back natural, 'cause she didn't have her grease, and left him in there. And he turned natural, too, and couldn't get out through the locked door.

Next morning the storekeeper found him sitting there like a rat, and asked him how he got in there. He said he greased in his mother's grease and follered her. And they asked him who was his mother, and he told. And they went and got her, and staked her, tied her to an iron stob, and tarred her and burnt her, set her on fire for being a witch. That was the custom of killing witches when they caught one.

123 *Skin Don't You Know Me?* (J. D. SUGGS)

Under Motif G229.1.1 Baughman enumerates twelve Negro variants and one white one of this well known tale, which has become a generalized account of catching the witch by filling her discarded skin with salt and red pepper. Sometimes, as here, this will be told as a localized happening (Bundle of Troubles, "Old Skinny," pp. 100-105; Drums and Shadows, pp. 80-81; Hurston, "Hoodoo in America," p. 394). Parsons, Antilles, no. 163, pp. 149-150, "She Takes Off Her Skin," gives two texts from Dominica and references. Puckett comments on the tradition, pp. 154-155. I have texts from John Blackamore, Carrie Eaton, Lulu Powell, E. L. Smith, and Carrie Williams. The efficacy of pepper and salt is presented in Hyatt nos. 9592-9596, 9624-9627, 9629-9645.

This old witch used to tantalize people out in the country. They didn't know she was a witch; but every day there'd be something missing— diamonds, jewelry. She'd come in through a keyhole, or a crack in the door. So this night she went to a big fine castle. And a man, we'll just call him Mr. John, he's just coming in from a party, about 2:30 A.M. Everybody else is asleep. He looked and he saw a lady standing right at his doorstep. "I'm just gonna stand here and see what she's gonna do." First she reaches up, pulls her hat off, lays it down. She pulls off her shoes, and she also lays them down. She undresses, lays the clothes all in the same heap. He seen her hands go up, and her skin begin to move upwards. Up it went, up it went, till it was about five feet in the air. Then it settled back to the ground. Nothing else moved.

"Oh, that's a curious sight." He goes up and examines the clothes. "Huh, this is old Grandma Jane's clothes, what stays over the hill." Then he feels the skin. "Hm, I don't know what this is, but if it's moisture I know how I'll find out. I'll get some pepper and salt and I'll put them on it." So he eased in the kitchen, gits his red pepper and salt, and sprinkles the hide good all over. "Now I'll see what's gonna happen." In a few minutes he seen the skin begin to work. Next he heard a whistle, and a voice said, "Skin don't you know me?" The skin was so hot she couldn't get in it. Three times he heard the whistle at the burning, and "Skin don't you know me?" Next thing the voice said was, "If you will wash this skin with soap and water, I'll give you all the diamonds and jewelry I've stolen from you. This is Grandma Jane." (She had looked and saw him.) Then he obeyed, washed it, and soaped it and greased it good for her. And she was the same old Grandma Jane when she got back into her skin.

Then she restored all their jewelry and became a poor old widowed woman. That salt had taken away all her power of witchcraft.

(They claim that salt kills the power—it holds the dampness, and the witch can't never get power enough to work. Same thing with hyp'tizing—some people got more salt in their blood than others.)

124 *The Cat-Witch* (MARY RICHARDSON)

For this widespread episode Baughman notes thirty-two examples, of which six are Negro, under Motif D702.1.1, "Cat's paw cut off: woman's hand missing:" Puckett refers to it, p. 149. The Southern Workman *gives variants, "Ten Witch Cats" in v. 10, no. 1 (Jan. 1881), p. 18; and "The Witch Cats," v. 24, no. 3 (March 1895), p. 50. I also have a text from Joe Thomas.*

This happened in slavery times, in North Carolina. I've heard my grandmother tell it more than enough.

My grandmother was cook and house-girl for this family of slaveowners —they must have been Bissits, 'cause she was a Bissit. Well, Old Marster had sheep, and he sheared his sheep and put the wool upstairs. And Old Miss accused the cook of stealing her wool. "Every day my wool gets smaller and smaller; somebody's taking my wool." She knowed nobody could get up there handy but the house-girl. So they took her out and tore up her back about the wool, and Old Marster give her a terrible whipping.

When grandma went upstairs to clean up, she'd often see a cat laying in the pile of wool. So she thought the cat laying there packed the wool, and made it look small. And she said to herself, she's going to cut off the cat's head with a butcher knife, if she catches her again. And sure enough she did. She grabbed the cat by her foot, her front foot, and hacked her foot with the knife, and cut it off. And the cat went running down the stairs, and out.

So she kilt the foot she cut off, and it turned natural, it turned to a hand. And the hand had a gold ring on the finger, with an initial in the ring. My grandmother carried the hand down to her Mistress, and showed it to her. Grandma could not read nor write, but Old Miss could, and she saw the initial on the ring. So it was an outcry; they begin to talk about it, like people do in a neighborhood, and they look around to see who lost her hand. And they found it was this rich white woman, who owned slaves, and was the wife of a young man hadn't been long married. (Witches don't stay long in one place; they travel.) Next morning she wouldn't get up to cook her husband's breakfast, 'cause she didn't have but one hand. And when he heard the talk, and saw the hand with his wife's gold ring, and found her in bed without a hand, he knew she was the cat-witch. And he said he didn't want her no longer.

So it was a custom of killing old witches. They took and fastened her to an iron stake, they staked her, and poured tar around her, and set her afire, and burnt her up.

She had studied witchcraft, and she wanted that wool, and could get places, like the wind, like a hant. She would slip out after her husband was in bed, go through keyholes, if necessary be a rat—they can change—and steal things, and bring them back.

Grandma told that for the truth.

125 *Rangtang* (ODESSA HALL)

Motifs G275.2, "Witch overcome by helpful dogs of hero"; B524.1.2, "Dogs rescue fleeing master from tree refuge"; and the African references under B421, "Helpful dog" apply here. Parsons has four texts in Andros Island, *no. 32, pp. 66-70, "The Old Witch and the*

Dogs," with references, and three in Sea Islands, *no. 73, pp. 80-83, "Escape Up the Tree." She comments on another similarly named text that it is "a European tale brought over long since by immigrants from the west coast of Africa. I have collected it in elaborate versions from Portuguese Negroes from the Cape Verde Islands. Among American Indians as well as Negroes it has a wide dispersal" ("Folk Tales from Students in Tuskegee Institute, Alabama," JAF XXXII, 1919, 397). Roberts has two variants, no. 3(a), "Alice and Ben" and (b), "Jack and his Dogs," for which he conjectures a Negro source. The fantastic names of the dogs especially distinguish this plot: Jimmie Bingo and Jim Bolden; Take um, Cut-Throat, and Suck-Blood; You-Know, I-Know, God-Knows; Cut-er-Throat, Suck-er-Blood, Crack-er-Bone, Smash-er-Meat; Wham, Jam, Jenny-Mo-Wham (the title story by Peggy Hendricks in* Folk Travelers, *ed. M. C. Boatright et al., TFSP XXV, 1953, 217-219); Bark and Berry, Jupiter and Kerry, and Darker-in-de-mawnin' ("Cindah Seed in You Pocket" in* Bundle of Troubles, *pp. 178-179).*

Once upon a time there was a little boy. And this little boy had two dogs, and one of them was named Dan and the other was named Rangtang. So one day his stepmother was going to send him over to his grandmother's. And he said, "Mother, let me take the dogs." But his mother told him, "No, you can't take the dogs." And then he started off. And the dogs was tied to the bed where she was lying. On the way he met some witches. And he climbed a tree. And he started to holler,

Here come a Rangtang, Rangtang,
Come along.

And then the witches started to cut the tree down. And he said,

Here come a Rangtang, Rangtang,
Come along.

And then the witches had the tree just about down. And then he called the dogs again,

Here come a Rangtang, Rangtang,
Come along.

And then the witches just about had the tree down. And the dogs started to bark. And the old lady got up and turned them loose.

And then the dogs they started where the boy was. And 'bout the time the witches got the tree cut down good, the dogs was there. And then the boy told them to arm the witches (to cut their arm off). So the dogs armed them. And then he said, "Leg 'em." And the dogs legged them. And then the boy got on out the tree and he searched them. And then the boy told the dogs to neck 'em. And so they cut their necks off. And then the boy was rich after he got the witches' money.

And then I stepped on some tin and the tin bend, and about that time I skated on away from there.

126 The Mermaid

Astonishingly, this firm tradition, for which I have eight good variants, has not previously been reported. Puckett says categorically that he has seldom found a belief in mermaids among Southern Negroes (137). Parsons, Sea Islands, no. 156, pp. 137-138, "The Mermaid," and Johnson, no. 13, pp. 148-150, "The Mermaid," belong to a quite separate cante-fable type. Beckwith, Jamaica, no. 111, p. 147, "The Boy and the Mermaid," contains one element of the American Negro legend, the question asked the human by the mermaid whether he eats fish (and also in this case meat). Baughman for Motif B81.2, "Mermaid marries man" finds only one example, from Vance Randolph, The Devil's Pretty Daughter, pp. 9-11, but this is an entirely different story. He gives one reference from Shropshire for Motif B81.13.4, "Mermaid gives mortals gold from sea bottom," a trait that occurs incidentally in just one of my texts. Baughman's only other mermaid motif to appear in my versions is B81.9.1, "Mermaid's hair reaches her waist" for which he has one English reference. My texts come from Silas Altheimer, Tobe Courtney, Sarah Hall, Sarah Jackson, Adelle Leonard, Mary Richardson, Mrs. E. L. Smith, and J. D. Suggs. Altheimer's text is printed in Pine Bluff, *pp. 73-74, and Mary Richardson's in* Midwest Folklore, *VI (1956), no. 19, pp. 17-18.*

a (J. D. SUGGS)

Before they had any steam, ships were sailing by sails, you know, across the Atlantic. The Atlantic was fifteen miles deep, and there were mermaids in those days. And if you called anybody's name on the ship, they would ax for it, "Give it to me." And if you didn't give it to them they would capsize the ship. So the captain had to change the men's names to different objects

—hatchet, ax, hammer, furniture. Whenever he wanted a man to do something, he had to call him, "Hammer, go on deck and look out." The mermaid would holler, "Give me hammer." So they throwed the hammer overboard to her, and the vessel would proceed on. The captain might say, "Ax, you go on down in the kindling room start a fire in the boiler; it's going dead." Then the mermaid says, "Give me ax." So they have to throw her an iron ax. Next day he says, "Suit of furniture, go down in the stateroom and make up those beds." And the mermaid yells, "Give me a suit of furniture." So they had to throw a whole suit of furniture overboard.

One day he made a mistake and forgot and said, "Sam, go in the kitchen and cook supper." The mermaid right away calls, "Give me Sam." They didn't have anything on die ship that was named Sam; so they had to throw Sam overboard. Soon as Sam hit the water she grabbed him. Her hair was so long she could wrap him up—he didn't even get wet. And she's swimming so fast he could catch breath under the water. When she gets home she goes in, unwraps Sam out of her hair, says: "Oooh, you sure do look nice. Do you like fish?" Sam says, "No, I won't even cook a fish." "Well, we'll get married." So they were married.

After a while Sam begin to step out with other mermaids. His girl friend became jealous of him and his wife, and they had a fight over Sam. The wife whipped her, and told her, "You can't see Sam never again." She says, "I'll get even with you." So one day Sam's girl friends asked him, didn't he want to go back to his native home. He says yes. So she grabs him, wraps him in her hair, and swum the same fastness as his wife did when she was carrying him, so he could catch breath. When she come to land she put him onto the ground, on the bank. "Now if he can't do me no good he sure won't do her none." That was Sam's experience in the mermaid's home in the bottom of the sea.

Then he told the others how nice her home was, all fixed up with the furniture and other things. There weren't any men down there—guess that's why they ain't any mermaids any more. Sam said they had purple lips, just like women are painted today. You see pictures of mermaids with lips like that. In old days people didn't wear lipstick, and I think they got the idea from seeing those pictures.

Sam told the people the mermaid's house was built like the alligator's. He digs in the bank at water level; then he goes up—nature teaches him how high to go—then digs down to water level again, and there he makes his home, in rooms ten to twenty feet long. The mermaid builds in the wall of the sea like the alligator. Sam stayed down there six years. If he hadn't got to co'ting he'd a been there yet, I guess.

b (MRS. E. L. SMITH)

My mother told us about the mermaid. If it's a story somebody was putting it out, we believed it for the truth.

The mermaids had different booths they stayed in. They'd go out and meet the ship and call for people by name. This one mermaid called for Aleck. And he was a colored man. So they knew the time was coming, or she'd wreck the ship. So they threw Aleck out, and she put her hair right over his face and carried him to her little booth. And she had everything in there he wanted to eat—beef, fruits. And she had rocks fixed for him to cook on, but she ate everything raw. She combed her hair all day and sang.

The water passed by and never came in. She'd set up on the bank and her tail was in the water. It was a blindfold of water. There was a bank for him to sit on. Every day she would ask him, "Aleck, do you like fish?" And he would say "No." They teach you to say that on the ships. They know that if she don't bring the man back in six months she done killed him. At the end of six months she says, "Aleck your ship is coming." And she'd pick him up and carry him on up, and ask for another one. And she'd ask for flour and meat, just as plain.

I don't see why they don't hear 'em now, or how they don't get those little raft boats after 'em. Maybe they do. Funny there wasn't no men there, just women.

Mother seed Aleck. He lived in Aberdeen, Mississippi. I seed a mermaid in Ringling Brothers Show.

c (SARAH "AUNT JIM" JACKSON)

Place not far from my home town, on the river bank— the Alabama River—they used to see the mermaid. When the boats was running on the Alabama River, steamboats would bring up groceries from Mobile to the farmers: caraway syrup, flour, sugar, rice. The boat came up to the wharf, and a fellow on the boat working there, a cabin-boy, saw the mermaid out in the water and laughed at her. From her navel up is a lady, down is a fish tail. She's got long hair.

He was on the flatform carrying the groceries to the wharf, and she slapped him with her tail and knocked him into the water. Then she took her hair and wrapped his face in it, so he wouldn't get drowned [gesture], and took him about half a mile downstream to her mermaid home. He stayed there eight or nine years. People claim he got sick down there. Everything they give him he just vomit, vomit, so they took him up to the land, wrapped in their hair, and left him on the bank. Then the mermaid riz up in the water, to see if he was sick enough to die. But he jumped up and run, and the mermaid couldn't follow him, 'cause she was to walk on her hands.

The people didn't know him 'cause he was so hairy. He didn't have on no clothes. But he knew them. He shaved up and got natural; he favored himself. But he looked like some kind of animal before. He nearly died in that desert down there.

I knew where that mermaid hole was. They had pretty stools for them to sit on. It's a place about as big as the gable end of this house, but you can't see it because it's dark as midnight. It's by the bank. And they lay their backs on the stools, and play around, and when they see people come they slide down into the water. It's the best kind of water, spring water.

You can paddle your skiff boat right into the hole; the water runs into the hole. But everybody's afraid to go in.

THE LORD AND THE DEVIL

For matters dark and mysterious the Southern Negro refers continuously to the Bible, his major reference work, and perhaps even his whole library. He may also own and consult the Seventh Book of Moses, the so-called Black Bible, as did the Reverend Lee, who quoted from it in a barbershop in Mound Bayou, Mississippi. "You taken an egg, handle it a thousand times, write certain Scriptures from the psalm of David on it, work it down to the size of a pea and swallow it, and then you can remember anything, cure people and work wonders." But the orthodox Bible contains sufficient allusion to miracles, ghosts, devilment, and providences to satisfy the average person.

Scripture serves to explain marvels, to censor the unrighteous, to illustrate a moral. References follow a highly selective thread, for the Southern Negro quotes not the abstract aphorisms of the Book of Proverbs or the epistles of Paul, but the concrete and vivid human scenes in the Gospels and Genesis and Exodus. A collector too far removed from the Word finds himself somewhat discomfited by these continual allusions, which his informants regard as common knowledge, and his embarrassment increases still more if he cannot distinguish between the Bible of the Church and the Bible of the folk. For the sacred tales he hears, while employing familiar characters, are apt to be apocryphal or revamped. At prayer meetings, revivals, and Sunday services, which they follow with fervent and active attention, Southern Negroes hear dramatic repetitions of Biblical episodes that permanently capture their imaginations. (Hearing me speak about the enthusiasm at a Baptist revival I had attended in Arkansas, Mr. and Mrs. Richardson remarked how "backward" and lacking in "the spirit" people were up North.) The oral folktales caught and crystallized in the Old and New Testaments are released and circulated again by devout Negro storytellers.

Scriptural scenes are thus retold with the freedom and flexibility of folk tradition. Occasionally Christian and Negro motifs mingle, in what the anthropologists name reinterpretation. Suggs calls the story of Moses in

Pharaoh's court, "How Hoodoo Lost His Hand," conceiving of the court sorcerers as hoodoo practitioners. The oft-repeated legend of why the Jews don't eat hog, Suggs told in two ways, and recognized the divergence between the Book and the folk. Some Biblical folktales enjoy as wide a currency as any secular tale, particularly how the Devil coined the word "Mhm," St. Peter and the stone that changed to bread, and God's punishment of the dog. These isolated episodes never combine into a connected sequence, as the reader of Stoney and Shelby's *Black Genesis* or the spectator at Marc Connelly's *Green Pastures* might conclude; they stand independent and unrelated, save for their common background of Christian myth. Their folk appeal lies largely in the portraits of the Devil as trickster and Christ as a master magician.

The moralistic folktale differs from the Biblical legend in applying the lessons in Scripture to contemporary events. It serves notice that the just wrath of God still operates to chastise wrongdoers who blaspheme or desecrate the Sabbath. The Puritans recounted many comparable judgments in their day, calling them "providences." One evening Mr. and Mrs. Smith reeled off between them seven judgments visited on Sabbath-breakers of their personal acquaintance, with the conviction of any colonial divine.

127 *Mangelizing* (J. D. SUGGS)

Motifs K1811, "Gods (saints) in disguise visit mortals," and Q1.1, "Gods (saints) in disguise reward hospitality and punish inhospitality" provide abundant references.

When the angels from heaven came down to earth, they could walk around and look just like men—that was called mangelizing. They might knock on your door; you see an old man; he asks you for something to eat. You tell your wife to cook something, and ask him in. He says No, he'll stay outside. You bring it to him, he hits what you bring him with his staff, and it smokes and goes up to heaven—just like priests send up incense with a prayer. When he hits with the staff, he turns to smoke too, and when you look back at him, he isn't there. For you being so kind, he is sending a blessing up to heaven. He always comes as an old, feeble man, never as a young man. When Christ came they did away with those burnt offerings.

After that other angels came down, who had never been to earth before. When they seen the daughters of men were so good-looking they wouldn't go back to heaven. They stayed down and became mighty men, giants in the world. And the children they bore came to be mighty men and giants in the world. These children were wicked and paid no attention to the Lord, and the world became wicked.

Norah was the only pure blood, from Adam and Eve, Norah and his wife and son. And then Norah began to preach and tell them there was going to come a flood, and he starts to build a ark. It had never rained before and they thought he was just talking foolishness. And so they were marrying and giving in marriage until Norah built the ark and closed up the door. And when the flood came up they'd go on the next floor and dance, and ask him to let them in. But he wouldn't. Then the flood destroyed them all, and nobody's ever had any angel blood since. Every human on earth that had any angel blood in him was drowned.

128 *How Hoodoo Lost His Hand* (J. D. SUGGS)

Suggs here supplies familiar Negro conjure terms, the "hoodoo" magician, and the "hand" that gives him power, to the Old Testament story of Moses in Pharaoh's court (Exodus, chs. 7-10). Roark Bradford presents a similar treatment in chs. 13 and 14 of Ol' Man Adam an' His Chillun (New York, 1928).

The Israelites was captured and carried down in bondage under Egypt. And Moses was born there. And they was killing all males, to keep the Hebrew children from multiplying so fast. And when Moses was born his mother kept, him hid three months. Then when she could keep him hid no longer, she made a basket of bulrushes and slime. And so she carried him down and put him in the river, where Pharaoh's daughters went down to bathe. When they seen him he was a fine Egyptian boy. Then the daughter carried him to the King, Pharaoh, and begged her daddy to let her keep him and 'dopt him. So he agreed. "Go out and find you a nurse, an Israelite woman, for they'd know how to take care of this baby." So she goes out and hires an Israelite woman, who was his mother.

So he waxed and grewed fast, and learned all the Egyptian words and languages. So Pharaoh made him a ruler then, when he seed how smart he was. So one day he walks out and he sees a Hebrew and a Egyptian fighting. So he killed this Egyptian, looked all around and seed nobody, and buried him in the sand. A couple of days after he went out and he seed two Hebrews fighting. He said, "Why do you all strive against one another, and you'se brothers?" One said, "You want to kill one of us like you did that Egyptian the other day?"

So Moses got scared and run away into Middin. He stayed there forty years and married this Ethiopian woman (which is a colored woman). One day he was out minding his father-in-law's sheep, and the Lord spoke unto Moses and said, "Pull off your shoes, for you is on holy ground. I want you to go back and deliver my children from Egypt." He said, "Moses, what is that you got in your hand?" Moses said, "It's a staff." He said, "Cast it on the ground." And it turned to a snake. And Moses fleed from it. The Lord said, "Go back and pick it up." So Moses picked it up, and it turned back to a staff. The Lord said, "Go back and wrought all these miracles in Egypt and deliver my children from bondage."

So Moses goes on back. He goes in to Pharaoh and told him what the Lord had told him to do. Pharaoh said, "Who is he?" "I can show you what He got power to do." And he cast his rod on the floor, and it turned into a serpent. Pharaoh said, "That ain't nothing. I got a magikin can do that." So he brought his magikins and soothsayers in, and they cast their rods on the floor. So theirs turned to snakes. And they crawled up to Moses' snake, and Moses' snake swallowed up their snake. And that's where hoodoo lost his hand, because theirs was the evil power and his was the good. They lost their rods, and he had his and theirs too.

129 St. Peter and the Stone (J. D. SUGGS)

See Hurston, Mules and Men, pp. 45-46, "How the Church Came To Be Split Up." Other variants were given me by Amos Cross, Iola Palmer, Mary Richardson, and Beulah Tate. Roark Bradford (see note above) tells a tale on "Nigger Deemus" in ch. 32.

Christ was traveling from Jerusalem to Bethlehem. Christ, knowing all things, knew the twelve disciples was getting hungry, though they didn't say a word. He just wanted to see what they would do. So he says, "All of you get a stone." Eleven of 'em stooped down and got a great big stone. Peter he picked up a little bitta one. Christ blessed the stone and said, "Be thou bread." And the stone turned to bread. Well, they all ate, and everybody was full but Peter.

That was about noon. And they traveled on till they got near to Nazareth. He says, "All of you get another stone." All of 'em got a little bitta stone. Peter got a great big one. Christ goes over to Peter, put his hand on the rock, and says, "Peter, upon this rock I'll build my church." Peter says: "No you won't, Lord. You're going to turn this rock into bread—I'm hungry."

130 *How the Turtle Got His Form* (T. V. MINOTT)

This is a variant of Type 751, "The Greedy Peasant Woman." Several motifs impinge upon it: Q292.1, "Inhospitality to saint (god) punished"; A2231.1.4, "Discourteous answer: tortoise's shell"; A2215.3, "Bowl placed on turtle's back: hence his shell"; D193, "Transformation: man to tortoise (turtle)."

It was during the time of Christ and he had gone to the houses begging for morsels of food. The woman of the household was baking bread, and she told him to go away, that she had nothing to give him. So he made a second round, and visited her again. At that time she was taking the bread out of the oven, and it had raised almost to the top, and she had quite a time extricating it. (That's why the Jews don't eat bread today.) He told her that he was Christ, and that God loveth a cheerful giver. She was so ashamed of herself that she fell to the floor on her stomach, using the kneading bowl to cover her face. Then Christ remarked that from thence on "Thou shalt crawl on thy stomach." The floor was made of flagstones, and that's what showed the markings on the turtle's stomach today.

I heard that from the gypsies forty years ago.

131 *How the Peckerwood Came to Be* (J. D. SUGGS)

This is Type 751A, "The Greedy Peasant Woman." Its rhythmic form indicates adaptation by a Negro preacher elaborating on a gospel text. The relevant motif is D153.1, "Transformation: man to woodpecker." See The Frank C. Brown Collection, I, p. 633, "The Origin of the Woodpecker." The reference to "stovecakes" (also "ashcakes") baked on the hearth represents a localization from Southern Negro culture. Baughman has eight references for Type 751A in Anglo-American tradition.

You know how the peckerwood came to be? I learned this from Professor Green in grade school.[14]

Once when the good St. Peter,
Whilst traveling around the earth,
Lived in this world below,

He walked about here preaching,
Jest as He did you know.
He came to the door of a cottage
Where a little woman was baking cakes
In ashes on the hearth.
He axed her for a stovecake
To give him a single one.
She taken a tiny scrap of dough,
She rolled and rolled it flat,
She baked it as thin as a wafer,
But she could not part from that.
For she said, "My cakes that seem so small
Yet they are too large to give away."
So she put them on the shelf.
And then the good St. Peter grew angry
For he was hungry and faint,
And surely such a woman
Were enough to try a saint.
For he said, "You shall get your food
As the birds do, by boring and boring
All day in the hard dry wood."
Then up through the chimley she went,
Never speaking a word, and out the top
Flew a woodpecker, for she was changed to a bird.
All of her clothes was burnt black as a charcoal
And a scarlet cap on her head,
And this is the lesson she teaches—
Live not for yourself alone
For you may be changed to a smaller thing,
A mean and selfish man.
And every country schoolboy
Have seen her up until this very day
Boring and boring for food.

132 *Why the Jews Don't Eat Hog* (J. D. SUGGS)

Pertinent motifs are A2287.1, "Jesus drives evil spirits into hogs: hence short snouts" and A1681.2, "Why Jews do not eat pork." I have variants from Mrs. John Grant and Mary Richardson.

There are two ways they tell this. One is the Bible, the other a story people make on the Jew, you know.

(a) A fellow come to Christ who had the evil spirits on him; he was insane. When the demons were on him—there were seven demons who were evil spirits of the Devil—he would cut himself up and cast himself into the fire. But when he seed Christ coming, on his way to Jerusalem, he knew that he could do something for him. So he fell down on his knees to Christ and axed him, "Good Master, do something for me." And the Lord told the demon, "Be thou out of him." The evil spirit said, "If you cast me out, suffer me to go into that head of swine." There were about five hundred feeding on the seacoast; a nobleman (we calls them rich men now) raised them. The spirit knew he would be destroyed if he didn't get into something else. So Jesus suffered him then to enter the swine. And they ran into the sea and was destroyed.

So the people turned against Christ, because he had destroyed the nobleman's hogs. They figured that that tormented and insane man was worth less than those hogs. Then that same devil entered into the nobleman. So Christ passed out of Jerusalem—he couldn't do no more good.

The Jews wouldn't eat hog no more. They knew devils were in swine. A hog could eat my corn and go across into that man's field and eat his, and make us fall out.

(b) Once Christ was traveling. He could tell a man anything he wanted to know, what he had in his bam, anything at all. So he came into a Jew's house. He told the people they could ask any question, like what was under a pot, and he didn't have to see it, but he could tell them what was under there. So one of 'em takes him in the house and was holding a conversation, while the Jew told his wife, "Slip out there and put our baby under the wash pot and then turn it down bottom upwards, so no one can see it." So he brings Christ out, and ax him, "You can guess everything, now what's under this pot?" Christ said, "It's a hog." Jew says, "No, it's a baby." The people begin to laugh and say, "We knowed you couldn't tell nothing. That's our little baby under that pot." Christ told him, "Set the pot up on its legs, the right side." And there was a hog in it instead of a baby. The Jew said, "I'll never eat no more hog."

He believes the hog will turn into a baby. Jews won't use lard or anything mat comes from a hog, in any way, shape, or fashion.

133 *Zacharias and the Sycamore Tree* (J. D. SUGGS)

See Botkin, Burden, pp. 13-14, "Nicodemus and the Sycamore Tree" for a variant.

Christ was on his way to Damascus. He was riding upon an ass. And the peoples around was all crowding to see Christ. Zacharias he was a low-statured man, nearly like a dwarf, so he goes up a sycamore tree (he could climb pretty good), so he could get a good view of Christ when he come along. No one seen him go up there. When Christ got along under the tree he looked up. Zacharias didn't know Christ knew his name or that he was up the tree—he'd never met him. But Christ told him: "Come down, Zacharias; you're too high. I'm going home with you and have dinner." And Zacharias come down in such a haste he skinned all the bark off a the tree. Now that's the reason a sycamore ain't got any hard bark like any other tree. It's just as slick as it can be.

134 *God Names the Dog* (TOMMY CARTER)

The closest motif here is A2231.1.1, "Discourteous answer: why cow (horse) is always eating." I have a variant from Walter Winfrey.

All the animals in the forest were holding a meeting. God was going to bless 'em all. At two meetings they'd had, the rabbit and the deer were always there first getting their little blessing. Every time the dog would git there, they'd done give away all the blessings. This one was set for Sunday at two o'clock and all of them was supposed to be there, and the fowls too. So the old hound dog taken out that Sunday, going with the crowd, and along the road he found a bone. He stopped, picked up the bone, and taken it in to the meeting. God blessed the deer to run fast, and the rabbit too. Then he looked over where the dog was just chewing on the bone, making a lot of noise. "For your disobedience I should name you a dog. And you should chew bones for the rest of your days."

This time the dog said to God: "You been giving out blessings all the time and I ain't got nothing. I don't give a damn about what you had in store for me. I'm going to eat this bone, and damn the rest."

135 *Samson and the Anvil* (J. D. SUGGS)

Baughman gives four references under Motif K18.1.2, "Throwing contest: trickster addresses Angel Gabriel or St. Peter, warns him to get out of way of missile trickster is about to throw." Three are Negro, one is white. South Carolina Folk Tales, *pp. 80-81, has for protagonists "Golias and the Devil." See also my notes to "The Fight," ante, tale 38.*

Samson was down to the blacksmith's shop. The blacksmith was showing him how hard his muscle was. Said he would throw his hammer seventy-five miles, and it would ring when it hit the object (like a shooting gallery). He throwed it, and it went b-a-n-g, b-a-n-g. So the anvil it weighs two hundred and fifty pounds. And Samson just reached down and grabbed the anvil and swinged it round his head, and yelled, "Look out, people five hundred miles from here; come an anvil."

So the blacksmith grabbed his arm and said, "Look Samson, don't throw my anvil away—that's all I got to make a living."

136 How the Devil Kept the Soul (MRS. JOHN GRANT)

See Hurston, Mules and Men, *pp. 204-205, "How the Devil Coined a Word." Variants were told me by Silas Altheimer, Nannie Demby, Al Simmons, Mrs. Smith, and Suggs.*

When God first created the earth, they said the Devil was loose down on earth, walking around and catching souls. He caught so many he had his both arms full, and one in his mouth. And he passed where a lady was washing, and she asked him, "Mr. Devil, are you coming back tomorrow?" And he says, "Yes." So he lost the soul he had in his mouth, and came back with only two. Then he studied a plan to hold the soul that he carried in his mouth. He put a stick in his mouth, and had the little devil ask him, "Mr. Devil, are you coming back tomorrow?" And he practiced saying the word Mhm. When he went the next day, he caught three souls, and passed the lady washing again. And she asked him, "Mr. Devil, are you coming back tomorrow?" He said, "Mhm." So he saved that soul.

That's where the word *Mhm* come from.

137 Seeing the Devil in Three Shapes (MARY RICHARDSON)

Puckett, pp. 550-552, discusses "Negro devil-forms," including the Devil as dog (p. 542). Cf. Barbara A. Woods, The Devil in Dog Form, a Partial Type-Index of Devil Legends (*Berkeley and Los Angeles, 1959*).

The Devil don't never sleep on his rights; he's always busy, trying to gain souls, trying to beat Jesus. I've heard lots of stories on the Devil.

I saw the Devil when I was praying to get religion. He struck my track, and ran me in the field. He looked just like an old hound dog. I was walking along the road, at night, and I heard the dog on my track barking, "Oooh." There was a man behind him telling him, "Heee." So I run into an old rotten house to keep him from ketching me. It was dilapidated, and the back door had creeled over. The front door was still standing up, and I run in that. And I saw him in there. He looked like a little old dark man, sitting on a sawed off block of wood. He was sitting by some bread he'd cooked; it looked as if it had been cooked in dishwater, it was so dingy and dirty. He asked me, "Are you hungry?" And I told him, "No, not so much." But I was afraid not to eat it. He cut it open and filled it full of butter and spread it on a plate. It tasted bitter as gall—that's the truth.

I put the plate on the table and tiptoed out the kitchen door. It looked like it was fixing to fall down, but I stooped where it was felled, and got through. The hound got on my track again; he knew I had come through the house. He chased me until I run into a green pasture lit up, like with electric lights. And he didn't come in there; when I stopped in the light, he stayed on the dark side.

The Devil's got a pack of hounds and he'll chase you. He took three shapes; he was the man and the dog on my tracks, and the little old man inside the house—all three were the Devil. I thought he run me because I didn't eat the bread he buttered for me. Why he struck my track to run me in there I don't know, 'cept that was just before I got converted.

The Bible tells me the Devil can kill you. He won't have anything to do with anything that's clean or nice or white. I ain't never seed no rot like in that house! Holes in the top, sides caving in—I don't see how he stayed in there, and it didn't rain or snow on him. The man in the house and the man with the dog were both colored. White folks say the colored are the Devil, because they're black, and black is dirty, mean, sinful, wicked. But it's not your skin that counts; it's your heart.

138 *Ben Weatherby Curses God* (J. D. SUGGS)

Motif Q221.3, "Blasphemy punished," applies here. Plentiful instances of "remarkable providences" in seventeenth-century America testify to the swift vengeance visited on the impious; see the section "Judgments" in Dorson, America Begins *(New York, 1966), pp. 124-146.*

When I was fifteen years old, living in Sallis Station, down in Mississippi, I went a-hunting with the boys. The dogs treed a coon, and we were following the dogs, when we come to a fallen tree. The whitegum trees when they fall stick up five or six feet high. It was dark, and we had just a lantern. William Russian had the lantern; so he gets on the log and jumps off first. Then Ben Weather-by jumped off, into the darkness, and he knocked his head against another tree, and knocked himself unconscious. When he regained consciousness, he commenced calling the Lord and the Devil, "Oh, Lord, oh, Devil, oh, Lord, oh, Devil." He thought he was going to die, and he wanted to make sure he'd have a friend wherever he was going. In a little while his head quit hurting and he said, "Oh, ain't neither one of you no good."

He used to cuss out God all the time. When it'd be too wet to plow, he'd cuss him for making it rain.

About six months after the coon hunt, he drowned during a spring flood of the Big Black River. He was in a boat with his brother, rowing back from feeding the hogs, and the cloudburst came. The boat flipped over in a whirlpool, and Ben went down. His brother, who was a good Christian and didn't never cuss God, he was pitched over to a tree, and hung on, with his back touching the water, till a white fellow swam a mile and a half for a boat and rescued him. The whole town was out there watching.

139 Hunting Possum on Sunday (MARY RICHARDSON)

Baughman under Motif Q223.6.2*, "Person is punished for hunting on Sunday" gives two Negro, two English, and one North Carolina white example.

There was a man had a habit of going hunting every night. He went Monday night, Tuesday night, Wednesday night, Thursday night, Friday night, Saturday night, and Sunday night too he went to hunting. So the dogs treed a possum one Sunday night. He shot the possum and it fell out the tree on the ground. The possum got up like a woman, and begin to talk to him. The huntsman got scared, and started to run. So the woman told the

249

huntsman, "You hunt e-very night." And he was running as fast as he could, and the woman kept walking along by his side. And the man says, "I sure is tired." The possum says, "I am too." And he says, "I'll be glad when I git to the house." And the possum says, "And so will I." When he got to the house he fell against the door. His wife opened the door and he told her, "No more hunting for me."

He didn't never go a-hunting again. He got home safe by his wife opening the door for him, but that hunt scared him out the woods.

140 *The White Quail* (E. L. SMITH)

Another instance of Motif Q223.6.2*, "Person is punished for hunting on Sunday." White as a symbolic color is cited under Motif Z132. Henry Nash Smith points out the symbolism of whiteness attached to the legendary White Steed of the prairies, and to Melville's white whale, in Virgin Land *(Cambridge, 1950), p. 79.*

Down in Georgia I worked together every day with a fellow, Walt Howard, for the same white man. Howard used to net quail for his boss. By netting the quail he'd catch them so they weren't bruised or hurt. The net is made out of fishing cord, and stakes crooked over hold the middle part up, about a foot off the ground. When the quail comes to your net, he won't fly over it, as long as you don't get off your mule, and he runs right down underneath the net till he gets to the end, which is closed up in kind of a chute. So all you have to do is pull up your stakes and fold the net together, and the quails' heads will be sticking out. Then you just take your thumb nail and press down tight on top of the bird's head, stick it through his brains, and kill him.

Walt's boss, Lee Callaway, told him about a white quail he'd seen, and promised Walt five dollars if he would go down to his place and catch him. Walt went down on Sunday during Christmas, and found the quail in the cornfield on the creek. He put his net down, went back on his mule to where he'd found the white quail, and drove him back to the net, along with the other quails in the bunch. This white one ran into the net first, and Walt was so glad to get him he jumped down from the mule and made all the rest fly. Then he brought him to the house, and his boss gave him the five dollars. Lee Callaway sent it to a neighbor of his, who was a big shot politician in Washington.

After Christmas that winter Walt took sick. He was lying in the bed, and the white quail 'peared out before him, and told him to "Catch me now." He turned over and laid on his other side. And this quail 'peared over on that side, and told him to "Catch me now." And after that, you couldn't get him to hunt no more on a Sunday. That broke him up hunting on a Sunday.

That's as true, as real as I'm sitting here.

141 Simon Fishing on Sunday (J. D. SUGGS)

Three Negro and two white references are given to this cante fable by Baughman under Motif Q2236.3*, "Punishment for fishing on Sunday." See also the Southern Workman, *v. 26, no. 11 (Nov. 1897), pp. 229-230, "Fish Stories," for two variants; and Talley, p. 177, "Fishing Simon" In* South Carolina Folk Tales, *pp. 106-107, "Fishing on Sunday" a voice speaking out of a bubble in the water thoroughly frightens the fisherman.*

Simon'd fish every day in the week and on Sunday. They'd been after him about that—"You shouldn't fish on Sunday." He said, "Oh, ain't nothing to that." So Simon digs him some worms, gets his pole and goes down to the lake. Baits his hook and throws it in the water. The fish grabbed it time it hit the water. Simon said, "I bet this is a big one." So the fish said,

 Pull me up, Simon. (*Whiny singsong*)
So Simon pulled him up. Said,
 Take me off your hook now, Simon.
Simon taken him off his hook. Said,
 Now take me home, Simon.
Simon taken him home. Said,
 Now scale me, Simon.
Simon scales him. Said,
 Now cut me open, Simon.
Simon cuts him open. Said,
 Now put grease in the skillet, Simon.
Simon greased the skillet. Said,
 Now put me on, Simon.
Simon put him on the skillet. Said,
 Now take me up, Simon.
Simon took him up. Said,
 Now eat me up, Simon.

Simon ate him. Said,
  Now lay down, Simon.
So Simon lay down. Said,
  Now bust open, Simon.
So Simon busted open.

That's the reason lotsa people won't fish on Sunday, for fear they'd catch a fish like Simon. After my father told me that I wouldn't even pick up a fish on Sunday. When the rain flooded the pond you could just pick up a fish on t'other side the road. We cooked fish every day it rained. But Sunday we'd go to church. When other boys went fishing Dad would say, "They're just like Simon."

142 *The Devil's Daughter* (J. D. SUGGS)

Unlike the previous narratives in this chapter which are all told as having actually occurred, this is a Märchen, a fictional tale of magic and the supernatural, with the Devil playing a key role. This is Type 313A, "The Girl as Helper in the Hero's Flight," popular among Negroes in the South and the West Indies. Flowers lists thirty-nine variants, including African, on the basis of Parsons' twenty-three texts and full references in Antilles, *no. 172, pp. 153-164, "The Devil's Daughter and Magic Flight." Roberts has a version, no. 8, "Jack and the Giant's Tasks." Herbert Halpert includes seven United States Negro references in his note (p. 198) to Richard Chase's example of Type 313C, "Jack and King Marock,"* The Jack Tales, *no. 15, pp. 135-150, and adds another in his note, pp. 169-170, to Randolph's title story,* The Devil's Pretty Daughter. *Andrew Lang discusses the worldwide appearance of the tale in* Custom *and* Myth (*London, 1901*), *pp. 87-102. I also have texts from Idell Moore, Mary Richardson, and Evelyn Thompson. Under Motif G530.2, "Help from ogre's daughter (or son)," Thompson refers to his own* Tales of the North American Indians (*Cambridge, 1929*), *325 n. 171, for numerous Indian examples. One of the main motifs in this tale, D672, "Obstacle flight," is found throughout folk literature.*

Fellow was going out to hunt for a job. And he was hunting the Devil, to get a job with him. At this particular time there were no shipping points to get your ticket at; so you had to go to this old lady to be shipped out on the eagle. She would tell you how many pounds of meat it would cost you to ship out on the eagle to see the Devil. So he goes to her, and she told him it would cost him four quarters of beef. Every time the eagle hollered he was to give it a quarter of the beef. She put him on the eagle, and it took off from the ground, rose and flew in the air. When the eagle had flown about one thousand miles he hollered. Fellow twisted his neck back and reaches in his sack and takes out one quarter of beef and gives it to him. Next one thousand he hollers, fellow gets another quarter of beef. Next one thousand eagle hollered again, he gives him another quarter. Eagle don't holler any more; he flies about another one thousand miles and then he lights. The fellow unmounts.

There's a lady standing on the ground. He says to her, "I'm looking for Mr. Devil; I'm hunting a job with him." She says: "Oh, that's my father. He'll give you a job all right, but you cannot do it. I've known 'em to come here and try, but none ever left. He would kill 'em because they could none of them do the job he give 'em. But anything he asks you to do, you try— I'll help you out."

In a couple of hours the Devil showed up. She says, "Here's a gentleman looking for a job." He said, "All right, I'll give him a job. Your first job in the morning is to go down and clear one hundred acres of ground by noon —cut all the trees down, pile 'em, and burn 'em all by noon."

Fellow rose early the next morning before breakfast, goes out, and cuts till about ten o'clock. The Devil's daughter came to bring him a drink of water. He said, "Well it's about noon, and I've only got one tree cut down and trimmed up." She says, "Give me the ax; I'll fix that." She goes to a small tree, and says: "Why not chop one lick on one side of the tree and one on the other side. When one tree falls, all of 'em will fall." (She was talking to the ax.) "When I trim one limb, I trim 'em all. When I light one branch, I light 'em all." And she says, "When that one branch bums up, all of 'em are burnt up." Then the whole one hundred acres were cleared—all the logs were cut, all the branches were trimmed, wasn't nothing left on the land.

Then they go back to the house; it's noon. Devil said, "Did you get your job done?" Fellow says, "Yes, go look." He looked out the door—the one hundred acres was cleared; wasn't nothing standing on it; it was ready for planting. Devil said, "Well, that was good." (He didn't know his daughter was doing the work 'cause she done got stuck on the fellow.) "In the morning I want you to break it, and plant it, and bring a mess of roasting ears for dinner when you come in."

Fellow was up early in the morning. He caught his team, hitches up, he plows and plows until about 11:30. The Devil's daughter comes to bring him a drink of water. She says, "Oh, you haven't over half an acre broke. I'll fix that. Give me the plow. When I plow one furrow (she's talking to the plow now), I plow them all. When I harrow it one inch, I harrows it all. When I plants one grain, I plants it all. Com, up; com, knee-high; com, waist-high; corn, head-high; com, tassel; com, shoots; com, silk; com, roasting ears. Now pull a mess of roasting ears and we'll come to the house."

She knew that her father's next plan would be to kill her boy friend; he was too smart; there wasn't nothing more he could ask him to do. She said: "Suppose we marry. I've got two fast horses, and while Dad's asleep we'll get up and catch them and run away and marry." So at twelve o'clock they ease out the bed, catches the horses; then they mounts them. "We're going back to your land and home and get married," she tells him. And she says to the horses, "Run, horses, run; five hundred miles a jump."

When daylight came they were far away from her home. She looks back. "Oh, look, yon comes Dad, and he's bound to overtake us." The man says, "What shall we do?" She says: "I'll fix that, I'll turn into a lake, and I'll be a duck on the water swimming, and you'll be the man shooting at me." The Devil passed them up; he had his boots on then and was telling them, "Step, boots, step, five hundred miles a step." He wore those boots out, and he had to go back to get his bull—he could only go one hundred miles a step going back. She said, "Let's go—father's gone back after that bull." And so they let out, telling the horses to jump five hundred miles a jump—they were the fastest horses in the world. But the bull he was faster than the boots or the horses. So they knowed he was going to catch them then.

In four hours she looked back, and seed her daddy coming on the bull. He's telling him, "Jump, bull, jump; two thousand miles a jump." She says, "Look, yon comes dad again, he's riding on the bull." Fellow says, "Oh what shall we do now?" She says, "Reach me one of those thorns." He reaches out to the thombush and hands it to her. She says: "When I plant one thorn I plant it all. Thorns up; four feet high; eight feet high; ten feet high; fifteen feet high; ten feet wide; fifteen feet wide; forty feet wide; sixty feet wide; one hundred miles long" (plumb across the country). When the Devil run up to the thorns his bull couldn't go through them. He says, "I'll get through there; I'll run back and git my ax." He was four years cutting through. Then he couldn't find no trace of his daughter and horses. But the fellow and his daughter were safely married, and were living at the man's home.

---

[14] But it didn't come from a book, Suggs added.

WONDERS

Freaks and oddities of nature generated a storylore in the New World from the time the first explorers marveled at its bizarre flora and fauna. In the colonial period one heard of snakes who hypnotized their prey, bears who sucked their paws to keep alive during the winter, porcupines who threw their quills at their enemies, and lascivious eagles who consorted with she-wolves. Some of this lore of natural history has persisted down to modern times and bred widely repeated legends. Three of the best known, familiar to white and colored people alike, turn up in the present group. One deals with a snake whose life is mysteriously coupled with that of a baby, another with a bear who is handed a baby by mistake in the dark, and a third with a girl who swallows a lizard egg that hatches inside her.

These and other marvels of the animal kingdom, ranging over human monstrosities and potent remedies, are told for gospel by narrators sensitive to the mysteries and enigmas of the physical universe.

143 *Stinging Snakes* (MRS. E. L. SMITH)

The Frank C. Brown Collection, *I, p. 637, gives "The Poisoned Tree," involving a horned snake, and also "The Coach-Whip Snake" Baughman assigns Motif B765.10, to "Coachwhip snake," with six references, all from the south. Usually the hoop snake is credited with poisoning trees, ax-handles, or hoe-handles, in a popular cycle of American tall tales; see, for example, Vance Randolph,* We Always Lie To Strangers *(New York, 1951), pp. 132-135. John Lawson told of the horn snake striking and killing a small locust tree in North Carolina, as far back as 1709* (America Begins, *ed. R. M. Dorson, New York, 1966, p. 105). A discussion of rattlesnakes, hoop snakes and stinging snakes by Thomas D. Clark, "The Snake in Mississippi Folk-Lore," appears in* Specimens of Mississippi Folk-Lore, *ed. A. P. Hudson (Ann Arbor, Mich., 1928), pp. 141-144.*

Down in Okolona, Mississippi, I was driving a wagon and team that I had borrowed from some white people. I was between twelve and thirteen. It was a beautiful new wagon—had a blue bed, with a rack on it to make it taller, and two big red horses. I had been to church and was carrying [driving] it home. (Don't know why white people had so much confidence in me.) In a little, low, marshy, swampy ground was this snake, about as thick as my arm and as long as that table. A schoolteacher named Thomas Word standing there told me to drive past him because the snake was by the side of the road and could kill the horses. I drove past about seventy-five feet, and walked back. He struck the snake with a stick. And the snake hit a swee' gum [sweet gum] tree with his stinger. (Swee' gum grows all around those nut trees, like hickory and chestnut—they must be kinfolks. It's a slow-burning wood, kind of sobby like.) I returned the wagon and then come back fifteen or twenty minutes later, riding boss's horses back to his other farm. And the green tree was wizzered—the leaves had turned yellow and dry, dead. It died dead, never did come back to life. And the snake died too, his stinger in the tree.

A coach whip turns over and over and trips you up, and wraps around you and whips you with his tail, 'cause they's awful long—seven or eight feet. One tripped my mother once, but she got loose before he could wrap around. Men would travel with their pocket knives open, and cut them in two.

There is a poison snake that takes the poison out of its mouth with its tail and throws it at a person.

144 *Joint Snakes* (MRS. E. L. SMITH)

Baughman gives seven references, all Southern, for Motif B765.7, "Jointed snake can join its segments when it is broken into pieces," and see Puckett, p. 44, and Randolph, We Always Lie to Strangers, *pp. 131-132.*

When we lived in Okolona, Mississippi, my mother used to tell us of joint snakes, about as big as my thumb, and long as my arm. You hit them with a stick, and they raise up in the middle and uncouple. Then the head part hides but the tail part has to stay there. Before sundown the head part comes back and finds its other part, feels along till it finds the end, then backs up like a freight train, and the two ends raise up and couple in the air —they have a little coupling thing in them. And they come down in one piece. He's a little candy-colored snake.

145 *The Snake and the Baby*

This widely known European and American belief tale is Type 285, "The Child and the Snake"; Grimm no. 105, pt. 1, Motif B765.6, "Snake eats milk and bread with child" Randolph, "The Little Boy and the Snake" in Who Blowed Up the Church House?, *pp. 87-89, has a detailed note by Herbert Halpert, pp. 206-207, which includes five Southern Negro references. See also Botkin, Burden, p. 128 (in the narrative of Ellen Betts, from Louisiana). I have another text from Mary Richardson. Clark comments (see note to "Stinging Snakes" tale 143), "The old classic story of the little girl who was found sitting on a doorstep sharing her bowl of mush with a large king snake is well known in Mississippi." Butler Waugh has written a doctoral dissertation on "The Child and the Snake, a Comparative Folktale Study" (Indiana University, 1959).*

a (MRS. E. L. SMITH)

They told us this in Mississippi. This little girl, about five years old, would take her milk and bread, which was cornbread crumbed into buttermilk, and go behind the house, where this rattlesnake was denned, and she would call him, "Jimmy," and feed him. The parents had trespassed her doing something, and they followed her and seen her rubbing his head and feeding him the milk and bread. They told her the snake would bite her. And she said, No, it was her Jimmy. So they fooled her away from the house, and her daddy took a gun and shot the snake. And she ran down the hill crying, "Daddy shot my Jimmy." She caught hold of the snake before he died, and he bit her, 'cause he didn't know her, you see. And she died in five minutes.

A lot of people thought he shouldn't have done that, until he saw how it worked out, 'cause the snake hadn't done any harm. So he lost his child by killing the snake.

b (J. D. SUGGS)

This was a bottle baby. They carried the baby to the field with its bottle, in the crib under the shade tree. When they came back, if the baby was woke, all the milk would be gone, if it wasn't woke only half would be gone. The field wasn't far from the house. When it got so it could walk it would go out in the yard and carry its bottle out there. When it came in the house the bottle would be empty, wouldn't be a bit in it. Then from three years old she quit the bottle but she would take milk in a cup and would always go outdoors to eat, but nobody paid her no attention. And when she got five years old she went outdoors, and her Dad seen this big snake. And she was reaching out her hand for it. When he ran outdoors with his gun the snake turned and went crawling off. He kills the snake and three days after, the baby it died.

It was a white baby, in Shreveport, Louisiana, not far from the Arkansas line. My a'ntie told my father and them about it.

(Maybe like a lodestone draws from metal and flesh, there was something between the snake and the baby.)

c (MARY RICHARDSON)

I heard of a woman working in the field, and left her baby at the house. Down in the South. When she came back she found the snake in the crib with the baby. The snake was laying with the baby to lick its mouth, they decided; it liked the smell of breast milk. She killed the snake, and the baby got poor and sick and weak, and dried up—wasn't nothing they could do for it.

The snake had been coming there every day—they could see signs of it. It would crawl out and hide when he heard the mother walking on the porch. He'd crawl out the crib from the baby. Oh, the baby was about six or seven months old.

They must have been partners. The snake took up with the baby. They should have let them grow up together, until the baby outgrowed the snake.

146 A Snake's Tongue

Puckett, pp. 267-268, talks about ways of keeping one's lover faithful Drums and Shadows, p. 95, reports that women frequently use love powders "so dat dey kin rule duh men."

They say if a woman measures your peter with a piece of string, and ties it round her leg, you can't get no stake up at all, you can't get ready at all, with no other woman but her.

A fellow told me, an older man from Baton Rouge, Louisiana, that he would kill a forked snake and take out its tongue, its forked tongue, and carry that with him all the time in his pocket, wrapped up in a little piece of rag. Then when he was with a woman, he'd pretend he was looking for the place, and he'd rub it against her, and then no other man could get her. He'd get ready, but as soon as he'd try, he'd fade away, melt away.

Tell you why I believe that. Down in Shaw, Mississippi, before I was married, there was a young girl, Duck, had a boy friend who cut logs, but she promised to go with me. He was trying to get together, and couldn't when I lived in town, but when I moved to the country as a cook, I'd know when he was out of town, and would drive in on a Sunday. We tried for half a day, but as soon as I got on top it dropped right away. We stripped stark buck naked, but I never could do nothing. That's the only time I failed.

147 The Bear and the Baby (MRS. E. L. SMITH)

> Other variants are Botkin, Burden, p. 13, "The Brown Bear and the Pickaninny"; "Richard's Tales," pp. 238-240, "The Bear and the Baby"; and Roberts no. 89, "The Bear and the Baby."

This was in Mississippi too, out at Baldwin, where there used to be bears in the big woods. This woman was visiting some of her sick neighbors. A man was low sick, and she would go sit up there with his wife, to help wait on him. Then on the way back her own husband would meet her, to take the baby over the fence at night—it was a tall rail fence. She had to take the baby with her 'cause he hadn't got home from work. This night she got to the crook in the fence and handed it to him, and then started to climb over. She handed it to a bear. When she said, "Here, Sam, take the baby," the bear just reached out and taken the baby. (They call a bear Sam, you know.) By the time she got over the fence the bear had gone off follering the fence road, and she went straight on home, trying to catch up. She found the door shut; so she asked her husband, "Sam, why did you shut the door?" He said, "I didn't shut the door, because I been asleep." She said, "What did you do with the baby?" He said, "I never took the baby, I slept too late to meet you."

They were afraid to go out that night, but early next morning they told the neighbors and went out to search for the baby, and found the bear at the end of the fence road lying on his back in a pile of leaves playing with the baby. He hadn't eaten him—wasn't hongry—a bear won't harm a baby unless he's hongry.

So one man took an ax and hit him in the head. They didn't know much about a gun then. (It was over fifty years ago; I was eight or nine years old.)

Bears stand up on their hind legs just like a man. And if one peeps in here, he can tell if you're goodhearted. He'll let a woman get close to him, he knows she's scary, but he won't let a man come close.

148 *Girl Swallows Lizard* (MRS. E. L. SMITH)

Under Motif B765.5, "Snake crawls from sleeper's mouth," Flowers gives a reference from St. Croix. Puckett discusses the possibility of snakes and lizards living inside the stomach, p. 250, and gives references to Campbell's Popular Tales of the West Highlands *and Lean's* Collectanea.

In Oxford, Mississippi, back in the 1920's Arthur Palmer Hudson heard accounts from his doctor, E. S. Bramlett, a locally prominent physician and surgeon, of Negro patients who complained they were suffering from the effects of swallowing bullfrogs alive. Dr. Bramlett had to fake an operation and produce a live bullfrog to show the patient. Another time he treated an old woman for rheumatism, who stoutly declared that a mouse had gnawed its way into the "j'int" of her shoulder. To pacify her, he let her see a bloody mouse when she came from under the anesthetic. I am grateful to Professor Hudson for this information, which he alludes to in his anthology, Humor of the Old Deep South *(New York, 1926), p. 127. Note how this evidence tallies with that of Suggs, ante tale 84, "How a Hoodoo Doctor Works," save that here natural rather than magical causes explain the presence of animals inside the patient.*

A spring lizard he's kind of short, like a dark snake. This girl in Mississippi swallowed one drinking at the spring. And it growed inside of her, and got so large till they thought she'd got "in the wrong path." And back in those days they mistreated you for anything like that. Well her brother was coming out through the yard from the field and happened to see her lying on the ground, just taking an evening nap, 'cause she didn't feel so good at times. And he seed what looked like a snake come out'n her mouth, like to choke her stiff. And he rushed in and told her mother and family, and they come out and took her to the hospital, they say in Memphis, Tennessee. They was so ashamed of having 'bused and dogged her.

I heard folks tell an old snake was in one person, and had prongs, about four feet long, and they had to hold it and it twisted and fit whiles they was pulling it out.

149 *The Greasy Man* (J. D. SUGGS)

Over one hundred "Apparitions" are referred to in Drums and Shadows *but do not include the counterparts to the following two specters. Queer spectral forms are mentioned by Puckett, p. 128.*

This happened in Fasonia, Mississippi, a small river town on Sunflower River, in 1910.

Everybody seen a strange man in the winter. He'd be sitting in the chair in front of the fire. (You know they had big fireplaces in the South, with a back log that would give a glow all night.) A fellow would see him, reach up in the rack over the bed for his gun, wake his wife up, and the man'd be gone. Every week somebody would see him—they commenced to laying for him; they'd fall asleep, and see him when they woke up. They called him the Greasy Man, because nobody could ketch him.

Mary Gise was the first one ever seen him. She woke up and seen him lying in the bed. Boy, she squalled. Then he disappeared. Folks said she was fogy, but then others began to see it all through that section, for twenty-five to thirty miles around. He was always sitting by the hearth, in a cane chair, with his back to the bed. He'd never come to the same house, never bothered no one, never took nothing.

150 *The Flying Man* (J. D. SUGGS)

I heard about the flying man up in Arkansas, at Jones-boro. The polices went up to him, and the faster they walked the faster he walked, until he just spread his arms and sailed right on off. And they never did catch him. Said he was faster than the planes. They told about him all through the South, in Alabama, Mississippi, Arkansas.

151 *The Twelve Days after Christmas* (MRS. E. L. SMITH)

Under Motif B251.1.2.3, "Cows kneel in stable at midnight of Eve of Old Christmas" Baughman gives three references, all in white tradition. The Frank C. Brown Collection, *I, p. 637, has "The Cows on Christmas Eve," and refers to Thomas Hardy's poem, "The Oxen." Helen Creighton locates the belief in six southern and eastern states, in* Folklore of Lunenburg County, Nova Scotia *(Ottawa, 1950), no. 46, p. 18, note 4, "Oxen."*

On Christmas day start to count twelve days, and they will represent the twelve months. And the first day is January, and watch that day the way it changes up, and the month will change the same way. And write it down so you don't forget. And continue that for the twelve days. After the twelve days it will come back to be the regular months. If that Christmas day is pretty then you're going to have a nice January. They'll all be different; there's going to be twelve changeable days. When I was a little girl I've sit down and wrote on a tablet what happened all day. Then when the month came up I'd say, "Daddy, do such and such, because it's going to be rainy." Just this year I did that, and I said they were going to have a hard time haying. And it was raining so, lots of people lost their hay. It came 99 per cent true. You know just about what the year in front of you is going to be like.

Then on the twelfth day is Old Christmas day. That night at twelve o'clock the horses (they don't go by this fast time you know; they go by standard time, and that must be God's time), they gets on their knees and moans and groans and prays. Giving God's thanks I imagine. It was handed down from my parents. My mother would let us stay up till twelve that night, and then those of us that was old enough she and papa took down to the barn. And there were three mules in the barn, and two or three cows, and a heifer, and an old sow. They were all lying down. At twelve o'clock they got up on their knees and groaned—you know how an animal makes a noise. Yes, they was on their knees about two or three minutes I guess. And they was all groaning at the same time in their own language. The sow was just falling down, to lay down, when I seed her.

I was about ten or eleven when I first seed that. But I've seen it since I was growed up too. I carried these kiddies here over to see the barn, at twelve o'clock. A German woman, Mrs. Crawflin, told my mother about it when I was five. I think that's how these calendar people know; they've heard it around.

Now don't tell those people it's Michigan time; it must be sun time.

152 *Buzzard's Grease* (MARY RICHARDSON)

Puckett, p. 389, notes that "Buzzard's grease is said to cure smallpox."

They say you rub buzzard's grease on you and you'll be just as soople as a buzzard. I reckon it would be the way you'd stink. My sister's husband's mother got a farmer to kill her a buzzard, and she buried it for three days, and then dug it up and plucked the feathers off. She heard it was good for rheumatism. So she boiled the meat and took off the grease and put it in a bowl. And her son come in and thought it was bacon grease; so he took him some out of the bowl and sopped it in syrup and ate it. He throwed it all up.

Well, my sister's mother-in-law tried it, and said it was a pure cure. I been in mind to try it myself, if I could get some one to kill a buzzard. It was against the law in my state to kill a buzzard.

153 *The Black Cat Bone* (DOROTHY FOWLER)

Belief that a black cat can render the possessor invisible is mentioned in Drums and Shadows, *p. 58; Marion E. Harmon,* Negro Wit and Humor (*Louisville, Ky., 1914*), *pp. 105-106, "The Trick Bone of a Cat"; Hurston, "Hoodoo in America," p. 396 ("How to Get the Black Cat Bone"); Puckett, pp. 256-258, "The 'Black Cat Bone.' " LeRoy Bolden, the Negro football star from Flint, turned in to the Michigan State University Folklore Archives this item. "In order to gain luck with the devil, get a black cat, put it in boiling water alive, and cool it. Then you must suck every bone. When you come to the right one, you will become invisible." Powerful testimony to the "Black Cat Lucky Bone" is given in Hyatt nos. 9063-9072, 9527-9528. See also Hurston,* Mules and Men, *pp. 272-273.*

Someone told a man in St. Louis, "If you take a real black cat and cook him alive, and then after he is well done, till all the meat is cooked off his bones, and eat from each one of the bones, before you're finished there's a magic bone in there." And this man thought he had gotten the magic bone that is supposed to make you invisible. After he had eaten the cat bone at midnight, he looked in the mirror and couldn't see himself.

So then he decided to go in broad open daylight and rob a store. And while he was robbing the store, the groceryman told him to put his drygoods and money back. The robber said, "Oh, no, he can't see me, because I've eaten a black cat bone." The grocery man heard him and answered, "Oh, so you've got a black cat bone," and he got his shotgun and sprinkled him with little pellets. The robber ran out crying, "Oh, you mean you can see me! I thought I was invisible."

154 *Curing the Thrash* (J. D. SUGGS)

The same treatment is reported in Vance Randolph, The Ozarks *(New York, 1931), pp. 95-96, and* Ozark Superstitions *(New York, 1947), p. 136. A friend of mine, Reda O'Brian, told me that her father, Wick Howard, born in the Kentucky hills and since living in Stockbridge, Michigan, had gone out looking for a man who had never seen his father, or a woman who had married without changing her name, to blow in the mouth of his grandchild afflicted with thrash.*

Most doctors say the child doesn't have the thrash. When they're three or four or five months they have it—it's white bumps that breaks out in the mouth—they can't even suck the breast or the bottle, they can't draw with their tongue. My boy died of the pneumonia (at twenty-two months) had the thrash, and my cousin, M. C. Clark in Vandalia, cured him by blowing in his mouth. Any child that has never seen its father can cure that way. Clark's father died before he was born. He's only twenty-six years old, he was in World War II. He came over to my house; my daughter went over and asked him to blow in the baby's mouth.

HORRORS

When the folklore collector approaches an informant, he customarily steers the discussion along predetermined lines. Looking for Child Ballads and European wonder tales, he eventually finds them and enlarges the store of already well-known materials. But the folksinger and storyteller make no such distinctions in their repertories, and our prejudgment may cost us intriguing items that do not match the established categories. American Negroes (and whites) relate local traditions, family history, and personal experiences with as much gusto as any folktale—and sometimes these localized and personalized narratives prove to be folktales in disguise.

Naturally enough, Southern-born Negroes refer frequently to slavery times, and repeat the more startling occurrences told them by their parents and grandparents who lived during the "peculiar institution." On my first meeting with E. L. Smith he recited the superman adventures of his maternal grandfather, Romey Howard, in escaping from the patterollers and bloodhounds that pursued runaway slaves. These wonderful exploits sounded like fiction, but Mr. Smith told them for literal truth, having them firsthand from his grandfather, a self-made folk hero, who thwarted and rendered ridiculous the white oppressor. (See tale 167.) Katy Pointer began relating the escape of her father from slavery within five minutes of our acquaintance, and her familiarity with every detail of the harrowing flight revealed plainly enough how often she had listened to and later repeated the saga. Brutal and inhuman acts of slave masters still burn in the breasts of generations born to freedom, fanned by the bellows of tradition (not that all memories of slavery life rankle, but shocking events live longest in the folk mind). Emancipation failed of course to end the injustice of white man to black; as Saint Elmo Bland said softly, "It seems to me I've lived pretty close to slavery," and the intimidation of freedmen and their children formed new atrocity stories. One must not identify the realistic shocker with race bitterness, however; any sensational crime attracts the folk historian and, if he be Negro, he naturally finds most material in the inhumanity to his people. But Suggs and Mary Richardson also talk about the man who sold his wife for stew beef, the robber disguised as a woman, and the drunkard who stomped on his child. How much of these stoutly upheld accounts should the listener believe? The disguised robber whom Suggs places in the Mississippi Delta attempts an identical holdup in the Kentucky mountains. Let us simply say that these grim incidents are all told for true, and could have happened.

155 *Grandmother Whipped* (MARY RICHARDSON)

Cruel whippings of slavery times are rife in Negro tradition. See Lay My Burden Down, ed. B. A. Botkin (Chicago, 1945), esp. pp. 163 ff., "Praying to the Right Man."

That was way back yonder in old slavery times. I heard my grandparents talk about it—I wouldn't took all they took, I'd a took the grave. My grandmother was working in a field (in North Carolina). They grubbed up all the ground instead of plowing it, they dug it up with grub-hoes. And she couldn't keep her breath up, she couldn't keep up with the gang, because she was pregnant. (They ought a left her at home.) And Marster took her hoe and dug a hole in the ground and laid her face foremost in the hole, and whipped her with a cat-o'-nine tails (a piece of leather split in nine parts, and every time they hit they hit you nine times).

He dug the hole so he wouldn't lose his little nigger. He didn't want to damage her but he wanted her to keep up with the gang. But she couldn't keep up; they had to help her at each end.

156 *The Escape of John Bennett* (JAMES A. COKER)

An early collection of runaway slave experiences was published by Benjamin Drew in The Refugee: or the Narratives of Fugitive Slaves in Canada *(Boston, 1856). Purportedly "Related by Themselves," they read too smoothly.*

I've talked to lots of them ex-slaves. John Bennett, whose boy Ed lives in Calvin now, used to tell me how he escaped; he was half white, tall and freckled, and wore his hair long. A hostler boy, a roustabout, crossed and mixed too, had a little education. He forged his own press, printed free papers, and wrote the magistrate's name on them. Then he stole a riding horse and rode to Kelbyware, sold it there, 'cause he needed money, and set out walking to Ohio. He'd sleep in the daytime, and travel at night, following the North Star. One night he got a chicken, cooked and ate it, started on, and saw he wasn't very far from Ohio. So he stopped in a cornfield by a spring, started to eat an ear, when he heard a dog a-barking. He knew he was on his trail. He ran and dumb a tree about one-fourth a mile off, to get away from the bloodhound. A man came along with the dog and said, "Come on down." "Don't shoot me." "I won't, but if you run you'll bite lead." John had an old double-barreled pistol himself. They went back to the spring together. The man set the gun down by the tree to get a gourd for a drink, and John walked around and grabbed it, and shot him with his own gun, "Pow." Then he shot the dog.

Next day he saw a colored man walking along the banks of the Ohio. He spoke to Bennett and said, "I'm a free man; I'm helping you fellows across." He rowed him across to a little house, which was a station on the underground railway. About ten of the farmers came around and gave Bennett little presents. The colored man rowed down a ways, then cut back to the Kentucky side. When John Bennett said he had shot that slave-hunter, they all cheered—so John Bennett said.

They sent him up to the next station, about twenty miles north. He made his way to Philadelfy, worked there a while, saved $150, came to Michigan, and settled on that farm across the creek, Mr. Steele.[15]

He told me that settin' right there. He said, "I don't care who knows I killed a man."

157 *The Escape of Isaac Berry* (KATY POINTER)

My father was a slave, born in Kentucky. When his master died, his slaves were divided out among his children. My grandmother and all of her children fell to one of the girls, who married James Pratt from Missouri, and went there with her slaves, near St. Louie (they call it St. Louis now). My father, Isaac Berry, ran away when he was twenty-seven, in 1859.

This Jim Pratt was a poor man and a gambler, and he would hire out his slaves. But it was the understanding that Mrs. Pratt's slaves wasn't ever to be whipped. My father farmed with the other slaves; one of his sisters cooked in the big house, the other cooked for the slaves. They had to cut all the nice meat off the ham, and give the bones to the slaves—hog heads and things like that, hambone, and cornbread—it was hearty food of course. The white folks had biscuits, but not the slaves. I can remember my father telling this to illustrate how different our life was to his.

You would see your brothers or sisters put on the block and auctioned off, like a steer or a hog. My father said that when Mr. Pratt sold one of his brothers, Harvey, down the river, it hurt him so that he decided to run away if he could.

Someone had given my father a little colt, and Mrs. Pratt said he could raise it himself. It was a natural "racker"—that's the way horses were taught to run. (Everybody rode horseback down there.) Jim Pratt sold the racker to pay a gambling debt. Then Mrs. Pratt called my father aside and told him, "I'm afraid Mr. Pratt will sell you too one day, down the river, and if you can run away, and think you can get away, you have my permission to go."

My father was a great hunter, for deer and wild turkeys, and he sold them to a lady in St. Louis who kept a hotel. (Her name was Mrs. Tousey.) She gave him a dollar and a half for a deer saddle, and then the rest of the deer he took back to Jim Pratt's folks, to help feed the slaves, you know. That way he saved up money enough to buy his food when he ran away. He had a friend, Albert Campbell, a free colored youngster, in Quincy, Illinois, who arranged to help him get across the Mississippi River by boat.

A white man had taught my father to play on the violin. He'd play "The Devil's Dream" and things like that—the colored people was great for dancing—and often when he went to play at a dance he wouldn't be back until Monday morning early. And there was nothing said so long as he got back in time. So he told Jim Pratt he was going to play at the dance, and left the farm Saturday night. He got a colored man to ride with him to the place where Albert Campbell would meet him with the boat. When he reached the Mississippi, which was quite a ways from the farm, the water was so high over the bank the boat couldn't get to him though he could see their light, and they could see his light.

Isaac hid in the brush along the river, away from the landing, all Saturday night and Sunday, without anything to eat. Then a white man came along in a boat, with his wife and two children, a boy and a girl. They were coming down the Mississippi. My father told them that he was working in Quincy and had to get across, and offered them a five-dollar gold piece. (A lot of the money was gold then.) It was the wife who said, "Let's carry him across or he'll lose his job; we can wait for breakfast." He helped row the boat across to Quincy. They'd have set the bloodhounds after him, if he hadn't crossed the river.

He got on the railroad and started walking. There was a $500 reward for him dead or alive. (Someone left a newspaper on the seat on the train when my mother come later on and she seen it. Jim Pratt followed him too, clear to Detroit.) He came to a little country store and waited until kind of late, then pulled his hat down over his face, and went in and bought a loaf of bread and some cheese—or sometimes only crackers. You see he didn't know how he'd have to be saving of his money.

He walked along the tracks, and hid in the daylight. Only once in all the time did he step in the daylight to wash and shave in a little river, and two white men stopped and asked him where he was going and where he was from. He told them he was going to Michigan City, and that he would sell his life dear, though they was two against one. You see he was afraid; he'd been afraid all his life. He laid out his razor—it was a long blade with a handle—and his revolver. And they said they wasn't going to bother him.

He walked to Ypsilanti on the railroad. His shoes was all wore out, and his socks, and his feet got all swelled up, and his legs all swelled up. (You know sometimes when I think about it I want to cry, a human being getting treated that way.)

When he got to Ypsilanti he met a colored man going to work; he had his dinner pail with him. And he asked my father, "Are you a runaway slave?" And my father said, "It's none of your business what I am." He was wore out with people asking him questions. The other man said, "I can see from your shoes that you've come a long way. You see that house up the railroad a ways—that's where I live. You go there and tell my wife to give you breakfast, and then you go to bed and stay there till I come home; I'll be home at six o'clock." So he went on to the house, and the old lady took care of him, and he went to bed and slept all day—he said his feet and legs were so sore. He was walking three weeks. That night the house couldn't hold all the colored people that came there. And they gave him carpet slippers and socks, and took up a collection and gave him quite a lot of money. In the morning one old fellow took him down to the railroad and said, "You get a ticket for Detroit, and when you get there take a ferry to Canada, just about a mile across the lake, and then you'll be under the lion's paw."

When he got to Windsor he looked up Aunt Celia Flenoy, a little black woman who was Albert Campbell's aunt. She got him a room with a colored man, and he got work on the street, at fifty cents a day. "I'm a free man now," he said.

158 *The Prison Farm* (MARY RICHARDSON)

Paul Green's dramas, Hymn to the Rising Sun *and* Potter's Field *(Scene 4) give an unbearable picture of Southern Negro convicts in the chain gangs.*

They had a colored prisoner farm at Walter Clark's place, three miles out of Clarksdale, Mississippi. I was the cook's helper, and saw some of what went on. Every time a prisoner came they whipped him, called it 'nitiating him, to let him know where his whipping post was; and they whipped him again before he went out to work, picking cotton or cleaning up woods. Prisoners got twenty-five cents a day and board till their fine was paid. They'd give him an extra gift for his work, though. They would make him lay on his stomach crost a barrel, and some would hold his head and the others his feet. And the whipping boss, a white man, would whip him with a strap of leather with round holes cut in it, to make blisters on the skin.

I seen them whip one man to death. He was a slim, skinny man, and they whipped him 'cause he couldn't pick two hundred pounds—that was his task and he couldn't never get it. So they whipped him morning and night until he couldn't work at all, just lay in his cage. The prisoners all slept in one room with double-deck beds 'side the walls. He couldn't even get out of bed to get his food. The feeder wasn't allowed to unlock the door, and each man had to come and get his pan; so he'd leave the sick man's in the window. I'd take the bread and roll it up in a piece of paper and throw it to his bunk, like a puppy. They told me I'd get prison for life if they found that out.

He died and they buried him in the farm cemetery, just like he was; didn't wash or change him. 'Cause the hole was too short they stomped on him, mashed, tramped, bent him down in there, and threw dirt on him.

159 *Burning a Murderer* (J. D. SUGGS)

The epilogue here refers to the well-known Negro belief that a lucky "hand" will ensure success in gambling; see Puckett, pp. 210, 234, 283; on p. 524 he mentions the discovery of a human finger in a conjure bag.

When they were building the Yellow Dog railroad, in 1904, I was working on the extra gang, laying steel. The proper name was the Yazoo and Mississippi Valley—the Y and M V. It followed the Sunflower River landings; the river would veer around, and the railroad went straight, and towns would spring up at the landings. This was in the Mississippi Delta. Every payday, once a month, the extra gangs would have a spree; there were five thousand men working on the railroad for a hundred miles, and a train would bring them to a hopjoint run by three white brothers out in the woods. There was no town there at all; later it became Darlings in Yellow Buck County.[16] Two of these Clarke brothers were twins; one of the twins and the third brother stayed out at the hopjoint, and the other twin kept in Marks, the county seat.

For three days during the spree nobody worked. The Clarkes sold whiskey out there, had gambling and dancing, and brought in women from all about—Memphis, Jackson, New Orleans, Yazoo City, St. Louis. They had bush arbors under which the men gambled, and tents where they danced and slept. Lights were made out of small ropes twisted into beer bottles filled with kerosene. A torch like that would burn all night; just stick a pin in the top and it keeps the flame from blowing out. The railroad company had to let the gangs go to the hop-joint and spend their money, so they'd have to go back to work. (White men won't work in the South, or just long enough to get a bossing job.)

A colored fellow was tending bar, and after payday night he saw how much money the Clarkes had collected. He goes out to Crenshaw, north of Darlings, where he knew a white fellow by the name of John Bell. He told Bell the Clarkes had made a big batch of money and he knew where they kept it. They planned to go down to Darlings next Sunday and kill the two white men, and the bartender could prove he was in Crenshaw at home. Then he would discover them dead Monday and report it.

So John Bell and the colored man killed the brothers at night. The next morning the bartender went out in the woods to allow time enough for him to get back (supposedly) from Crenshaw. Then he come back and spread the news at Crenshaw. The sheriff followed him back down to Darlings. When they got in, both of the Clarkes was in bed with their bodies cut up with a butcher knife and their heads knocked in. The law noticed a spot of blood on the Negro's shoe, that he hadn't wiped off. (Blood is hard to get off.) So they arrested him, on suspicions. They questioned him about three hours that day. He broke down and confessed that he did it. They carried him back to Crenshaw, and he dug up the money where he had hid it. He had five thousand dollars, and the white fellow had six thousand.

So that goes like wildfire, you know, 'cause when anything happens in the country it spreads fast. The railroad men went up and down the line telling the extra gangs and picked them up and brought them back to the hopjoint where they had their good times.

I reckon over five thousand people was there when the law brought the fellow back. The white peoples of Crenshaw and Marks made Captain Carre superintendent, to hold the crowd back; he'd been a captain in the Spanish-American War. He was a great friend to the Clarkes, too. There wasn't any police, just the high sheriff from Marks with two deputies, and a couple of constables from Crenshaw. They deputized Captain Carre.

The burning took place right in the woods, among the big oaks and hickory. They cleared enough to put down the big tent and the little tents all around, tied to the trees with poles, and benches of planks were notched between the trees.

Then Captain Carre told the crowd: "You section men, the foremens, the straw bosses, take your gangs back. Just the citizens come around (the white people), because when a man gets burning he's liable to blame anybody, and a shooting might start. Put your guns down; if he tries to get loose I'll shoot him." Captain Carre turned to the colored man and said, "If you tell us who did it, we won't burn you." They knowed one man couldn't have killed both brothers with one lick. He said nobody had helped him.

So they drove four iron posts in the ground, and they chained his legs and arms both. He was a nice-looking brown-skinned fellow, about twenty-five. They wrapped him in the bedding and the wooden bed of the murdered men, and put enough coal oil on to start the burning slowly. The fire kept getting closer and hotter, and when the wind blew, it blew the fire in toward the man. (Just like in the story of the Bear meeting trouble.)[17] When it got high enough to reach above his head, then he said, "John Bell."

After the burning we came up and saw the bones and heart.

They went and got John Bell that night and he confessed, and they gave him life imprisonment.

The next day we were working right down below Darlings. So the twin brother came along by us, with a Winchester 44 on his shoulder, just like a person grieving. He goes out in the woods where his brothers were killed, but there was nothing there—everything was demonstrated and gone. It must have been about ten o'clock when he passed us going to work. So we ate dinner, and we was setting down talking and worrying about where we was going next payday. Some of them said Captain Carre was going to run a special train out to Clarks-dale. The foreman, Jim Biddy, looked up and seed this fellow staggering in the woods toward us. "Look at that fellow over there!" He knew he couldn't be drunk, because there was no whiskey in there. He'd forgot about the brother going through. So we all ran over to him, and saw he was covered with blood and didn't have his gun. It was one o'clock then, and he'd passed about ten o'clock, and the place was only twenty minutes away. We went back and found his gun on the spot. He didn't know what had happened. There was no scar on him, but blood on his head and shirt, in the same place where his brother had been cut.

The foreman put him on a lever car and took him back to Marks. His head kept hurting; he knowed he had a lick somehow. Some believed it was 'cause he was a twin; some thought somebody up in a tree hit him to get the rest of the money. After I seen moving pictures I saw how they could jump out of a tree and knock a man down. Before that I believed he had suffered the same hurts as his twin brother, by being in the same place his twin was killed.

They say any time you get a part of a dead man it brings you luck. Lots of men went up to the body after it was burned, and took finger joints and leg bones and teeth, everything but the heart; it wouldn't burn. They broke them up and took the dust from the bones and sewed it up in bags—they call them tobies, or mojos. Gamblers use them for luck.

Sometimes they'll go to a grave and get the dust or the bones, to make a mojo. People sell the mojos, for a "gambling hand." You rub it on your own hand before you shoot the dice. A bad man's bones are the best, one who got kilt being bad.

160 *Killing Colored Brakesmen* (J. D. SUGGS)

Many post-Civil War recollections in Botkin, Lay My Burden Down, *deal with Ku Klux Klan violence; see pp. 255ff.*

In 1914, during the summer, all extra conductors were being laid off, and so they paid middle-class white hoodlums three hundred dollars for every colored brakesman or fireman that was killed. Then the extras could get their jobs when there were no conductor runs. After 1910, colored men had seniority, and they were making as much money as the whites. Arthur Tyler, a friend of mine, was first to get killed, at Lake Connate [Cormorant] twenty miles south of Memphis, where the Yellow Dog branches off from the main Y and M V. They shot him at night, when he was lining up the switch and looking over his train as it was pulling out. Nothing you can do; you got a cannon in your side. Will Winder they killed at Phillips City. I stayed with him seven years. They shot him through and through, burned his clothes all off except for his watch in his side pocket and his greenbacks in his bib pocket. Next morning they found a white man dead alongside of him; Will must have been shot with his gun in his hand. Will'd told his wife: "I'm going to look over my train tonight if they kill me. I'm not going to let Mr. Watson do it any more." At night the regular white conductors would look over the train, to protect the colored brakesmen.

Next one they killed was my first cousin, Alious Clark, at Ackerman, near Birmingham, Alabama. He was taking water at the water tank. That's when I quit. Five hundred of us all quit and went up to Chicago.

A mulatto named Lee Legins, a brakesman on the 58, a manifest, looked just like the conductor. The train was going south out of Memphis on the high line, and the hoodlums were so anxious to kill him—it was such a good train—they didn't wait for it to get to Mississippi, but shot him from the willows as he was walking back to the caboose. The engineer saw the conductor fall off (they thought it was the colored brakesman); so he took the train right back to Memphis and got the bloodhounds, and they caught the two fellows did the shooting. That broke it up. Give 'em life imprisonment.

When they killed Arthur Tyler they pinned a note to him saying: "Let this be a lesson to all nigger brakesmen. If you don't get down we're going to meet you at some water tank or secret place and shoot you down like rabbits. K.K.K."

161 The Man Who Sold His Wife for Beef (MARY RICHARDSON)

Suggs is my only other informant to speak of this butchery. He says it occurred at Itta Bena, Mississippi, and that the woman was big and heavy, weighing about two hundred and sixty pounds. See Pine Bluff, pp. 219-220, "Sells Wife for Beef." If this is a folktale, as I suspect, it would fall under Motif S100, "Revolting murders or mutilations."

275

Now this ain't no joke. It happened in Clarksdale, Mississippi, when I was about sixteen—I'm seventy-one now. This man worked on share-crop on a plantation. And he was always beating his wife. Any time he'd get fretted with her, he'd beat her and run the kids off; he'd get his neck up, and want to kill 'em all. And they knew it; they'd cut out and leave the house.

So this one night he decided he'd kill her, he'd finish her off. He was jealous mad that she didn't do things she didn't have time to do, or ought to have did. He was a liquor-head, a whiskey-headed man. So he pulled her head back in the chair and cut her throat from one ear to the other, with his pocketknife, and left her head in the back of the chair and her feet against the wall. And then he lit out after the kids. He couldn't find them—they ran to the neighbors for the night—so he came back and decided to make steak out of her, to get him a dollar or two. So he skinned her and put the bony parts in a sack and buried it in the smokehouse—the hands and feet, the head, the parts that would have betrayed it was a human. But the blood ran down on the floor, and the woman what the kids spent the night with saw that next morning when she brought them home.

He cut up the hips, the fleshy part, and laid them in his little springwagon, and went on down the road hollering, "Fresh beef." When he'd get to a house, a woman'd come out and buy a pound or two, and put it on for dinner. (They thought it was cow meat.) But it wouldn't cook done enough to eat for dinner; it swole and toughened. Some of 'em made gravy or soup from it, and left it on for supper. Everybody that eat it was sick, vomiting, about heaving themselves to death. They had to have the doctor. There was one doctor for the whole plantation, about three hundred families, close to a thousand head of people. Since he kept hearing the same thing, he decided to examine the meat to see what it was making so many people sick. He tested it, and said it was human flesh.

Then they started looking for this man. He'd disappeared. And they couldn't find his wife. He'd told his nearest neighbor she was visiting her mother. It wasn't three days before they had their hands on him. Then he told what he'd did with her. Damnation pushed it out of him. (When they get through with you in that jail, with the sweatbox, the hotbox, you're glad to tell. They put you in a dark dungeon, chain you down, punish you till you come to your milk.) They put him in jail, and hung him.

After they hung him they buried him at Mt. Avery Church, not in a casket, just in a little hole in the ground. And they didn't put enough dirt on him, so the dogs scratched him, and the odor was so bad the people didn't want to pass the cemetery. They had to go put more dirt on him, to hold the odor down.

162 *Embalming a Live Man* (J. D. SUGGS)

Dalton Trumbo's play, "The Meanest Man in Town," produced in London in 1951, was based on this motif. Here the horror story verges in the direction of the humorous; a whole cycle of Negro jocular tales revolves around the cooling-board, on which a dead man suddenly sits up, when the cord binding him snaps, or because he has only been in a coma. See post, tale 197.

Years ago they didn't have doctors to test whether a fellow was dead or not. This man went off in a trance overnight; he hadn't been sick at all. So they carried him to the undertaker shop. The undertaker put on his embalming clothes, then put a little shirt on the dead man, and got ready to draw the blood and food from the intestines. When he popped the needle to him up come the dead man. The first place he seen the light he ran for it, and that was the door. The embalmer was right behind him with his needle and his alcohol, saying "Whenever I catch you, I'm sure going to embalm you." He wanted his money. But he never did catch the dead man.

163 *Dies after Bath* (MARY RICHARDSON)

A timber cruiser in the Upper Peninsula told me of a woman who came to town after seventeen years in the woods, was given a bath by her neighbors, and died (see Dorson, Bloodstoppers and Bearwalkers, *Cambridge, 1952, p. 207).*

This is the truth. An old man named Ollie Knight lived on King and Annison's place, about three miles from Friar's Point, Mississippi. He hadn't had a bath in so long, his feet was rusty and had scales, and his foot wouldn't hardly bend.

He got married to a girl named Charlotte who wasn't very bright, didn't have much sense. She was about seventeen, a stout, healthy-looking ox girl, and he was in his sixties or seventies. His neighbors come in and give him a shave, a bath, a haircut, for the wedding. And before day he was dead.

The boys on the place all said when he got the dirt off him he froze to death.

She lost him 'fore she got him.

164 *A Drunkard's Doom* (J. D. SUGGS)

Temperance fables and songs have roots deep in the nineteenth century; see, for example, "Father's a Drunkard, and Mother Is Dead," in The Genteel Female, *ed. Clifton J. Furness (New York, 1931), pp. 97-98.*

I heard Sam Jones preach in Durant, Mississippi, in 1908. He was the biggest evangelist preacher we ever had. He had a tent with sixty choir singers. He preached in every big city in the South. Mississippi is a dry state today because of him.

He told about a drunkard who came home so drunk he didn't know his own baby; he thought it was the dog in the front room. He stomped the baby to death; then he goes down into the kitchen where his wife was preparing supper for him, and axed her, "Where's our baby?" She says, "In the front room." He says, "No, I stomped a dog out there." So he and her goes back up to the front room. She picks up the baby, and cries: "See what you have done. You've kilt our only baby." So he drew his revolver from his pocket, put it to his temple, and shot his own brains out. His wife takes the baby, walks across the street to the saloonkeeper, and says: "Mr. Saloonkeeper, you have murdered my husband. Here's my little baby; you have murdered my baby. Now please take your dagger and dagger me to my heart." The saloonkeeper walked behind the bar, gets him a five-gallon can of gasoline, sprinkles it over the house, taken a match, struck it and throwed it into the gasoline. Then he reaches under the counter, pulls out his revolver, puts it to his own temple, and blows his brains out.

Now you see the harm that liquor will do to a man. It caused him to murder his baby, himself, killed the saloonkeeper, and burned the building.

165 *The Disguised Robber* (J. D. SUGGS)

Here is a fine example of the allegedly true happening that conceals a migratory legend. Roberts no. 104c (same title) gives an identical account from the Pine Mountain of eastern Kentucky.

Directly after the Civil War, robbers were very bad down South. Finally they had to get the Rangers to clean 'em out. Well, in 1870, Mr. Silas Smith went to Durant to sell cotton. (My father worked for him; he was a big landholder in Mississippi. That's where I grew up and went to school.) He sold about a hundred dollars' worth, and started back the twenty-five miles to his plantation. The road ran through a swamp for about ten miles, with no house around for the whole stretch. People always tried to get through there before night, because that's where the robbers held 'em up, after they'd come to town to get food. Mr. Smith had bought him a pair of swift horses, swift as there were in the country, and bought him a double-rigged hack (a buggy pulled by two horses they call a hack). That was for fast speeding through that ten miles.

So when he was leaving town that evening, he got even with an old lady with a walking cane, a bonnet over her head, and a basket on her arm. (Old people used to carry little old hand baskets with 'em for their knitting, about a foot long, made out of cane; they even carried 'em to church, with something to eat for the kids.) Well, the lady axed him to let her ride. He said yes, and she climbed up in the hack. He kinda noticed it was funny she kept her head from him all the time, and didn't talk much. Whenever he would ax a question she never would speak, just nod her head.

About two miles out of town, the horseflies began to bite the horses. Whenever a horsefly bites a horse it always hurts him awful bad; he nearly goes into spasms. When the horse made his lunge, that snatched the woman over backwards. Mr. Smith looked at Grandma to see if she was about to fall out. And her bonnet had flew back offa her jowls, and he discovered that she was a man; he could see a stub of beard under the bonnet. (It was a bonnet that come out about six or eight inches off the face, had slips of cardboard set in to hold it out; it was ribbed, and the tail was sewed onto the bonnet and covered the shoulders and the cheeks—like Little Red Riding Hood.) He pretended like he hadn't seen nothing and just drove on. Meanwhile he kept fooling around trying to work his hat till it could fall off, by turning his head and getting the horses to prance. Finally one of the horses gave a jerk and his hat blew off. He says, "Grandma, will you go out and get my hat? I know you can't see to hold these horses." And she just bowed her head, "Yes." Whiles she's going back after the hat, he give the horses a lash with the buggy whip. When he looked back, she'd done got out that dress, and her head lay back and she was waving her hands begging for him to stop. But he done lick the horses and they was splitting the wind.

When he got in home, his wife came out and met him. He was telling her about the old grandma got in the wagon with him coming out of town.

"Here's her basket and her knitting here, in the back." He picks up the basket and looks in it, to give it to his wife, and there's two Colt 44's in there, and eight hundred dollars in cash money. So the robber's plan was to wait till they got to the woods, then shoot him in the head and have those fine horses. But instead, Mr. Smith got all his money.

166 *The Death Car* (JOHN BERRY)

At the annual Old Settlers Day at Mecosta, I delivered a talk on folklore, couched in general terms, without any specific reference to Negro tales. It occurred to me to give, as an example of a widely believed modern city legend, the story of the "Death Car," several versions of which turned up each year in my folklore classes. In every instance, an automobile had been sold at a reduced price because its owner had died at the wheel and the smell of death could not be removed. Localized all over the United States, the variants always stopped short of actual confirmation; someone had heard from someone else about the car. To my utter surprise, that evening at a local dance, strapping John Berry, grandson of the fugitive slave Isaac (see tale 157), pulled me aside and said: "You got that story wrong. It happened right here, you know." And he and his pals, including Clifford Cross who bought the Death Car, gave me the first authenticated account of the phantom tale ever to come my way.

It first came to my attention from my colleague, Russel B. Nye, who had heard the Buick dealer in Lansing complain of many telephone calls asking about the depreciated car in which a man had died. The Indiana University Folklore Archives now has thirty-three variants, placing the tragedy not only in various Michigan cities (twenty-three) but also in California (five), New Jersey (two), Illinois, Iowa, Maine, and Wisconsin, Usually the car is a Buick, although five Cadillacs are reported. Death occurs from suicide, heart attack, or a hunting accident, with only one suspicion of murder mentioned. The price of the car varies from twenty to six hundred dollars.

A white fellow from around here, named Demings, committed suicide in his car back in 1938. He had a 1929 Model-A Ford, painted all over with birds and fish; it would catch your eye right away. He was going with a girl who didn't care much for him, Nellie Boyers, and it seems they had a fight when he took her on a date to the Ionia State Fair. When he came back he pulled off the road into the brush, stuck a gas hose onto the tailpipe, turned the motor on, and sniffed the other end of the hose. He must have prepared for it, because he had the cracks under the seat and on the floorboards all chinked up with concrete, to keep the gas from escaping. He killed himself in August, and no one found him till October, in the hunting season. A guide kept going out to that spot where Demings had parked; he'd see the car and say, "That fellow's always hunting when I am." Finally he took a close-up look, and smelled the body.

A used-car dealer in Remus sold the car at a reduced price to Clifford Cross. Cliff did everything possible to get the smell out; he upholstered it, fumigated it, but nothing worked, and in the middle of winter he would have to drive around with the window wide open. I said one time, "If I'm going to freeze to death driving with you I'd rather be out on my feet," and I got out. Another time a little white dog crawled inside while Cliff was getting gas, and started to bark from the back seat after he drove off. Cliff thought it was the dead man's ghost, and he stopped that car and shot out like the Devil was after him. Finally he give up trying to get the smell out, and turned the car in for junk.

---

[15] Said to Fred Steele, who had brought me to Coker's house.

[16] Darling (*sic*) and Marks are in present Quitman County. "Yellow Buck" may be Yalobusha County.

[17] Told by Suggs, *ante*, tale 5.

PROTEST TALES

While the term "protest song" has entered the vocabulary of folklorists, an equivalent phrase for the folktale remains to be coined. Numerous traditional tales, involving the grievances of minority groups and the lower classes, might well be designated "protest tales." Sometimes these narratives center about proletarian heroes, who champion the cause of peasant and crofter against an overweening aristocracy. Often they take the form of grim jests, as in the body of Jewish folk humor growing around Russian and Nazi persecutions. In the richly diversified story lore of American Negroes, certain tales inevitably reflect their racial humiliations. These too appear in comic garb, and sometimes are told by white men, just as non-Jews have adopted Jewish stories.

The note of protest may be directly sounded with sharp and bitter irony. My leading informant of protest tales, E. M. Moore, a building contractor in Pine Bluff, regarded his narrations as a true expression of Southern Negro suffering. A discrimination incident, where I was refused curb service for having colored people in my car, suggested to John Courtney the fearful yam of John fighting the bulldogs. In other tales a gentle humor cushions the ugly facts, and pictures ignorant country Negroes who cannot recognize a bathtub, or a train, or a traffic light. Here the protest sounds more faintly, but such episodes pass comment on the society that denies learning and opportunity to some of its members. Sometimes this ignorance is feigned, to avoid penalties. "Those white folks made us lie. We had to lie to live," one descendant of a slave remarked to me. My new acquaintances fully understood the ironies of the American dilemma, and revealed to me amazing instances of how Bilbo and Huey Long befriended their people, in the midst of savagely anti-Negro public utterances. The protest tales reflect these ironies, and sometimes favor the Southern white man over his Northern counterpart.

A shift in stereotypes emerges in this group of stories. First comes the naive and gullible rural Negro, then the knowing and crafty city boy who outwits the white man by playing dumb, and finally the proud self-supporting "new Negro," who tells his former boss, "I'm sopping my own gravy now." This change in plot mirrors the gradual ascent of the colored man in American society. A similar pattern appears in comic anecdotes Indians have told about their relations with white men.[18]

Few variants as yet can be found for these protest tales among the numerous printed examples of Negro folkstories. Collectors avoid them, or fail to inquire for them, or do not know of them, and continue to gather texts about Brer Rabbit and graveyard hants. But these serio-comic yams of protest enjoy wide oral currency, and deserve attention both as oral folklore and as documents of social attitudes.

167 *Outrunning the Patterolls* (E. L. SMITH)

For references to the system of white patrols on the slave plantations see Botkin, Burden, *"Poor White-Trash Pater oilers" pp 168-169. The informant says, "I often think that the system of paterollers and bloodhounds did more to bring on the war and the wrath of the Lord than anything else." Suggs has an anecdote on "Fooling the Padderol," where the slave being whipped at night swings under the tree trunk he is tied to and screams when the whip hits the wood* (Pine Bluff, *pp. 175-176, "Fooling the Padderoll"). A slave's escape from the patterollers by dancing is told on tape in the University of Arkansas Folklore Archives (Lula Campbell, reel 167, item 5).*

In slavery times the Marster paid poor white men, patterolls they called them, to catch their slaves when they ran away. You had to have a pass to go from farm to farm, and if they caught you without a pass they'd whip you. My grandfather, Romey Howard, never would stay to whom he was give; he'd run back to his Old Marsa.

My grandfather told us he could outrun bloodhounds, till they were too tired to jump over the fence. Then he'd let the fence down so they could get through, circle around in the field back to the fence, and put it up again. When he'd get tired of fooling with 'em, he'd go into this cemetery, and raise up the top on the marble stones, and stretch out under it and slide the slab back over him. When the dogs tracked him up there the patterolls would call the dogs off and say it was a ghost—they was scared, you see.

Four patterolls died owing him a whipping—Zach Clark, Johnson Memmel, Tom Hawkins, Dr. Sanders. They caught him one night and stripped him and laid him on a rock and said, "Fresh meat tonight." And when he was taking off his last piece of clothes he knew they couldn't hold him then; he slid right off that rock and ran. But this white patteroll, John, was about as fast, and he'd get close enough to rake Romey in the back with his fingers, but he couldn't get no hold. So Romey'd bend over and run on out from under him.

He got back to his mistress (Mrs. Becky Sanders) buck naked. And told her he wouldn't let no one-gallus man[19] whip him. She was just getting him clothes when the patterolls came up. They told her to let him go up to the gin-house (where they ginned cotton) and race John back to the house, and they'd never whip him when they'd ketch him out, if he outrun John.

When John was about halfway to the house Romey was going through the front door.

168 *John In Alabama* (JOHN COURTNEY)

John went to Alabama for a vacation. And while he was there he got into some trouble with a white man. John was telling his friends how they do over here in Arkansas, how they treat the colored better. So this white fellow was passing by, and he taken it up, and he wanted to know where John was from. So John told him he wasn't speaking to him.

So he said, "You know who you speaking to, nigger?" So John told him he didn't care. He stepped right up to John and knocked him down. John knocked his leg out from under him and crawled over under him. So they seed John was going to win that fight. Up came the laws. They arrested John. Then they carried him to the place to punish. Buried him in the ground up to his shoulder. Got two bulldogs and turned them loose on John. John was nodding his head so fast they stopped those dogs, called John, told John to fight those two bulldogs fair.

169 *John Dodges White Man* (TOBE COURTNEY)

Although this tale contains the same motif of the skillful dodger as the preceding, it is I believe a separate type. Two close variants were told me in Michigan, by Walter Winfrey and J. D. Suggs (whose text is in Pine Bluff, *no. 19, pp. 182-183). In Winfrey's text the Negro dodges the fists of Bob Fitzsimmons, former world's heavyweight boxing champion.*

Two men were traveling, John and his partner. And they got loud-talking, stiff-talking you know, after they had some drinks—John was a wise-head, say things he had no business. So a white man heard him and took it up, jumped on John and beat him up a little. His partner said, "Say listen, there ain't a man in the world can beat me up that way."

So the white man asked him, "Say, what you got to do with it?"

John told him, "I got nothing to do with it, but there ain't a man in the world can beat me up that way, nobody."

So the white man jumped on him and commenced hitting at him. And John commenced a-dodging. The white man hit at him till he got tired, he said, "Hold your head still, nigger."

John said, "Boss, I'm a dodging son-of-a-bitch, ain't I?"

170 Making the Negro Jump (E. M. MOORE)

This happened up at Corning, Arkansas. A Negro was passing through there. It was cotton picking time, but no Negroes lived there, and weren't allowed there. They didn't want to pick this Negro up and make him go to picking cotton. So one big white man walked out to the railroad as he was walking by, with a pistol in one hand and a quirt in the other. So he called him over, told him to come over. Said, "Don't you know we don't allow no niggers through here?"

He said, "No, Boss, I didn't know it."

He said, "I'm not going to kill you, I'm just going to whip you, and make you remember this place, so you don't ever come through here again." And he said, "Well, before I whip you, I'm going to see if you can jump this fence." He had a six foot fence there, and he told the Negro, he says, "Now when I tell you to go over this fence," he say, "you go over. And when I say 'Back again,' you jump back on this side." He said, "Now if you attempt to run, I'm going to kill you." So he drilled him on it. "Have you got it now? When I say 'Over,' you jump over. And when I say 'Back again,' you come back and don't touch that fence. And when I say 'Halt,' you stop."

So they got started. He said, "Over." The Negro jumped over. He said, "Back again." The Negro jumped back. "Over. Back again. Over. Back again." And as the Negro was jumping back again he hollered "Halt," and caught him right up over the fence. So the Negro knew the white man meant for him to do what he had told him to do. The poor Negro just had to hang up there in the air over the fence.

171 *Fast Departure* (E. M. MOORE)

This also happened up at Corning, Arkansas. At that time Corning didn't allow Negroes in the little town. This colored man was walking up the railroad track. Some white man caught him and held him until the gang came. They first thought they would whip him, but then later decided to make him dance. When the Negro had danced until he was just about out of breath, one big-hat-wearing white man said, "Nigger, if we don't whip you, will you catch the next train coming through here, and leave and never be caught here again?"

He said, "Boss, if you just don't whip me, and let me go, I'll catch that train that's already done gone."

172 *The New Dance Step* (J. D. SUGGS)

This told for true episode seems a variant of the two preceding narratives, but with the Negroes triumphing.

Morehouse, Missouri, was a big sawmill town on Little River. Every time a colored fellow come through they made him dance and run—the young white fellows did, eighteen to twenty-one. These two colored boys come along, and they made them dance, and then chuck rocks at 'em and run 'em out of town. One of the white fellows, John, was in the bunch, told me they was the best dancers he ever saw. They were gone about five or six months. One day the same two boys come back along there. John said to the gang, "Here come the same two, let's make them dance again today." "Boys, I want you to dance some for me today."

They says "Okay," just sets their suitcases down. And the white fellows begin to pat for them (to make the music). They done all kinds of dancing. After awhile one of 'em stopped, said "Did you ever see that step, Get Your Gun?"

He said, "No."

The colored boy said, "If we had our light shoes on we'd show you something. That beats any step we know."

They said, "Well get your light shoes out; we sure wants to see that."

They went to the suitcases, unlocked it, retched in like they was going to get the shoes. Both of 'em come up with a gun at the same time. Said, "Now let's see you all dance." John said none of them couldn't dance at all. He said they just made them jump up and down for forty minutes till they couldn't get their feets hardly off the ground. Said then they just picked up their suitcases, said "That's pretty good, boys," and walked off.

And they never did bother nobody after that. (My cousin moved out in '27, and I went there in '25—this was the year before. There was no coloreds there when I went there. He come out there to see me, and went to work for the same man I did.)

173 *A Fine for Killing Two Negroes* (J. D. SUGGS)

Ted Uptegrove, who runs the colored tavern in Cass, told me this happened in Hazlehurst, Mississippi, near the Gulf of Mexico. He said there was three bad fellows there, an old man and his two sons, who was just as bad as they could be. They were after a white fellow named Willie, that had been to the country and whipped one of them. So they were riding to town on their mules, when they come on Willie. He had a thirty-thirty Winchester. They made a shot before they got to him. Next shot Willie made, he killed the old man, and the second boy he went to running and Willie shot him through the hip and killed him, and the other boy he hid behind the mule. And Willie shot at him and killed the mule.

They had the trial, and fined Willie five dollars for killing the mule and a nickel for killing the two colored men.

174 *Old Missy, the Mule and the Buggy*

An exaggerative folktale has here grown out of realities of Southern mores. The mule obviously represents the colored man, as Suggs' parenthetical comment makes clear. Compare Hyatt no. 10606, p. 637, "They say down in Georgia if a black man sees a white mule he must bow to it." Suggs' story "The Fast Runner," post, tale 222, in similar vein develops a tall tale from the consequences resulting when a colored man strikes a white man.

a (J. D. SUGGS)

Old Missy was going to town to carry some eggs. So she was driving a mule to a buggy. The mule got scared and runned away and throwed Old Missy out. It didn't kill her, just bruised her up a little. So they got the mule and buggy and drove it up to town, and had the mule and buggy tried. They found the mule guilty for running away with the buggy, and the buggy guilty for running away and throwing Old Missy out. So the J. P. he sentences the mule to be hung, and sent the buggy to the penitentiary for life.

(Anything happened to Old Missy you going to suffer for it, right or wrong. It's the middle class what had to work you had to worry about—the big shots let you do anything, the doctors, lawyers. They won't work. Old Missy was working, she was going to town to carry eggs. The middle class don't like the colored because they won't get out of a job, and that makes them prejudiced. If the colored got money they won't work for nothing. There's fifty colored folks to one white in the South. But the rich colored men can fry the poor ones just like the whites do. Since the war things is better. The white boys didn't like saying "Yes, sir" and "No, sir" in the army.)

b (JOHN COURTNEY)

White lady in the state of Georgia (we give Georgia a hard name here), went to a livery stable and rented a black mule and a black buggy. She went out for a drive, round the skirts of town. Mule seed a book of paper and he ran away, broke her leg and arm. They executed the mule, sentenced the buggy to lifetime in the state penitentiary, bind the harness over to circuit court.

175 *Its and Ifs* (HAROLD LEE)

Two colored men were talking to themselves. One was a farmer, the other had quit. He said he wasn't going to farm any more, there were too many its and ifs. The ifs were, *if* the boll weevils don't eat it up, *if* the worms don't eat it up, *if* the drouth don't come, he'll make a good crop, for the man to take with the pencil and pad.

The its were: to plow *it*, to plant *it*, to chop *it*, to poison *it*, to pick *it*, to weigh *it*, haul *it* to the gin, sell *it*, and the man behind the desk take *it*.

176 *Gifts from Heaven* (HAROLD LEE)

Cf. Hurston, Mules and Men, *p. 102, "De Reason Niggers Is Working So Hard"; and "Colored Man, Jew and White Man," by*

Tommy Carter, ante, *tale 70(a).*
It was raining, and after the rains subsided two packages was seen. Two men ran to see what it was. After discovering a plow and a hoe in one package, one ex-clamored real loud, "This is a gift from heaven."

The other fellow said, "Look what I have, a pencil and a scratch pad and a cushion."

So the retired farmer says, "That's why I stopped farming. After all my hard work, the fellow behind the desk gets it all."

177 *Mistake in Account* (E. M. MOORE)

A similar theme appears in J. Mason Brewer, The Word on the Brazos, *pp. 92-93, "Uncle Si, His Bossman, and Hell," but in that case the deluded slave emerges on top.*

It was on a large plantation in Mississippi, all Negro tenants. This man would settle with them seven or eight years. And one Negro, George Jackson, couldn't read or write. Neither could his wife. But they lived on the main road that led from where most tenants on the place lived, up to the headquarters. So this year the Boss decided to settle. And this particular man, the Boss gave him a statement and a check pinned to the statement for $750. He carried his statement and his check home. He and his wife looked over it. With that being the first settlement they had had in seven years they didn't know what to do with it. Living on the main road where all the Negroes had to pass his house to go down to the headquarters or the office, some of the Negroes could read or write, or could figure. After going home with their statements, several of them found mistakes. They passed back by George Jackson's house going back to have their mistakes corrected. George Jackson being one of the busybodies, he asked everyone that came by, "Hey buddy, where you gwine?"

So they would all tell him, "Well I found a mistake in my account, and I'm going back to have it corrected."

And after so many of them had found mistakes, something just told him that there was a mistake in his account. So he went in and told his wife Mandy, said, "Do you know, I believe there is a mistake in our account. You give it here." And he went back to the office to talk to the Boss.

When he walked in the office the Boss said, "Well Uncle George, what's your trouble?"

And he says, "I think there is a mistake in my account."

The Boss knew George Jackson couldn't read or figure. He was just coming back because others were saying they were coming back. He decided to have some fun off him. He took the statement and looked over it for a little while. Called George Jackson over to the desk. He said, "Well Uncle George, I did discover a mistake here." He said, "I find here that I paid you $20 too much."

George said, "I knowed it, I knowed it, I knowed it."

178 *White Man's Ice* (EDNA NELSON)

This colored man had worked up a nice trade selling ice in a community. And all the people in that community, both white and colored, was buying from him. The white man began selling ice too, since the colored man doing so well he thought he would go in there and get him some customers.

So when the white woman saw the colored woman had changed to the white man—the white woman was still buying from the colored man—she said, "Now why did you stop buying from John, he was so courteous and nice, and we did business with him a long time?"

"Well I tell you truth Miz George, I tell you just why I changed—that white man's ice is just colder than that nigger's ice."

(They told that tale to try to get colored people to patronize each other, when their things were just as good as the white man's.)

179 *Running the Red Light* (TILMAN C. COTHRAN)

E. M. Moore has the arrested Negro tell the judge, "Boss, I thought the red light was a Christmas bell."

The colored man was arrested in a town in Mississippi for crossing a red light. He explained, "I saw all the white folks going on the green light, I thought the red light was for us colored folks." The judge let him off.

(Frequently educated Negroes will pretend to be ignorant to fool the white man.)

180 *Educating the White Folk* (TILMAN C. COTHRAN)

The appropriation for the Negro school was used for the White school. The superintendent explained this to the Negro principal, who of course couldn't make a direct protest. So he said, "The one thing we need most of all is educated white folk."

181 *Never Seen a Bathtub* (E. M. MOORE)

A Negro in Mississippi had lived on a plantation all his life, had reached the age of seventy-five. So the Boss called him in and told him, says, "John, you've been on this farm all your life, even before I was born." Says, "I'm going to stop you from work now. I'm going to build you a little house in town, you and your wife, and take care of you the rest of your life."

So he did build the house and move them to town, but he moved them in before the house was completed. A day or two after they moved in, the Boss just called one of the plumbing companies and told them to take a bathtub out there, and to leave it on the front porch. So a day or two later the truck driver from the plantation went by the man's house to take something. And he told the truck driver to tell the Boss that the white man brought that boat out there, but he didn't bring the oars to it.

182 *Po' Thing* (JOHN COURTNEY)

Close variants with the same title are in Pine Bluff, *pp. 237-238, from J. D. Suggs, and in "Negro Tales of Mary Richardson," no. 22, p. 19. This tale deserves a separate type number alongside Type 1315, "The Steamship thought to be the Devil." In variants told me by Walter Winfrey and Idell Moore a handcart and a bull are mistaken for a train. Joe D. Heardley told me of a family running in fright from a streetcar, thinking it a train that had jumped the track, and Clarence Grier gave me one about the Irishman in Philadelphia who thought a streetcar was Pat's house on wheels, because it had the same number.*

Old man Sam and his wife he was the father of fourteen children. And he had never carried his wife and children to town. So in the spring of the year he loaded them all up in the wagon and 'cided to take them to town. When they all reached town, he unloaded them outa the wagon, and begin walking around showing them. So after they'd looked the town over, he 'cided to take them round to the station. That was to let them see the train —they had never seed a train. Pretty soon after they got around there, the train showed up in sight. So when the train showed up in sight, when the train blowed the stop whistle, wasn't no one standing there but he and his wife. His children done scattered all over town. Some was going and meeting the people, shaking hands you know, glad to see each other. She done backed up again the station as far back as she could go. When the train run up and stop, it say, "Choo, choo, choo, choo."

Sam's wife say, "Po' thing. Done run so much, so tired, hot and sweating. Won't anybody pay it no 'tention." And she take off her big old straw hat, her Bill Bailey, and commenced fanning it. "Po' thing, I know she's tired."

183 *John and the Twelve Jews* (JOHN COURTNEY)

Fellow folklorist D. K. Wilgus gave me a variant to this one, when I passed through Bowling Green, Kentucky. His shortened version has only two Jewish business men; each thinks the other has tipped George who, when he finally gets the twenty-five dollars, says, "Now I know that you Jews didn't crucify Christ, you just scared him to death"

Once upon a time there was twelve Jews and they had a porter boy. His name was John. John had been traveling all over the United States with those Jews, and everywhere they go you know, where they get off y'know, they tip John you know. And John would have something to help support hisself in the place y'know while he was there. So they went to Chicago y'know. They came from New York to Chicago. They give John, oh, a big pocket of money. John had a big time y'know. And they all got ready to go y'know, he'd go get all of 'em their grips y'know, and he'd put 'em, load 'em all on the train y'know. And then John he'd be standing there when they'd get on y'know. And when the last one get on, why John he get right on up behind the boss, y'know. And he say, "Okay John, you all loaded and ready to go?"

So John traveled with them y'know for quite a bit of time, like he'd been with 'em for years. So they left Chicago for Los Angeles, California. And so John loaded their things. So when they got to Los Angeles, the train pulled up, the porter put the box down. John got off y'know, and John took all their grips off y'know and set 'em down, taken 'em off. John got all their grips sorted out y'know before they came out. Okay. The first big boss came out y'know, he came right down y'know, his coat fastened, picks his two grips y'know, and never looked back. John looked at him y'know. Okay. Here comes the other, the second one. He come down, he picks up his two grips y'know, never looked back, steps right on.

John said, "Well, maybe the other one's got the money." So here come the third one down. He picks up his grips, step down, and never looked back. So John still thought about it y'know, getting worried about the money. And so here come the fourth one. The fourth one picked up his grips, and he never looked back. Fifth one came down and picked up his grips. He never looked back. John ain't got nothing. So here come the sixth man. The sixth man come down, he picks up his grips, never looked back. So John begin to frown, "That's half of 'em y'know." So John looked all around y'know at the porter and the porter looked at him y'know. And so John looked, "Here come the seventh one down." And he done the same thing, the seventh. He picked up his grips. The eighth one, he picked up his, and he ain't looked back. John just kept frowning. So the ninth one he picked up his ones. He never looked back. The tenth one did the same. The eleventh man he was a big, heavy-sot, great big feller. He wagged down, he got his grips y'know, and he looked back at John. John he never said a word. John all frowned up. "That's the eleventh man y'know." John said, "Well maybe Old Boss is got the last one." Old Boss is long, tall. He come down y'know, he's *tall*. He picks up his grips. John looks at him. So he picks up his grips and set 'em over there on the side, y'know, and he turned around to John. Run his hand in his pocket, got his billfold out y'know.

John says, "Cap'n," says, "let me tell you something." Says, "Y'know they just telling a damn lie on you-all." Say, "I. . I. . I thought that like hell y'know, for a long time. I'se been thinking it like hell." Said, "But I'm going to tell you," said, "they sure told a damn lie. They say you-all killed Christ. But you didn't kill him."

He said, "What's the matter, John?"

He said, "You-all just worried hell out of him."

184 *Eating Farther Down the Hog* (REV. MRS. L. R. TOLER)

Two other texts were given me by J. D. Suggs (printed ante, tale 56, as an Old Marster tale) and Lulu Powell. These variants have the colored man eating further up the hog. Lulu Powell heard the tale from her minister in the First Baptist Church in Vandalia. "He was making the point how we had progressed in our church work."

There was a man named John Ashe, cut wood for a living, usually would accept just a hog head—raised in a country where they grew hogs. So one day somebody gave him a piece of shoulder—tasted pretty good to him, never tasted it before. Passed by one of his old friends, she'd killed a couple of hogs. Children called out, "Mammy, here comes Uncle John."

She called out, "Children, tell Uncle John I'll give him a hog head to cut a load of wood."

Children said, "Uncle John."

He just throwed up the back of his hand, wouldn't stop. Finally their mother came out, called "John, John—give you two hog heads for the one load of wood."

He kept on going, said, "Children, tell your mammy I'm eating further down the hog now."

185 *I'm Sopping My Own Gravy Now* (E. M. MOORE)

The Negro worked for the Southern doctor. The doctor would leave home before breakfast every morning and the Negro would carry breakfast to the office. One morning the doctor was sitting looking out the window from his upstairs office. He saw the Negro coming down the street with his breakfast. He took a biscuit from the plate and sopped the biscuit in the doctor's gravy and ate it. When he reached the office, the doctor whipped him, told him he was fired. "I don't allow a nigger to sop out of my gravy. Get out and get you some gravy of your own to sop."

The Negro left and moved to Arkansas (from Mississippi). The first year he was in Arkansas, farming was good. He made money, he bought a pair of mules and some plow tools. The next year farming was good. He started buying forty acres of land, paid for his mules, his forty acres of land, bought a horse and buggy and nice clothes. The next year he drove back to the same town in Mississippi. He saw the doctor he had worked for when he lived in Mississippi. The doctor wanted to know who he was driving for when he saw him in the new buggy with the nice horse.

He said, "I'm driving for myself."

He said, "What are you doing now, John?"

He said, "I'm farming."

He said, "Who for, John?"

He said, "Myself."

He said, "Whose buggy and horse is that?"

He said, "They belong to me."

"And you're farming for yourself?"

"Yessir."

"Own your own mules?"

"Yessir."

"Own your own land?"

"Yessir."

"Well John, tell me, what are you doing in Arkansas?"

"Sir, I'm sopping my own gravy."

186 The Mulatto (JOHN BLACKAMORE)

This curious story appears in sharply localized form in Brewer, Brazos, "The Mulatto Boys and the Religious Test," pp. 72-74. Its key idea, the currency in Southern Negro culture of the saying "I'll pay you Saturday if the Lord spares me and nothing happens," appears in other tales; see ante, tale 70(c).

During slavery times the master had intercourses with his colored woman, his slave, and their baby was half-white, half-colored—what they calls a mulatto. When he grew up the colored people didn't hang around with him too much and neither did the white people; that's why he had to get away—he didn't have no peace on either side. So he decided to buy him a nice suit, and some shirts, and some shoes (the colored people didn't have shoes), and get himself a haircut and shave; he had nice coal-black hair. His color was real light but not as light as the white man; so they didn't know what he was. But after he got all sharp, he could go in the white restaurant and the white rest room.

So he decided he'd try to get him one of those important jobs. He had pretty good book learning, so he goes to the bank and applies for a job. Well, he worked around there and he done real good. Since he was doing so good they wanted to find out all they could about him, so they could bring him up to a higher position. But whenever anybody talked to him about his personal life he would always evade them, and talks about something else. Finally one day the rumor got around that he might be half-white and half-colored. So the bank president said: "Well, we can't let that happen here—we don't use colored employees. We got to find out what he really is." He decided that when the fourth of July holiday rolled around, and the bank closed at three o'clock, he'd find out whether the man was really colored or not.

On July 3, the president asked everyone to come and work the next day. Everybody told him they would. But he had the manager standing at the door to tell them different when they come out the bank. Then the manager gave the president the O.K. sign when each one passed him. Finally this mulatto come up. And he says as he goes out, "I'll be here in the morning if the Lord spares me and nothing don't happen." So the president knew he was colored, and discharged him.

187 *The Light Child* (E. M. MOORE)

Another ending was given me by Jesse Burnett at Sodus, Michigan; the Boss assures John his wife must have got scared by a white cow, which marked her baby so that it was born white.

A farmer on a Mississippi plantation had thirteen children. He and his wife both were very dark. The thirteen children were between their colors and the fourteenth child was very light. The father was very disturbed about the color of Ms child, so much so he wasn't pleasant with the Boss on the place. So the Boss decided he'd go out and talk with him about it. He told him, said, "John, I've discovered you just aren't the same John you've been for the last twenty years. I want you to tell me what's wrong."

He said, "Well, you know all my thirteen children are of the same color, and the fourteenth child came up half white." And he said, "I just can't understand it."

"I don't think you ought to let that worry you, John." He said, "You know I have a herd of sheep, to be exact four hundred. They all are supposed to be white, but every now and then one comes up black. But I don't worry about it. They're my sheep and these are your children. So I don't think you ought to worry about your children. I want you to make me a promise, that you don't worry about them. Now will you make me that promise?"

"Yes, under one condition. If you stay out of my house, I'll stay out of your pasture."

188 *The Hobo's Experience* (JOHN BLACKAMORE)

Tommy Carter's variant has the colored hobo out West knocking on a Chinaman's door; the Chinaman says, "Do you like rabbit?" "Yes" "You catch him, I cook him." E. M. Moore gave me a text close to Blackamore's, printed in Pine Bluff, *p. 114.*

One day we was out cutting timber, and a man came along looking for work, and my dad gave him a job. So we started early the next morning, about five o'clock A.M., without any breakfast. Along around ten o'clock I made the expression that I was hungry. So Ray asked me what was the matter. He says, "You couldn't be hungry, 'cause when you do without food about three days, then you begin to get hungry." So he begins to telling me about his experiences as a hobo.

He said he'd been on the road about a week, stopped at a dozen different houses, couldn't get anything to eat, 'cause it was during depression in the South. He was so hungry he got too weak to ride the freight train. So he decided he'd get off the train and walk. He came upon a bag full of orange peelings someone had thrown off a passenger train. So he got the bag and opened it, wiped the ants off, and ate the peelings hisself. Well, he walked on down the railroad track about five miles further, till he saw a nice beautiful ranchhouse off the railroad about a quarter of a mile. So he decided he'd go over there and try to beg him a feed. After he got there, being tired of asking the people for food at the houses he'd gone to and getting turned down, he thought he'd try another way of begging. So when he got to the front yard he just fell down on the front yard and commenced to eating the grass. He really wasn't nipping grass; he was trying to impress the lady of the house that he was hungry. So the lady of the house came to the door and spoke to him, and asked him what he was doing. He told her he hadn't had any food in over a week, but he figured if she'd give him a little salt it would make the grass taste better. So she said, "Poor man! Well, you come on out into the back." He just knows he was going to get some food. So she met him at the back door with a teacup of salt, and told him, "If you got to eat grass, eat it around here, it's taller than out in front."

189 *I'm Glad I'm Back Home* (BILLY JACK TYLER)

The present tale is told by both Southern Whites and Negroes. Professor Thelma James of Wayne University informs me that Senator Tom Connolly of Texas told it for political purposes, and has had it printed in the Congressional Record. *A similar text appears in Fred W. Allsopp,* Folklore of Romantic Arkansas, *2 vols. (The Grolier Society, 1931), II, 184-185, "Dat Sho" Sounded Good to Dis Ole Nigger" told on a newly freed plantation darky.*

There was a boy and he had a brother that had been in Chicago for a period of about five years. And he kept on writing to his brother and telling him that when he made enough money he would send for him, for he was doing fine. In about a month after that his brother send him a ticket. And he went on up and got him a job. He had been working for about three months, when work got short on the job and they turned him off. So he went to his brother's house, and axed him could he stay with him until he was able to get another job. His brother told him he just had enough room and enough food for his wife and family. And he told him to go farther. The reason he had wanted to go to the North in the first place was because the discrimination down South. He had heard that when you in the North, everybody's created equal. As he was walking down the alley he knocked on the front door of the house. A white lady came to the door and said, "Good morning, sir. Something I can do for you?"

He said, "Yes mam. I'm hongry and I wonder would you give me something to eat."

And she said, "No, because I just do have enough for my husband and my kids."

He walked on and he passed several houses through St. Louis, and he come to a house and knocked on the door. And he never noticed the sign up on the wall, that read like this: "If you have lost your way this is not a information bureau."

He kept on walking until he came to the Mason-Dixie line. And he came up to a house in Tennessee. And he noticed he had crossed the state line, and he said, "Tennessee's the place for me." He knocked on the door.

A big fat white man came to the door and said, "What can I do for you, nigger?"

Said, "Boss-man, I'm hongry."

Said, "Bring your black self to the back door and I'll give you something to eat."

Said, "Thanks God, I'm back home."

(In the South they'll always feed the colored people if they're hungry. Up North it's each for himself.)

190 *Bill Adams and Georgia the Peach State* (BILLY JACK TYLER)

Bill Adams he was born and reared in Illinois. He was eighteen years old then, and he thought it was about time for him to travel some. And he had read about Georgia in his school books, so he thought he would go to Georgia. So he got his little clothes together and put them in a paper bag. He got on a train and hoboed to Albany, Georgia. And he didn't like it there so he went on further, hoboed to Atlanta. He hitchhiked a ride from out of Atlanta, about eight miles out in the rural to a little old country town that had a few little junk stores. And he had got lonesome so he thought he would sing a song. Before he begin singing he saw a tall rednecked man coming down the streets. And he began .singing,

"Just Molly and me
And baby makes three.
We're happy as we
In our blue heaven."

And the rednecked with a strong expression, "What did you say, nigger?"
"I didn't say nothing, white folks."
He called out again in a harsh voice, "What did you say, nigger?"
"All I said, white folks,

"Just Molly and you-all
No niggers at all.
You-all happy as you-all
In you-all's blue heaven."

(I heard it in several different arrangements but that's the only one I remember.)

191 *The Governor's Convention* (REV. MRS. L. R. TOLER)

The governor of Mississippi called a convention of all the governors. And he wanted to show them the colored people were treated all right in the South. So he called the old colored man over and said, "Sam, when you're hongry we take care of you, don't we?"
"Yessuh, Boss."
"And when you need a new suit, we give you one, don't we?"
"Yessuh, Boss."
"And if you need some money, we'll put some in your pocket, won't we?"
"Yessuh, Boss."
"All right now Sam, just step up to this mike here and tell all the people how we take care of you."
Sam he goes to the mike, and he says, "Who am I talking to, Boss?"
And the governor says, "You're talking to Washington, D. C, and New York, and the high country up north."
"You mean I'm not talking to Alabama, Georgia, Mississippi?"

"No, Sam."
So Sam hollers into the mike, "HELP! HELP! HELP!"

---

[18] Described in my article "Comic Indian Anecdotes," *Southern Folklore Quarterly,* X (June 1946), 113–128.

[19] A white man so poor he had only one suspender to hold up his trousers.

SCARE TALES

Colored people delight in relating ghost and hant scares in the friendly warmth and safety of their hearths. Oscar Saunders and Fred Steele fairly split their sides matching frights they had fled from on lonely paths and in abandoned dwellings; and yet Saunders readily confessed that the frightful hants rising on the desolate creek where ten years before a fellow had drunk rat poison—"Rough on Rats"—was simply the white side of his oilskin laprobe thrown up by the wind. Natural explanations for their fears only amuse storyteller and audience all the more; believing in hants, they can laugh at their error, but be prepared to run as speedily next time.

This attitude explains the popularity of several hanted-house tales told as fiction. Especially popular is the unsuccessful attempt of a daring man to pass one night in the house of terror, a story I heard in ten variants. The armchair listener laughs hugely at Rufus's increasing trepidation when limbs drop down the chimney—because he, the listener, is far away. Other relished scary tales deal with obstinate or "hardheaded" ghosts who outstay their welcome and with dead men laid out on the cooling board before burial who mysteriously come to life.

192 *Waiting for Rufus* (JOE D. HEARDLEY)

Variations on a comic tale of frights that scare a man from a haunted house circulate widely in American white and Negro tradition. Believed tales of haunted houses have generated this very popular folk-tale, an American oikotype of Type 326, "The Youth Who Wanted to Learn What Fear Is." Baughman places it under Motif J1495.2, "When Caleb Comes. Man attempts to stay in haunted house all night. One cat after another enters . . ." Five of his seven references are Negro. Roberts gives thirteen variants, pp. 109-134. See Randolph, "Three Black Cats," in Who Blowed Up the Church House?, *pp. 163-164, and note, p. 223, which gives five Negro references. Blackamore's text is printed in* Western Folklore, *XIII (1954), 167-168, "The Hanted House" and Suggs' in* Pine Bluff, *p. 264, "Wait Till Martin Comes." I have other examples from Herman Baker, Tommy Carter, Sarah Hall, Idell Moore, Lulu Powell, William Smith, and Florine Strong. Abrahams, Jungle, pp. 187-188, "You Seen Willy," is a text from Philadelphia.*

This is 'bout, "Is you going to stay here till Rufus comes?"

There was a fellow called Emmick Hassen of Rankin County, Mississippi. He builds a new house and couldn't get nobody to live in it but one night. Everybody would run away before day. So we was all in town while they was sitting around talking (just a small country town), and he said he'd give $250 to anybody who stayed in it overnight. It wasn't none of us would stay in it. So here come one of those old gamblers, old coon can players, old skinners. He'd been in a game and got broke, and he wanted some money. He came up there and heard us talking about this house that Emmick built. So he got interested and asked us where was Emmick at. We taken him to Emmick. Emmick told him he'd give him anything he wanted to eat or to have while he stayed there just one night, and the $250. And he told Emmick he wanted a nickel box of matches, a gallon of gasoline, one slab of sowbelly, a pound of lard, three dozen eggs, a gallon of quart oil (or kerosene), and a ax. That's all he wanted.

So he went in that evening, and cut him down a bunch of trees, and built him a log heap fire. Had his lamp burning good. Round about two-thirty in the morning he just knowed he had the $250. Whiles he was sitting there with his hat pulled down over his eyes, a little cat come through a little hole in the door, walked up to him, walked around, touched him on the leg, and asked him, "Are you going to stay here till Rufus comes?" So he run the little kitten out, pulled his hat back over his eyes. Then a little monkey come in, commenced to playing all around the house, hopped up on his knees, looked in his eyes, and asked him, "Are you going to stay here till Rufus comes?" He took his pistol out, stuck it in the monkey's ears, his nose, his eyes, told him he'd blow his brains out if he didn't get out. Out the monkey went. He pulled the hat back over his eyes.

And a big gorilla walked in, knocked the door down, and touched rum on the shoulder. He opened his eyes and the gorilla asked him, "Are you going to stay here till Rufus comes?" So then he moved the gorilla over out of his way, busted the pound heap of lard on the skillet over the log heap of fire, broke the three dozen eggs in the skillet, throwed the slab of sowbelly in the skillet and fried and eat that. Then the gorilla walked up to him, touched him on the shoulder and said, "Say, Buddy, is you going to stay here till Rufus comes?" Then he taken his pistol out and showed it to the gorilla and told him he'd kill him if he didn't get out. So then the gorilla reached in the log heap of fire, pulled out the skillet, and drank all the hot grease. Then he threw the skillet back in the fire. Next he reached over and got one of those red hot charcoals, and commenced to clean his teeth. So then he touched this fellow on the shoulder again and said, "Now, this is the third time I asked you, is you going to stay here till Rufus comes?" He said, "No, Rufus is here now." And he left.

193 *Waiting for Martin* (JULIA COURTNEY)

Like the preceding tale, this one represents a humorous outgrowth from Type 326, "The Youth Who Wanted to Learn What Fear Is." Other Märchen likewise require the hero to endure horrors in an enchanted dwelling (Motif D758.1); see e. g. Types 400, 401, 402.

You see that ghost was named Martin. See it was a hanted house, could no one stay there. And so they put up money to see could they find someone to stay in the house. And so everyone would go to stay in that house couldn't stay there. And so one of the mens went in town, quite natchally was telling about the hanted house. And so the preacher came along. The man said to himself, if anyone could stay in the hanted house, it should be a preacher. So he saw the preacher, and he axed the preacher, was he afraid of a hanted house. And the preacher says, "Why no, everywhere I go I reads my Bible." So this man takes him on back there to this man what owned this house. So when they got there the man told him how much money he had for everyone that stayed in the hanted house.

So that night the preacher got his grip and his Bible and went on over to the hanted house. He went on in and he sat down. He opened his Bible, and the preacher began to read. And the verse he was reading was very familiar to everybody. The preacher said, "In those days came John the Baptist preaching in the wilderness of Judea. Repent for the Kingdom of Heaven is at hand." So he read it for a long time. After a while he heard a door squeak. He kept reading his Bible. He read it, "In those days come John the Baptist preaching in the wilderness of Judey."

The spook come on by and just said, "How de do." He kept reading and he never looked up. Way after a while he heard another door open. That spook come on by. The preacher began reading just a little bit faster.

"In those days come John the Baptist preaching in the wilderness of Judey."

After a while he heard another one. This time didn't no door open, but he heard footsteps. He began reading just a little bit faster.

"In those days come John the Baptist preaching in the wilderness of Judey."

This spook got even with him and stopped. He said, "Mister," he said, "will you be here when Martin come?" The preacher kept reading.

"In those days come John the Baptist preaching in the wilderness of Judey."

He's getting scared.

So way after a while the hant touched him again. He said, "Will you be here when Martin comes?"

The preacher kind of looked up slyly and axed, "Who Martin? Sure I'll be here when he comes." (He's trying to bluff this spook you see.)

Way after while the preacher began to read faster an' faster. This time he heard the turriblest noises of all. This was Martin. Martin dug on up to the preacher he did. This time the preacher put his finger on the Bible.

"In those days come John the Baptist preaching in the wilderness of Judey."

(See he didn't want to look up.)

Martin stood there and listened at him read. After a while Martin shook him. Preacher kept reading. He wouldn't look up. He kept tetching the preacher on the shoulder, and arter a while Martin wouldn't go away, the preacher looked up. And when he looked and saw Martin's face, instead of reading "In those days come John the Baptist," the preacher begin to tremble. And every which a way he turn Martin was there. The preacher finally couldn't get out the room. The preacher says, "Oh mama." Way arter a while, he was so scared, he hollered, "Oh papa." Martin was chasing the preacher so bad till when he did get a chance he grabbed his Bible and grip and got going. And no one ever saw the preacher again.

(He figgered he'd just take a gait he could hold that was familiar to the spirits.)

194 *I'm Going to Fall* (JOHN COURTNEY)

See the references under Motif H1411.1, "Fear test: staying in haunted house where corpse drops piecemeal down chimney. Dead man's members call out to hero, 'Shall we fall, or shall we not?' " This trait also occurs as an episode in Type 326, "The Youth Who Wanted to Learn What Fear Is" and appears as tale no. 4 in the classic collection of Household Tales by the Brothers Grimm. Mention of variants of Type 326 where the spectral limbs announce their fall is in Johannes Bolte and George Polívka, Anmerkungen zu den Kinder- u. Hausmärchen der Bruder Grimm, *vol. I (Leipzig, 1913), p. 30, n. I. A good text is in the* Southern Workman, *v. 27, no. 3. (March 1898), p. 57, "The Boy and the Ghost." A poor boy stays in a haunted house, which is offered to anyone who passes the night there. He cooks his supper, and a leg up the chimney says, "I am going to drop." "I don't keer jes' so's you don' drap in my soup." The whole man finally drops; the boy goes to bed, legs pull him under the house and show him money. A very close text is in A. M. Bacon and E. C. Parsons, "Folk-Lore from Elizabeth City County, Virginia," JAF XXV (1922), no. 50, p. 290, "The Dismembered Ghost."*

Under "I'm Hauling Sand," Abrahams, Jungle, *pp. 188-190, gives two variants in which the spectral voice comes through the window. A variation of Type 326 from a Portuguese Negro living on the New England coast, interestingly localized, and with the present episode, is in Elsie C. Parsons,* Folk-Lore from the Cape Verde Islands, Part I, *MAFLS XV (1923), no. 81, pp. 241-244, "As Broad as He Was Long."*

Some travelers in olden time traveled with a yoke of oxen. So they come to this old house. So they 'cided they'd put up for the night there. They took out everything and got the cook vessels, 'cided they would cook them something to eat. So they cooked the bread. Then John put his meat on. Just about time his meat begin to cook, something holler,

"I'm going to fall." [*Very high*]

They looked around, looked at one another. Say,

"What was that?" He just kept hollering,

"I'm going to fall."

So John thought it was some of the boys trying to kid him, said, "That's not none of us, that's up high, whatsever it is." So he hollered again,

"I'm going to fall."

So that made John mad. John hollered back, "Fall then."

That time down he come into that skillet, and down went the skillet, and knocked his meat and fire and everything, and out went the boys. John whirled and got away from there.

195 *Haunted Castle* (J. D. SUGGS)

This tale begins like the preceding one with Motif H1411.1, "Fear test: staying in haunted house where corpse drops piecemeal down chimney." It then shifts into a sober use of Motif E371.5*, "Ghost of woman returns to reveal hidden treasure," for which Baughman cites one Negro reference. See "The Spirit and the Treasure," from Katy Pointer, ante, tale 114, for a realistic use of this theme with a male revenant.

There was a hanted castle [pronounced castul]—nobody could not stay there. It was a fine place, well furnished, everything comfortable, so that's why people would want to stay there. A fellow would be coming along, walking, asking for a place to stay—"You can stay there, if you can stay there all night you can have it." That's why so many people tried it, but none of them stayed out the night.

The fellow goes in, everything's all fixed up, he sat at a big table looking at a book—there was plenty of books there—says, "I'll set up all night." A leg dropped down on the table. Just looked over and another leg dropped down. He looked back and a right arm dropped down, by the side of it. Then a left arm drops down. He looks off and he looks jack—a body dropped down. Well he looks at his book, he looks back, a head drops down. So there was a whole woman laying there on the table. Out he goes. [Slap of the hands to indicate rapid flight]

Next week here come along another man hunting a place to stay. Says "There's a castle over there, if you can stay all night you can have it."

"Well I know I can stay." So he goes in, light the lamp, set on that table, reach over and get him a book, begin to read. It was kind of cold, in the fall of the year, he had a fire going.

In walked a big black cat. Say "Phew, it's cold tonight." He looked at him, went back to reading his book.

After awhile in walks a big old rooster, no feathers but on his neck and head. He says, "Boys, ain't got here yet?"

The cat says, "Naw."

After awhile he look up, in come a little bitty kitten with the mange and the sore eyes. He turned his back to the fire (just the way a cat does). He says in a low whiny voice, "You gonna start now or wait till Martin comes?"

Up jumped the man, say "I won't be here when Martin comes."

So he was gone. Next two or three nights here comes an old poor man, raggedy—he had a Bible under his arm. He axed him, "Is there anywhere I can stay tonight?"

Man says, "Yeah, see that house there, you can stay there all night."

"Okay, I thanks." So he goes and makes him a fire, open his sack, get him a cold lunch; a little piece of bread he got, and meat. So he goes over to the table with his Bible and begun to read. So down come a leg on the table. Well the man he looked up and he just move around a little further, went back to reading. Next time he looked up it was the right leg. Well he just moved around a little bit further, goes back to reading again. Next time he looked up it was the arm dropped down. He looks up, goes back to reading. Next time he looks up a body drops down. Bloh—it was kinda heavy. Next time he looked up a head dropped down and united to the body. He just looked around and went back to reading. Next time he looked around there was a woman, she was dressed up and standing on the floor.

Said "What in the name of the Lord do you wants yere?" That's what he axed her.

So she pointed to the door, said "Follow me." They went outdoors, and there was a big apple tree, and she pointed straight down by it, said "Dig here," Said, "Go to the house and get ye a spade—you'll find one in the closet there. You go and get your spade and come back and begin to dig." He digs about seven feet, and he hit a pot. It was about a ten gallon pot. Under the cover it was full of gold. The lady say, "That's why I been coming back. I wanted to give it to some poor person that needed it. I was murdered for money but no one never did find it."

(The others was wicked people, no doubt they was gamblers and murderers—she kept coming back till somebody axed her what she wanted. But he was a Christian, he had a Bible and said, "In the Name of the Lord.")

196 Hardheaded Ghost

Similar texts of stubborn ghosts occur in Ray B. Browne, "Negro Folktales from Alabama" Southern Folklore Quarterly, XVIII (June 1954), p. 130, no. 1, "The Hard Headed Ghost" (living brother pretends he is dead twin's ghost to pacify grieving father); item 8, reel

167 in the University of Arkansas Folklore Archives, told by Mrs. Theresa Warren, Brinkley, Arkansas, 14 Nov. 1953, collected by Mary Celestia Parler (prankster pretends to be ghost of grieving father's dead son); Arthur H. Fauset, "Negro Folk Tales from the South," JAF XL (1927), 270 (text 2 of "The Ghost Walks"); Abrahams, Jungle, pp. 228-229, "Too Much Grief" (parents pray to see dead son, then ask him to go back).

a (JOHN COURTNEY)

They say if your people die while you're young and can't remember, after you get up some size you go to a two-headed woman and she'll call 'em up and let you talk with them. And so fellow by the name of Joe wanted to see his mother and father, had never seen them. So they went to this old lady and told her to call up his father, he wanted to talk with him. So she called him up, and in a few minutes up come his father. So when he got pretty close to her Joe commenced looking at him. So Joe kept looking at him. After a while Joe begin to back up. Joe said, "That's enough, that's enough, I just wanted to see you." So he kept coming you know. Joe say, "I told you to go back, I told you to go back. That's the reason you're dead now, your head is hard."

(Head hard or head long means you go looking for trouble.)

b (TOBE COURTNEY)

Brother died and he was away, and he told them to hold the burying till he got there. But they couldn't wait, they had to bury him. So when he come and they done bury him, he went to praying to the Lord, "Lord, let me see my brother." He hadn't seen him in a long time. And he'd go out to the grave every morning and evening, where he was buried at, praying to see him. At last one evening he went out, and met his brother. He just looked and peeped—it was dusk dark you know—said, "Brother is that you?" [Gesture of looking hard, first on one side then on other] He said that two or three times. Brother just kept a-coming. He said, "Go back brother, I done seed you now." Brother kept coming. Said, "Brother that's how come you dead now, you so hard-headed."

(A schoolteacher told that during the service. Everybody in church just looked like they'd fall out.)

197 On the Cooling Board

Other Negro cooling-board stories were told me in Michigan by John Courtney (Pine Bluff, pp. 84-85), Mary Richardson ("Negro Tales of Mary Richardson" no. 21, pp. 18-19), Willie Sewall, and J. D. Suggs (Pine Bluff, p. 217). All the texts in common derive from the old custom, explained by the storytellers, of shrouding the corpse and laying it on the cooling board all night, while the family sits around, sings, prays, and drinks coffee till daybreak. Richardson and Suggs both lay the tale in their home state, Mississippi, and tell it as truth, although Richardson has the apparently dead man revive from a trance, while with Suggs a trickster stands the dead man up in a corner. Sewall has a seemingly dead man come to while the family are eating baked potatoes, and say, 'I'll take one if it's soft.' He was an old man without teeth. Clear Rock tells how he ran from a corpse on the cooling-board who asked for a potato, in John Lomax, Adventures of a Ballad Hunter *(New York, 1947), pp. 182-184.*

Baughman's Motif J1769.2, "Dead man is thought to be alive," is applicable here, although extracted from a different complex.

a (TOBE COURTNEY)

It was at the church at a wake. In them days they'd have a prayer meeting in the night. Long about the turn of the night John was praying—he was the last of 'em that prayed that night. John you know was in a big way of praying.

"O Lord, have mercy tonight." [*High*]

John when he was praying kept his eyes shut all the time.

"Oh Lord, bless the relatives of this bereaved family." [*High*]

John heard a little rumbling but he thought it was shouting. So after a while he heard a door open, so John when he hollered again he opened his eyes, and there was a fellow sitting up on the cooling board. John looked up and saw him. Everybody done gone but John on his knees. John said, "Hah, hah (say) don't you move, hah hah (say) don't you move, if you ain't dead you will die."

He's moving toward the door all the time, and when he got a space to move he went on outa there.

b (JULIA COURTNEY)

Back in the olden times when anyone died there wasn't any embalming then. They kept the bodies at home. After they bathed them and dress 'em, they lay on the cooling board. And that's why they would stay until they got the casket to put 'em in.

So that night all the people went to the wake. And they sit up until late that night. There was one man there was very sleepyheaded. He slept from the time he get there until everybody was about gone. And he still was 'sleep. So it was two of the mens left there wasn't fraid of dead people. So they 'tided that they would scare this sleepyhead man. They had a few baked potatoes, so they stood the dead man up, peeled a potato, and put it in his mouth. And then they went outside and called this sleepy man. He was pretty hard to wake up. Then they knocked on the wall. That time he heard the noise. He woke up and looked all round and wasn't anyone in the room but him and the dead man. So when he saw the dead man he knew he was dead, and he was 'fraid of dead people.

He looked at the dead man and kind of laughed, and said, "You eating 'tater." He looked at him again and backed up.

And this time he said again, "You eating 'tater." This time he got the door open, and was a cotton patch all around the house.

He broke out in the field and begin to say,
  "You eating 'tater."
And fur as they heard him he kept saying,
  "You eating 'tater."
until he got home.

c (WALTER WINFREY)

This humpback died, and the people came over to wash him up, clean him up, lay him out on the cooling board. So he couldn't lay flat on the board and he lay with his head up and his feet up. Other fellow said, "Tell you what, we'll tie him down, put a string around his head and another around his neck." And they got out on their knees, begin to pray over this feller. And the string from his neck broke and that made him set up, just like a man sitting up you know.

So one guy happened to look up and he seen him sitting up, so he went on out the door. The next guy, he happened to look up, so he went on out,

310

eased out the door. So finally the whole bunch got out and left nobody but the preacher. So he was still down on his knees praying. And when he said "Amen" and raised up, he looked right into this dead fellow's face. So he jumped up and grabbed at his pistol, put it on this fellow and said, "Lay down or I'll kill you again."

198 *The One-Legged Grave Robber* (MARY RICHARDSON)

This unusual story impinges on several popular American tales: the lame man who beats the dogs home on the hunt (Baughman X143.1 gives four Negro examples) or outraces his servant back to the house (see ante, *tale 58, "Old Boss Wants Into Heaven" from John Blackamore); the darer who spends the night on the grave and dies of fear when he pins himself accidentally to the earth (Baughman, Motif N384.2(a) has extensive references); and the buried woman resuscitated by grave robbers (Type 990, "The Seemingly Dead Revives"). Mary Richardson told this narrative during a tape recording (see Dorson, "A Negro Storytelling Session on Tape" pp. 207-208) after Mr. and Mrs. Smith had related tales with the motif of the fast running crippled man. Motif Q212.2, "Grave-robbing punished," is also relevant here.*

Old Mistress died, and when they carried her to the cemetery they put a watch on her, and a gold ring on her finger. And too they put some money in there to pay her fare across Jerdan's River. Well, there was a one-legg'd man lived with the white people and worked in the yard, he wanted the jewelry, but he couldn't get down there on his one leg. And there was a two-legg'd man stayed on the place who wanted it too, but he was afraid to go alone to the cemetery. So he said to the one-legg'd man: "Come on go with me. I'll wheelbarrow you down there tonight, and we'll dig her up and get that jewelry offa her. You don't have to do nothing but just sit in the wheelbarrow; I'll do the digging." So the other says, "All right."

Come night, the two-legg'd man wheelbarrowed him down back of the field, where his old mistress was buried. So he said, "You just sit there; I'll dig the dirt offa her, get down to the coffin, and I'll open it." He taken the dirt off the top of the coffin, and got down to where the box was nailed on top. So he said: "Phew, I'm about here, about got to her. I just believe I'll rest some now, and then we'll lift her out again, and set her up, and take the jewelry off her." So he sits down on the coffin. But they hadn't driv all the

311

nails down right good, and when he aimed to get up, his pants caught a nail. The one-legg'd man standing up on the top said. "What's the matter, John, is she got you?" John didn't say nothing. He tried to get up again, and the nail caught again and pulled tight. So the one-legg'd man repleats [sic], "Is she got you?" John said, "I don't know whether she got me or no, but when I get loose I ain't got time to fool with that wheelbarrow."

So the one-legg'd man says, "Well, I'll go on." And he gets outa the wheelbarrow and starts to the house on his hands and one foot, and he beat the two-legg'd man to the house.

They ran off so fast, they left the cemetery open, and left the wheelbarrow down at Old Miss's grave. So the two-legg'd man crept down there next morning to get it—the wheelbarrow would have betrayed them. And they never got the gold or jewelry off her. But the one-legg'd man beat the two-legg'd man to the house.

FOOL TALES

Visibly the Southern Negro possesses a hair-trigger sense of humor. He relishes a comic story vastly, meets it more than halfway, and laughs with body and soul at even a simple wheeze.[20] Such at any rate has been my experience on numerous field trips. While the dirty joke travels among colored people as readily as among whites, unsoiled jests enjoy great favor with colored people. One jocular pattern involves the gullible and credulous country Negro who plays a fool role, perhaps on a visit to town much like the New England Yankee farmers of an earlier day. In his selection of European folktales, the Negro again shows a penchant for ridiculous scenes. He delights in those Old World fictions that tell of simple-minded girls and old maids who commit follies in quest of husbands. Fools, simpletons, and numskulls parade through the various categories of Negro humorous tales. They may be little boys, white sheriffs, or overly literal dunces, all testifying to the obtuseness of man.

199 *The Fool Discovered* (JULIA COURTNEY)

The only printed analogue besides my own three texts seems to be in Straight Texas, *ed. J. F. Dobie and M. C. Boatright, PTFS, XIII (1937), pp. 159-160, "A Still Tongue Makes a Wise Head" from A. W. Eddins, and condensed in Boatright,* Folk Laughter on the American Frontier (*New York, 1949*), *p. 107. In the variants told me by Mrs. E. L. Smith (printed in* Negro Folktales in Michigan, *p. 194*) *and by J.D. Suggs (printed in* Pine Bluff, *p. 260*) *the little boy is told to say nothing so people will not learn he is a fool. The general Motif J2460, "Literal obedience," in the section of the Motif-Index on Literal Fools, applies here.*

His father didn't have but just that one little boy, and he raised him up in the country. And everything the little boy done, everybody said he was a fool. So his daddy 'tided to take him to town. So he taken him to town and left him on the comer, Main Street, and told the boy, "Speak to everybody."

The people begin to come to town slowly. The boy began to speak slowly. He said, "Good mo'ning. Good mo'ning. Good mo'ning." Begin to be more and more people. He began to speak "Good mo'ning," little faster. Begin to get so many of 'em on the streets, he begin to speak faster and faster, all day long.

That evening two ladies come by and said, "He been standing there all day saying 'Good mo'ning,' and this is evening. He ain't nothing but a fool."

The little boy heard what they said about him. So when his daddy come, he told his daddy, "They found out I was a fool." His daddy taken him home.

Next day his daddy brought him back to town again. In the part of town he put him in they had a little peanut stand. Was a mighty few people in that end of town, but they were friendly. So they begin to speak to the little boy, "Hi little boy." Little boy didn't say anything.

So some little children went where he was and they spoke to him. So one of the kids axed the little boy, "Do you want some peanuts?" The little boy still didn't say anything. He stayed there all day.

More and more people spoke to him. "Hi little boy." [*Cutely*] He still didn't say anything.

Way after while some of the same people come along that evening that had passed that morning. They spoke again to the little boy. "Hi little boy." The little boy still didn't say anything. So they said that he wasn't nothing but a fool because he wouldn't talk to anyone.

So his father come after him. When the little boy saw his father coming he runned and met his daddy and said, "Daddy, daddy, they found out I was a fool after all."

200 *The Boy Who Had Never Seen Women* (MRS. E. L. SMITH)

Type 1678 and Motif T371, "The Boy who had Never Seen a Woman," give wide references, including Boccaccio, but exclusive of North America. Halpert has a New Jersey white text, no. 241, and cites North and South Carolina forms in his note, p. 211, to Randolph's tale, "The Woman-Hater's Son," in The Devil's Pretty Daughter, *pp. 120-122. A variant told me by Walter Winfrey describes the girls as "pumpkins."*

There was a boy in Alabama, I think, they raised never to see a girl till he was twenty-one—they was kind of 'sperimenting. He was raised by mens. So when he was twenty-one his daddy carried him to where the high school children would pass by when they came home for dinner at noon. And he seen them from the windows coming along so pretty, with their ribbons and long hair ('cause they had long hair in those days), and smiling and playing. And he said, "Daddy, Daddy, come here. Looky looky, what are those?" (*Very high*) "Those are ducks." "Give me one, Daddy." "Which one do you want?" "It don't make no difference, daddy, any one."

So it's better to let them grow up with each other, so they can pick a little.

201 *Little Boy Sees Lion* (BEN JONES)

A close variant from Harrison Stanfill is in Pine Bluff, *p. 91. The general motif is J1750, "One animal mistaken for another."*

There was a widow woman that preacher loved to go home with him. And she was boasting to him how truthful her Johnny was, and smart, and never told a lie. So it was a fellow by the name of Sam Jones had a big shepherd dog, and had sheared him and left a switch in his tail. So Johnny he walks out on the porch, and seen this dog walking down the street, and he said, "Look mama, there's a lion coming down the street."

So his mother walked out, and she recognized the dog and said, "Johnny, shame on you, I just told the preacher you never told a lie. Now you come and told a lie in front of him, and you must go up and pray and ask the Lord to forgive you."

So Johnny went upstairs and prayed and asked the Lord to forgive him for that lie. So he stayed awhile and said, "Mama, can I come down now?" Says, "The Lord done heard me pray."

So she said, "Come down and tell us what the Lord said to you."

So he said, "The Lord said, when he first seed that dog he thought he was a lion too."

202 *Young Man in the Morning* (MARY RICHARDSON)

Type 1479, Motif X753, "The Youth Promises to Marry the Old Maid," synopsize the tale as given here, and report it from Russia, Estonia, and Finland. See Hurston,* Mules and Men, *pp. 216-217, "How the Squinch Owl Came to Be"; Parsons, "Guildford," no. 49, p.*

194, "Woman on House-Top." The old woman's cry on the house-top is thus presented by other informants: "I'm shivering cold tonight, but I'm going to marry a young man in the morning, and I'm going to play rat-trap tomorrow night" (Georgia Slim Germany); "I'm going to freeze all night tonight but I'll marry a young man tomorrow night" (Mrs. Smith); "Oooh yes, but young man in the morning" (J. D. Suggs); "Young m-a-a-a-n tomorrow night" (Archie Tyler in Cleveland, Mississippi); "Cold wet sheet tonight, but young man in the morning" (Rev. J. H. Lee in Mound Bayou, Mississsippi).

An old lady lived in the country was anxious to get married, but was too old, like me. And there was a young man come through the yard mornings, who she wanted to marry. So he told her, "If you wet your sheet and wrap it around you, and stay on the roof all night tonight, I'll marry you in the morning."

And she was fool enough to try it. She wrapped the wet sheet around her and went upon the roof, and sat there and shivered. The young man stayed in the house to make sure she stayed on the roof. Through the night he could hear her shivering and saying:

    Oooooh, oooooh,
    Young man in the morning.

She meant she'd just make it till morning, if she didn't freeze. (She sure was dumb.) Every time she said it she'd get weaker. So about three o'clock in the morning the sheet was ice, and the young man heard her rolling off the roof of the house and hit the ground in the yard, froze stiff. And when she landed he says, "What a blessing. No old woman for me."

203 Nearsighted Old Lady (JULIA COURTNEY)

This is Type 1456, "The Blind Fiancée" and Motif K1984.5, "Blind fiancée betrays self." See E. C. Parsons, Folk-Lore of the Sea Islands, South Carolina, MAFLS XVI (1923), no. 117, p. 114, "The Blind Old Woman," and note summarizing a variant in the records of the Hampton Folk-Lore Society, and referring to another published in JAF by Portia Smiley, "Folk-Lore from Virginia, South Carolina, Georgia, Alabama, and Florida," XXXII (1919), no. 17, p. 365 (same title). In the Ozark text of Vance Randolph, who says the tale is known throughout the region (note, p. 206, in Who Blowed Up the Church House?; see pp. 86-87 for "The Pin in the Gatepost"), a nearsighted but goodlooking young girl sets her cap for a rich old man. Negro variants I collected appear in Negro Folktales in Michigan, *p. 192, "The Old Lady with Poor Eyesight," from Mary Richardson; in "Negro Tales from Bolivar County, Mississippi," no. 15, p. 113, "Old Lady Who Couldn't See Well," from Rev. J. H. Lee; and in* Pine Bluff, *pp. 100-101, from Tobe Courtney.*

A man wanted to marry a woman that could see real good. So he started to cou'ting on her. (You know how it is, some old people want to be real young.) He done cou'ted all around and every time he come on one she couldn't see like she oughta. That was his idea y'see. So someone was telling him about this wealthy woman. So he 'cided he'd go and see her. When he got to her home he introduced hisself to her. She introduced herself to him, and axed him in. They made good friends, and from time to time he would go and see her. He cou'ted her for a long time, until at last one time he went to her home, she invited him over one night. So when he got there, she had a maid to fix him some tea. They drank tea together, laughed and talked. And so she had a maid to understand you know, to stick a needle up in the gatepost. So 'bout time she figgered she had the needle out there, she got up an' stretched, "Ho ho, let's walk out on the porch and set in the cool." So when they gotten out there and set down, they had no more sit down good when she played like, "Look like to me I see something out there on that gatepost." And she called to her maid and said, "Go out there and look on that gatepost." Said, "Look like to me I see something out there shining."

So her maid went on out there and played like she's looking for it. But she knew it was there. After while the maid said, "It's a needle." So the maid brought it to her.

The man began to like her better. He says, "You're the very one I want, someone can see real good."

That night he axed her to marry. The next day, she had plenty money, boy she put a wedding out, because she wanted a husband badder than he wanted a wife. The night of the wedding come. She had her maid just to cook up much food. And they prepared a big dining room table. Unbeknownst to her mistress she set a great big old white pitcher of milk on the comer of the table betweenst the bride and groom. And OP Mistress had a big white cat too. Everyone circled around the table and sit down and began to eat. They had been eating a good while, when suddenly she happened to kinda glaze around and see this pitcher a milk. She slapped the pitcher of milk off the table, and says, "Get off from here, you nasty stinking cat you."

So he found out then she couldn't see at all. So he had married her then, but that was the separation. So she still didn't have her husband.

(I thought that was one of the most precious stories when I heard it. When we were cou'ting we told sweet stories, no nasty ones.)

I just know how that dining room floor was messed, and all them guests.

204 *Three More Bigger Fools* (JULIA COURTNEY)

This tale includes Types 1450, "Clever Elsie" 1384, "The Husband Hunts Three Persons as Stupid as His Wife"; 1210, "The Cow is Taken to the-Roof to Graze"; 1245, "Sunlight carried in a Bag into the Windowless House," and 1286, "Jumping into the Breeches," which are often joined. Baughman reports these as among the most popular folktales in England and the United States. Three characteristic Negro examples of this combination are in Parsons, Folk-Lore of the Sea Islands, South Carolina, no. 87, pp. 94-97, "Three More Damn Fools," who gives further references. Emelyn E. Gardner notes these Negro variants at the end of her extended commentary on a text, "The Four Fools," in Folklore from the Schoharie Hills, New York (Ann Arbor, 1937), pp. 163-172. West Indies texts of Type 1450 from Andros Island, Barbados, Guadaloupe, Jamaica, and Puerto Rico are cited in Flowers. A version close to the present one is in "Negro Tales of Mary Richardson," no. 29, pp. 23-24. Mrs. E. L. Smith told me Type 1450 by itself. An engaged couple goes down to the spring to get water, and falls to studying what to name the first baby; each successive member of the family asks "What's the matter with yourance?" and joins the brown study, until a neighbor man says, "That's easy, if it's a girl name it Puss, and if it's a boy name it Dick." Suggs has a tale of three fools, Pine Bluff, pp. 260-261. The present text differs from those of Richardson and Smith in that the silly woman worries about the father of her children rather than about the name of her baby.

Two old peoples had young daughter. So the one daughter had a boy friend whom was cou'ting her, name was John. So John one day axed the girl to marry him. So the girl come home and told her mother and father, "I and John is going to get married." The next day her mother was fixing to cook dinner. She sent the girl down to the next house to draw some molasses. (They had sorghum molasses in sixty gallon barrels in those days. We had a sharecropper house didn't no one stay in it, and we kept things in it.)

So when she got there she set her bucket down under the barrel and poured the stopper out the barrel, and the molasses begin to run slowly. So she sit down and begin to think about her marriage. She said, "If John and I marry, who will be the father of our first two children?" So she sit down and begin to cry.

She stayed down there so long until her mother thought she'd go and see her daughter. When she got there she saw the girl was crying. So she axed the girl, "Honey, what you crying for?"

And the girl told her, "I was just studying, mother; if John and I marry, who would be the father of our first two children?"

Her mother said, "Well, that's something to think about." And the old lady sit down and begin to think too. "If my daughter marry, who would be the father of the first two children?"

Twelve o'clock come, the old man come home from work, father's gone out in the store, and wasn't nothing done. He said, "Mhm, wonder what happened to the old lady?" He decided that he would go and see. When he got there the molasses had run the bucket over, all over the floor, and running off the porch. He went on in, and when he got in there he axed what was the matter.

And so the old lady told him, "I sent the baby down here to get some molasses to make molasses bread for dinner. And when she got in here, and turned the 'lasses on, she said she sit down and begin to think, if her and John marry who would be the father of their first two children."

So the old man said, "That's something to think about." He sit down and begin to think too. So all three of 'em was sitting down thinking about the same thing.

Way after while salesman come along. He stopped at the house and honked his horn. No one come to the door, but he knew someone was there by seeing the 'lasses running out the house, into the road. So he decided he'd go and see where the molasses was coming from ('cause the people wasn't saying anything). So he saw the three of 'em sitting down, not either one of them saying a word. So he axed 'em, "What's the matter with you-all?"

So the old man told him. "We was all thinking, if our daughter would marry John, who would be the father of her first two children?"

So the man said, "I'm going on down the road a little further, and if I find three more fools, bigger than your daughter, I'll come back and marry her."

So he left and went on down the road about a mile further. And the first thing he saw was a old raggedy shangle-topped house with long moss on top. One of the boys was in front had a long rope, the other one was behind the house with a stick beating the cow, trying to make her climb up upon the house and eat the moss off. The man said, "That ain't the way to do that." Said, "Take the rope off the cow, and put her back in the lot and cut the moss off the top of the house, and carry to the cow."

So then he went back and got in his car, and drove down the road just a little further. This time this old lady had scrubbed her house, and the way she scrubbed her house, she took the bucket and went to the pump, and pumped it full of water, and just dosled it in there. She put so much water in her house, until she couldn't sweep it all out. So the old man 'cided he would get the wheelbarrow and roll the sun in to dry it. This time the man told him, "Let you h'ist your windows, that's the way to dry your house."

So then he got on his journey again, and went 'bout a mile further, And before he gotten there, he saw a man standing way by. And then he'd run and jump. When he gotten there, he saw the man had his pants with a rope tied on each side of 'em. So he told the man, "That ain't the way to put no pants on. Take the ropes off of it, and put one foot in each leg." This time the salesman thought about the pretty girl that was studying, if her and John marry, who would be the father of their first two children.

So he went back there and told the girl that "I have found three more bigger fools than you was. So now I come back to marry you."

205 The Silly Girl (GRACE BEDFORD)

Here the previous tale-types are combined (save for the two forgotten episodes of Types 1245 and 1286) with Type 1541, "Tor the Long Winter" (Motif K362.1) and Type 1653A, "Guarding the Door" (Motif K335.1.1.1, "Door falls on robbers from tree"). The 1541-1653A combination appears in Par-sons, Folk-Lore of the Sea Islands, South Carolina, *no. 147, p. 132, "Mr. Hard-Times," text 1; and in Halpert,* Folktales and Legends from the New Jersey Pines, *no. 178, "Mr. Time-of-Need; Above the Robbers," who gives full references* (*vol. II, pp. 661-663*). *A text of "Mr. Hard Times" I collected from Archie Tyler appears in "Negro Tales from Bolivar County, Mississippi" no. 19, pp. 114-115. Mrs. E. L. Smith in Calvin told me a variant of "Mr. Hard Times" in which the child of a "widder woman" gives the money she had saved in her old black stocking to the stranger. Grimm no. 59, "Frederick and Catherine," contains pretty much the 1541-1653A story, with a foolish wife giving her husband's money away and then luckily rescuing it from the robbers with the aid of the house-door. Flowers reports eleven variants of Type 1653 from the West Indies, and five of Type 1541; two of the latter, from Andros Island and Antigua, have the 1653 ending of the robbers under the tree.*

(I heard this from my mother and father. They were both very good storytellers. My mother's people came from South Carolina and my father's from Georgia. They were born in Arkansas. Doesn't it sound like a mountain story?)

A traveling salesman was going around from house to house in the country. And come dinner time he asked this lady to prepare him some food. She consented to fix him a ham dinner, and sent the girl to the smokehouse for the ham. Lena was twenty-five years old and she'd never been married. She was called an old maid, back there then. Out in the smokehouse were great big hams and they were hanging from the rafters. Lena stared up at the hams and said to herself, "If those hams would fall on me I'd never get a chance to marry." And she stayed so long, her mother she came out to see.

And when the daughter told the mother what detained her, her mother said the same thing, "If one of those hams would fall on you, you'd never get a chance to marry."

And the father gets alarmed on the front porch, so he goes around the back to see what's the trouble, and he agrees with them.

"Oh yes, that's true, if one of those hams should fall on you, you'd never get a chance to marry."

And that's the way the salesman finds them, all three of them staring at the ham, saying "Oh yes, if the ham should fall you'd never get a chance to marry."

So he tells them, "Well if I can find two other people as silly as you, I'll come back and marry the girl."

Finally he comes to a house where a handful of green grass is growing in the eaves, and the people are trying to pull the cow on top of the house to eat the sprig, or bunch, of green grass.

(I can't recall the second one.)

After he finds the two other silly incidents, he goes back and marries the girl. But her silliness pays off—have you heard that?

Every so often he would bring her a few coins of money and tell her to keep it for Mr. Hard Times. She, thinking it was a person, a man, was very anxious for Mr. Hard Times to come, so she could give him the money. Finally one day a hobo passed, begging for food. He asked her, he was hungry, could she give him some bread and he would cut her some wood. And she asked him if he was Mr. Hard Times. He said, "I surely am."

So she said (You notice each part of the story seems to belong to a different age. Each one adds his part as he tells it. I'm trying to tell it as it was told to me), "I have something better for you than just a piece of bread. My husband has been saving for you." She goes inside, gets the coins and gives them to him.

Soon after her husband comes home, and she tells him, "Oh, Mr. Hard Times came, and I gave him the coins." He was startled. And so he asked her which way he went, and started down the road after him. And he told her to come on with him and "pull the door to behind you." (In those days they hooked it on.) She was coming along so slowly behind him he looked back and saw her carrying the door on her back. Then he took the door so they could go faster.

Night came and they had to stop. It was in the woods, and he put the door up in the tree and they lay down on it. It was a shiny new door, because it came from a new house—they were just married. Some robbers came and settled under this tree to count their money. And they got so loud and quarreling over the money the girl was wakened, and she became frightened and screaming. She began twisting, and the door lost its balance and fell down on them. Just as they looked up, the white skirt and apron looked ghostly, and the shiny door, and she screaming, and they just left.

So they got more money than they lost.

206 *Three Wishes* (WALTER WINFREY)

Motif 12071, "Three foolish wishes," which also turns up in Type 750A, "The Wishes." This story is best known in the version of Grimm no. 87, "The Poor Man and the Rich Man." Randolph has it as "The Three Wishes," in Who Blowed Up the Church House?, *pp. 139-140, and note, p. 217. It appears to be enjoying a modern revival in the present burlesque form. I collected a text in Maine, printed in my* Buying the Wind *(Chicago, 1964), p. 83.*

This was a cowboy, and he wanted to be a strong man. So he saddled his horse and went down the street riding along. A snake crossed the path before him, and he taken his gun out to shoot it. So the snake says, "Mr. Cowboy, don't shoot me, and I'll make you any deal that you want me to." So the cowboy says: "All right. Make me three wishes." The snake tells him, "Go ahead and wish." So the cowboy says: "I wisht I had muscles like Joe Louis. And I'd like to have features like Clark Gable." And he says, "I'd like to be as strong as this stud I'm riding."

So the snake says, "Okay, you go home, go to bed early, get up in the morning and see if you've got your wishes."

So the cowboy got up the next morning; he throwed his bathrobe back; he says, "I got the muscles like Joe Louis." He looked in the mirror, and he says, "I got the features like Clark Gable." Then he pulled his bathrobe back again and looks down. He says, "Well, I'll be durned; I forgot I was riding a mare."

207 *Dreaming Contest* (HAROLD LEE)

Under Motif K66 "Dream Contests" Baughman lists one Master and Negro and four Indian and white man examples. The Negro variant in J. Mason Brewer, "How John Stopped His Boss-man from Dreaming" Mexican Border Ballads and Other Lore, PTFS XXI (1946), pp. 89-90, has John get the best of the officious planter. Usually the white man out-dreams the Indian; the earliest version involves Sir William Johnson and Hendrick, king of the Mohawk nation. See my "Comic Indian Anecdotes" Southern Folklore Quarterly, X (June 1946), 122, quoting from The Merry Fellow's Companion; or American Jest Book (Harrisburgh, 1797); and Harold W. Thompson, Body, Boots and Britches (Philadelphia, 1940), p. 177, who takes the tale from Funny Stories: or the American Jester (New York, 1804), and gives variants attached to other persons.

Dreams is very significant with us you know. We both were farmers, wealthy, and I had a piece of property you wanted, and you were figuring how to outwit me out of it. You figured I like to dream, and my dreams were so insignificant and minor, you thought you'd make my dreams come true if I made your dreams come true.

I would have such unsignificant dreams as about hunting and fishing and how many chickens I had and all. About three or four weeks I was just dreaming about how many fish I'd caught, and ducks I'd shot, and snakes I'd killed. And all that time you wasn't dreaming nothing. So it comes the time you dreamed that all my children was working for you, had left school, all my money was yours, and property, livestock, feedstuff, my wife was working for you and I your horseman.

I had to make that dream true. In the course of time you noticed me not dreaming no more. About six months I was quiet, singing my songs, doing my work. Finally one morning I woke you up, telling you I had a dream. I dreamed that my kids were back in school, that I had all my money back, my property, livestock, foodstuff, and everything you owned was mine, and I dreamed that I ain't going dream no more.

208 *Hunting Partners* (GRACE BEDFORD)

Baughman under Motif X584.2* summarizes this episode, and gives three references, two from Texas (Negro) and one from Canada. See the Fables of Aesop, *trans. S. A. Handford (Penguin Books: Melbourne, London, Baltimore, 1954), no. 177, p. 181, "Share and Share Alike."*

My uncle used to tell a tale about the fellows going hunting. (Guess this was back in the times of slavery.) There were two fellows hunting, one could shoot very well, the other one couldn't. The bears were bad in that locality, and everybody was encouraged to shoot the bears. The one who could shoot well shot the bear. The other fellow who couldn't shoot so well said, "Oh look what we've done, we've killed the bear."

The good shooter said, "We nothing, I killed that bear, and that's the way it's going to be."

So old Marster had a big fine horse in the pea patch. He was trigger happy, and shot the horse, thinking it was a bear. When he see what he had done, he said, "Look what we done."

The little one said, "*We* nothing. You did it, and that's the way it's going to be."

209 *Who Darket the Hole?* (SILAS ALTHEIMER)

This is Motif X1133.3.2, "If the wolf's tail breaks." Halpert appends to a non-Negro text in Folktales and Legends from the New Jersey Pines, *no. 187, p. 699, references from Alabama, Georgia, North Carolina, South Carolina, Texas, and Virginia (all Negro), and Newfoundland, Nova Scotia, Ontario, and Scotland. See Bacon and Parsons, "Folk-Lore from Elizabeth City County, Virginia," no. 54, p. 292, "What Darkens the Hole?", for a text and two references. Suggs ends the tale with Type 1900, "How the Man Came out of a Tree Stump" (Pine Bluff, pp. 253-254). I also have a close variant from E. M. Moore (Pine Bluff, pp. 87-88).*

Sambo and Jim Bungum were straggling through the woods one day looking for muscadines and wild grapes. And finally they came upon an embankment with a ditch below and a large stump up above, where there was high ground, which went down into the hole. And the stump was hollow at the top. So Jim Bungum went down and peeped into the big hole below, and saw some bear cubs. So he decided to go in, to get him one of the cubs. In the meantime the bear at some distance had seen them. The bear came in great haste, and she chased Sambo round and round a good while. And finally the bear quit chasing Sambo, and stuck her head in the stump on the high ground. And she started down the hole from the embankment. And so when she got part way down Sambo grabbed her by the tail and held her.

And so Jim Bungum down below said, "Sambo, who darket de hole?"

Sambo says, "If tail hold slip you'll see who darket de hole."

210 *Greasing the Baby* (ARCHIE "BILLY JACK" TYLER)

Motif J2465, "Disastrous following of instructions," is present here. In a tale from St. Martin in the West Indies, a sick man, told by the doctor to place a plaster on his chest to relieve his cold, places it on his trunk (Parsons, Antilles, Part III, no. 16, p. 410, "Trunk").

There was an old man and an old lady that lived in Arkansas. In the first part of the winter their baby had her first cold and they didn't know what it was. So the old man decided to carry the baby to the doctor. When he got to the doctor's office, the doctor told him wasn't anything wrong with the baby but a chest cold. He told them to take the baby and grease his chest and warm him by the fire. The old man carried the baby back home and told the old lady to grease the baby and warm him by the fire because he had to go back to town, and it would be dark before he could get back. After he had gone, the old lady greased the baby all over and put him in a frying pan. And as the baby began to cook, the skin drawed up on his forehead. And it looked as if he was grinning.

And the old lady said, "Grin and endure it, child, grin and endure it." By that time the old man had made it home, and he axed the old lady, how was the baby getting along. She said, "You will be surprised to see how he is grinning in that frying pan in the stove." And the old man repeated what she said: "Grin and endure it, child, grin and endure it."

211 *Ketch Me John* (JOHN COURTNEY)

Paul climbed up a great tall pole, and had to climb up there to do some work. John told him, say, "Hell I wouldn't go up there." John kept prevailing with him not to go. So Paul climbed to just about the top of it, and he lost his holt.

And Paul lost his holt, he commenced to hollering to John,
    "Ketch me John. [*Very high*]
    Ketch me John, ketch me."
So John wasn't paying no attention. After a while John looked up, and Paul was pretty close to the ground then. John grabbed the rake, said, "I'll just level a place for this son-of-a-bitch, 'cause I see he's going to splatter all over everything."

212 *Oh Lord Oh Devil* (J. D. SUGGS)

This incident also appears in a localized tale by Suggs, ante, no. 138.

A fellow was topping a tree (cut the top out so it will spread and make shade—it's dangerous but there's big money in it). Well he stepped on a rotten limb and it broke. Here he come tumbling down. He hit on one limb, that would break his fall. Say "Oh Lord, oh Devil." About that time he'd fall offa that limb down on another. He was falling awful slow. He was hollering all the time, "Oh Lord, oh Devil, oh Lord, oh Devil." So he fell and hit the ground and he didn't get much of a jar, the limbs had broke his fall, and he didn't have to fall more'n five feet to hit the ground.

People asked him, "Why were you calling on the Lord first and then the Devil, what were you calling on both of 'em for?"

He said, "Well, I hadn't been too good, and neither too bad, so I didn't know which one of 'em's hands I was going to fall into. So I called on both of 'em." So he'd be right, didn't care what hand he fall into.

213 *The Bootlegger* (J. D. SUGGS)

This seems like a plausible enough incident, but it is a traveling story. See Randolph, Who Blowed Up the Church House?, *pp. 70-72, "The Vinegar Jug" Randolph refers to one close Ozark variant, p. 200. In Brewer,* Worser Days, *p. 66, "The Deputy Sheriff and the Negro Bootlegger," the trick is pulled by a Negro from Wilkesboro, N. C.*

The revenue man in prohibiting days was out trying to catch a bootlegger. So, Sam (I know his right name but I won't call his name personally) was coming down Lawton Street; and the revenue man, the agent, we'll say, he was on the corner, looking shabby. "Say, boy," the agent called to Sam, "come here." Sam goes over to him and the agent flashes a ten-dollar bill. He says, "I'll give you this if you get me a quart of whiskey." Sam says, "Yessir, but a quart will cost you forty dollars." So he gives Sam forty dollars. Sam has a shoebox under his arm. He asks the agent, "Will you hold this shoebox till I go around the corner? I'll be right back." So the law he taken the box and held it for Sam, while Sam went to get the whiskey. Sam stayed so long, he said, "I'm going to see what's in this box." So there was his quart of whiskey. He had his quart of whiskey, Sam had his forty dollars, but the law hasn't got his man yet.

That's true, sure enough; that happened in St. Louis.

214 *The Monkey Who Impitated His Master* (J. D. SUGGS)

The first episode is the well known story of "Big 'Fraid and Little 'Fraid," Type 1676A and Motif K1682.1. Baughman reports seventeen examples, including Negro texts from Florida, Pennsylvania, Louisiana, and Virginia. Getting the remainder of the tale is another matter however. The Motif-Index gives one West African and one West Indies example for Motif K585, "Fatal game: shaving necks. Dupe's head cut off." Botkin, Burden, *p. 23, "Fatal Imitation," alone*

combines these two motifs of the imitating monkey. The middle episode
of the monkey running off with the train I have not found anywhere.

Mr. Jones had a monkey, a pet monkey, and everything Mr. Jones would do, he would do. But Mr. Jones didn't know the monkey was impitating him all the time. Mr. Jones was a engineer, that was his job.

One night Mr. Jones hears some boys coming down the road. He lived close to the cemetery; so he thought, "I'll just have some fun outa those boys; I'll play ghost, hant." So he grabs him a sheet right quick and out the back door he went. And his pet monkey grabbed him a towel, and out the door he went behind Mr. Jones. Mr. Jones lay down covered up in the sheet but he never looked back; he hadn't no suspicion at all. The monkey lay down right behind him and wrapped up in the towel like his master. One boy said, "Look, yonder's a hant, a great big one." Next boy says, "Yeah, and a little hant is laying behind the big hant; there's two of them." Mr, Jones looked behind him and he seen the monkey and thought it was a little hant, and he got up and started to running, and the monkey ran right behind him. The boys commenced hollering, "Run, big hant; little hant gonna catch you." They thought the little hant was after the big one. So Mr. Jones run home and jumps in his bed. And the monkey run in the house right behind him and jumps in his bed too. Mr. Jones don't know yet the monkey was with him.

So the next night the engineer was called out to take his train on its run. The monkey he eased on behind him and gets up on the coal tender. So the train pulls out. They run about forty miles before they get to another town, where they had to stop to get orders. So while they're getting the orders they all stand around behind the depot talking, and the fireman he's standing around too. The monkey seed how the engineer had started off, so he pulls the throttle and off she goes. None of the crew knew what the matter was, till the monkey stuck his head out the window, like he seen the engineer doing, with his left hand on the throttle, and then they knew what was happening. So the operator ran back and commenced sending messages down the road ahead of him: "All trains take the side track, for the monkey has the main line." So the monkey ran about sixty miles before the steam run out; he didn't have nobody to fire for him.

That's how Mr. Jones found out the monkey was tricking him. Well, he didn't want to give him away and he didn't want to sell him; so when he got home he studied up a scheme to get rid of him. He gets some soap and his bresh and lathers his face good. Then he shaves the lather off. Next he takes the razor and jerks the back of it across his throat quick. Then he lays it down and walks out. So the monkey he had slipped in there and watched him, and as soon as Mr. Jones walks out he lathers. Well, it only takes him two or three strokes to get the suds off his face. So he takes the razor then, but he didn't turn it over like his master had; he tuck the blade and jerked it across his throat, and committed suicide. So his master got rid of him without selling or killing him or giving him away. He tricked the monkey for trying to impitate him.

(That's what happens when a fellow tries to impitate another.)

215 *The Animals in Night Quarters* (J. D. SUGGS)

Type 130 bears this title, and refers to Motif K1161, "Animals hidden in various parts of a house attack owner." This is Grimm no. 27, well known in Europe. Richard Chase has a text in The Jack Tales *(Boston, 1943), no. 4, "Jack and the Robbers," annotated by Herbert Halpert, p. 191, who lists five white references and one Negro from the United States, and another Negro source from the Bahamas. Roberts has the tale as his no. 1, "The Animals and the Robbers," and refers also to J. M. Carrière,* Tales from the French Folk-Lore of Missouri *(Evanston and Chicago, 1937), no. 1, pp. 19-21, "P'tsit Jean."*

Well, there was a fellow traveling once, a hobo, a drifter, who'd been up around the wheat harvests. He seen a house down the road there, and it was raining and cold; so he decided to go in and stay all night. It was dark in there, and he pushes the door open and walks in. The goat was coming out and butted him. Before he could get up the goose grabbed him and commenced hitting him with his wings. Down came the cat, right across his head he went, as he was making for the door. That fuss woke the rooster up —it was about twelve o'clock—and he began to crow—"Urh-urh-urh." By that time the man got up and out the door he went.

Down the road he run, up to another house. Ran up to the door and told the man: "There's robbers or hants in the next house. As soon as I got in the door, one man knocked me down with a maul. Another man carded me in the head with his cards." (He thought it was a carding machine to get knots out of wool.) "Another man setting on the end of the log said, 'Bring the rascal up here.' " (*Chanted*)

And the one that owned the house said, "Why that weren't nothing; that's where I keep my goat and my goose and my cat and my rooster."

216 *I Eat a Barrel of Pickle* (EFFIE DEAN HALL)

Type 2028 and Motif 233.4, "The Troll who was Cut Open." Curiously, this seldom reported story (Thompson says it is well known in Scandinavia and an analogue has been found in east Africa, The Folktale, p. 231) is collected in four variants by Roberts, no. 77a-d. Richard Chase has a text in Grandfather Tales *(Boston, 1948), no. 7, pp. 75-79, "Sody Sallyraytus." Three of Roberts's texts and Chase's have a bear as the gluttonous creature; Roberts's third variant is a "Greedy Fat Man."*

I eat a barrel of pickle,
I drink a barrel of wine,
I'll eat you if I catch you.

There's a man he was real big and fat. He ate a barrel of pickle; he drank a barrel of wine, every day. And so one day he met a little girl, and she say, "What makes you so big and fat?" He says, "I eat a barrel of pickle, I drink a barrel of wine, and I'll eat you if I catch you." And he chased her, and he caught her, and he ate her up.

And then he met a little boy. The boy said, "What makes you so big and fat?" He said, "I eat a barrel of pickle, I drink a barrel of wine, and I'll eat you if I catch you." And he caught him and he ate him up.

And then he met an old lady. She said, "What makes you so big and fat?" He said, "I eat a barrel of pickle, I drink a barrel of wine, and I'll eat you if I catch you." And so he caught her and ate her up.

And then he met an old farmer. The farmer said, "What makes you so big and fat?" He said, "I eat a barrel of pickle, I drink a barrel of wine, and I'll eat you if I catch you." And he caught him and he ate him up.

And then he met a rabbit. The rabbit said, "Mister, what makes you so big and fat?" He said, "I eat a barrel of pickle, I drink a barrel of wine, and I'll eat you if I catch you." And he went to chasing the rabbit. And he couldn't catch him. And they went running and running. And this old man he fell over a barbed wire fence, and he fell and bust open. And all the people got out of him.

See that pumpkin? Go get it,
And I'll make you a coach out of it.

217 *Johnny's Story* (EFFIE DEAN HALL)

This story suggests Type 1360B, "Flight of the Woman and her Lover from the Stable," especially the first two episodes, where a man who has observed the pair enters the woman's house, and relates the situation at the meal in the form of a tale. Effie Dean had another amorous tale along this line, "Harry and Such as That and Some of 'Em," where hidden lovers are flushed out by the accidental calling of their names (see Smiley no. 31, p. 372, "Three Sweethearts"). This idea is found in Abrahams, pp. 201-202, "Himself Discovered." Motif K1550, "Husband outwits adulteress and paramour," fits here.

Once there was a man and his wife. And this lady she was going with another man. And every time her husband would go away the man would come over to her house. So one day the husband was going to work. He saw a boy setting on the side of the road. The boy's name was Johnny. And he axed the boy, "What are you good for?" And the boy says, "All for catching up with womens and their devilment." And he said: "I want you to go over to my house and stay. And I want you to tell me everything that goes on."

So that evening the other man comes over, and the woman she cooked him a pig and some big biscuits. But the husband came home early, and he says, "Johnny, tell me a story." And the boy said: "One day I was traveling, and I got mighty hungry. And there was a hawk came by, and went to running a hog. And he ran him up a tree. And the hog was throwing apples at the hawk, about as big as those biscuits up in the chimney. And the hog was built about as big as that pig up in the chimley. And the hog was scared of him, as that man up under the bed is a-scared of you." And the man ran from up under there, and the husband was trying to catch him.

And about that time I stepped on a pin, and slipped on away from there.

---

[20] Newbell N. Puckett comments in similar vein on Negro humor, in *Folk Beliefs of the Southern Negro* (Chapel Hill, 1926), p. 49, "Negro Jokes."

LYING TALES

"They's what we call gallyfloppers," Mrs. Smith remarked after telling a big story, of the kind ordinarily called Münchausens, long bows, windies, or just tall tales. Southern Negroes have adopted this favorite American species of folktale with a ready relish for its solemn exaggeration, and spin familiar "lies" about giant vegetables, excessively lazy loafers, fabulous marksmen and clever bedbugs. Only a few tall tales seem to enjoy more Negro than white popularity, such as the whopper about the oversized mosquito or "gallinipper." Suggs surprised me, though, with his picture of Brother Bill, a Negro cowboy, careening down Main Street on a panther, and performing desperado feats in exact replica of the superman cowboy, Pecos Bill. The first Pecos Bill article appeared in 1923, and books later expanded its content, but in the manner of synthetic Paul Bunyan fabrication. However, Suggs claims to have heard the Brother Bill saga in Texas in 1908, and John Blackamore knew the same exploits about the colored cowhand as a rhymed "toastie;" so apparently a genuine precedent to Pecos Bill exists in Negro tall-tale humor, consistent even to the Texas locale and the name of Bill. On the other hand, the heroic exploits that one might expect to hear about John Henry defeating the steam drill with his hammer fail to materialize.

218 *The Lucky Shot* (J. D. SUGGS)

Two of the most popular American tall tales are here combined, Type 1890, "The Lucky Shot," whose numerous variants Baughman has arranged into seven subdivisions, and Type 1917, Motif 1785.1, "The Stretching and Shrinking Harness," for which he reports twenty-five North American examples. Hurston Mules and Men, *pp. 151-153, "Tall Hunting Story," also has the combination. I have six New England examples of Type 1890, continuing from the eighteenth to the twentieth century, in "Jonathan Draws the Long Bow," New England Quarterly, XVI (1943), 253-259.*

Fellow went out hunting. He didn't have but one shell. And he happened to look up, and first thing he seed was ten ducks sitting on one limb. He looked over to one side before he shot, and saw a panter standing there. He looked over on his left—there was a big buck standing there. He looked behind, and there was a covey of partridge right behind him. He didn't know which one to shoot at. He looked straight in front of him and he seed a big bear coming towards him. He knowed he had to shoot the bear, for the bear would kill him—he knowed that. So he cocked both muzzles of a double-barreled muzzle loader, pulled both triggers the same time. The shot killed the bear. The ramrod shot out and hit the limb and caught the ducks' toes before they could fly away. And the hammer on the left, it flew off and killed the deer. The right hammer, it flew off and killed the panter. He kicked his overcoat off, and smothered the covey of partridges.

So he wondered how he was going to get all this game home. He had a big knife he'd made at the blacksmith's shop, that he carried with him. So he cut him down two saplings to make him a sled with slip elms (pussy willows) across, and tied it with the bark. Then he skinned the deer, and cut it in strips about three inches wide. That was for his harnesses, so he could pull the sled. So he begin to pull, going home with his game. When he got home he didn't see a sign of the sled—the skin had done stretched. So he just tied the harnesses to the gatepost. He said: "I'm hungry. I'll go eat a snack and then go back for it." The sunshine came out bright and hot. So he went to the door and looked. Here come his sled and all his game on it slowly dragging up. The sun had dried the harnesses while he was eating.

219 *Dead-Shot Ben Jackson* (J. D. SUGGS)

Personal brags of hunting, shooting and fighting form standard themes in American folk humor. The tradition is especially manifest in the tales about Davy Crockett; see my Davy Crockett, American Comic Legend (*New York, 1939*), *particularly the chapters on "Davy Conquering Beast" and "Davy Conquering Man."*

Ben Jackson was the turriblest man for telling lies. He had us laughing till it hurt; he could carry expression with everything he said, and he never missed a word. He did timber work, cutting staves for the mill, and when work quit, he had the floor. He came from Virginia, but I knew him down at Indianola, Mississippi.

Ben told us he was hunting at a lake once. He said: "I sat down there and rested, looking for a squirrel. And a big land-beast, which was a cow, went down to the water to get a drink. And a big water-animal, which was a alligator, hit her with his tail and knocked her in. And I said to myself, 'Doggone the luck in the thirteen hells; I can't set here and let a water-animal destroy a land-beast thataway.' I up with my Winchester, and I shot him thirty-two times under his left eyelid before he could wink his eye."

They had pump Winchesters in those days too.

While he was dancing a square dance at Fasonia, he stepped on a fellow's foot. The fellow cussed him and called him a bad name, and up with his 45. "I had a little bitty 32, and I shot him five times. And he wouldn't fall. I walks over to him, taken my little bitty 32, and knocked him down. And I told him, 'Doggone the luck in the thirteen hells; now lay down and die like a man.' "

220 *Brother Bill* (J. D. SUGGS)

"The Saga of Pecos Bill" was first written up by Edward O'Reilly in the Century Magazine *in 1923 (v. 106, pp. 827-833). Although the Pecos Bill legend has been challenged on the same grounds as that of Paul Bunyan (thus see Brent Ashabranner, "Pecos Bill—An Appraisal," in* Western Folklore, *XI, 1952, 20-24) it now appears that the panther-riding cowboy did exist in oral tradition. John Blackamore told me the Brother Bill yarn as a toastie, and see Talley, p. 94, "Wild Negro Bill."*

John was telling about his brother Bill. Bill was a colored cowboy out on a ranch in El Paso, Texas. John he stayed in town. He hadn't seen Bill in a long time.

"I looked down the road and seed Brother Bill coming down on a bobcat. He had two guns, one on each side; he had barbed wire for his bridle reins (on his naked hands too) and a five rattlesnake, a diamond-back rattlesnake for a riding whip (that's the baddest snake we got in the United States). He run up to the drugstore, and jumped down and ran inside to the pharmacy. Told the man to give him a big glass of glycerine mixed with twenty sticks of dynamite. Pharmacist he made it and handed it to him. Bill turns it up and drinks it down, all in one gulp. Reaches on each side and gets his two guns. Went a walking down the street yelling, 'I'm a bad man.' Killed him twenty men. Came back and got on his bobcat. He left town, and I haven't heard from my brother Bill since."

221 *Turning the Buffalo Around* (J. D. SUGGS)

This is Type 1889B, Motif X11242, "Hunter Turns Animal Inside Out," for which Baughman lists nine American examples.
When I was in Wyoming in 1923 I heard an Indian tell how he was running from a buffalo. (There used to be lots of buffalo there.) It was seventy-five acres across the plain to a big oak tree, and the bull was right behind him as he was running around the tree. And he run so fast he caught up with the bull, and run his hand down his throat and caught him by the tail, and turned him wrongside out, and the bull went running right back the other way.

222 *The Fast Runner* (J. D. SUGGS)

"Lies concerning speed," Motif X1796, are reported by Baughman, such as the Negro tale of the man who heard a bullet twice; once when it passed him, and the second time when he passed it: X1796.2.2*(b). Mistaking a buck for a man with a chair on his head is a common Negro tale, told on the Irishman. See, for example, Bacon and Parsons, no. 73, p. 301, "Chair on his head!* Baughman gives one reference under J1785.8*, "Deer thought to be devil with chair on his head." Clear Rock tacks on fabulous evidence of his running ability to two conventional scare stories, in John A. Lomax, Adventures of a Ballad Hunter *(New York, 1947), pp. 182-185.*
A colored feller slapped a white man in Arkansas. That was in a log camp about five miles from town. So he lit out, and run to town to catch a train. It was night when he got to town. So he asked the depot agent how long 'fore he'd get a train. Agent told him the train had been gone about thirty minutes. So he taken off down the railroad at night, running on his foot. He caught up with a deer, a doe. Said, "Boy, did you slap a white man too?" So he just run on off and left the deer. (He thought it was a man.)
So he hits the hard road then, the paved road. He caught up with a Cadillac, making eighty miles an hour. Driver told him, "Get in, I'll give you a lift." He got in, never stopped running. The driver shoved the Cadillac down to ninety miles an hour. Said, "Is this all the fastest it can

run? I was making faster than that." So he jumps out the Cadillac, ran over to the airport.

Plane was taking off, making ninety miles an hour, just leaving the ground. He got in, said, "Hey, pilot, how fast is we going now?" Pilot said, "Four hundred miles an hour." Colored man said, "I was going faster than that myself." He grabbed him a parachute and bailed out—that was a little too slow for him.

When he landed, he landed right by a big old buck on the ground. So him and that buck run side by side—he done scared the buck, and he was scared hisself. He said: "Say mister, you must a slapped a white man too in Arkansas. If you're going to run why don't you take those rocking chairs off your head?"

So he went off and never came back to Arkansas.

223 *Two Lazy Men* (J. D. SUGGS)

Under Motif W111.5.10.1, "Lazy man is being taken to poorhouse. . . . 'Is the corn shelled?' ", Baughman lists two Negro examples, and white texts from Ontario, Maine, New York, New Jersey, Texas, Indiana, and Arkansas. See also Parsons, Antilles, no. 338, p. 320, "Too Lazy to Live," for references and three texts (the third, from Haiti, is closest; lazy man asks, "Is the rice husked?"). Johnson, Folk Culture, no. 15, pp. 151-152, "Too Lazy to Live," refers to a hundred-year-old variant of Monk Lewis. A seventeenth-century instance of an emigrant to New England too lazy to live, who became his servant's servant, and chose half a cake a day without work to a whole cake with work, is told by Christopher Levett (see America Begins, ed. Dorson, New York, 1966, pp. 114-115).

This man was so lazy he wouldn't work, he wouldn't do nothing. He just lay down side of the road. Everybody heard about him being lazy. Fellow said, "Hey, Bill, come over here; here's twenty dollars I'll give you." Bill says, "No, no, bring it over here." "No, but if you be laying there still when I come back I'll give you one hundred dollars." Bill was laying in the shade, you see; sun was mighty hot and he'd have to come into the sun to get the twenty-dollar bill. When the fellow came back Bill was still laying there. "All right, here's the hundred dollars—come and get it." Bill told him, "No—you bring it over here." "No, I won't—you'll have to come and get it." So Bill said, "Well, just lay it down over there—a puff of wind might blow it over."

Another one was even lazier. He wouldn't work, and they were going to bury him alive. They put him in the hearse, and started for the cemetery. An old lady come along and said, "Where you going with Tom?" (His name was Lazy Tom.) "Well, he's so lazy he won't work to get something to eat and we're going to bury him alive." She said, "Don't do that; I got some meat and bread for him." Tom said, "Madam, is it cooked?" "No, it's not cooked." "Well, drive on, boys."

They went on and another lady stopped the hearse, and asked where they were going with Lazy Tom. When they told her she said: "Don't bury him for that. I'll give him a chicken already cooked." He wanted to know was it chewed up. She told him, no, it wasn't chewed up, but she had run it through a sausage mill. He asked her, "Was it swallowed?" "No." Lazy Tom told 'em, "Drive on, boys." So they buried him alive.

224 *The Old Man* (MRS. E. L. SMITH)

Type 726, "The Oldest on the Farm" and Motif F571.2, "Sending to the older" W. A. Clouston has a comparative note on this motif in his Popular Tales and Fictions (*New York, 1887*), *II, 96-98, "Sending One to an Older and the Oldest Person," with European and Asiatic references. A lovely variation was told by tennis champion Vic Seixas at the 1955 Davis Cup Dinner. A young player of merit looking for a game finds only an older man in his forties on the courts. He plays with him and is beaten. The stranger then tells him that his father, at 65, is even better. The young man plays and loses to the father, who recommends his own father, at 104, as better still. A game is arranged, but the old man fails to appear. It seems he was getting married that morning. "But why did he want to get married at his age?" asks the young player. "He didn't want to," he is told* (World Tennis, *v. 2, no. 11, April 1955, p. 44). I have two Maine texts in* Buying the Wind (*Chicago, 1964), pp. 86-87.*

There was a man a hundred and one years old standing outside the house crying, just crying. And two more men seed him crying, and walked up and asked him what was he crying about. He said his daddy whipped him. They asked him where was his daddy. He said, "He's sitting around the chimney corner making baskets." And they went around and asked him what did he whip his son for. And he said heM sassed his grandfather. And they asked him where his grandfather was. He said he was sitting out in the sun. And they went out there, and he was just a wrinkle.

225 *Aunt Dinah* (J. D. SUGGS)

Motif W125, "Gluttony," is used here in a tall-tale context.

Aunt Dinah stayed in a little house off from Ben Jackson, in Georgia. Said a lady come over to the house, and hold his mother Aunt Dinah was dead.

I said, "Mama, can I go with you over there?" She said, "No, Ben. I know how you are about laughing." So I told her, "Mama, I won't laugh." She says, "Okay, come on." I walked up to the door. There sat Aunt Dinah in a chair. She was stiff dead. She had her lap full of peanut hulls, and all around her was peanut hulls, and she had both hands full of peanuts, and her mouth was full of peanuts. And that tickled me so bad I fell out the door backwards, laughing. They took me up and carried me home. I laughed all that day, and all that night, and all day the next day, and about ten o'clock that night I went to sleep. And when I woke up, I was very tickled the next morning.

226 *The Frozen Mule* (JOE D. HEARDLEY)

Baughman reports this as one of the most popular American tales, Negro and white, with 22 examples. He gives it the motif X1633.1, "Heat causes corn to pop in crib or in field. Animals . . . think the popping corn is snow, freezes to death."

There was a mule once; his name was Charlie. And my uncle told me, "You been a bad boy; now you take Charlie and go down lay that corn by, and I'm only gonna give you 50 cents." And that was the third of July. And we had to have it all laid by the fourth. So I went on down there, but instead of my laying the corn by, I taken the ears off it and rode away on the mule. Sometimes he'd get tired and put his feet on my shoulders and I'd help him along. We'd sleep together and eat together. So we got up to Tennessee to a place called Nashville. We were going to Covert, Michigan. People told us, mules don't live up there—it's too cold up north. We had never seen no snow. While we were talking we got to Missouri, and folks asked us whose mule that was. I said, "Mine." "Well, he can't live in Michigan." We got to

338

Indiana. "Where are you and that mule going? No mules live here." "Well, we're going to Michigan." Charlie was still, just listening. We got by—stole a few roasting ears, and tomatoes—and landed here in Covert about the eighteenth of July, that hot day, you know.

They wouldn't let me bring that mule in town; so I carried him out in the country, and turned him over to a farmer to keep him in his shed. That was the hottest day in over a hundred years in Michigan. While Charles was eating he peeked through the crack, and saw the corn, the dry corn popping, and flying about. And he thought it was snowing, like he'd heard the people talking about on the way up. So he walked over to the corner and lay down and froze to death.

227 *The Gallinipper* (J. D. SUGGS)

Baughman gathers together mosquito tall tales under Motif X1286.1.3, "Large mosquito has long bill," and refers to three examples, one Negro and two white for (c), "Mosquito bores through tree with long bill to get at man standing with back to tree." For variations on this idea (as distinct from the mosquito's bill being bradded so that he flies away with an iron pot), see Fauset, "South," III, no. 2, p. 261, "Catching the Gallinipper"; Jones, Negro Myths, no. 9, p. 22, "De Ole Man an de Gallinipper" (it pulls up the tree by the roots); Hurston, Mules and Men, pp. 134-135 (its bones fence in ten acres). Other stories using "gallinipper" in the sense of a ferocious mosquito are in The Frank C. Brown Collection, I, p. 703, "The Gallinipper"; and Parsons, Sea Islands, no. 94, p. 99, "Gallinipper on the Bridge." I have another text from John Blackamore, printed in Western Folklore, XIII (1954), 169.

They were talking about how bad mosquitoes was. One said he'd seen mosquitoes as long as your finger. The other said: "Shaw, that ain't nothing. I was cutting timber down on the Panama when they were putting the canal through. As I was standing side of a tree about five feet thick through, I heard a big roaring coming through the woods. It was a gallinipper coming right at me. I jumped behind this big five foot tree. He missed me and lammed into that tree and stuck his bill plumb through it. I happened to have my sledge hammer in my hand what I drive wedges with; so I lammed it—bam! And I bradded it there on that side of the tree, and he couldn't get loose.

"Well, I went back about ten weeks after that, and he had rotted. Well, I had a five-acre farm, a little five-acre spot of land there. So I had his bones hauled up to build me a fence. I had enough bones to fence in the five acres, with some f~w small ones left over."

(When the gallinipper hits you, you feel as if someone struck a match to your head. You hits yourself so hard trying to smack him you near knocks yourself out.)

228 *The Clever Chinch Bugs* (J. D. SUGGS)

"Bob White in Chicago told me this" Suggs recalled. A well-told variant, "The Michigan Bedbug Story," localized in Kalamazoo, Michigan, was printed in the Wisconsin Superior Chronicle *for Oct. 6, 1857, credited to the* Grand River Eagle, *and has received a modern reprinting in* Michigan History, *XXXIII, 1949, p. 255. After the hotel guest tarred the ceiling as well as the floor, the bedbugs built bridges of straw to cross the tar. This last touch is used in two variants in A. H. Fauset,* Folklore from Nova Scotia, *MAFLS XXIV, 1931, no. 89, pp. 73-74, "Bugs." In an Ozark text in Randolph,* The Devil's Pretty Daughter, *"The Drummer's Magic Circle," pp. 148-149, the hotel guest outwits the bedbugs with his circle of molasses, but as H. Halpert points out in his note, p. 222, the usual variants result in triumph for the bugs. Here again Suggs switches from third to first person.*

Fellow went to the rooming house to stay all night. So they gave him a room right next to the kitchen. So he goes to bed, but the chinches begin to bite. So he felt like they were two or three hundred the way they were biting. "So I'll just get out of bed and take and make me a pallet on the floor." He knowed he'd get rid of 'em then. (They hatched in the wooden bed.) "Well here they come, a line of 'em." He say, "Well I know what I'll do. I'll just go there in the kitchen and get me some syrup, and pour them all around me. They sure will stick up when they crawl up in that."

So I lays down and goes to sleep with that ring of molasses around me. So I felt something hit me in the face and I woke up. "Tip tap, tip tap." Do you know what they had done? They had chmbed up the wall, run across the ceiling, so they got over me, then they was dropping, like drops of rain, over in the ring where I was lying. But there wasn't a single one that misjudged his drop, and dropped in the syrup. So I didn't get to sleep at all that night.

[Business of looking up at the ceiling, wiping face]

PREACHERS

Throughout medieval and modern times, priest and parson have served as butts for innumerable lampoons, gibes, and jests. Being learned and exalted figures, clothed in sanctity yet dealing directly with the folk, clergymen formed natural targets for the satire of their less favored brethren. Their alleged pomposity, greed, unchastity, and hypocrisy made fine joke material for the humor of deflation and irreverence. Among the white population of the United States, parson jokes evoke little response, for the decline of the church and the closing of the gulf between ministry and laity have removed the ingredients for laughter. In the Negro South, however, conditions comparable to the European peasant village can be found. Unlettered men take religion seriously, and daily associate with their spiritual leader. By "preacher" (the term habitually used), the Negro means the singing, exhorting, hypnotic Baptist layman who had been called from the ranks to guide the flock. On the hottest of summer nights, while the congregation swelters in shirtsleeves and cotton dresses, the preacher keeps on his dark suit coat. He works at a regular job like any other man—preachers I have met collect junk, labor on the roads, and sweat in the assembly line—but retains his meed of respect and title of "Reverend." Jackleg preachers float about looking for a church or an occasional invitation to conduct service. Preachers themselves know many preacher stories, and, indeed, to dominate their audiences must excel at storytelling, singing, and chanting.

Much preacher humor revolves about the half-chanted, half-shouted sermon, in which the congregation participates with enthusiastic responses and choruses. A stock situation in older European jokelore deals with a layman's literal and highly embarrassing retort to the pulpit message, and this verbal play is adopted with relish by Negro humorists. In one variation the preacher finds his prophetic text coming true all too soon, when he calls Gabriel to blow his horn for Judgment Day, and a boy in the gallery promptly responds. A young bride from Mississippi solemnly avowed that her minister lost his front teeth during the excitement of his sermon, and adapted the hymn, "You must reach out for the Lord," with such fine literal effect that he recaptured his fallen dentures.

While preacher anecdotes are infrequently told for true, they remain firmly set in the social realities of revivals, baptizings, and house visits. The preacher's fondness for chicken induces a separate spate of jocular tales; the farmer's sons, or the barnyard fowls, resent the preacher's presence at Sunday dinner, since he always gets a chicken and eats the best parts himself, and they contrive ways to keep him from his dinner. Various tricks to catch the preacher in a lie are popular, but he is spared more serious shortcomings, such as the articlerical satirists of the Renaissance delighted to expose. Gibes at particular excesses of different sects—the Baptists' emphasis on immersion, the Methodists' habit of passing the plate, the Campbellites' rule for eating fish—provide staple subjects for comedy. Curiously I heard no jokes about Seventh Day Adventists, now vigorously established in Calvin and Benton Harbor, whose devout, abstemious ways would seem to invite ridicule.

Some familiar floating jests get attached to the preacher, in the way that all central folktale characters attract the passing story. But the Negro preacher joke conveys a special flavor by including the ecstatic chant of the Baptist service.

229 *A Sermon* (BILL FRANKLIN)

James Weldon Johnson's introduction to his God's Trombones (*New York, 1927*), *comments perceptively on Negro folk sermons. Puckett has some suggestive remarks on "The Sermon," pp. 533-534, and "A Slipperance uv de Tongue," pp. 534-536. The finest rendition I know of a Negro preacher carried away by his own imagery is Dean Faulkner's record. "The Eagle—He Flew" (World of Fun Records S-251-A: E2-QC-4074). Another delicious recording, this time by a white dialectician, Holman Willis, porfraying the preacher's improvisation from an unfamiliar text, is "The Psaltree Sermon" (Dialect Records Co., Roanoke, Va., CS 057395, 1948).*

The preacher was talking on the modern inventions of the day. He said, "The first thing I want to call to your attention is the automobile. It travels up and down the road seventy-five, eighty-five, a hundred miles up and down the road, and first thing you know, ramjam-bammed into a telegraph pole, kills up eight or ten people every day."

Tlie deacon said, "A-men, brother." [*chanted*].

"Next thing I want to call to your attention is the railroad train. It travels seventy-eighty miles up and down those steel rails. First thing you know it's ramjambammed into a telegraph pole, kills up eight or ten people every day."

Old deacon says, "Amen, brother—amen—amen."

"Next thing I want to tell you about is the airplane flying around up there in the air, going two hundred, three hundred, four hundred miles an hour. First thing you know it's ramjambammed into a telegraph pole, kills up eight or ten people every day."

"Goddamn," says the deacon.

230 *Hell on Gums* (J. D. SUGGS)

A non-Negro variant in the Indiana University Folklore Archives has the evangelist warning "There will be weeping and wailing and gnashing of teeth." An old lady shouts, "Sir, I have no teeth." "Madam, teeth will he provided" (Verne Hohl, Spring 1954). Suggs tells another preacher retort, where the excited old sister exclaims that if she had wings like a juney bug she would fly to heaven; oh no, says the preacher, a peckerwood would catch you before you got half-way.

The preacher is preaching. "Oh, sisters, don't you know it's going to be terrible when that last day comes. If you ain't got your soul right, the Devil going to have a red hot iron down there." (*Singsong*) And one old sister saying "Um-mmm." Preacher goes on, "He's going to take that redhot iron and put it in your teeth and bore and bore."

Old sister jumped up and said, "Thank God, I ain't got no teeth."

Preacher said, "Yes, sister, but it's going to be hell on gums."

231 *Blow, Gabriel, Blow* (J. D. SUGGS)

Variants are in Brewer, Brazos, pp. 98-100, "Gabriel and the Elder's Goat"; Fauset, "Philadelphia" no. 54, p. 552, "Gabriel Blows His Horn"; Roberts no. 68, "Gabriel's Horn"; Abrahams, pp. 193-194, "Gabriel Blows his Horn." I have other texts from Joe Heardley and Walter Winfrey, in both of which the preacher's coattails catch in the door as he rushes out; he begs Gabriel, or the Lord, to let him go.

This is Type 1833J, "Preacher Says: 'Let Gabriel Blow His Horn!'"
proposed by Baughman, who gives two references.

The preacher was carrying on a revival and getting converts. He taken for his text and was preaching, "Sisters and Brothers, won't you be glad when the good Lord sends Gabriel to blow his trumpet!" (*Deep singsong*)

The old sister said, "Yes, will I be glad when old Gab'l blow his trumpet." (*High-pitched, ecstatic*)

Preacher says, "Gab'l gonna place one foot on the sea and one on dry land, and declare that times have been will be no more. Now blow, Gab'l."

A little boy hears that in the loft, and blows his horn. "Too-o-ot." (*Softly*)

The preacher thought he'd heard it. He looked up and said, "Blow, Gab'l," so he'd be sure.

The boy blowed loudly then—"Drrrr."

Out they all go, just running over one another to get outdoors, the preacher too. There was a hogpen right next to the church, belonged to a neighbor's house, and big old hog was in there. The preacher run right into the hogpen, and he scared the hog. And the hog jumped up and started hasseling, "Hahuhahuha." And the preacher said, "It wasn't none of me; the fellow started that, he's gone."

232 *What Did Paul Say?* (J. D. SUGGS)

Baughman reports this tale, Type 1833A, Motif X435.1, "What Says David?" as one of the most popular of English and American stories, and notes twenty-four variants. Abrahams has a text in Jungle, *pp. 186-187. I have variants from Mrs. I. E. Edwards ("Negro Tales from Bolivar County, Mississippi" no. 14, pp. 112-113), Lulu Powell, and Willie Sewall.*

Well there was a preacher you know, way down South—he was a preacher of the Hardshell Baptist church. So his brother Deacon Jones, he's making moonshine whiskey. Well he's always get it on credit. So he gets up this Sunday morning, he's going have a big day there. He wanted to preach a good sermon but he had to get half drunk you know. And so he says, "Hey son, go and tell Brother Paul to send me a pint of good whiskey. I'm going preach some today." Say "Now listen, when you come in, get there 'fore I start." And says, "Now I'll come out the back." Say "When you come, I'll go out the back, you go back and you give it to me;"

So he says, "All right, Dad." So he goes out. So while he stayed so long, the preacher father kept waiting on him, waiting on him, he didn't come, so he had to open up the revival, his meeting.

He says, "Well now, Sisters and Brothers," say "what did Paul say?" Say "I seen Paul when he was coming down from Gotha." [*Chanted*]

Sister say, "Yes I did." [*Chanted*]

Here come his son walking in. He [the preacher] say, "What did Paul say?" [*Loud*]

Boy just kept walking up to him, shaking his head. He said, "What did Paul say?" [*Chanted*]

He said, "Now listen Dad, Paul say you pay him for that first quart of whiskey you had and he'll let you have another'n."

So, he hadn't paid for the first one. So the father got so mad, he just walked right out of the back of the poolpit [pulpit] hollering "What did Paul say?" Just went right out of the back of the door, hollering "What did Paul say?"

233 *Abraham, What Is Thou Got in Thy Bosom?* (J. D. SUGGS)

This is another form of Type 1833A, in which the jest is turned on the parishioner rather than the preacher. Parsons, Antilles, no. 339, p. 321, "Whatsoever in Thy Bosom," gives two references.

Abraham was late coming to church, and on the way he passed a brother deacon's smokehouse—he'd gone on to church—where they keep the big smoked hams. So he put one of the big hams under his overcoat, and went on to the church.

The preacher was preaching from the text: "What hast thou got in thy bosom, Abraham? The Lord said, Thou shalt not steal, thou shalt not commit adultery. Now tell me Abraham, what hast thou got in thy bosom?"

He was pointing at the audience; so Abraham thought he was pointing at him and said, "Well, I'll confess it's a ham. I was just going by Brother Jones's house and I thought I'd help myself to a ham. But I was wrong, I shouldn't have stole it."

(He didn't wait for the preacher to explain he was talking about Lazarus in Abraham's bosom. Lazarus was the poor man who went to heaven because he had faith; he was the faithfulest man in the world. The rich man went to hell and looked off and saw Lazarus in Abraham's bosom.)

234 *Preacher Loses Teeth* (RUBY BOOTH)

This supposedly true incident can be considered a variation of Type 1833A with the preacher applying the sermon to himself.

My pastor at the Baptist church in Vicksburg, Mississippi—Mt. Zion Missionary Baptist Church No. 4—lost his teeth in church the morning I was baptized. At the service afterward he was delivering his second sermon. He was groaning and squalling real loud.

"*Ohhhh Lord, Ohhh.*" And his teeth fell out onto the Bible and slid to the floor. Afterwards he struck out on the hymn, "Father, I stretch out my hand to Thee," and reached out his hand and replaced the teeth in his mouth.

I had on a white suit, and it was as black as the bottom on a shoe when I got home. I was laughing so hard, I fell right out on the floor.

235 *Preacher Steals Pocketbook* (IOLA PALMER)

This suggests Type 1831, "The Parson and Sexton at Mass" where the two connivers communicate by chanting. Abrahams has a close text, Jungle, p. 193, "The Preacher Bends Down."

Preacher was in the pulpit preaching one Sunday, and a lady kept jumping up and shouting. So finally she threw her pocketbook into the pulpit. So he said, "Preaching time's over, now it's praying time." Every time they'd go to pray he'd inch over toward the pocketbook. When he finally got the pocketbook he saw one deacon watching. Then he said, "Praying time is over," and everyone got up and started singing.

After the singing finished, and the people were getting ready to go, he made this announcement for next Sunday: "My text will be, 'All that sees and says nothing, it shall be divided among them.' "

236 *Swimology* (J. D. SUGGS)

A variant is in Fauset, "South," V, no. 15, p. 273, "Bible and Swimming." Amos Cross also told me the story.

The preacher had to go across the lake to the church, and the boy rowed him across. This Sunday morning a new preacher walked down to the boat, says: "Good morning son. Are you the one carries 'em across the lake to the church?" Boy says, "Yessa, parson." So the preacher gets in the boat. He asks, "What do you charge, son?" "Twenty-five cents a person." So the parson gives him a quarter. Boy shoved off from the bank. Preacher says, "Sonny, you ever go to Sunday school?" Boy answers, "I hate to tell you, parson, but I never did." "Did you ever learn the Ten Commandments?" "I hate to tell you parson, but I never did." Preacher said, "Son, you lost half your life then." Then he asks him: "Son, did you ever learn theology? Did you ever learn geography?" "No." "That's too bad, son; you lost half your life."

About that time the boy paddled on a snag up there in the lake, and capsized the boat. Out went the parson. Boy, he commenced swimming off. Parson went down. When he come up the boy hollered to him, "Say, parson, you ever learn swimology?" Parson said, "No, son, I never did." "Well, parson, I hate to tell you but you lost all of your life."

237 *Baptizing a Hard Candidate* (WALTER WINFREY)

See Brewer, Brazos, pp. 54-56, "Sister Sadie Washington's Littlest Boy," and Abrahams, Jungle, p. 196, "Baptism and Belief."

There was a preacher running a revival, and he had several candidates to join the church. And so he told all the candidates to be ready Sunday; he was going to have a baptizing. So he baptized all of 'em and they come out praising the Lord. The last one he had to baptize was one of them stubborn-head guys. So the preacher raised his right hand and said, "I baptize this my brother in the name of the Father and the Son and the Holy Ghost." And the fellow come up wiping the water out of his face. And so they carried him down again. (The preacher and the deacon get one on each side. The preacher gets hold of the chest and one arm, and the deacon the other arm, and they carry him backwards in the water.) And the candidate goes down again, and the preacher blesses him.

When he comes up the second time the deacon says to him, "Say something, say something." So the candidate asks him, "What shall I say?" He tells him, "Say, 'I believe.' " So the preacher raises his right hand up the third time and says, "I baptize this my brother in the name of the Father and the Son and the Holy Ghost."

When he comes up the third time, wiping the water off his face, he says, "I believe, I believe." And the preacher says, "You believe what?" And he says, "I believe you sons of bitches is trying to drown me."

238 *Uncle Bill Objects* (J. D. SUGGS)

The general Motifs W167, "Stubbornness" and J2470, "Metaphors literally interpreted" fit here.

The deacon board of the church met, and the president called them to order. "Well, we're ready for new business." One of the deacons gets up, says: "Brother Moderator, this church been standing here so long moss is done growed all over the top; the moss is about five feet deep. I think we ought to put a new cover on it. And if I'm in order, I motion we get money out of the treasury and have a new top put on the church." Brother Bill gets up, says: "I object, Brother Moderator. Because I'm ninety years old, and I been sitting under this church here forty years, and it's good enough for me."

Another deacon gets up, says, "Brother Moderator, look at these old benches. They're so rough, they tear the ladies' silk dresses. We need smooth lumber, like the other churches have. And if I'm in order, I motion we throw these old benches out, and get some new ones." Brother Bill says: "Brother Moderator, I object. Because I been setting on these benches forty-odd years, and it's good enough for me."

Then a third brother gets up, says: "Brother Moderator, look at these old windows, they just got shutters, no glass in 'em like other churches. We should get glass in 'em and tear these old shutters off." Brother Bill gets up. "Brother Moderator, I been lookng out of these windows forty-odd years and they're good enough for me."

Well then the senior deacon he gets up. Says: "Brother Moderator, Brother Bill's a good old Christian. And if I'm in order I will motion, when Brother Bill die, the good Lord will take him into heaven." Brother Bill says: "I object. I've been living here ninety years, and this is good enough for me."

(He objected himself out of heaven. There's people like that, just contrary, object to everything. I've noticed among everybody, black and white people but more among my people; they're like a barrel of lobsters—you don't need to cover them up—if one can't get out himself he won't let the others out. If one man can't get hisself a good job he don't want no one else to get it.)

239 *The Campbellite, Methodist, and Baptist Preachers* (BEN JONES)

They were having a community fish fry, and some of the boys wanted to play a joke on the denominations. They had the Campbellite, Methodist,

Baptist. So the first fish they caught was a grinner. The boys said, "That's a Campbellite fish."

So the Campbellite preacher wanted to know why. Said, "He's a grinder, can't stand much when you get him out the water."

The next one they caught was a fish-eel. So he said, "That's a Methodist fish."

So the Methodist preacher he wanted to know why he called him a Methodist fish.

So he said he was so slick you couldn't do nothing with him when you got him outa the water. (Methodists are very slick in the Bible and all.)

So they caught two more and they didn't name them. So the Baptist preacher wanted to know did they ever catch any Baptist fish.

He told them, "Not yet, we catch them at the stillery."

240 *The Baptist, Methodist, and Presbyterian Preachers* (BILL BAKER)

In Brewer, Brazos, pp. 64-66, "The Haunted Church and the Sermon on Tithing," hants depart when the plate is passed.

There was a big Baptist state convention. The delegates was so numerous they couldn't hardly take care of all of them. And there was three preachers left didn't have nowhere to stay, a Baptist preacher, a Methodist preacher, and a Presbyterian preacher. The lady told them she had fixed a room in a nearby house (she didn't tell them it was hanted), and they could take their meals with her.

They came for meeting that night and set down and begin to talk. Eventually the hants commenced to coming in. The Baptist preacher began singing. The more he sing the more the hants came in. The Presbyterian preacher he begin praying. And the more he prayed the more he hants come in. He says to the Methodist preacher, "Now doc, it's your floor." And the Methodist preacher say, "Let's take up a collection," and the hants begin to leave.

IRISHMEN

Negroes savor jokes about Irishmen. Silly stories about Pat and Mike became a commonplace in American humor following the mid-nineteenth century Irish immigration, when the green and hapless sons of Erin replaced the Yankee bumpkin as fool characters, stumbling and bobbling then-way through an America of big cities and puzzling machines. The comic Irishman of stage farce and folk anecdote had his day and vanished before new stereotypes of later immigrant waves, but somehow he lingered on in the repertoires of Southern Negroes, Kentucky hillfolk, and no doubt other unreported pockets. Perhaps because these groups remain close to the social situation where the uneducated and the untraveled commit follies, they relish the absurd mistakes of noodle Irishmen. Frequently colored folk turn the jest upon themselves, and laugh at the reaction of a country Negro to a train or streetcar, while Northern Negroes will refer amusedly to the ignorance of their Southern cousins.

Negro jokes about Irishmen include noodle anecdotes transplanted from the Old World, and extraneous plots fastened onto Pat and Mike because of their notoriety. In the first class fall various incidents of mistaken identity: Pat mistakes the cries of frogs for human voices, or thinks a turtle is a watch, or is gulled into believing a pumpkin is a mule's egg. From medieval times comes the legend about three travelers whose slight knowledge of the foreign language manages to get them convicted of murder—a misadventure told about Walloons in England in the twelfth century, but applied by John Blackamore to three Irish hoboes just landed in the United States. On the other hand, if one secures enough variants of the more popular Negro jokes about sharpers, braggarts, and even the animals, he will sooner or later find the "Ahshman" involved.

241 Irishman at the Dance (SILAS ALTHEIMER)

For Irish jokes from White sources see Herbert Halpert, "Aggressive Humor on the East Branch," New York Folklore Quarterly, II (1946), 86-97; and Leonard Roberts, Eastern Kentucky

Folktales: A Collection and a Study (*University of Kentucky doctoral dissertation, 1953*), nos. 42-55. *A large Negro collection is in A. M. Bacon and E. C. Parsons, "Folk-lore from Elizabeth City County, Virginia," JAF XXXV (1922), nos. 72-108, pp. 300-310. An early Negro collection appeared in the* Southern Workman, *XXVIII (May, 1899), pp. 190-194, reprinted in JAF XII (1899), 226-228. A resemblance to the present story occurs in Roberts no. 52, "Irishman and the Fiddler," where the dunce thinks the fiddle is a cat being tortured by the fiddler (Motif J1772.26*).*

A slave from the Old States (Carolina and Virginia) told me this when I was a child, when the railroads first began to build, sixty years ago.

There were building a road through Virginia and the Carolinas, and the contractor had many slaves and some white men, Irishmen. And there was one Irishman, Pat, had recently come from Ireland, and never seen a colored man. A dance was given in the area, and the white men were invited to the dance. They had to go through a bottom and across a creek to reach the seat of the dance. And of course when they arrived Pat went in and took his seat, and stood very still in one place, and the other boys began to talk to the many beautiful girls at the dance, and choosing their partners.

There was a big black man sitting in the corner, with red eyes, and he was tuning his fiddle. And after a while when the dancers were ready, they were all assembled on the floor. The fiddler began to play and the dancers began to move around the room, promenading we'd call it. Pat sat there and all at once he jumped up, he couldn't stand it any longer, and so he ran out. He got lost, and he tramped around the whole night in the mud, and fell in the lagoon. So he pulled himself out, and next morning, just before day, when the train was heating up to go out, Pat coursed in, all muddy and wet, about seven o'clock. So the boys began to laugh and tease him about leaving the dance. "Well Pat, how did you enjoy the dance?" They didn't know what had become of him.

When they asked him, Pat gave his conception of the dance. He said, "When I got there, there were many beautiful girls there. And the boys began to enjoy theirselves, chatting with the young ladies. But the Devil was sitting in one corner, and he had a little red babe in his arms. And he pulled its ears, and it was all I could do to sit there. And finally he picked up a stick and whaled the baby across the back, and of all the racket I ever heard, there it was. And the people were flying around, hunting the door. And no one could find it but me."

242 The Irishman and the Pumpkin (MARVIN RICE)

Type 1319, Motif 11772.1, "Pumpkin thought to be Ass's Egg." Flowers gives two Southern Negro references and one from Trinidad. Randolph, Who Blowed Up the Church House? *pp. 144-145, "The Mare's Nest," is annotated by Herbert Halpert, p. 218, who gives twelve United States references, of which three are Negro, and Randolph supplies a fourth. Roberts no. 146 is "The Irishman and the Pumpkin." Clyde E. Henson has a variant from East Liverpool, Ohio, in* Folk-Lore, *LXIII (1952), 37-38. I have other texts from Shorty Hankins and J. D. Suggs, the latter printed in* Pine Bluff, *p. 252.*

This Irishman was passing another white fellow's house, just as he come out from the field carrying a big pumpkin. The Irishman asked him, "What have you there, John?" He said, "This is a mule egg." "What do you want for the mule egg." And John says, "Being as it is you, though this mule egg is worth ten dollars I'll let you have it for five, seeing as we're old pals." Irishman said: "Feth-er-me-Christ, that's a deal. Now what would I have to do to get a mule?" John told him: "You have to sit on it till it hatches out. You take this home and in the big breshheap in back of your house build you a big nest, put your egg in the nest, and sit there until it hatches out." "How long will it take?" "Oh, about a week or ten days."

He taken the egg, put it in his nest, and begin sitting and sitting. After a while he got discouraged. It turned cold and he had to put on his raincoat. He sat for three weeks, and said, "Well I'll sit this night and if it isn't hatched by morning I'll quit." He got up off it the next morning, looked at the egg, and said, "Fether-me-Christ, this egg has rotted." And he tossed it over in the bresh-pile. A rabbit started out. He looked and seed the rabbit and thought it was a colt, and begin to yell, "Cupcallee, cupcallee, here's yo' mammy, here's yo' mammy."

John seed him the next day after and asked him did his egg ever hatch out. He said, "Yes, by Jesus; the little son of a gun jumped out running like hell."

243 The Irishman and the Frogs (J. D. SUGGS)

The second part of this tale is Motif J1851.1.1, "Numskull throws money to frogs so that they can count it," which corresponds to the first episode in Type 1642, "The Good Bargain" Baughman gives two Negro references out of eight under Motif J1811.5* (c), "Frogs' cries misunderstood" In Alcée Fortier, Louisiana Folk-Tales, MAFLS II, 1895, "The Irishman and the Frogs," no. 5, p. 21, the Irishman first throws his jug to the frogs, then enters the water and drowns. I have other texts from Carrie Williams and Andrew W. Smith.

Pat been to town to buy his tobacco and groceries for the weekend. So he buys a caddy of tobacco (that's about twelve pounds). It was a warm night in May, warm and cloudy. (Frogs begin to holler in May when it gets cloudy). Pat walked up on the bridge, the bullfrog commenced to holler, "Knee-deep, knee-deep." [*Bass*]

Pat was afraid of the bridge, and when they said knee-deep he thought he'd wade. He kept getting deeper till it was over his head, so he scrambled back and went over the bridge, said "You don't know what you're talking about, it's head deep." He crosses the bridge then, buys the tobacco.

When he's coming back and gets to the bridge the little frogs holler, "Chew-tobacco, chew-tobacco, chew-tobacco," and they keep a-hollering. So he th'owed the whole pack in there, a piece at a time, told them to take all the tobacco.

Then he thought about his money, said "Veil, I'll just count my money to see how much I have to buy me tobacco tomorrow." He counted, "One-two-three-four-five."

Old frog said, "Tenk, tenk, tenk, tenk." [*Deep*] He counts it the second time up to five. He thought the frog was saying, "It ain't."

So he th'owed it in there and said, "Veil, count it yourself." So the next day he had to go back to town and when he looks over there he seen the tobacco laying on water—it done swelled up. Said, "They take the darndest big chews of tobacco in little fellows I ever seen."

(The water gets in the leaves and swells them.)

244 *The Three Irishmen Who Couldn't Speak English* (JOHN BLACKAMORE)

A perfect example of Type 1697, "We Three; For Money" (Motif C495.2.2). Baughman gives references to Westmorland, New Jersey, and Indiana texts. See Flowers for a Dominican example, "Lo Tre Haitiano." Bolte and Polívka reprint a fourteenth-century Latin text from John Bromyard (II, 564), in which three Walloons traveling in England talk themselves into a confession of murder. Halpert has two New Jersey white texts, no. 165 A and B, one on Irishmen and one on Dutchmen, and further notes a New Mexican Spanish and an Irish parallel.

These three Irishmen fresh over from Ireland didn't know anything about America. They didn't even know the language. Not having any money, they just came stowaway on a cow-boat from Ireland. So when they got to America they didn't have no way of getting around. They drifted in with a bunch of hoboes, and they all caught a freight train together.

So the hoboes started shooting dice. One fellow he picked up the dice and rolled them out, and he caught craps. So the guy betting with him who had him faded, yelled out, "We three." The three Irishmen looked at each other. The way he said it they figured them were important words; so they were going to keep that in mind.

Whenever you throw craps you always get another shot. So the next point the fellow caught was six. The other guy says, "Six months in the county jail." (That was just an expression of speech among the crapshooters you know.) He said it kind of low so they didn't get it all; all they got was "six months." Then the man shooting dice threw a seven; so he loses. But he didn't want to pay this other guy. This fellow tells him, "Give me my money or I'm going to kill you." So after they started arguing that kind of frightened the Irishmen (they couldn't understand what was happening). Well, the fellow fading the thrower said again, "I'm going to kill you." That didn't even rest on their mind. The one shooting the dice said, "The quicker the better." Then everything got quieter. All the other hoboes in there knew there might be a fight and somebody would get killed. So the Irishmen remembered those words.

The hobo that had faded the shooter cut his head off with his knife. All three of the Irishmen backed off into the other end of the car, and sat down. Everybody else got off the car 'cause they knew when the police found the dead body somebody would have to go to jail for it, maybe all; they were breaking the law riding the car. The three Irishmen didn't know; they thought everybody in America rode like that. The train was running, but hoboes know how to get off.

355

When the train gets to the stop at the next town, the police come around in the empty cars looking for hoboes, to put 'em in jail or put 'em to work. So when they come to the car where the three Irishmen were, they found them still waiting, thinking the train was going on. The police ordered them out; they didn't move. So the police climbed in the car, and saw the dead man with his throat cut. One of the officers tells them, "Get up and come on out." He motioned to them, and they come out. Then he asked them who done it. Since they didn't know but three words in American, which was "We three," "Six months," "The quicker the better," all three of them said at the same time, "We three." Then the officer says, "How long you been in the United States?" He knew they were migrants from the way they looked. All three of them said again at the same time, "Six months" (although they'd been there less than three days).

So the police got them together and hurried them off to jail. Got 'em in jail, had a judge come over and look at 'em. The officer told the jury what they'd told him. So the judge said, "Well, we have no alternative but to hang them." Next morning the jailer went in and give them fried chicken and all the fixings, and started out of the jail with them. They had been talking among themselves, but he couldn't understand what they were saying. So they said again, "We three, six months." The jailer hauled off and shoved them when they said that, and told them, "We're going to hang you." All three of them said together, "The quicker the better." So they were hung.

(They knew too much after all. They knew just enough about America to get hung.)

BIBLIOGRAPHY

For a long stretch the bibliography of American Negro tales was identified with the South. Fauset did publish Negro folktales from Nova Scotia in a memoir and from Philadelphia in an article. An unpubhshed dissertation by Herbert Halpert (see below) contains "Transplanted Southern Negro Tales" in New Jersey. Additions to the literature that mark a new advance in authentic reproduction are the transcripts from tape recordings of Richard Smith's stories (from Texas) and the records of Dean Faulkner (from South Carolina). For full cross-referencing of American Negro texts, the work of Elsie Clews Parsons still stands paramount. A proper recognition of some basic groupings in the Negro repertoire is first made by Fauset in his article "Negro Folk Tales from the South." The *Southern Workman*, published by Hampton Institute, conducted a folklore department in the 1880's and 1890's, which provides some valid early texts. The recent collection of Abrahams from Philadelphia is of the first importance.

The following works are referred to by short title in the notes.

Indexes and Reference Works

Aarne, Antti, and Stith Thompson, *The Types of the Folk-Tale*. Helsinki, 1961.

Baughman, Ernest W., *Type and Motif-Index of the Folktales of England and North America*. The Hague, 1966.

Bolte, Johannes, and Georg Polívka, *Anmerkungen zu den Kinderund Hausmärchen der Bruder Grimm*. 5 vols. Leipzig, 1913-1932.

Flowers, Helen L., *A Classification of the Folktale of the West Indies by Types and Motifs*. Indiana University doctoral dissertation, 1952.

Klipple, May A., *African Folktales with Foreign Analogues*. Indiana University doctoral dissertation, 1938, abstracted by Stith Thompson.

Thompson, Stith, *Motif-Index of Folk-Literature*. 6 vols. Bloomington, Indiana, 1955-58.

—— *The Folktale*. New York, 1946.

Collections

A few important tale collections from United States white tradition are included, which show overlappings with Negro folk narrative, for example, Brown, Halpert, Randolph, Roberts.*

Abrahams, Roger D., *Deep Down in the Jungle* . . . *Negro Narrative Folklore from the Streets of Philadelphia*. Hatboro, Penna., 1964.

Backus, Emma M., "Animal Tales from North Carolina," JAF 11 (1898), 284-291.

—— "Tales of the Rabbit from Georgia Negroes," JAF 12 (1899), 108-115.

Backus, Emma M., and Ethel H. Leitner, "Negro Tales from Georgia," JAF 25 (1912), 125-136.

Bacon, A. M., and E. C. Parsons, "Folk-Lore from Elizabeth City county, Virginia," JAF 35 (1922), 250-327.

Beckwith, Martha W., *Jamaica Anansi Stories*, MAFLS 17 (1924).

Botkin, B. A., ed. *Lay My Burden Down, A Folk History of Slavery*, Chicago, 1945

Brewer, J. Mason, ed. *Humorous Folk Tales of the South Carolina Negro*, Orangeburg, S. C., 1945.

———— "John Tales," Mexican Border Ballads and Other Lore, ed. M. C. Boat-right, PTFS 21 (1946), 81-104.

———— "Juneteenth," *Tone the Bell Easy*, ed. J. F. Dobie, PTFS 10 (1932), 9-54.

———— *The Word on the Brazos. Negro Preacher Tales from the Brazos Bottoms of Texas.* Austin, Texas, 1953.

———— *Worser Days and Better Times. The Folklore of the North Carolina Negro.* Chicago, 1965.

Browne, Ray B., "Negro Folktales from Alabama," *Southern Folklore Quarterly*, 18 (1954), 129-134.

Bundle of Troubles and Other Tarheel Tales. By workers of the Writers' Program of the Works Projects Administration in the State of North Carolina, ed. W. C. Hendricks. Durham, N. C, 1943.

Christensen, Mrs. A. M. H., *Afro-American Folk Lore. Told Round Cabin Fires on the Sea Islands of South Carolina.* Boston, 1892.

Cox, John Harrington, "Negro Tales from West Virginia," JAF 47 (1934), 341-349.

* Abbreviations: JAF—Journal of American Folklore; MAFLS—Memoirs of the American Folklore Society; PTFS—Publications of the Texas Folklore Society.

Crowley, Daniel J., *I Could Talk Old-Story Good: Creativity in Bahamian Folklore.* Berkeley and Los Angeles, 1966.

Davis, Henry C, "Negro Folk-Lore in South Carolina," JAF 27 (1914), 241-254.

Dorson, Richard M., "King Beast of the Forest Meets Man," *Southern Folklore Quarterly*, 17 (1954), 118-128.

————*Negro Folktales in Michigan*, Cambridge, Mass., 1956.

———— "Negro Songs from the Repertoire of J. D. Suggs," *Folklore and Folk Music Archivist*, IX (Fall 1966), 3-39. Music transcription by George List, headnotes by Neil Rosenberg.

———— "A Negro Storytelling Session on Tape," *Midwest Folklore*, 3 (1953), 201-212.

————"Negro Tales" [of John Blackamore], *Western Folklore*, 13 (1954), 77-97, 160-169, 256-259.

———— "Negro Tales of Mary Richardson," *Midwest Folklore*, 6 (1956), 1-26.

————"Negro Tales from Bolivar County, Mississippi," *Southern Folklore Quarterly*, 19 (1955), 104-116.

————*Negro Tales from Pine Bluff, Arkansas, and Calvin, Michigan*, Bloomington, Indiana, 1958.

————"Negro Witch Stories on Tape," *Midwest Folklore*, 2 (1952), 229-241.

Drums and Shadows. Survival Studies among the Georgia Coastal Negroes. By the Savannah Unit of the Georgia Writers' Project of the Works Projects Administration. Athens, Ga., 1940.

Eddins, A. W., "Anecdotes from the Brazos Bottoms," *Straight Texas*, ed. J. F. Dobie and M. C. Boatright, PTFS 13 (1937), 86-105.

————"Brazos Bottoms Philosophy," *Southwestern Lore*, ed. J. F. Dobie, PTFS 9 (1931), 153-164.

Emmons, Martha, "Confidences from Old Nacogdoches," *Follow de Drinkin' Gou'd*, ed. J. F. Dobie, PTFS 7 (1928), 119-134.

Faulkner, W. J., "Dean Faulkner Folk Story Series," World of Fun Records S251, S252, S253, distributed by the Methodist Publishing House, Nashville, Tennessee, with four page leaflet, "Uncle Simon's Folk Tales."

Fauset, Arthur Huff, *Folklore from Nova Scotia*, MAFLS 24 (1931).

—— "Negro Folk Tales from the South. (Alabama, Mississippi, Louisiana)," JAF 40 (1927), 213-303.

————"Tales and Riddles Collected' in Philadelphia," JAF 41 (1928), 529-557.

"Folklore from St. Helena, South Carolina," JAF 38 (1925), 217-238.

"Folk-Tales from Students in the Georgia State College," JAF 32 (1919), 402-405.

"Folk-Tales from Students in Tuskegee Institute, Alabama," JAF 32 (1919), 397-401.

Fortier, Alcée, *Louisiana Folk-Tales*, MAFLS 2 (1895).

The Frank C. Brown Collection of North Carolina Folklore, Vol. 1. Durham, N. C, 1952. "Folk Tales and Legends," ed. Stith Thompson, pp. 619-704.

Halpert, Herbert N., *Folktales and Legends from the New Jersey Fines: A Collection and a Study*, 2 vols.: Indiana University doctoral dissertation, 1947.

Harris, Joel Chandler, *Daddy Jake the Runaway, and Short Stories Told After Dark*. New York, 1889.

———— *Nights With Uncle Remus: Myths and Legends of the Old Plantation*, New York, 1883.

—— *Told By Uncle Remus: New Stories of the Old Plantation*. New York, 1905.

———————— *Uncle Remus and His Friends: Old Plantation Stories, Songs, and Ballads of Negro Character*. Boston and New York, 1892.

———————— *Uncle Remus, His Songs and His Sayings: The Folk-Lore of the Old Plantation*. New York, 1881.

Hurston, Zora Neale, *Mules and Men*. Philadelphia and London, 1935.

Hyatt, Harry M., *Folk-Lore from Adams County, Illinois*. New York, 1935.

Johnson, Guy B., *Folk Culture on St. Helena Island, South Carolina*. Chapel Hill, N. C., 1930.

Jones, Charles C, *Negro Myths from the Georgia Coast, Told in the Vernacular*. Boston and New York, 1888.

Parsons, Elsie Clews, "Folk-Lore from Aiken, South Carolina." JAF 34 (1921), 1-39.

———— *Folk-Lore of the Antilles, French and English*, Part III, MAFLS 26 (1943).

————"Folk-Tales Collected at Miami, Fla.," JAF 30 (1917), 222-227.

————*Folk-Lore of the Sea Islands, South Carolina*, MAFLS 16 (1923).

————*Folk-Tales of Andros Island, Bahamas*, MAFLS 13 (1918).

———— "Tales from Guildford County, North Carolina," JAF 30 (1917), 168-200.

———— "Tales from Maryland and Pennsylvania," JAF 30 (1917), 209-217.

Puckett, Newbell Niles, *Folk Beliefs of the Southern Negro*. Chapel Hill, N. C., 1926.

Randolph, Vance, *The Devil's Pretty Daughter and other Ozark Folk Tales*. New York, 1955.

———— *Who Blowed Up the Church House? and other Ozark Folk Tales*. New York, 1952.

Roberts, Leonard W., *Eastern Kentucky Folktales: A Collection and a Study*. University of Kentucky doctoral dissertation, 1953. (Published as *South from Hell-fer-Sartin*, Lexington, Kentucky, 1955, with the same numbering for the tales.)

Smiley, Portia, "Folk-Lore from Virginia, South Carolina, Georgia, Alabama, and Florida," JAF 32 (1919), 357-383.

Smith, Richard, "Richard's Tales," *Folk Travelers, Ballads, Tales, and Talk*, ed. M. C. Boatright, W. M. Hudson, A. Maxwell, PFTS 25 (1953), 220-253 (recorded by John L. Sinclair, transcribed by Stella A. Sinclair).

South Carolina Folk Tales: Stories of Animals and Supernatural Beings. Compiled by Workers of the Writers' Program of the Works Projects Administration in the State of South Carolina, Columbia, S. C. 1941.

Southern Workman and Hampton School Record. Hampton, Va., Vols. 20-33. December 1893 to January 1904, department of "Folklore and Ethnology."

Speers, Mary W. F., "Maryland and Virginia Folk-Lore," JAF 25 (1912), 284-286.

Stewart, Sadie E., "Seven Folk-Tales from the Sea Islands, South Carolina," JAF 32 (1919), 394-396.

Talley, Thomas W., *Negro Folk Rhymes*. New York, 1922.

Vann, William H., "Two Negro Folk Tales," *Backwoods to Border*, ed. M. C. Boatright and D. Day, PTFS 18 (1943), 172-180.

INDEX OF MOTIFS

References are to Thompson's index, save where (B) refers to Baughman's index.

A. MYTHOLOGICAL MOTIFS

A1661.2, "Why the white man has short hair" Ch. III, No. 72
A1671.1, "Why the Negro works" Ch. III, No. 70
A1681.2, "Why Jews do not eat pork" Ch. VII, No. 132
A2215.3, "Bowl place,d on turtle's back; hence his shell" Ch. VII, No. 130
A2216.1, "Bear fishes through ice with tail: hencelackstail" Ch. I, No. 11
A2231.1, "Discourteous answer: why cow (horse) is always eating" Ch. VII, No. 134
A2231.1.4, "Discourteous answer: tortoise's shell" Ch. VII, No. 130
A2287.1, "Jesus drives evil spirits into hogs: hence short snouts" Ch. VII, No. 132
A2317.3, "Why buzzard is bald" Ch. I, No. 24
A2317.11, "Why john-crow has bald head" Ch. I, No. 24
A2325.1, "Why rabbit has long ears" Ch. I, No. 11
A2378.4.1, "Why hare has short tail" Ch. I, No. 11
A2494.4.4, "Enmity between dog and rabbit" Ch. I, No. 14

B. ANIMALS

B81.9.1, "Mermaid's hair reaches her waist" Ch. VI, No. 126
B81.13.4, "Mermaid gives mortals gold from sea bottom" (B) Ch. VI, No. 126
B210.2, "Talking animal or object refuses to talk on demand. Discoverer is unable to prove his claims: is beaten" (B) Ch. II, Nos. 49, 50, 51, 52
B251.1.2.3, "Cows kneel in stable at midnight of Eve of Old Christmas" (B) Ch. VIII, No. 151
B421, "Helpful dog" Ch. VI, No. 125
B524.1.2, "Dogs rescue fleeing master from tree refuge" Ch. VI, No. 125
B765.5, "Snake crawls from sleepers mouth" Ch. VIII, No. 148
B765.6, "Snake eats milk and bread with child" Ch. VIII, No. 145
B765.7, "Jointed snake can join its segments when it is broken into pieces" (B) Ch. VIII, No. 144
B765.10, "Coachwhip snake" (B) Ch. VIII, No. 143

C. TABU

C495.2.2, " 'We three'—'For gold'—'That is right': phrases of foreign language" (B) Ch. xv, No. 260

D. MAGIC

D153.1, "Transformation: man to woodpecker" Ch. VII, No. 131
D193, "Tranformation: man to tortoise (turtle)" Ch. VII, No. 130
D615, "Transformation combat" Ch. II, No. 45
D672, "Obstacle flight" Ch. VII, 142
D702.1.1, "Cat's paw cut off: woman's hand missing" (B) Ch. VI, No. 124
D758.1, "Disenchantment by three nights' silence under punishment" Ch. XI, No. 193
D1719.1, "Contest in magic" Ch. IV, No. 100

E. THE DEAD

E272, "Road-ghosts" (B) Ch. V, 110
E275, "Ghost haunts place of great accident or misfortune" Ch. V, 110
E291.1, "Person burying treasure kills person to supply guardian ghost" Ch. V, No. 116

E293.1(b), "Ghost appears to apple stealers, stares at them until they drop apples and flee" (B) Ch. V, 109

E321, "Dead husband's friendly return" Ch. V, No. 108

E323.1, "Dead mother returns to see baby" Ch. V, No. 111

E337.1.1, "Murder sounds heard just as they must have happened at time of death" (B) Ch. V, No. 104

E337.1.1(o), "Cries of persons executed innocently" (B) Ch. V, No. 106

E338.1(fa), "Ghost walks in bedroom, disturbing occupants (B) Ch. V, No. 107

E371.4*, "Ghost of man returns to point out buried treasure" (B) Ch. V, Nos. 114, 116, 117

E371.5*, "Ghost of woman returns to reveal hidden treasure" (B) Ch. XI, No. 195

E421.3, "Luminous ghosts" Ch. V, 111

E422.4.4, "Revenant in female dress" (B) Ch. V, No. 102

E422.4.4(a), "Female revenant in white clothing" (B) Ch. V, Nos. 103, 111

E535.4, "Phantom railway train" (B) Ch. V, No. 105

E632.1, "Speaking bones of murdered person reveal murder" Ch. II, No. 50

F. MARVELS

F571.2, "Sending to the older" Ch. XIII, No. 225

G. OGRES

G229.1.1, "Witch who is out of skin is prevented from re-entering it when person salts or peppers skin" (B) Ch. VI, No. 123

G241.2, "Witch rides on person" (B) Ch. VI, No. 120

G242.7, "Mistakes made by person traveling with witches. . . ." (B) Ch. VI, No. 122

G263.4, "Witch causes sickness" (B) Ch. IV, No. 82

G275.2, "Witch overcome by helpful dogs of hero" Ch. VI, No. 125

G530.2, "Help from ogre's daughter (or son)" Ch. VII, No. 142

H. TESTS

H1376.5, "Questfor trouble" Ch. I, No. 5

H1411.1, "Fear Test: staying in haunted house where corpse drops piecemeal down chimney. . . ." Ch. XI, No. 194

J. THE WISE AND THE FOOLISH

J17, "Animal learns through experience to fear men" Ch. I, No. 18

J217.0.1.1, "Trickster overhears man praying for death to take him" (B) Ch. II, No. 47

J551.5, "Magpie tells a man that his wife has eaten an eel" Ch. I, No. 34a

J955.1, "Frog tries in vain to be as big as ox" Ch. I, No. 21

J1172.3, "Ungrateful animal returned to captivity" Ch. I, No. 22

J1260, "Repartee based on church or clergy" Ch. II, No. 43

J1341.11, "Hired men sing of displeasure with food; change song when food is improved (cante fable)" (B) Ch. n, No. 57

J1390, "Retorts concerning thefts" Ch. II, Nos. 42, 43, 44

J1473.1, "The 999 gold pieces" Ch. II, No. 55

J1495.2, "When Caleb Comes. . . ." (B) Ch. XI, No. 192

J1750, "One animal mistaken for another" Ch. II, No. 68 Ch. XII, No. 201

J1759.3, "Numskull thinks lightning bugs are mosquitoes carrying lanterns to find victims" (B) Ch. XV, 258

J1769.2, "Dead man is thought to be alive" (B) Ch. XI, No. 197

J1772.1, "Pumpkin thought to be ass's egg" Ch. XV, No. 253

J1772.26*, "Violin thought to be cat" . Ch. XV, No. 252

J1781.2, "The watch mistaken for the devil's eye" (B) Ch. XV, No. 254

J1785,8*, "Deer thought to be devil with chair on his head" (B) Ch. XIII, No. 222

X584.2*, "Man without gun accompanies hunter. Every time hunter kills an animal the one without the gun says, 'We killed a (rabbit).' This goes on until hunter kills a mule thinking it a deer. He says, 'We killed a mule.' The other says, 'We nothing; you killed that mule' " (B) Ch. XII, No. 208

X753, "A youth promises to marry an old maid if she will sit all night on the roof" Ch. XII, No. 202

X936(b), "Lie: person with remarkable hearing" (B) Ch. XV, No. 255

X938, "Lie: person of remarkable sight" Ch. XIII, No. 224

X938(a), "Lie: person of remarkable sight" (B) Ch. XV, No. 255

X1124.2, "Hunter turns animal inside out" (B) Ch. XIII, No, 221

X1133.3.2, "If the wolf's tail breaks" (B) Ch. XII, No. 209

X1215.2, "Lie: large dog' (B) Ch. XIII, No. 231

X1286.1.3, "Large mosquito has long bill" (B) Ch. XIII, No. 232

X1401.1(b), "Animals eat into large vegetable, live there for some time" (B) Ch. XIII, No. 228

X1401.2(g), "Large vegetable must be sawed up into pieces . . . ." (B) Ch. XIII, No. 229

X1402.1*, "Lie: the fast-growing vine" (B) Ch. XIII, No. 228

X1423, "Lies about cabbages" Ch. XIII, No. 230

X1633.1, "Heat causes corn to pop in crib or in field" (B) Ch. XIII, 227

X1785.1, "The stretching and shrinking harness" (B) Ch. XIII, No. 218

X1796, "Lies concerning speed". See in (B) X1796.2.2*(b), "Man hears bullet twice when he is shot at: once when the bullet passes him, again when he passes the bullet" Ch. XIII, No. 222

Z. MISCELLANEOUS GROUPS OF MOTIFS

Z33.4, "The fat troll (wolf)" Ch. XII, No. 216

Z71.5, "Formulistic number: seven" Ch. IV, No. 89

Z132, "War personified" Ch. VII, 140

INDEX OF TALE TYPES

IV. FORMULA TALES